BALL OF COLLUSION

ALSO BY ANDREW C. McCARTHY

Willful Blindness: A Memoir of the Jihad

The Grand Jihad: How Islam and the Left Sabotage America

Spring Fever: The Illusion of Islamic Democracy

*Faithless Execution: Building the Political Case
for Obama's Impeachment*

ANDREW C. McCARTHY

BALL OF COLLUSION

THE PLOT TO RIG AN ELECTION AND DESTROY A PRESIDENCY

ENCOUNTER BOOKS NEW YORK · LONDON

First American edition published in 2019 by Encounter Books,
an activity of Encounter for Culture and Education, Inc.,
a nonprofit, tax exempt corporation.
Encounter Books website address: www.encounterbooks.com

Manufactured in the United States and printed on
acid-free paper. The paper used in this publication meets
the minimum requirements of ANSI/NISO Z39.48—1992
(R 1997) (Permanence of Paper).

FIRST AMERICAN EDITION

LIBRARY OF CONGRESS CATALOGING-IN-PUBLICATION DATA

Names: McCarthy, Andrew C., author.
Title: Ball of collusion : the plot to rig an election and destroy a
presidency / by Andrew C. McCarthy.
Description: First American edition. | New York : Encounter Books, 2019.
|
Includes bibliographical references and index.
Identifiers: LCCN 2019024876 (print) | LCCN 2019024877 (ebook) |
ISBN 9781641770255 (hardcover) | ISBN 9781641770262 (ebook)
Subjects: LCSH: Presidents--United States--Election--2016. | Clinton,
Hillary Rodham. | Trump, Donald, 1946- | United States--Politics and
government--2008-2016. | United States--Politics and government--2016-
Classification: LCC E911 .M388 2019 (print) | LCC E911 (ebook) |
DDC 324.973/0905--dc23
LC record available at https://lccn.loc.gov/2019024876
LC ebook record available at https://lccn.loc.gov/2019024877

Table of Contents

Introduction

T his is a story about hubris. Sure, there's plenty of collusion. But hubris is the more fitting word. This is a story about what happens when those we trust to be the guardians of our system anoint themselves the masters of our system. For our own good, of course.

As for *collusion*, that word we've heard so incessantly from pundits and leaky government officials, Special Counsel Robert Mueller has rendered his judgment that there was none—at least, not the collusion he was hunting for. There really was a collusion plot, though. And it really did target our election system. It absolutely sought to usurp our capacity for self-determination. It was just not the collusion you've been told about. It was not "Donald Trump's collusion with Russia."

Here is the real collusion scheme: In 2016, the incumbent Democratic administration of President Barack Obama put the awesome powers of the United States government's law-enforcement and intelligence apparatus in the service of the Hillary Rodham Clinton presidential campaign, the Democratic party, and the progressive Beltway establishment. This scheme had two parts: Plan A, the objective; and Plan B, a fail-safe strategy in case Plan A imploded—which all the smartest people were supremely confident would never, ever happen...which is why you could bet the ranch that it would.

Plan A was to get Mrs. Clinton elected president of the United States. This required exonerating her, at least ostensibly, from well-founded allegations that were both felonious and politically disqualifying.

Plan B was the insurance policy: an investigation that Donald Trump, in the highly unlikely event he were elected, would be powerless to shut down. An investigation that would simultaneously monitor and taint him. An investigation that internalized Clinton campaign–generated opposition research, limning Trump and his campaign as complicit in Russian espionage. An investigation that would hunt for a crime under the guise of counterintelligence, build an impeachment case under the guise of hunting for a crime, and seek to make Trump un-reelectable under the guise of building an impeachment case.

The Clinton-Emails Caper

Upon becoming President Obama's secretary of state, Clinton improperly set up a private, nonsecure system for email communications. It featured her own personal server, stored in her home and, later, maintained by a private contractor headquartered in Colorado. Secretary Clinton used this private email system for all of her official State Department communications, notwithstanding that doing so (a) violated government regulations (which, as the department head, she was responsible for enforcing); (b) violated governmental recordkeeping and record-production obligations imposed by federal law; and (c) made it inevitable—due to the nature of her responsibilities—that streams of classified information would flow through and be stored in the nonsecure system.

This lack of security meant that top-secret intelligence—some of it classified at the highest levels, some of it involving Clinton's communications with the president of the United States and other top national-security officials—became accessible to people who were not cleared to see it. Accessible not just to those lacking security clearance, but also to hostile actors, including foreign-intelligence services and anti-American hackers.

When asked, nearly two years after leaving office, to surrender copies of her emails (by an Obama State Department under pressure from congressional investigators and Freedom of Information Act claimants), Clinton caused tens of thousands of her emails to be destroyed. Not just deleted. *Destroyed*. As in: purged with a special software program ("BleachBit") designed to shred electronic documents. The aim was to prevent their being recovered. Ever. By anyone.

In all, Clinton undertook to destroy over 30,000 emails, even though some of them had been demanded by congressional subpoena. And this would not be a Clinton story if we failed to note that, in the time-honored family tradition, Hillary lied her head off about the substance of the destroyed emails: We were to believe that, in thousands upon thousands of email exchanges, one of the busiest public officials and most obsessively political creatures on the planet had lolled her days away gabbing about yoga routines, family vacations, and her daughter's wedding.

The FBI was eventually able to reassemble portions of the tens of thousands of purged emails. "Several thousand," the FBI's then-director James Comey reported, were "work-related," and at least three of them were classified.¹ We will never have a final count because, in extirpating her correspondence, Clinton and her subordinates took extraordinary measures to defeat forensic investigation. And why not? After all, if you had discussed some earth-shattering development in yoga—perhaps a secret breakthrough in *utthita trikonasana!*—you wouldn't just delete that, right? You'd want to make certain that all the king's horses and all the king's men—and all the prying FBI agents, the nosy congressional committees, and those ferrets down at Judicial Watch—couldn't put those emails together again.

Doesn't everybody BleachBit their deleted emails?

Even the emails Clinton deigned to turn over were rife with classified intelligence. They also contained other government information that, though not classified, is supposed to be kept on the government's secure system because it is sensitive.

Mrs. Clinton's misconduct appears to have transgressed several federal criminal laws. Among the most obvious are those making it a felony to mishandle classified information, convert and destroy government records, and obstruct congressional investigations. Plainly, while the classified information offenses are the most egregious, they are not the only crimes—just the only ones we ever heard much about.

Why? It was a brilliant play, really. Clinton-friendly government officials and media spoke only about the classified information in the emails Clinton surrendered. That she massively destroyed records of State Department business, and that the purge occurred after a congressional investigative committee issued a preservation letter and a subpoena, were largely ignored. It was a simple strategy: first, focus obsessively on classified information issues so that other misconduct would fade into trivia and irrelevance; second, find ways to undermine the classified information allegations so that the emails debacle would disappear as a source of potential criminal jeopardy; and finally, maintain that the lack of criminal charges erased Clinton's national security recklessness and rules-don't-apply-to-me arrogance as campaign issues.

President Obama took care of undermining any classified information prosecution. He had a deep interest in doing so: He had knowingly communicated with his secretary of state through the private system, and he had misled the public about it—claiming to have learned about Clinton's private email practices from news reports, like everyone else. All of that could be neatly buried in two steps. First, invoke executive privilege (without calling it that—too Nixonian) to seal the Obama–Clinton emails from public view. Second, ensure that the Clinton-emails case would never be prosecuted. If Clinton was never accused of criminal conduct, then Obama's role as a minor participant would not become evidence in a criminal case.[2]

In April 2016, on national television, the president made clear that he did not believe an indictment should be filed against former Secretary Clinton, who, by then, was the inevitable Democratic presidential nominee. Obama explained that, in his considered judgment, Clinton meant no harm to national security. Plus, the intelligence involved, though technically categorized as "classified," was not really, you know, the supersecret stuff—"There's 'classified,'" Obama scoffed, "and then there's *classified*."[3] It was a classic Obama straw man. The criminal provisions pertinent to Clinton's case did not require proof of intent to harm the United States, only that she was trusted with access to intelligence and nevertheless mishandled it, either intentionally or through gross negligence.[4] Moreover, no one was accusing Clinton of trying to damage national security. That is a different, more serious criminal offense that was not on the table. It was as if Obama were claiming that a bank robber was somehow not guilty of the bank robbery because she hadn't murdered anyone while committing it.

Of course Mrs. Clinton hadn't set out with a purpose to harm the country. Her purpose, with a 2016 presidential bid in the works, was to conceal her communications as secretary of state from Congress and the public. Hillary Clinton had been under criminal investigation before—indeed, when she was first lady in 1995, she was very nearly indicted for obstruction and making false statements by Independent Counsel Kenneth Starr.[5] Mrs. Clinton knew that leaving a paper trail, especially one that documents conversations, is how shady characters get themselves jammed up with the law.

During her tenure, the State Department had an intriguingly cozy relationship with the Clinton Foundation, the enterprise through which Mrs. Clinton and her husband, former President Bill Clinton, had become fabulously rich by monetizing their outsize political influence. Do you suppose that maybe, just maybe, *that* could be a better explanation than yoga routines for why, when it came to her stored emails, Clinton decided to scorch the earth and poison the wells?

Several bureaucrats and military officials have been prosecuted and severely disciplined for failing to safeguard the national-defense intelligence to which they were given privileged access. None of them wanted to harm the nation. Lack of malevolent motive was no defense, however, because it formed no part of the offense they were cited for committing. Yet, for the putative Democratic nominee, the Obama administration effectively rewrote the law.

There was no way on God's green earth that the Obama Justice Department was ever going to authorize a prosecution involving conduct that would embarrass the president. Nor was it ever going to indict Obama's former secretary of state—certainly not after Obama, revered by Democrats and pundits as a first-rate lawyer, had pronounced her not guilty, had provided a legal rationale for exoneration, and had endorsed her as his successor. There was no way an indictment was going to be approved by Obama's attorney general, Loretta Lynch—the same Loretta Lynch who rose to prominence when she was appointed to a coveted U.S. attorney post by, yes, President Bill Clinton. The same Loretta Lynch who knew she stood a good chance of remaining attorney general if there were a President Hillary Clinton.

Approve an *indictment*? Lynch did not even allow the FBI to refer to its probe of Clinton as an *investigation*. She instructed Comey to describe it as a "matter," as if the issue were a parking ticket, or maybe a yoga routine. "I guess you're the Federal Bureau of *Matters*, now," a colleague tartly ribbed the director.[6] The Bureau could run down all the, er, matters it wanted (within severe limits imposed by the Justice Department). Hillary Clinton was not going to be charged, period. Lisa Page, an FBI lawyer who worked on the Clinton-emails investigation (and who became a notorious figure during the Trump–Russia investigation), told congressional investigators that the Obama Justice Department repeatedly rejected the FBI's efforts to make a case against Clinton for mishandling classified information.[7]

Wonder of wonders: The "no intent to harm the United States" rationale President Obama had glibly posited in insisting Clinton had done nothing wrong was echoed in the ensuing months by his subordinates. Justice Department officials leaked to their media friends that Clinton was unlikely to be charged because there was scant evidence of intent to harm the United States.[8] Meanwhile, very shortly after Obama's public statements about Clinton's case, FBI Director James Comey and his closest advisers began drafting remarks exonerating Mrs. Clinton. Over a dozen critical witnesses, *including Clinton herself*, had not yet been interviewed. Salient evidence had not yet been examined. No matter. With the end of the story already written, the rest was just details. When Director Comey finally announced that Clinton would not be indicted, his rationalizations were indistinguishable from Obama's.

Comey took a page out of Obama's book. The director acknowledged that "several thousand work-related emails"—i.e., records of the United States Department of State—were among the thousands of emails Clinton had cordoned off from the government's filing system, deleted, and ultimately destroyed. He claimed, however, that prosecution was not warranted because the Bureau "found no evidence that any of the additional work-related emails were intentionally deleted *in an effort to conceal them.*" As implausible as that rationalization was (Comey did not address the many motives Clinton might have to conceal documents she had gone to extraordinary lengths to cordon off from State Department recordkeeping), it was legally irrelevant. Just as the classified information laws do not require prosecutors to show a motive to harm the United States, the statute criminalizing the theft or destruction of government records does not require proof of a motive to conceal the records. Government officials, particularly those trusted to run government departments, are not allowed to embezzle or destroy records, period.[9]

Comey's public exoneration of the former secretary of state took place right after Independence Day, with Election Day on the horizon. It was a press conference, held a little over a week after a shameful tarmac *tête-à-tête* between Attorney General Lynch and former President Clinton, and just three days after a perfunctory interview of Mrs. Clinton during which the Justice Department permitted Clinton's coconspirators to sit in as her lawyers. The press conference was a breathtaking departure from Justice Department rules: The FBI director cleared Clinton on the charges even though the Bureau has no authority to make charging decisions (that's the Justice Department's job). Yet he did so only after excoriating Clinton in a detailed, factual description of her misconduct. This, notwithstanding that law-enforcement officials are generally barred from commenting publicly on the evidence against uncharged persons—in fact, they routinely refuse even to acknowledge the existence of any investigation.

Notably, there was no excoriation of the president. Nor even mild criticism. Initially, the Bureau planned a mention of Clinton's communication with "President Obama" from the territory of a foreign adversary (i.e., a place where an unprotected communication could easily be hacked). In the editing process, the reference to Obama was changed to "another senior government official." When Comey finally made his public remarks, though, he omitted the episode entirely.[10]

Clinton's Problem: Clinton

Thus "exonerated," the former first lady was on her way to the Oval Office—this time as president. Or so she thought—as did the Obama White House, the Justice Department, the State Department, the FBI, the intelligence agencies, every progressive activist from Boston Harbor to Silicon Valley, and every political pundit from the Beltway to the Upper West Side. Alas, there was just one problem—a problem the president and his myrmidons could not fix for Mrs. Clinton.

That problem was *Mrs. Clinton.*

As would have been manifest to less politicized eyes, she was an atrocious candidate. Clinton was the same fundamentally flawed, deeply dishonest, broadly unpopular candidate she had been in 2008, when she couldn't convince *Democrats* to support her. You may recall this as the reason there was a President Barack Obama in the first place. You say, "Hey, wait a second. Donald Trump was fundamentally flawed, deeply dishonest, and broadly unpopular, too." Maybe so, but if hammering away at an opponent's malignance is the path to victory, shouldn't you perhaps nominate a candidate who doesn't mirror his defects?

The only differences between the "It's My Turn" Senator *Hillary!* of 2008 and the "Stronger Together" Secretary Clinton who expected a 2016 coronation was that she now had hanging around her neck the Benghazi debacle, a desultory tenure as secretary of state, a shades-of-2008 inability to convince Democrats that she was the preferable candidate (this time, not in comparison to a charismatic young progressive, but to a seventy-five-year-old self-proclaimed socialist who had joined the Democratic Party about five minutes ago), whispers that her health was deteriorating, and an email scandal that smacked of both national-security recklessness and rules-don't-apply-to-me arrogance—precisely the kind of controversy that reminded Americans of how exhausting the last scandal-plagued Clinton administration had been.

The Obama administration's exoneration gambit came up snake eyes because of Clinton herself. Democrats can con themselves (and attempt to con everyone else) into believing that her failure is due to Vladimir Putin's perfidy or Trump's demagoguery. In the real world, though, Clinton lost because of her epic shortcomings. Trump acolytes maintain that their man is the only Republican who could have beaten Hillary Clinton. In truth, Democrats are right to wonder whether they managed to nominate the only candidate who could have lost to Donald Trump.

In the event, the American people disrupted Plan A. By a hair...not even with a popular majority. Democrats incessantly remind us that Mrs. Clinton "won the popular vote" (which is like a losing football team bragging that it *gained the most yards*, when the relevant metric is *scoring the most points*). Have you noticed, though, that Democrats and their media echo chamber avoid saying Clinton won a popular *majority*? She didn't. Every presidential election has a winner because the Constitution's design assures it. This time around, though, no candidate could claim to be most people's preference. Clinton amassed nearly three million more votes than Trump, but that was good for just 48 percent of the popular vote. A majority of American voters preferred someone else; or, in the *minima de malis* terms of the 2016 election, a majority of Americans opposed Clinton.[11] Of course, looking at it that way, Trump was opposed by an even larger majority of Americans. Yet his 46 percent share consisted of sixty-three million voters, perfectly enough dispersed to win thirty states. These included the rustbelt battlegrounds of Michigan, Pennsylvania, and Wisconsin, where, had there been a shift of just 77,744 votes—about half a percentage point—we would not have been talking about a populist revolt, but about how a longtime pillar of the Washington establishment had cruised to the victory confidently predicted by all the polls.[12]

Trump's haul was enough to cobble together a win in the Electoral College. That is the Constitution's metric, and rightly so. The increasingly left-leaning power centers of the Democratic party want an electorate that reflects New York and San Francisco; our fundamental law, by contrast, demands one that reflects America, broadly. The Electoral College system invests our entire, richly diverse country, not just its urban centers, in the contest to lead our government. Columnist George Will states the matter with characteristic clarity: "[T]he Electoral College shapes the character of majorities by helping to generate those that are neither geographically nor ideologically narrow, and that depict, more than the popular vote does, national decisiveness."[13]

Trump and Russia

This particular act of national decisiveness was not the one the Beltway was banking on. Of course, if Clinton had prevailed as expected, we would never have heard tell of the collusion narrative. But unwilling to take defeat lying down, and aware that its anti-Trump machinations would be exposed once the new president took office, the fabled "deep state" responded by hyping an imaginary Trump–Russia espionage conspiracy.

I use the above scare quotes advisedly. Invocations of the "deep state" by Trump votaries are overkill. I first encountered the term, years before Trump entered electoral politics, while researching post-Ottoman Turkey. To have any chance of success, Kemal Ata-turk's experiment in secularizing an Islamic society required a notorious but surreptitious power center that prevented Muslim fundamentalists from undoing cultural and political Westernization. This "deep state" was an elite inner sanctum of top government, military, and judicial officials. Notwithstanding Turkey's ostensibly democratic system, it stood ever ready to preserve the Kemalist establishment, whether by military coup or more subtle forms of intimidation.[14]

This book contends that the Obama administration, abetted by Washington's politically progressive order, exploited its control of law-enforcement and intelligence agencies to help Clinton and undermine Trump. This was a scandalous abuse of power. That's bad enough. There is no need to hyperbolize what happened into a deep state coup, or to trivialize what life in an authoritarian society with a real deep state is like. Let's not forget: Trump *is* president. The officials who politicized their law-enforcement and intelligence duties *have been* removed, whether by dismissal or in the ordinary transition of power from one administration to the next. Trump's political opponents would be delighted to remove him from office, but as a practical matter, that is a pipe dream. They will have to content themselves with a democratic election and the result will stand, regardless of how the political establishment feels about it.

Now that the special prosecutor has delivered his report, can we say the collusion narrative was a "hoax"? Many do, as does the president. There is a lot to be said for this assessment, particularly insofar as it relates to the essential allegation: a Trump–Russia cyberespionage conspiracy to "steal the election." There has never been any real evidence of this, just the sometimes lurid, sometimes laughable innuendo known as the "Steele dossier," a slapdash collection of "intelligence" reporting, crafted by a former British spy and his former journalist partners, the anti-Trump partisans Christopher Steele and Glenn Simpson, whose work was commissioned by the Clinton campaign.

The standard dictionary definition of *hoax* is "something accepted or established by fraud or fabrication." A traitorous calumny largely based on fabricated intelligence fits that bill. Nevertheless, the word "hoax" is carrying a lot of freight in Trump World—a clean bill of

health in which any hint that conduct was objectionable, that Russia
ties were unsavory, is ridiculed as a #NeverTrump hallucination. I
think one should be able to see the president as exonerated on a libel-
ous allegation that smacked of treason without sticking one's head in
the sand about his strange ingratiation of Putin; about the seamy dots
connecting Kremlin cronies to Trump-campaign officials and business
partners; and about the fact that the Putin regime did offer, and the
Trump campaign did eagerly hope to receive, campaign dirt on Hillary
Clinton. The latter "collusion" did not rise to the level of a criminal
agreement. But the facts that it was not consummated, and that Putin
may very well have been playing Trump, do not erase the collaboration. That is why *collusion* is a weasel word that should not be con-
founded, or used interchangeably, with *conspiracy*.

Here's what matters in our democratic republic: Trump's blandishments toward Russia were not hidden from voters. Ties between the
Trump and Putin orbits were not merely covered by the media; they
were given a criminally corrupt spin, one that the evidence has not
borne out. The problem for Clinton was that Russia was simply not a
salient issue in the campaign. That is not easy for us to remember after
two years of Democrat-media Russo-mania. In the event, however, Russia barely registered, not just because other issues were weightier but
because raising it would have been counterproductive for Democrats.

Trump promoted his anticipation of a good relationship with the
Russian strongman as a campaign asset. The candidate's business
dealings with Russian oligarchs were widely reported on. So was his
skepticism about the North Atlantic Treaty Organization (NATO), the
premier Western alliance formed to oppose the Soviet Union and the
bane of Putin's revanchist ambitions. That skepticism provoked sten-
torian opposition to his candidacy from both the globalist Left and
elements of the Reaganite Right. Moreover, Paul Manafort was scan-
dalously removed as Trump's campaign chairman just three months
before the election when the media exposed his lucrative lobbying
work for Ukraine's Kremlin-backed former president, whose ouster
triggered the Russian aggression that continues to this day.

In addition, just weeks before the election, a Clinton-campaign media blitz claimed that Russia's hacking of Democratic National Com-

mittee email accounts could be part of a coordinated Trump–Putin strategy: Kremlin help for the Republican nominee in exchange for his lifting of economic sanctions against Russia if he won. The blitz was goosed along by Obama's Central Intelligence Agency: The CIA's then-Director John Brennan spun up then-Senate Minority Leader Harry Reid (D., Nev.) with allegations that Trump's campaign was tied to the Russian government, while Michael Morell, a Clinton booster who had been the Agency's Acting Director, publicly described Trump as an "unwitting agent" of the Kremlin.[15]

Political campaigns and elections are how we sort through such claims and policy disputes. We decide who is fit for office at the ballot box. The Justice Department, the FBI, and U.S. intelligence agencies are servants of the public, not a check on the public—much less a check on the public to be wielded by a presidential candidate's political opposition. Personally, I found Donald Trump's indulgence toward Putin, an anti-American dictator who runs his country like a mafia don, to be contemptible. That is one of several reasons why, out of seventeen potential Republican presidential nominees, Trump was much closer to the bottom than the top of my preference list. But nobody elected the federal government and its sprawling administrative state to decide whom to place at the top of the federal government and its sprawling administrative state. That is a decision for the sovereign, *the American people* exercising the franchise, not the administrators of the government they elect.

It is not that Trump's take on Russia was popular. It is that 2016 voters decided that Russia was a low priority in the greater scheme of things. That should not surprise us because Democrats, too, regarded Russia as a trifling concern... right up until Mrs. Clinton lost and they unexpectedly found themselves in need of a scapegoat.

The investigation was thus "trumped up," as it were. As president, Donald Trump has been refreshingly tough on Moscow—considerably tougher than his predecessors over the past quarter century. Yes, candidate Trump's Russophilic commentary disturbed national-security conservatives, yours truly among them. Still, it is simply a fact that, in recent American history, a longing for conciliation with Moscow's rogue regime has been standard fare. To be sure, Trump's rhetoric—

unabashedly solipsistic, off the cuff, and sometimes inattentive, uninformed, or flatly untrue—is more jarring than that of conventional politicians. Not content merely to hope aloud for better relations, he has gone so far as to defend Putin by drawing a moral equivalence between the Kremlin's political assassinations of dissenters and our government's covert national-defense operations.[16] But while Trump's logorrhea is often hair-raising, his policy positions (with a few exceptions not relevant here) tend to be quotidian. That should not surprise us either, the Democrats' Chicken Little routine notwithstanding. President Trump spent most of his politically active life prior to running for office as a nonideological centrist who thought "Bill Clinton was a great president," and who donated mostly to Democrats (such as Hillary Clinton and Chuck Schumer) and moderate Republicans (such as the late John McCain).[17] His "Let's try to get along" approach to Putin during the campaign was utterly conventional.

Ever since the Soviet Union dissolved in 1991, it has been bipartisan Beltway wisdom that Russia is an essentially normal country with which we can do business—a "strategic partner," as President George W. Bush's administration delusionally put it in May 2008 upon submitting to Congress its U.S.–Russian Civilian Nuclear Power Agreement, four months before withdrawing the pact in humiliation when Russia, being Russia, seized territory in neighboring Georgia. But not to worry: President Obama revived the agreement 4610 if you're keeping score, that's in between Russia's annexations in Georgia and its annexations in Ukraine.[18]

From *Perestroika* through Putin, our government's perception transformed from Red Menace to *La Vie en Rose*. From George H. W. Bush's "Chicken Kiev" speech through Barack Obama's hot-mic promise of "more flexibility" on the Kremlin's agenda of hamstringing America, Washington has regarded the regime in Moscow as a democratically-reforming, capitalism-friendly potential ally. For a fleeting moment in the 2012 campaign, GOP nominee Mitt Romney had the temerity to limn Russia as, "without question, our number-one geopolitical foe"; who could forget President Obama's censorious retort: "The 1980s are now calling to ask for their foreign policy back because the Cold War has been over for 20 years."[19]

On Russia, as on many things, Trump can be his own worst enemy and it is hard to feel sorry for him. To paraphrase Lenin, his opponents are trying to hang him with rope that he supplied. But his blandishments were not criminal. Given the Beltway establishment's canoodling with the Kremlin right up until his election, Trump was like the guy left without a chair when the music stopped.

Voters, however, were not fooled. Those who cared about Russia as an election issue knew that the incumbent Democratic administration had regularly kowtowed to the Kremlin, including in the cause of kowtowing to Iran. Secretary Clinton had been that administration's point person on relations with Moscow for four years. Among her "accomplishments" was the promotion of Skolkovo, a suburb of Moscow slated to evolve into Russia's Silicon Valley. With the State Department's guidance, American technology companies (most of them Clinton Foundation donors and Bill Clinton speech sponsors) joined with Russian backers (some of them also Clinton Foundation donors) to develop state-of-the-art tech for the venture. The result? The Defense Department and the FBI assess Skolkovo as a boon for Russia's military and cyber capabilities.[20] (Did I mention that our intelligence agencies attribute Moscow's interference in political campaigns throughout the West to its military and cyber capabilities?)

Candidate Clinton and her husband had disturbing Russia ties, too. In an episode that oozed self-dealing, Secretary Clinton helped greenlight Russia's acquisition of a fifth of U.S. uranium stock, through its state-controlled energy giant, Rosatom—even though the Justice Department had an active racketeering investigation against Rosatom's American subsidiary, and even though the United States does not produce nearly enough uranium to meet our own energy needs.[21] While approval was pending, a Russian bank that promotes Rosatom paid Bill Clinton $500,000 for a short speech in Moscow. The former president met with Putin and his factotum, Dmitry Medvedev, during the trip—which may have mooted a planned get-together with a Rosatom board member. The uranium stock sold to Rosatom had been held by Uranium One, a company controlled by Clinton backers. Their acquisition of the valuable uranium assets eventually sold to Russia was due to Bill Clinton's intercession with Kazakhstan's Kremlin-allied dictator in 2005, after which an eye-popping $145 million flowed into the Clinton Foundation.²²

The public's indifference to Russia as a 2016 campaign issue can be summed up in one word: *Clinton*. Again, it is the word that explains virtually every Democratic failure to exploit Trump's vulnerabilities.

Until Trump was elected, indifference to Russia and the possibility of foreign interference in our political campaign was the standard government position, too. President Obama and his intelligence agencies were thoroughly informed about Russia's cyber operations, which mostly—but not exclusively—targeted Democratic campaigns. Yet the administration took no meaningful action. Obama publicly scoffed at the notion that the Kremlin could affect the outcome of a presidential election. Clinton took great umbrage, during the final debate between the candidates, at Trump's refusal to concede that the election could be anything but fair and legitimate—a message echoed by Obama. With Hillary a shoo-in to win, Democrats were not going to permit any intimation that the process was rigged.

Republicans knew all about Trump's wheedling of Putin. It was not a secret. Indeed, many Republicans were chagrined over the nomination precisely because they detected in Trump's Russia rhetoric traces of an isolationist streak, antithetical to GOP doctrine that America's prosperity hinges on our standing as the fully engaged leader of the free world. That most of these Republicans "came home" on Election Day was not due to a sudden comfort level found with Trump, but to disdain for Clinton—particularly after eight years of a foreign policy marked by American retreat and decline, a policy she'd helped steer.

The Trump–Russia tale was no secret. Voters, however, were far more animated by the question of which candidate should be trusted to fill the Supreme Court seat left open by Justice Antonin Scalia's death in February 2016. Should it be the avowedly progressive Democrat, or the Republican who'd committed to appoint conservative jurists in the Scalia mold? The vacancy concentrated the electorate's mind on the gravity of the Supreme Court's work; the ideological deadlock that hamstrung its capacity to decide major cases; and the advanced ages of several justices, making it highly likely that the next president would make multiple appointments and shape the philosophical bent of the judiciary for a generation to come.

Beyond that, the attention of Americans was consumed by the future of health care, the challenges of border security and illegal immigration, safety from terrorist attacks, the weak recovery from the financial crisis, the tension between maintaining low crime rates and addressing calls for criminal-justice reform, the opioid crisis, and the anxieties of middle-class Americans. The question of which candidate was apt to be *weaker* on Russia, a shell of its former Soviet self, was a comparative nonfactor. It's not that nobody knew. Nobody cared...least of all Democrats, for whom the matter of Russian aggression would have been shoved right back in the appeasement drawer the moment Clinton's slam-dunk victory was announced the night of November 8.

But she lost, so we've had three years of collusion narrative.

This is a book about that narrative. It is a complex, fascinating story about storytelling: about how critical it is in Information Age politics, and how dangerous it can be when the government dabbles in it, politicizing intelligence and putting its partisan thumb on the scale of electoral politics.

Writing a book about a still-moving target means having to break off a piece for study while history is still unfolding. Shortly before we went to press, Special Counsel Mueller published his voluminous report. Like Mueller's appointment, which we address toward the end, the report marks a significant shift in focus from collusion to alleged obstruction. The obstruction allegations will not be grist for courtroom prosecution, and my own view is that they are not prosecutable. In our constitutional system, responsibility for addressing alleged presidential misconduct is vested in Congress, in the impeachment process—the subject of my 2014 book, *Faithless Execution.*

The obstruction and impeachment dynamic is still playing out. It is beyond the scope of this book...except to the extent that collusion is what got us there. It is the collusion narrative by which Donald Trump's opponents hoped to defeat him, and if they could not defeat him, to undermine his presidency—in hopes of defeating him next time.

CHAPTER ONE

The Collusion Fable

"The 1980s are now calling to ask for their foreign policy back."

Thus spoke President Barack Obama just a couple of weeks before Election Day 2012. With the race still thought to be tight, he had come to the candidates' final debate loaded for bear. Earlier in the campaign, his Republican rival, former Massachusetts Governor Mitt Romney, had had the temerity to pronounce that Russia was, "without question, our number-one geopolitical foe." The incumbent president regarded this as an absurd anachronism. So that night, he brought the snark. Hadn't anyone informed Romney that "the Cold War's been over for twenty years"? Obama tut-tutted that this Republican nostalgia for the foreign policy of the 1980s was of a piece with the GOP's desire to revive the "social policy of the 1950s and the economic policies of the 1920s."

Yes, that was your Democratic Party standard-bearer, what seems like only yesterday. No longer was this the party of Harry Truman and John F. Kennedy. To Obama-era Democrats, arguing that Russia was a real threat, that it longed for a return to Soviet hegemony, was akin to calling for the return of Jim Crow and the adoption of protectionist practices that helped ignite the Great Depression.

But then Hillary Clinton lost the 2016 election, and Democrats decided they'd best return that call from the 1980s, after all. Turns out Russia—the Russia against whose serial aggressions Obama took little meaningful action throughout his eight years in office—really is our Numero Uno geopolitical foe. Turns out the Cold War isn't "so last century." Since November 8, 2016, in ever-evolving Democratic dogma, Russia has gone from a quaint obsession of neo-con warmongers to an existential threat on the order of Climate Change!

As is generally the case, neither extreme of political posturing has been accurate. Romney was right that Putin's Russia is a significant rival on the world stage. Whether it is "number one" on the tally sheet is debatable. To figure that out, we'd have to make judgment calls about all the threats we face—immediate versus long-term, forcible versus other forms of aggression, ideological versus transactional, and so on. No need to dawdle over that. It suffices to say that the Russian regime is a serious adversary. It has a formidable nuclear arsenal, as well as highly capable military and intelligence forces. Its default posture is anti-American (though it is biddable). It cooperates effectively with other anti-American regimes and factions. Its veto power in the United Nations Security Council complicates our government's capacity to act in American interests. It has a Soviet iciness about the use of terrorism and forges alliances with terrorists in the pursuit of its interests. The regime is ruthless in its determination to remain in power, it has revanchist ambitions, and it is shrewd in testing the West's resolve—or lack of same—to respond to incremental aggressions that implicate NATO and other commitments.

At the same time, Putin's Russia is not the Soviet Union. The Cold War really is over. We are not in a bipolar global order, rivaled by a tyrannical Soviet empire. Modern Russia is a fading country. Its first-rate weaponry, armed forces, and intelligence agencies scarcely obscure its third-rate economy, declining population, pervasive societal dysfunction (high levels of drunkenness, disease, and unemployment), and lowering life expectancy.[1] Behind the façade of democratic elections and constitutional restraints, Russia has less a principled system of government than a marriage of rulers, oligarchs, and organized crime. To endure, Vladimir Putin's regime must terrorize the Russian people. Nevertheless, it is a pale imitation of the brutal Soviet behemoth that imploded nearly thirty years ago when the Berlin Wall fell, the Iron Curtain lifted, and tens of millions of enslaved subjects broke free.

Does Russia have the wherewithal to "interfere in our elections," as the media–Democrat trope puts it? If by "interference"—or its frequently invoked synonym, "meddling"—we refer to the ability to inject propaganda and attempt to influence the campaign debate, then *of course* it can interfere. And it does. That is what capable governments do to other countries. It is not only what the Soviet Union always did, and what Putin's Russia does throughout the West and in other parts of the world of consequence to Russian interests; *it is what our own government does.*

This calls for a bit of international-law throat-clearing. The United Nations has long proclaimed, "No State has the right to intervene, directly or indirectly, for any reason whatever, in the internal or external affairs of any State."[2] Yet, interference is not deemed to rise to a prohibited intervention unless it not only involves a matter committed exclusively to another state's prerogative, but is also *coercive*. That is, as Creighton Law School Professor Sean Watts observes, "the operation must force the target State into a course of action it would not otherwise undertake."[3] Russia, of course, is alleged to have interfered in the 2016 U.S. presidential campaign by such "cyberespionage" operations as hacking email accounts and social-media messaging. Hacking is clearly a crime, and Special Counsel Robert Mueller's staff theorizes that internet electioneering and propaganda by foreign actors may also rise to the level of criminal conspiracy.[4] As an international-law matter, however, Russia's election interference, provocative and obnoxious as it was, cannot conceivably be said to have "coerced" the United States.

We must concede, moreover, that the United States is among the most active participants in the election-interference game. "We've been doing this kind of thing since the CIA was created in 1947," Loch K. Johnson, an acclaimed scholar of U.S. intelligence, told *The New York Times* in 2018. "We've used posters, pamphlets, mailers, banners—you name it. We've planted false information in foreign newspapers. We've used what the British call 'King George's cavalry': suitcases of cash."[5]

Democrats, moreover, conveniently forget that they've historically *welcomed* such mischief-making. As historian Steven F. Hayward recounts, President Jimmy Carter used such emissaries as billionaire industrialist Armand Hammer and National Security Adviser Zbigniew Brzezinski to seek Soviet accommodations that could help in the 1980 campaign against Ronald Reagan. This mirrored the tactics of the 1976 campaign, during which Democratic eminence Averell Harriman conveyed to the Soviet foreign ministry that Carter was anxious to negotiate and would be more agreeable to deal with than then-President Gerald Ford.[6]

By the 1984 campaign, it was the renowned "Lion of the Senate," Ted Kennedy, pleading with Soviet leader Yuri Andropov for help in the Democrats' futile effort to stop the Reagan landslide. The Hoover Institution's Peter Robinson, a Reagan speechwriter, provided details of the unabashed quid pro quo, outlined in a 1983 KGB memorandum. Through his confidant, former Democratic Senator John Tunney, Kennedy told Andropov, "The only real potential threats to Reagan are problems of war and peace and Soviet-American relations. ... These issues... will without a doubt become the most important of the election campaign." Kennedy offered to visit Andropov in Moscow to provide Soviet officials with pointers on the challenges of nuclear disarmament "so they may be better prepared and more convincing during appearances in the USA." Having thus offered to update their propaganda, Kennedy further proposed arranging to have television networks give Andropov airtime for "a direct appeal... to the American people." Tunney went on to advise the Russians that, while his friend wanted to run for president in 1988, "Kennedy does not discount that during the 1984 campaign, the Democratic Party may officially turn to him to lead the fight against Republicans and elect their candidate president."[7]

Now *that's* some collusion right there.

There is nothing unusual about it, though. President Bill Clinton labored to ensure that Russia's reformer President (and Putin patron) Boris Yeltsin would not be defeated by a Soviet-style Communist in 1996.[8] President Obama sedulously worked against Israeli Prime Minister Benjamin Netanyahu, first attempting to force progressives into his right-leaning governing coalition, then dedicating U.S. taxpayer funds to a failed effort to defeat Netanyahu in 2015. Nothing new there: Clinton had unsuccessfully tried to defeat Netanyahu nearly twenty years earlier, later telling Israeli television, "I tried to do it in a way that didn't overtly involve me."[9]

As these things go, it would have been shocking if Moscow had *not* attempted to meddle in our 2016 election. Putting aside the Russians' general penchant for anti-American mischief-making, in 2011 Putin had publicly blamed then–Secretary of State Hillary Clinton for inciting unrest following Russia's typically rigged Parliamentary elections.[10] So, the 2016 campaign was not just business as usual. There was an element of score-settling. And with Putin being a canny strongman, the point was to sow discord and make life difficult for what he fully expected would be the new Clinton administration. There are good reasons to doubt the sincerity of assurances by Kremlin-tied operatives that Putin wanted Trump to win. Russia's modus operandi in the West is to agitate minority factions it believes are going to lose—whether it would prefer to see them to win or not. That is how Moscow sows discord in the society and makes it more difficult for the incumbent government to pursue its interests. But even if we accept at face value Russian assertions that Putin wanted Trump to win, there is no reason to think Putin believed Trump would win.

Nobody did. Not even Donald Trump himself.[11]

Collusion with Russia: A Bipartisan Affair

Let's put aside the time-honored international sport of meddling in other countries' elections. Let's stick with collusion with Russia: a quarter-century long, Bipartisan Beltway melody, right up until on November 8, 2016.

Cro-Magnon blowhards like myself have never warmed up to Moscow. So we've complained about the New Thinking, regardless of whether it was incumbent Republicans or Democrats delusionally portraying Russia as a perfectly normal country with which to do business, make lots of money, and even ally ourselves.[12]

Washington, however, has preferred to stay delusional.

The unsustainability of the Communist system, under the pressure of Reagan's military buildup and support of anti-Communist movements, made the Evil Empire's disintegration inevitable. Yet, gifted a historic opportunity to dance on the grave of Soviet tyranny, our government's bipartisan foreign-policy establishment punted. Rather than call the culprits to account and make an enduring record of the hundreds of millions killed and enslaved, successive administrations embraced and propped up Moscow as a force for global stability. The Soviet Union hadn't quite finished crumbling when President George H. W. Bush gave his infamous "Chicken Kiev" speech, trying to persuade Ukraine *not* to break away from Moscow.[13] It was a harbinger of things to come: Presidents Bill Clinton, George W. Bush, and

Barack Obama all enticed Ukraine to give up its means of self-defense on the false assurance that we would—with Russia's help!—protect it from aggression—an assurance premised on the pie-in-the-sky theory that there would, of course, be no Russian aggression.[14]

Given Ukraine's prominence in the Trump–Russia collusion narrative developed by the Hillary Clinton campaign, it is worth recalling Bill Clinton's collusion with Russia in the "Trilateral Statement": a joint declaration between Clinton and Boris Yeltsin, along with Britain, purporting to guarantee Ukraine's security. Why would Kiev need to keep its nuclear arsenal when its neighbor, Moscow, had reformed? The Iron Curtain was history, history itself was supposedly at its happy democratic ending, and it was now all about paying out the "peace dividend."[15] Throughout his eight-year tenure, Clinton flaunted his warm relationship with Yeltsin, committing to support Moscow with financial assistance, including subsidies to adjust decommissioned military officers and nuclear scientists to the new order. In 1997, the U.S. president prevailed upon our G-7 allies to make it the G-8 by admitting Russia, giving it greater influence over global trendsetting by the world's leading economies, despite the fact that Russia was not one of them.[16]

Then there was President George W. Bush peering into Vladimir Putin's soul and finding a "trustworthy" ally. Secretary of State Condoleezza Rice joined our new "strategic partner" in an agreement to help Russia amass the technology, material, and equipment needed to improve its nuclear research and power production—for "civilian" purposes only, of course. Bush enthusiastically seconded Clinton's proposal that Russia be admitted to the World Trade Organization, even though its corrupt economic policies and practices undermine the market-based norms the WTO is meant to fortify.[17]

Meanwhile, up-and-coming Democratic Senator Barack Obama was working bipartisan magic with Senate Republicans, pushing Kiev to think bolder than just giving up its nukes; Ukraine needed to surrender its conventional arsenals, too. But wait, what about protection from possible Russian invasions? Please...that was foreign-policy thinking for a bygone time.[18]

Naturally, Putin humiliated the Bush administration and Congress's bipartisan Russia accommodationists by invading Georgia, annexing swaths of its territory in Abkhazia and South Ossetia. The White House quietly withdrew the ballyhooed U.S.–Russia Civilian Nuclear Power Agreement from congressional consideration.[19]

Collusion with Russia: The Obama Reset

That brings us to the Obama years, the era of the "Russia Reset"— announced with great ceremony by Secretary of State Hillary Clinton, brandishing a red plastic "reset" push button that she presented to her counterpart, Foreign Minister Sergey Lavrov. Oops: The button was mislabeled *Peregruzka* (the Russian word for "overcharge") rather than *Perezagruzka* ("reset"). As investigative journalist Claudia Rosett observes, the Kremlin still keeps the button on display in a museum at the Foreign Ministry, "less a souvenir of U.S.–Russia camaraderie than a symbol of American folly."[20]

Even as Putin continued his Georgian occupation, Obama kicked off the Reset by shelving Bush's plans for missile-defense installations in Eastern Europe.[21] Further courting the Russian dictator, the president revived the civilian nuclear-power agreement in 2010, insisting that the pact advanced U.S. national security. It was just the beginning of the administration's promotion of Russia's key industrial sectors, improving our declining but dangerous rival's military and cyber capabilities and fortifying its capacity to extort the European nations and former Soviet republics that rely on Russia for their power needs.

Why? Because "Trade with Russia Is a Win-Win." That was the headline of Secretary Clinton's June 2012 *Wall Street Journal* op-ed, applauding Russia's formal entry into the WTO.[22] It was crucial, she explained, because Russia was just a great place for Americans to do business, and our commerce could now blossom since the Obama administration had made Moscow "a normal trading partner." Sure, the Putin regime posed many challenges, but Clinton maintained that "it is in our long-term strategic interest to collaborate with Russia in areas where our interests overlap."

Collaborate? That sounds almost like *collu*—well, never mind.

Obama and Clinton somehow decided that one of these collaborative areas should be technology. Under the secretary's guidance as point person of the Obama administration's "U.S.–Russia Bilateral Presidential Commission," the State Department teamed up with Russia's Foreign Ministry to help erect Moscow's version of Silicon Valley—Skolkovo. It's unlikely Putin could believe his good fortune: The project was like an espionage operation in broad daylight, openly enhancing Russia's military and cyber capabilities.

The Defense Department's European Command (EUCOM) put it this way:

> Skolkovo is an ambitious enterprise, aiming to promote technology transfer generally, by inbound direct investment, and occasionally, through selected acquisitions. As such, *Skolkovo is arguably an overt alternative to clandestine industrial espionage*—with the additional distinction that it can achieve such a transfer on a much larger scale and more efficiently. Implicit in Russia's development of Skolkovo is a critical question—a question that Russia may be asking itself—why bother spying on foreign companies and government laboratories if they will voluntarily hand over all the expertise Russia seeks?

Recognizing Russia's "current pursuit of external aggression and internal repression," which marked what it generously regarded as the Kremlin's "previous course toward democracy and cooperation with the West," EUCOM stressed caution against "*the risks that Russia could leverage transferred scientific knowledge to modernize and strengthen its military.*"[23]

Ya think? The U.S. Army's Foreign Military Studies Program at Fort Leavenworth concluded that Skolkovo was a "vehicle for world-wide technology transfer to Russia in the areas of information technology, biomedicine, energy, satellite and space technology, and nuclear technology." Moscow has made it unabashedly clear, moreover, that "not all of the center's efforts are civilian in nature": The project was deeply involved in military activities, including the development of a hypersonic cruise missile engine.[24] As investigative journalist John Solomon notes, the FBI ended up warning several American tech companies that entanglement with Skolkovo risked wide-ranging intellectual property theft. The agent in charge of the Bureau's Boston field office even took the extraordinary step of publishing a business journal op-ed, depicting Skolkovo as "a means for the Russian government to access our nation's sensitive or classified research development facilities and dual-use technologies with military and commercial application."[25]

Why would our government do such a thing? At the time this was all going on, Clinton's State Department issued its annual country-by-country findings on the state of civil liberties. Russia was found to be using technology "to monitor and control the internet." The State Department elaborated that official corruption was rampant, security services engaged in sweeping surveillance of communications, journalists were under siege, dissidents were arbitrarily detained—and some even tortured and killed.[26]

What was Secretary Clinton thinking?

As we've seen, most of the time, she was thinking about the Clinton Foundation, and money (I'd say not in that order, but it's pretty much the same order). Putin's regime dangled billions of dollars to invest in Skolkovo companies. Secretary Clinton immediately went to work attracting both corporate contributors and businesses deemed worthy of Russian investment.

The investigative journalist Peter Schweizer has done yeoman's work exposing the grimy interplay between the Clinton Foundation and the State Department. By 2012, the last year of Secretary Clinton's tenure, 60 percent of the "key partners" identified for the Skolkovo venture (seventeen out of twenty-eight) had "made financial commitments to the Clinton Foundation, totaling tens of millions of dollars, or sponsored speeches by Bill Clinton." Russians tied to Skolkovo also gave to the Clinton Foundation, including Viktor Vekselberg, a billionaire confidant of Putin's who was chosen to run the Skolkovo Foundation.[27]

There is symmetry here. Again, no one would sensibly say that Secretary Clinton *wanted* to make Russia a more capable adversary—and, as things turned out, I'd wager that strengthening the regime's cyber proficiency would be something she'd regret (if she were given to that kind of introspection). But it is like the irresponsible mishandling of top-secret information, and the storing and transmission of any sensitive government information, classified or otherwise, on a nonsecure server system: It's not that Clinton didn't know what she was doing or that she didn't apprehend the risks; it is that she had other priorities and threw caution to the wind—pretty much the textbook definition of gross negligence. She wasn't alone: this was not Secretary Clinton's administration, but President Obama's. He calculated that abetting and appeasing Russia was a price worth paying for "help" on the Iran deal and in Syria. And while there is some reason to believe Clinton was marginally harder on Russian aggression than Obama, it is a simple thing to rationalize doing the wrong thing when making waves is hard. So, you convince yourself that building Russia into a modern economy will somehow change the nature of the regime (instead of enriching and fortifying it). Plus, there was money to be made.

Collusion with Russia: Uranium One

That, naturally, is where the Clinton Foundation came in. And while Skolkovo is not a pretty story, Uranium One is even worse, involving the surrender to Putin's regime of fully one-fifth of the United States' uranium-mining stock, an outrage concealed by the tanking of a criminal investigation into the American subsidiary of Russia's state-controlled nuclear-energy and uranium-mining conglomerate, Rosatom.

Once again, Peter Schweizer's *Clinton Cash* has exposed much of this scandal, this time supplemented by excellent reporting from *The New York Times*.[28] Significant background of the story predates the Obama years, involving more of Washington's history of "collusion with Russia."

The United States government has been conducting uranium commerce with Russia since the Soviet Union imploded. In 1992, the Bush administration agreed with the nascent Russian federation that U.S. nuclear providers would be permitted to purchase uranium from Russia's disassembled nuclear warheads (after it had been down-blended from its highly enriched weapons-grade level). Uranium is a key component of nuclear power, from which the United States derives about 20 percent of our total electrical power, generated by approximately ninety-nine commercial reactors operating at sixty-one nuclear power plants in thirty states. Relatively speaking, our country does not have vast uranium resources. We currently produce only about 7 percent of the uranium we need and must import the rest; in 2017, for example, Russia accounted for 18 percent.[29]

In 2005, under the guise of the Clinton Foundation's mobilization to address the incidence of HIV/AIDS in Kazakhstan (where the virus was nearly nonexistent), Bill Clinton helped his Canadian billionaire pal Frank Giustra convince the ruling despot, Nursultan Nazarbayev, to grant coveted uranium-mining rights to Giustra's company, Ur-Asia Energy. Ur-Asia had no background in this highly competitive but potentially lucrative business. Nazarbayev, a former Communist party apparatchik, has ruled Kazakhstan for almost thirty years, and is notorious for human rights abuses and looting the treasury.[30]

In the months that followed, Giustra gave an astonishing $31.3 million to the Clinton Foundation and pledged $100 million more. With the Kazakh rights secured, Ur-Asia was able to expand its holdings and attract new investors. One was Ian Telfer, who also donated $2.35 million to the Clinton Foundation. Ur-Asia merged with Uranium One, a South African company, in a $3.5 billion deal. Telfer became Uranium One's chairman. The new company proceeded to buy up major uranium assets in the United States.

Meanwhile, as tends to happen in dictatorships, Nazarbayev turned on the head of Kazakhstan's uranium agency (Kazatomprom), who was arrested for selling valuable mining rights to such foreign entities as Ur-Asia/Uranium One. This was likely done at the urging of Russia, the neighborhood bully. Rosatom, the Kremlin-controlled nuclear-energy and uranium extraction conglomerate, was hoping to grab the Kazakh mines—whether by taking them outright or by taking over Uranium One.

The arrest, which happened a few months after Obama took office, had Uranium One's Clinton Foundation investors deeply concerned that the Kazakh mining rights would be lost. Uranium One turned to Secretary Clinton's State Department for help. As State Department cables disclosed by WikiLeaks show, Uranium One officials wanted more than a U.S. government statement to the media; they pressed for written confirmation that their mining licenses were valid. The State Department leapt into action: An energy officer from the U.S. embassy immediately held meetings with the Kazakh regime. A few days later, it was announced that Russia's Rosatom had purchased 17 percent of Uranium One. Problem solved.

Well, not quite. Rosatom was only fleetingly satisfied. Russia wanted a controlling interest in Uranium One. That would mean a controlling interest not just in the Afghan mines but in the U.S. assets that Uranium One had acquired—amounting to 20 percent of total U.S. uranium stock.

On this point, much of the anti-Clinton (and pro-Trump) coverage in conservative media has misaimed its focus.[31] The tendency is to hype the U.S. uranium assets and the fact that uranium can be used to make nuclear bombs. But Russia did not need our uranium for weapons purposes—no more than Newcastle needs our coal. Rather, to generate wealth, Putin's regime has long sought to develop and exploit its capacity as a commercial energy producer. The Kremlin was no doubt delighted at the opportunity to grab American uranium stocks: As I've already noted, we do not produce enough uranium for our domestic electricity needs, so anytime Putin takes from us something we need, it potentially becomes a leverage point for him and thus a problem for us. But in the greater scheme of things, the U.S. assets were a comparatively small objective next to the Kremlin's real target: the copious Kazakh stocks Uranium One owned.

Still, because Russia's move on Uranium One implicated significant U.S. uranium assets, federal law required approval by the Committee on Foreign Investment in the United States. CFIUS is a powerful tribunal, composed of the leaders of fourteen U.S. government agencies involved in national security and commerce. In 2010, these included not only Secretary of State Hillary Clinton, who had cultivated a reputation as a hawk opposed to such foreign purchases, but Attorney General Eric Holder. This is important because, at the very time the Uranium One transaction was under consideration, the Justice Department and the FBI were conducting an investigation of Rosatom's ongoing U.S. racketeering, extortion, and money-laundering scheme.

The Russian commercial agent responsible for the sale and transportation of uranium to the United States is a subsidiary of Rosatom known as "Tenex" (formally, JSC Techsnabexport). Tenex (and, by extension, Rosatom) has an American arm called "Tenam USA," based in Bethesda, Maryland. Around the time President Obama came to power, the Russian official in charge of Tenam was Vadim Mikerin. The Obama administration reportedly issued a visa for Mikerin in 2010, but a racketeering investigation led by the FBI determined that he was already operating here in 2009.

As Tenam's general director, Mikerin was responsible for arranging and managing Rosatom/Tenex's contracts with American uranium purchasers. This gave him tremendous leverage over the U.S. companies. With the assistance of several confederates, Mikerin used this leverage to extort and defraud the U.S. contractors into paying inflated prices for uranium. The proceeds were then laundered through shell companies and secret bank accounts in Latvia, Cyprus, Switzerland, and the Seychelles Islands—though sometimes transactions were handled in cash, with the skim divided into envelopes stuffed with thousands of dollars. The inflated payments served two purposes: they enriched Kremlin-connected energy officials in the United States and in Russia to the tune of millions of dollars; and they compromised the American companies that paid the bribes, rendering players in U.S. nuclear energy—a sector critical to national security—vulnerable to blackmail by Moscow.

To further the Kremlin's push for nuclear-energy expansion, Mikerin sought to retain a lobbyist. Naturally, he planned not only to use the lobbyist's services but to extort kickbacks, just as he did with U.S. energy companies with which he dealt. Aided by an associate connected to Russian organized-crime groups, Mikerin found his lobbyist—a man named William Douglas Campbell. Mikerin's solicitation in 2009 made Campbell uncomfortable, worried that he'd end up on the wrong side of the law. He contacted the FBI and revealed what he knew. From then on, he became the Bureau's informant, and the Justice Department ultimately relied on his information to arrest and prosecute Mikerin and his conspirators.

Interestingly, at the time Campbell started cooperating, the FBI was led by director Robert Mueller, the special counsel who investigated whether *Trump* had colluded with Russia. The case against Russia's subsidiary, Tenam, was centered in Maryland, where the U.S. attorney was Rod Rosenstein—President Trump's deputy attorney general through most of Mueller's Trump–Russia investigation.

Thanks to Campbell's work, the FBI was able to understand and monitor the racketeering enterprise almost from the start. By mid-May 2010, it could already prove the scheme and three separate extortionate payments Mikerin had squeezed out of the informant.

Keeping Congress in the Dark

Meanwhile, congressional opposition to Russia's potential acquisition of American uranium resources began to stir. As Peter Schweizer noted in *Clinton Cash*,[32] four senior House members steeped in national-security issues—Peter King (R., N.Y.), Ileana Ros-Lehtinen (R., Fla.), Spencer Bachus (R., Ala.), and Howard McKeon (R., Calif.)—voiced grave concerns, pointing out that Rosatom had helped Iran, America's sworn enemy, build its Bushehr nuclear reactor. The members concluded that "the take-over of essential US nuclear resources by a government-owned Russian agency...would not advance the national security interests of the United States." Republican Senator John Barrasso objected to Kremlin control of uranium assets in his state of Wyoming, warning of Russia's "disturbing record of supporting nuclear programs in countries that are openly hostile to the United States, specifically Iran and Venezuela." The House began moving a bill "expressing disfavor of the Congress" regarding Obama's revival of the nuclear-cooperation agreement Bush had abandoned.

Clearly, in this atmosphere, disclosure of the racketeering enterprise that Rosatom's American subsidiary was, at that very moment, carrying out would have been the death knell of the asset transfer to Russia. It would also likely have ended the "reset" initiative in which Obama and Clinton were deeply invested—an agenda that contemplated Kremlin-friendly deals on nuclear-arms control and accommodation of the nuclear program of Russia's ally, Iran. Nothing, however, would be allowed to disturb the reset. It appears that no disclosure of Russia's racketeering and strong-arming was made to CFIUS or to Congress—not by Secretary Clinton, not by Attorney General Holder, and certainly not by President Obama. In October 2010, CFIUS gave its blessing to Rosatom's acquisition of Uranium One.

A Sweetheart Plea Helps the Case Disappear

Even though the FBI had an informant collecting damning information, and had a prosecutable case against Mikerin by early 2010, the extortion racket against American energy companies was permitted to continue into the summer of 2014. It was only then that, finally, Mikerin and his confederates were arrested. Why then? Months earlier, in March 2014, Russia annexed Crimea. Putin also began massing forces on the Ukrainian border, coordinating and conducting attacks, ultimately taking control of territory. Clearly, the pie-in-the-sky Obama reset was dead. Furthermore, the prosecution of Mikerin's racketeering scheme had been so delayed that the Justice Department risked losing the ability to charge the 2009 felonies because of the five-year statute of limitations on most federal crimes.

Still, a lid needed to be kept on the case. It would have made for an epic Obama administration scandal, and a body blow to Hillary Clinton's presidential hopes, if in the midst of Russia's 2014 aggression, public attention had been drawn to the failure, four years earlier, to prosecute a national-security case in order to protect Russia's takeover of U.S. nuclear assets…in a transaction that had significant ramifications for Clinton Foundation investors.

And, lo and behold, the case disappeared without fanfare, much less a public trial. Think about that. The investigation of Russian racketeering in the American energy sector was the kind of spectacular success over which the FBI and Justice Department typically do a bells-'n'-whistles victory lap: the big self-congratulatory press conference followed by the media-intensive prosecutions—and, of course, more press conferences.

Here . . . crickets.

The Justice Department and FBI had little to say when Mikerin and his coconspirators were arrested. They quietly negotiated guilty pleas that were announced just before Labor Day. It was arranged that Mikerin would be sentenced just before Christmas. All under the radar.

How desperate was the Obama Justice Department to plead the case out? Mikerin was arrested on a complaint describing a racketeering scheme that stretched back to 2004 and included extortion, fraud, and money laundering. Yet he was permitted to plead guilty to a single count of money-laundering conspiracy.

Except it was not really money-laundering conspiracy.

Under federal law, that crime carries a penalty of *up to twenty years' imprisonment*, not only for conspiracy but for each act of money laundering.[33] But Mikerin was not made to plead guilty to this charge. He was permitted to plead guilty to an offense charged under the catch-all federal conspiracy provision, Section 371, which criminalizes agreements to commit any crime against the United States—an offense carrying a penalty of *zero to five years' imprisonment*.[34]

The Justice Department instructs prosecutors that when Congress has given a federal offense its own conspiracy provision with a heightened punishment (as it has for money laundering, racketeering, narcotics trafficking, and other serious crimes), they may not charge a Section 371 conspiracy. That statute is for less serious conspiracy cases. To invoke it for money laundering caps the sentence way below Congress's intent for that behavior. It signals to the court that the prosecutor does not regard the offense as major.

Yet, that is exactly what Rosenstein's office did, in a plea agreement his prosecutors cosigned with attorneys from the Justice Department's Fraud Section—then run by Andrew Weissmann, later Mueller's top deputy in the Trump–Russia investigation.[35]

As we'll see at many junctures, it's a small world.

Mikerin thus faced no RICO charges, no extortion or fraud charges. The plea agreement is careful not to mention any of the extortions in 2009 and 2010, before CFIUS approved Rosatom's acquisition of U.S. uranium stock. Mikerin just had to plead guilty to a nominal "money laundering" conspiracy charge. Insulated from Congress's prescribed money-laundering sentence, he got a term of just four years' imprisonment. The deal was a steal for him. It also spared the Obama administration a full public airing of the facts.[36]

Democrats Never Bought the Rigged Election Nonsense

"*Horrifying!*" As we've seen, candidates can get chirpy at final presidential debates less than three weeks from Election Day, and Hillary

Clinton was no exception. What "horror" had her inveighing so? The very thought that her Republican rival would question the legitimacy of the presidential election.[37]

Donald Trump being Donald Trump, he wouldn't budge. He would not pledge to accept the election results *a priori*. Okay, no, Trump didn't use the phase *a priori*. But he did speculate that the electoral process could be rigged. Until he saw how it played out, the Republican nominee said, he could not concede that the outcome would be on the up-and-up.

First, he reaffirmed an allegation for which he'd already been roundly condemned: foreigners could swing the election—specifical ly, "millions" of ineligible voters, an allusion to illegal immigration, the piñata of Trump's campaign. Second, he complained about the gross one-sidedness of the media's campaign coverage: scathing when it came to him; between inattentive and fawning when it came to his opponent, whose considerable sins were airbrushed away. Third, he claimed there was deep corruption: Clinton, he maintained, should not have been permitted to run given the evidence of felony mis-conduct uncovered in her email scandal. Instead of prosecuting her, law-enforcement agencies of the Democratic administration bent over backwards to give her a pass, and congressional Democrats closed ranks around her, conducting themselves in committee hearings more like her defense lawyers than investigators searching for the truth.

A flabbergasted Clinton responded that she was shocked—horri-fied—to hear Trump "talking down our democracy" this way. This was a top theme in her campaign's closing days: The election was absolutely legitimate; Trump was traitorously condemnable for refusing to say so.

Of course, Clinton and the Democrats who parroted her would prefer that you forget that now. And given her strained relationship with the truth, they're right to suspect that you'd never retain any-thing she said for very long. The media–Democrat caterwauling over Trump's election-rigging spiel was not rooted in patriotic commitment to the American democratic tradition of accepting election outcomes. They said what they said because they fully expected to win. The polls all said they would. Mrs. Clinton and her backers, President Obama included, would not abide a taint of illegitimacy affixing itself to her inevitable presidency.

Except it wasn't so inevitable. And when Clinton lost, they changed their tune about election-rigging. Suddenly, the inconceivable, the heresy-even-to-hint-at, was to be taken as gospel: The outcome was illegitimate! *Russia hacked the election!*

There was, however, a very inconvenient problem for this narrative: Everything of significance that is known to the U.S. government about Russian meddling was already known in those preelection weeks when Clinton and the Democrats were vouching for the integrity of the process and condemning Trump for even hesitating to endorse it.

By now, the story is well known.[38] Russia's cyberespionage operations began in 2014, long before Donald Trump's entry into the race. By summer 2015, hackers believed to be connected to Russian intelligence agencies had access to DNC computer networks, and the FBI began warning DNC officials of this in September of that year—albeit with a lack of urgency that now seems stunning. In March 2016 came the hacking of a private email account belonging to John Podesta, Mrs. Clinton's campaign chairman, who was sufficiently versed in cyber-privacy issues to have authored a 2014 report on the subject while serving as a top Obama White House adviser.

U.S. intelligence agencies were intimately aware of the penetrations. Obama's national intelligence director, James Clapper, publicly acknowledged that hackers appeared to have targeted presidential campaigns. By August 2016, CIA Director John Brennan interpreted streams of foreign intelligence to indicate that Putin had personally ordered the cyber thefts with the intention of at least damaging Clinton, if not flipping the election to Trump. In a phone call, Brennan is said to have admonished Alexander Bortnikov, the head of Russia's security service (the FSB), to desist. The next month, in a face-to-face confrontation (through interpreters) at an international conference in China, Obama warned Putin that "we knew what he was doing and [he] better stop it or else." Meanwhile, the administration conducted numerous high-level, close-hold meetings, weighing several options including retaliatory cyberattacks.

Ultimately, Obama decided to do nothing. The president's political allies and media admirers are now embarrassed about his inaction—"It is the hardest thing about my entire time in government to defend. I feel like we sort of choked," one anonymous senior administration official told *The Washington Post*. As ever, though, they remain apologists for their man, portraying a pained POTUS, fearful that any action he took would make matters worse, or be perceived as political, or otherwise undermine confidence in the election.

What, then, is the collusion narrative? And what's their story now? It is pretty much the same story they rebuked Trump for telling. They peddle a three-part rigged-election claim: (1) foreign interference, not by illegal aliens who may have voted but by Russians who did not affect the voting process; (2) one-sided press coverage—they mean the *Russian propaganda press* and the WikiLeaks release of DNC and John Podesta emails, which they'd now have you believe had more influence on Americans than did the media–Democrat complex and the grudging State Department release of Hillary Clinton's own emails; and (3) the corruption that lifted a low-character candidate who should not have been allowed to run but who received extraordinary government assistance—not from the Obama Justice Department but from the Putin regime.

To assess the Democratic narrative as bunk is not to excuse Russian duplicity, which many of us were warning about while Bush was embracing Putin as a strategic partner and while Obama was "resetting" with all due "flexibility."

By late October, the Russian "cyberespionage" effort to meddle in the election was well known. In the same debate in which Clinton rebuked Trump for refusing to concede the election's legitimacy, she attacked her rival as "Putin's puppet" and cited the finding of government agencies that Russia sought to interfere in the election. Clinton was not at all concerned that Putin's shenanigans would have any actual impact on the election. She invoked them because she thought it was *helpful* to her campaign—an opportunity to portray Trump as ripe for rolling by the Russian regime.

And how could she have taken any other position? None other than President Obama himself observed that there was nothing unusual about Russian scheming to influence American elections, which he said "dates back to the Soviet Union."[39] Obama deftly avoided mentioning that past scheming had never gotten much media traction because the Soviets had been more favorably disposed towards Democrats. While he blamed the Putin regime for hacking emails during the 2016 campaign, Obama described this as "fairly routine." He acknowledged, moreover, that it was publicly notorious well in advance of the election—which, of course, is why Clinton had been able to exploit it in a nationally televised debate three weeks prior to November 8.

What happened here is very simple: Russia was unimportant to Democrats, and was indeed avoided by Democrats, until they needed to rationalize a stunning defeat. Prior to the election, Democrats had little interest in mentioning "Russia" or "Putin." Of course, they sputtered out the words when they had no choice—when, not wanting to address the substance of embarrassing emails, they had to shift attention to the nefarious theft of those emails.

Beyond that, attention to the Kremlin was bad news for Clinton. It invited scrutiny of the Clinton Foundation's suspicious foreign dealings, Bill Clinton's lucrative speech racket, Hillary's biddable State Department, and Russia's acquisition of major U.S. uranium supplies. It conjured embarrassing memories of the "Russia Reset," during which the supine Obama administration watched Putin capture territory in Eastern Europe and muscle his way into the Middle East, all while arming and aligning with Iran. It called to mind the intriguing relationship between Podesta (the Clinton-campaign chairman and former Obama White House official) and Putin's circle—specifically, a $35 million investment by a Putin-created venture capital firm, Rusnano, into a small Massachusetts energy company, Joule Energy, just two months after Podesta joined Joule's board.[40]

So, while Donald Trump's Russia rhetoric ranged from the unseemly (blowing kisses at an anti-American thug) to the delusional (the notion that Russia, Iran's new friend, could be a reliable ally against jihadism) to the reprehensible (moral equivalence between the murderous Putin regime and American national-defense operations), Clinton's own Russia baggage rendered her unable to exploit it.

It was only afterward, after she lost a contest she thought she had in the bag, that the election turned illegitimate.

CHAPTER TWO

What Investigation . . .
and What Started It?

"ox News anchor Chris Wallace burst viewers' bubble," crowed The Daily Beast. The media–Democrat complex was popping its buttons because Fox News's highly regarded anchor had delivered his audience the purportedly devastating and unimpeachably factual news that the Trump–Russia investigation did not begin with the infamous Steele dossier. [1]

Wallace was reacting to a clip of Rush Limbaugh's observation, in a then-recent Fox News interview, that the Obama Justice Department and the FBI "began an investigation based on a phony dossier created and written by associates of Hillary Clinton"—the Steele dossier. No, Wallace countered, "The Trump investigation did not start with the FISA warrant and Carter Page and the dossier." To the contrary, "It started in June and July of 2016 when George Papadopoulos had spoken to a Russian agent and spoke to an Australian diplomat and said he had heard they had information on—dirt on Hillary Clinton."

I am a Chris Wallace fan and was one long before I became a contributor at Fox News. The Fox firmament is fairly described as right-leaning, and its prime-time options are laden with opinion programming. The network's best product, though, is its straight news coverage. Wallace is at the top of the class: a fact-driven journalist who prizes getting it right over getting it Right. Still, his snapshot of the Trump–Russia investigation's Origin Story—a tale designed to defy accurate rendering—was woefully incomplete.

The Origin Story has been the subject of cacophonous debate, foreign intrigue, spy games, stonewalling, and media scripting. In a sense, in scoffing at the claim that everything flows from the Carter Page FISA warrant, which was substantially based on the Steele dossier, Wallace and others *have to be right*. No investigation ever starts with a FISA warrant.

A good deal of gumshoe effort is generally needed to get an investigation to the point where a warrant may be sought. The warrant permits what is still called "wiretapping" and "bugging," the lexicon of a bygone technological time. In Justice Department lingo, such monitoring is known as "elsur," short for *electronic surveillance*. Today, it involves eavesdropping not just on people's phone calls and backroom meetings; there are emails, texts, social-media posts, and the like—torrents of communications by wire, cable, satellite, and all manner of complex telecom. Caught in the mix are providers from the legacy phone companies, to newer telecoms, to such social-media sites such as Facebook, Twitter, and Instagram. Gone are the days of simple analog technology transmitting waves of sound by hard wire; modern communications technology zooms packets of digital data, disassembled and reassembled, across vast global networks. Now, investigators are vexed by apps that scramble the packets in order to defeat eavesdropping, to say nothing of the legal and technological challenges posed by millions of seemingly indiscriminate communications racing through the internet's "upstream," which we'll encounter in Chapter Five.

The pejorative term for intruding on these communications is *spying*. To get a judicial warrant permitting it, whether in a criminal or a counterintelligence probe, is no layup. Such a warrant is sought at an advanced stage of an investigation because agents must work hard to corroborate the factual claims on which they will ask a judge to base the legally mandated probable-cause finding. Further, Congress has prescribed numerous approval hoops, including sign-offs by top officials at the FBI and the Justice Department. These agencies and the Foreign Intelligence Surveillance Court, in turn, impose additional vetting procedures. As a practical matter, a proper application may not be made to the court until a considerable amount of investigative grunt work has been done.

Even those, like my friend Rush Limbaugh, who stress the foundational role of the so-called "dossier" and the Carter Page FISA warrant, acknowledge that, although the FBI began receiving Christopher Steele's reports (eventually compiled into the dossier) in July 2016, no warrant was sought until October, three months later. The problem is not that the FBI *did not try* to verify Steele's information; it is that the Bureau *was not able* to verify it (in addition to having good reasons to know that parts of it were ridiculous, that Steele's credibility was suspect, and that Steele himself did not claim that his information was accurate—just worrisome and worthy of further investigation).

That said, to concede that the Trump–Russia investigation did not begin with the dossier-fueled spying on Page is not an admission that it commenced in the early summer of 2016, due to reports about Papadopoulos. In truth, by then it had been going on for several months—since at least the latter half of 2015, not long after Donald Trump entered the GOP nomination chase and before most anyone had ever heard of George Papadopoulos.

More Than One Investigation

Just as with *collusion*, there is confusion about what the ambiguous term *investigation* means in the variegated context of Russia-gate.

There is, for example, the *FISA investigation*. FISA surveillance is classified, and our knowledge of its extent in the Trump–Russia investigation remains incomplete. We do know, however, that there was a FISA investigation of Page.[2] In Justice Department and FBI parlance, it is common to refer to a "FISA investigation" (just as in organized crime, prosecutors and agents speak of a "wiretap investigation") as if it were an entity separate and apart from the preexisting, overarching investigation that generated the probable-cause evidence for the FISA coverage. The FISA surveillance is not actually separate, but it is spoken of as such because elsur has a legal process of its own, involving court applications and reports that do not necessarily affect the rest of the investigation. Other investigative techniques, such as physical surveillance (i.e., following people around), using informants, conducting interviews, and some methods of gathering business and financial records, do not require court warrants, even though these techniques are typically used in tandem with, and informed by, court-authorized electronic surveillance.

To refer to "the investigation" in Russia-gate is also confusing because the FBI investigation was not the only one. The CIA and allied foreign-intelligence services—especially Britain's spy agencies—did a fair amount of Trump–Russia probing before the FBI got involved.

Herculean efforts are still being made to obscure this history, the telling of which could expose some foreign "collusion" in the 2016 campaign that Democrats and other Trump detractors are not so anxious to broadcast. More importantly, it could lead to tit-for-tat revelations about clandestine American misadventures, to say nothing of the rupturing of intelligence-sharing arrangements critical to U.S. national security.

The CIA is not supposed to involve itself in American political campaigns, much less spy on Americans. Our intelligence community is not supposed to circumvent federal privacy laws by using allied intelligence services as a cat's paw: nod-and-wink encouragement to friendly foreign agencies that investigate Americans then pass the information along to U.S. agencies. Our closest intelligence allies—Britain, Canada, Australia, and New Zealand, which with the United States comprise the "Five Eyes"—pledge not to spy on each other's government officials. Yet, the oft-heard claim that they do not monitor each other's citizens is fiction. In 2016, at least some of the Five Eyes deemed Donald Trump and his campaign fair game.[3]

I believe the complicity of our allies, particularly Britain, partially explains why (as this book is written) President Trump has refrained from unsealing and publicizing most memoranda, files, and court documents pertaining to the Trump–Russia investigation's origins. (I use the plural, *origins*, advisedly, as there may not have been a single bigbang moment.) Trump's reluctance to disclose is also explained by a desire to avoid more accusations that he was obstructing the FBI and the Mueller probe.

There is also the likelihood that disclosure, even if not incriminating, would be embarrassing for Trump. In nearly twenty years as a prosecutor, I wrote and litigated hundreds of search and eavesdropping warrant applications. Naturally, an application reflects the theory underlying the government's investigation. The Obama administration's theory was that Trump was involved in personal (i.e., sexual), financial, and possibly criminal misconduct (even espionage) that made him subject to blackmail by the Kremlin. We must therefore deduce that the intelligence agencies' memoranda spell out these suspicions. Even if the suspicions are untrue, the president could obviously be wounded politically by the disclosure of FBI and CIA documents describing him as compromised and traitorous.

Let us not forget: John Brennan, Obama's former White House intelligence adviser and CIA director who blazed the Trump–Russia trail, has publicly accused Trump of *treason*, and of being "wholly in the pocket of Putin." He leveled these hyper-partisan slanders in a way that intimates insider knowledge.[4] This is, to say the least, despicable conduct by a former official trusted with access to classified intelligence. But here's what matters for our present purposes: (1), since Brennan had considerable influence over the government's intelligence analyses, we should assume Trump would not be flattered by their public release; and (2), the Justice Department and intelligence community's virulent opposition to disclosure of their files renders it very difficult to chart when and how the international, multiagency investigations of suspected Trump–Putin ties began.

When Did It Start and Who Was the Target?

Even if we just consider the investigation led by the Justice Department and the FBI, there has been sleight of hand about how things got rolling. Politicized misdirection, of course, was a signature feature of the Obama Justice Department. Recall the Clinton-emails probe: The Justice Department was a de facto Clinton-campaign adjunct (and a not very subtle one), camouflaging the existence and criminal nature of the probe, with Attorney General Lynch ordering FBI Director Comey to describe the effort as a "matter" rather than an investigation. Similar dissimulations marked the Trump–Russia probe.

Before there was a Trump angle, the FBI was conducting a counterintelligence investigation of Russia's cyberespionage. That evolved into an investigation of Russia's influence operation against the 2016 campaign—which, for transparently partisan purposes, has been tirelessly described by the media, Democrats, and government officials as an "investigation of Russia's interference in the *election*," notwithstanding that there was no tampering with the voting process. This inquiry came to include the Trump–Russia angle, thanks to the exertions of CIA Director Brennan and his counterparts in British and European intelligence services—likeminded in their transnational-progressive alarm at Trump's NATO-bashing and overt infatuation with Putin.

Many informed people refer to late July 2016, when the FBI formally opened a counterintelligence investigation code-named "Crossfire Hurricane," as the commencement of the probe. That, however, is just a bookkeeping entry—sheer form over substance. The truth is that Trump–Russia investigative activity, even by the FBI, was ongoing well before an investigative file was established.

The FBI is cute about this, too, drawing untenable distinctions between when key "evidence," such as the Steele dossier, was given to the Bureau, versus when the dossier purportedly first came to the attention of what the Bureau calls its "closely held investigative team" at headquarters. For example, FBI leadership long maintained that its headquarters team did not learn about the Steele dossier until mid-September 2016, less than a month before it sought the Page FISA warrant. This claim is regurgitated by Democrats, who maintain, to quote Rep. Adam Schiff (now the chairman of the House Intelligence Committee), that the dossier "**played no role** in launching the FBI's counterintelligence investigation" (bold underlining in original).[5]

Nonsense. Steele began supplying his reports to the FBI on July 5, 2016—ironically, the same day as Director Comey's Hillary Clinton press conference. In London that day, Steele gave the "intelligence" he had by then compiled to Michael Gaeta, the Bureau's Rome-based legal attaché, whom Steele knew from the FIFA soccer investigation. Huddling with Steele was so important to Agent Gaeta that he took pains to get the green light from his superiors and the State Department for this sudden trip to Britain. Steele proceeded to tell him that the Republican presidential nominee was in Putin's pocket. Is it possible that Gaeta decided to sit on this astonishing information rather than alert his chain of command? Not at the FBI I worked investigations with for almost twenty years.

But even if you buy that unlikely story, Steele and his dossier coauthor, Glenn Simpson, informed Bruce Ohr, a high-ranking Justice Department official, of their Trump–Russia allegations that summer.

As we'll see, these conversations occurred both before and after the FBI formally opened "Crossfire Hurricane" in late July. The allegation against Trump cannot have been much of a surprise to Ohr: Not only were Steele and Simpson longtime acquaintances of his, Ohr's wife Nellie—a Russia scholar, CIA contractor, and Hillary Clinton supporter—had been hired by Simpson as a Fusion GPS contractor. She was collaborating with Simpson and Steele on the Clinton campaign's anti-Trump project.

Steele dilated on his Trump–Russia allegations at a breakfast meeting with Bruce and Nellie Ohr in Washington on Saturday, July 30—just one day before Crossfire Hurricane was formally opened. After the meeting, Ohr promptly called FBI Deputy Director Andrew McCabe (an old friend and colleague from their days investigating organized crime in New York) to pass along Steele's alarming claims. Within either hours or a few days (Bruce Ohr's congressional testimony is murky on the timing), Ohr was at FBI headquarters, meeting with McCabe and the latter's counsel, Lisa Page—who had worked for Ohr at the Justice Department for several years, investigating international organized crime (particularly the Russian variety). McCabe and Page put Ohr in touch with the lead Trump–Russia investigator, Agent Peter Strzok. Over the ensuing months, the FBI both took information directly from Steele and used Ohr as a conduit for information from Steele.

Who started which investigation, when, and why? These are unsettled questions. So is the most significant question: Exactly who was under investigation? Common sense tells us that the principal subject was Donald Trump. It is risible to suggest that the immense international investigative effort here was triggered by concerns over Carter Page, whom Russian spies dismissed as an "idiot" when dealing with him in 2013; twenty-eight-year-old George Papadopoulos, who was still touting participation in the "Model U.N." on his paltry résumé; or even Paul Manafort, whose labors for Russia-friendly Ukrainians had been well known for years. The fact that Donald Trump could become president, and then did become president, was what animated the Obama administration and allied governments. But this obvious fact was the subject of gamesmanship before and after the 2016 election.

Democrats and the media assert that Page parted ways with the Trump campaign weeks before FISA surveillance was authorized on October 21, 2016[6] (though they conveniently avoid noting that what prompted the severance was the recent push by Brennan, Simpson, and Steele to draw the attention of Capitol Hill and the media to the dossier's allegations). Put aside that the Trump campaign was so chaotic and disorganized that it was difficult to tell whether low-level supporters were "in" or "around" it. *Page was surveilled precisely because of his connection to the Trump campaign.* The FBI's Page warrant applications explicitly stated the Bureau's belief that "Page and perhaps other individuals associated with Candidate #1's [i.e., Trump's] campaign" were collaborating in Russia's espionage. The Bureau was relying on Steele, who claimed that Page was an emissary running messages between the Trump and Putin camps in an elaborate scheme of campaign influence operations and corrupt payoffs.

More to the point, once a court authorizes eavesdropping, agents may not only intercept communications prospectively. They may also *seize past communications*—such as stored emails, text messages, and social-media posts. Manifestly, the FBI hoped the warrant would help them go backwards. Of particular interest was Page's July 2016 Russia trip, during which, according to the dossier, he met with high-ranking Putin confidants—a claim that Page vehemently denies and that has never been verified. Page was the subject of the surveillance, but he was never the objective. Investigators saw him as a window into *Trump's* ties to Russia.

After the election, the Obama administration confronted a different challenge: how to keep the investigation alive after Trump took office, at which point he would have the power to shut it down. This was done by telling him he was not under investigation—notwithstanding that he was the central figure in the investigation. The probe was structured so that, even though Trump's name would not formally appear on any investigative file or list of targets proposed for court surveillance, by pursuing the investigation of the named targets, the FBI would incidentally gather evidence against Trump. The Bureau disingenuously elevated form over substance, telling the president he was not a suspect (which merely meant, "we haven't opened a case file on you") even as it homed in on his campaign in hopes of proving the Trump–Russia conspiracy of Steele's imagination.

Then, a few days after Comey's May 9, 2017, firing, Acting FBI Director Andrew McCabe formally opened a criminal investigation against Trump for suspected obstruction—even though, inconveniently, two days after Comey's firing, McCabe testified to Congress that no one had attempted to obstruct the Bureau's Russia investigation. In essence, McCabe's action merely caused the FBI's files to reflect what had long been reality: Under the guise of the Russia counterintelligence probe, and in the absence of any hard evidence of criminal activity, the FBI was examining whether the president (a) had been in a criminal conspiracy with Russia and (b) was covering it up. A few days later, however, when Deputy Attorney General Rod Rosenstein appointed Mueller, the Trump–Russia investigation was effectively wrested from FBI control and entrusted to the special counsel. Adopting Comey's public announcement of the probe (in March 2017 testimony), Rosenstein described it as a "counterintelligence" investigation...although Rosenstein also adopted Comey's slippery caveat that the "counterintelligence" probe would include an "assessment" of whether any crimes had been committed—i.e., it was an *investigation* hoping to find a predicate *crime*, even though no one dared call it a *criminal investigation*.

When did the investigation start? Why did it start? What kind of investigation was it? It has proved impossible to get straight answers to these questions.

The Investigation ... and the Narrative

Why is so much time and energy spent on fixing the origination of the Trump–Russia investigation? It is not just that the government is withholding documentation. The "when it all began" question is driven by the political battle to dictate the narrative.

That should never be the case. Questions about when and why an investigation starts involve matters of objective fact. Here, though, the cone of top-secret intelligence hides that information. Trump antagonists want the probe to be seen as triggered by an episode that colorably raises suspicions of a Trump–Russia espionage plot. This would attest to the investigators' good faith and paint Trump as the villain, even if there was not enough evidence to prove criminal collusion. Trump partisans, by contrast, want the font of collusion to be a fraudulent episode. This paints the president as a victim and the investigators as perpetrators of a hoax, even if there is evidence of unsavory but noncriminal collusion.

If the media has now decided that the president's fans are over-emphasizing Carter Page and the role of the Steele dossier, that is a self-serving case of amnesia. It was Trump antagonists who started that game.

"Trump Adviser's Visit to Moscow Got the F.B.I.'s Attention." That was the page-one headline *The New York Times* ran on April 20, 2017. There followed a breathless report that "a catalyst for the F.B.I. investigation into connections between Russia and President Trump's campaign" was a July 2016 visit to Moscow by Carter Page. It was due to the Moscow trip by Page, dubbed a Trump "foreign policy adviser," that "the F.B.I. obtained a warrant from the Foreign Intelligence Surveillance Court" during the stretch run of the presidential campaign.

No fewer than six of the *Times*'s top reporters, along with a researcher, worked their anonymous "current and former law enforcement and intelligence officials" in order to generate this blockbuster. With these leaks, the paper confidently reported: "*From the Russia trip of the once-obscure Mr. Page* grew a wide-ranging investigation, now accompanied by two congressional inquiries, that has cast a shadow over the early months of the Trump administration" (emphasis added).

Oh sure, the *Times* acknowledged, there might have been a couple of other factors involved. "Paul Manafort, then Mr. Trump's campaign manager [i.e., at the time of Page's trip], was already under criminal investigation in connection with payments from a pro-Russian political party in Ukraine."[7] And "WikiLeaks and two websites later identified as Russian intelligence fronts had begun releasing emails obtained when Democratic Party servers were hacked." But the trigger for the investigation—its main "catalyst"—was Page. George Papadopoulos? Somehow, despite this centipede of journalistic legwork and this chorus of insider intel sources, the name Papadopoulos does not appear in the *Times*'s story.

So imagine the dizzy spell seven months later—a slightly early case of New Year's reverie—when the *Times* premiered its Origin Story 2.0, the Papadopoulos yarn, under the headline "How the Russia Inquiry Began: A Campaign Aide, Drinks and Talk of Political Dirt." This time, with a mere six doughty journalists (no seventh wheel researcher on this holiday weekend), the Gray Lady explained that it was actually young George who triggered the FBI's massive probe by . . . wait for it . . . a night of boozy blather in London. Papadopoulos, an unknown figure back when he had pled guilty a few weeks before the *Times*'s new blockbuster, was now elevated to "the improbable match that set off a blaze that has consumed the first year of the Trump administration."

Wait a second, *what happened to Carter Page?* Well, if you were willing to hang in there through the first thirty-six paragraphs of the new 3,000-word story, you found a fleeting mention: "A trip to Moscow by another adviser, Carter Page, also raised concerns at the F.B.I."[8] *You don't say!*

What actually happened to Page is obvious. The dossier that was the script for the first media–Democrat Origin Story, starring Page, collapsed. Recall that Steele's reports, based on anonymous Russian sources, alleged that (a) there was an explicit Trump–Russia conspiracy to interfere in the 2016 election; (b) the conspiracy included Russian hacking of Democratic email accounts in which Trump-campaign officials, including Manafort and Page, were complicit; and (c) Page met with two top Kremlin operatives on the Moscow trip—operatives who discussed with him a quid pro quo arrangement to drop sanctions against Russia, floated the possibility of providing the Trump campaign with "*kompromat*" (compromising information) on Hillary Clinton, and warned that Trump better be careful because the Putin regime had a *kompromat* file on him, too.

In the months after the *Times*'s big report on Page's Moscow trip, we learned that the dossier was actually an opposition-research project paid for by the Hillary Clinton campaign and the Democratic National Committee.[9] We found out that the FBI regarded the most notorious dossier allegations as "salacious and unverified"—and if this was true when former FBI Director Comey testified to it in June

2017, it had to have been true eight months earlier, when the Page surveillance warrant was first sought.[10] It emerged that in England, where he was being sued for libel, Steele had explained to a court that the dossier was merely a compilation of bits of "raw intelligence" that were "unverified" and that he passed along because they "warranted further investigation." The ardently anti-Trump former spy claimed to be worried that there might be national-security threats, not that there really were any such threats. That, he now says, was for the FBI to figure out.[11]

Of course, the FBI hadn't figured it out. In seeking court warrants, the Bureau had trusted Steele. As Judiciary Committee Senators Charles Grassley (R., Iowa) and Lindsey Graham (R., S.C.) have recounted:

> When asked at the March 2017 briefing [of Judiciary Committee leaders] why the FBI relied on the dossier in the FISA applications absent meaningful corroboration—and in light of the highly political motives surrounding its creation—then-Director [James] Comey stated that the FBI included the dossier allegations about Carter Page in the FISA applications because Mr. Steele himself was considered reliable due to his past work with the Bureau.[12]

Yet the Obama Justice Department and the FBI concealed from the Foreign Intelligence Surveillance Court the Clinton campaign's sponsorship of Steele's work. Moreover, the Justice Department stonewalled House inquiries about whether dossier allegations were used in applying for the Page surveillance warrant...even though, shortly before the *Times* ran its April 2017 Page extravaganza, unnamed "US officials briefed on the [Russia] investigation" had leaked to CNN that the dossier had indeed been used to obtain the FISA warrant.[13] And even when the Justice Department grudgingly acknowledged to the court that Steele had been officially removed from the investigation (over press contacts that the FBI had implausibly denied in the original FISA warrant application), the judges were not told that the FBI was still relying on him as an informant, using Bruce Ohr as their cutout.

While the dossier's lack of heft became increasingly clear, Page—an

Annapolis grad and a former naval-intelligence officer who has never been accused of a crime and has never met Donald Trump[14]—became a public fixture, vigorously and credibly denying Steele's allegations. To be sure, Page's views about Russia are accommodationist: He has been an investor in the Russian energy sector and blamed United States policies for tensions with the Putin regime. But while that might qualify him for a job at the State Department, we are talking here about a job as the point man in a traitorous anti-American plot. Not only did Page insist he was unacquainted with Igor Sechin and Igor Divyekin, the highly placed Russians with whom Steele placed him at Moscow meetings, he also maintained that he had never met Manafort, who supposedly directed him in the Trump–Russia espionage plot. While the Justice Department and FBI had stressed to the court that Russia tried to recruit Page as an asset in 2013, they apparently low-keyed (if they mentioned it at all) the fact that *Page had cooperated with the Justice Department in the investigation of the Russian spies.* To say the least, such cooperation would not exactly commend Page for later Russian reliance on him to convey corrupt messages between the Kremlin and Trump. Not only had information from Page been used by the Justice Department against Russian spies in the arrest complaint; Victor Podobnyy, the Russian recruiter, was quoted referring to Page as an "idiot."[15]

In the months after the *Times*'s big Page story, the dossier came to appear fraudulent. The notion that Page could have played the role assigned to him strained credibility, and even a cynic who believed Donald Trump was open to conspiring with Russia had to admit that the Kremlin had agents far better positioned than Page for an approach to him.[16]

We will come to Papadopoulos in due course. For now, what is remarkable is that, in pivoting to Papadopoulos seven months after its Page story melted, the Newspaper of Record tut-tutted that it was not the dossier that "so alarmed American officials to provoke the F.B.I. to open a counterintelligence investigation into the Trump campaign months before the presidential election." This reliance on the dossier, the *Times* now said, was a false claim that "Mr. Trump and other politicians have alleged." Somehow omitted from the report were the inconvenient details that it was the *Times* itself that led the charge in claiming it was Page's trip to Moscow that provoked the investigation, and that it was the Steele dossier that so alarmed the FBI about that trip.

CHAPTER THREE

An Old Story: Beltway Consultants as Agents of the Kremlin

'We are now of the belief that this model can greatly benefit the Putin Government if employed at the correct levels with the appropriate commitment to success." So wrote Paul Manafort in 2005. He was writing to Oleg Deripaska, a Russian aluminum oligarch and close confidant of Vladimir Putin, the Russian dictator. Manafort's memorandum pitched Deripaska on a strategy to improve the image of Putin's regime in the United States, Europe, and former Soviet republics.[1]

He did not write these words as a clandestine agent of Russia. He wrote them as a political consultant. This distinction is a key to piercing the Trump–Russia "collusion" veil, to understanding the narrative's foundational fallacy.

As we've seen, for a quarter century prior to Donald Trump's entry into the 2016 campaign, the bipartisan Beltway regarded collusion with Russia as a boon to world peace, global prosperity, and American security. Nirvana commenced when the Soviet Union disintegrated in December 1991. Suddenly, a gravy train roared through the badlands of "gangster capitalism,"[2] the terrain of vast mineral and commodity wealth—the spoils of a fallen empire—that became available to the shrewdest and most ruthless bidders. In the aftermath, there emerged a marriage: On one side were fabulously wealthy Russian and Ukrainian "oligarchs," many of whom had risen from nothing through alliances with organized-crime chieftains and corrupt government officials. On the other side were well-connected American political operatives—lawyers and lobbyists tied to both political parties.

It has been a perverse arrangement. It reeks of corruption. How much more unseemly does it get? One moment, a former director of the FBI is giving a speech in Moscow about how vital it is for Americans and Russians to align in the battle to "beat organized crime." Then, in the blink of an eye, that same former top Fed—William Sessions, driven from office over a slew of ethical lapses—is a lawyer representing the Russian mafia's "Boss of Bosses" in a $150 million racketeering scheme to defraud American investors?[3]

Here's what you need to remember: Most of this whoring is legal. "Unsavory but Legal" is a fact of Swamp life. The guys with their snouts in the trough are the same guys who write and enforce the laws, the benefits accruing as they glide between the "public service" and the private lobbying sides of the revolving door—the door between political office and political consultancy, between law enforcement and law evasion.

Unsavory but Legal is to Washington what *Semper Fi* is to the Marines.

On Capitol Hill, high-profile, low-impact, good-governance legislation is the tribute vice pays to virtue. Thus, technically speaking, there are some pertinent laws on the books, such as the Foreign Agents Registration Act, a set of provisions dating to 1938. If taken seriously, FARA requires individuals who do advocacy work in the United States on behalf of foreign entities to disclose these relationships and activities to the Justice Department. Noncompliance is a felony, calling for up to five years' imprisonment.[4] But FARA is not taken seriously—or at least it wasn't prior to the appointment of a special counsel to investigate the Trump campaign. In the half-century prior to the 2016 election, the Justice Department won a whopping three—count 'em, *three*—convictions, out of just seven attempts to prosecute FARA violations.[5] Sparse as that is, FARA has been a prosecutorial juggernaut compared to the Logan Act, which—as we shall see—the Obama Justice Department and FBI also trotted out to justify investigating the Trump campaign. An almost certainly unconstitutional artifact of the late eighteenth century (in fact, a companion of the notorious Alien and Sedition Acts), the Logan Act purports to criminalize foreign-policy freelancing by U.S. citizens. It has *never* resulted in a successful prosecution—there have been two unsuccessful indictments, the last one nearly 170 years ago.[6]

But I digress.

Ever since the Soviet Union collapsed, influential Republican and Democratic elected officials, agency administrators, and political operatives have put on their lobbying hats to flack for Ukrainian and Russian billionaires and the partisan factions they patronize. Everyone knew the lobbyists were doing it. And everyone knew it was sleazy. But it was sleazy because the money was dirty, not because there was espionage afoot.

The political consultants were cashing in on Washington's utopian dream of installing a Western political order and free market economies in the former Soviet empire. The Ukrainian oligarchs toward whom Republican consultants gravitated were leveraging Moscow against Kiev. There's a salient distinction, though: The magnates were oft-time Putin allies, but that did not make them Kremlin agents. They did not want Ukraine to be dominated by Russia. The oligarchs, mostly concentrated in the Donbas region of eastern Ukraine, have always wanted their country to enjoy friendly relations with Moscow. Hostilities with a covetous and far more powerful neighbor is bad for business.[7] Yet, the oligarchs want Ukraine to be independent. *Really* independent, as in *federalized*. They want to reign over semiautonomous Ukrainian regions, persisting in their monopoly grips on key economic sectors. To accomplish this, they need to delay and limit Ukraine's integration into the European Union, the strong preference of Kiev and western Ukraine, as well as of Western Europe and the United States.

It has been a delicate dance. To thrive, the oligarchs have needed good relations with the West, too. That is why buying up Washington lobbyists (and no small number of EU political wizards) was essential. Let's clarify what the "collusion" narrative distorts, though. Yes, it is true that the oligarchs' interests frequently line up with the Kremlin's obsession to prevent former Soviet satellites, and especially Ukraine, from going West. *But the oligarchs are not the Kremlin.* They have their own agenda, and it has often involved playing Europe against Moscow. The tycoons have governmental cronies and customer bases on both sides of the East–West tinderbox. To keep the gravy train rolling, they must avoid being swallowed up by either.

While Washington political consultants do the oligarchs' bidding, the former make the latter salable by nudging them in a pro-Western direction. You do not have to be a Kremlin apologist (I most certainly am not[8]) to grasp the absurdity of the "collusion" narrative's premise: namely, that being a lobbyist for Ukrainian oligarchs who prioritize good relations with Moscow is the same thing as being a clandestine agent of Russia.[9] For the Obama Justice Department and FBI to have exploited the United States government's national-security spying powers on such a risible pretext was to criminalize disputes over foreign policy—a politicization of investigative authorities, a gross abuse of power.[10]

The tensions between Moscow and Kiev, between Russia and the West, make for a dynamic political context. Because of their clients' shifting needs and transient preferences, the consultants have often found themselves on Russia's side of some policy dispute or another. Regardless of whether one agrees with them, the consultants contend their work promotes good American relations with Moscow and eases Ukrainian tensions (and the Kremlin's stoking thereof). Is this just a rationalization for cashing in? Well, there's no shortage of that. Still, it cannot be gainsaid that these Russia–Ukraine tensions, left to fester, could explode into major war. At flashpoints, they have already have burst into significant hostilities.

It's complicated, and therefore ripe for distortion.

Most Americans are not familiar with the fraught history and politics of Ukraine. They know little about the netherworld of Washington political lobbying for foreign interests—especially for despots and Mafiosi-turned-magnates. When Hillary Clinton lost an election, and it came time for her progressive sympathizers and Republican anti-Trump agitators to pin her defeat on Russian espionage, it was easy to craft a narrative that painted Trump political consultants who'd worked for Ukrainian and Russian oligarchs as Putin's puppets. All that was necessary was for the rest of us to forget the last quarter century, to develop amnesia about Washington's projection of post-Soviet Russia as a political and business partner, an effort that Mrs. Clinton herself had been in up to her neck.[11]

That sets the stage. Now let's get to the villain out of central casting.

The Lobbyist

Paul Manafort was the very model of a well-connected GOP establishment operator and lobbyist. By the time he wrote the aforementioned 2005 memo to Oleg Deripaska, he had been in the political consultancy biz for three decades. He cut his teeth on the 1976 campaign of President Gerald R. Ford, as a twenty-seven-year-old convention floor manager helping the incumbent president stave off a grassroots conservative insurgency, the primary challenge of Ronald Reagan. Not one to fuss over ideology, by 1980 Manafort was working for Reagan's victorious campaign.

With Republicans back in power, Manafort dove into the lucrative lobbying business with an array of fellow GOP consultants. These included his pal Roger Stone, a Nixon devotee who reveled in "the dark arts" of politics, and whose 1977 campaign to lead the Young Republicans National Federation was managed by Manafort.[12] Over time, other Manafort partners included Charles Black and Rick Davis, Republican establishment stalwarts who worked as top advisers to GOP campaigns going back to Reagan and who eventually teamed up to run Senator John McCain's unsuccessful 2008 White House bid.

Manafort had been an adviser to the failed 1996 Republican presidential campaign of Senator Bob Dole, a McCain ally. With all these connections, it is unsurprising that McCain initially wanted Manafort to run the 2008 GOP convention. He thought better of it, though, because too much media attention had been drawn to Manafort's sideline specialty: prettying up despicable foreign tyrants for American and Western consumption...and, of course, for financial aid. The consultant's client list was a who's who of global abominations: Mobuto Sese Seko of Zaire, Ferdinand Marcos of the Philippines, Jonas Savimbi of Angola, and so on.[13] The Faustian bargain paid fabulously well.

It was the same bargain that led him to Oleg Deripaska. In that, Manafort was far from alone. The gravy train was filled to capacity, though you'd never know it from the revisionist history painted after Trump's 2016 victory.

In the gangster capitalism era, Deripaska had cornered the Russian aluminum market. Besides concerns arising from his Kremlin connections, American national-security officials harbored suspicions that Deripaska had amassed his fortune through the usual mafia methods—murder, extortion, kickbacks—even though his criminal record was spotless (not exactly a clean bill of health when it comes to insiders of corrupt regimes). He was accordingly denied a visa to come to the United States.

Thus did Bob Dole go to work for Deripaska in 2003, well before Manafort entered the picture. The law firm at which the GOP former Senate leader and presidential standard-bearer had landed managed to rake in over half a million dollars—without being accused of espionage!—while persuading the State Department to lift visa restrictions against Deripaska. That was finally done in 2005, but by the next year, the travel ban was reinstated at the FBI's insistence. At that point, the billionaire turned to Manafort's lobbying partner, Rick Davis, to set up meetings with John McCain and other U.S. senators in a new attempt to get the visa renewed. Eventually, the FBI not only relented but, in 2009, actually recommended that the Kremlin-tied oligarch be admitted into the United States. The Bureau, you see, had calculated that Deripaska might be in a position to help rescue Robert Levinson, an FBI agent believed to be detained in Iran. The effort failed, but Deripaska is said to have cooperated enthusiastically, even to have spent $25 million of his own money in the cause.

If you're keeping score, the FBI director at the time was Robert Mueller.

The Spy

By 2015, the former British spy Christopher Steele, who would later help both Hillary Clinton's campaign and the FBI concoct the Trump–Russia narrative, was lobbying the Justice Department on Deripaska's behalf, arranging meetings between the oligarch and such high-ranking anti-racketeering officials as Bruce Ohr (who would later become Steele's conduit to the FBI, while Ohr's wife collaborated with Steele on the anti-Trump dossier). Sure, Steele had been running MI6's Russia desk even as Putin's regime murdered defector Alexander Litvinen-ko on British soil in 2006. By 2012, though, Steele had traversed the British version of the revolving door, seamlessly shifting to the highly remunerative private intelligence business. He gladly accepted a re-tainer to help Deripaska—often called "Putin's oligarch"—defend against a lawsuit brought by a business rival, and, well, one thing led to another...

Despite Steele's touting of Deripaska as a potential informant for the United States, the Justice Department apparently lost interest when the magnate told investigators that (a) their notions about or-ganized crime in Russia were all wet, and (b) although he had no love lost for Manafort, his swindling former business partner, their theory of Manafort as the linchpin of Trump–Russia collusion was "prepos-terous." No matter: For Steele, it was on to the next thing. In 2017, he induced yet another D.C. lobbyist—Adam Waldman, Deripaska's FARA-registered agent since 2009—to reach out on the oligarch's be-half to Senate Democrats investigating Manafort's role in the collu-sion caper.[14]

Unsavory but Legal: that's how close observers viewed the Wash-ington pastime of lobbying for bad guys with Kremlin connections, at least before Donald Trump came along.

The Journalist

One of those close observers was Glenn Simpson, the investigative re-porter who eventually collaborated with his friend Chris Steele on the anti-Trump dossier. Back in 2007, as McCain readied his presidential run, Simpson and his wife, Mary Jacoby (a journalist with longstand-ing Clinton ties through her Little Rock–based family), coauthored a *Wall Street Journal* feature: "How Lobbyists Help Ex-Soviets Woo Washington."[15] The meticulously researched report explored the work Manafort and such Swamp luminaries as Senator Dole, former FBI Director Sessions, and Haley Barbour (the former GOP chairman and Mississippi Governor) had done on behalf of Russian and Ukrainian oligarchs, politicians, and organized-crime figures. In a follow-up report on McCain's ties to Manafort's lobbying firm, Simpson and

Jacoby acknowledged that "working for foreign interests is legal, but it can be politically hazardous for lobbyists and the politicians they advise."[16] Ain't that the truth!

By 2016, Simpson was running the private intelligence firm Fusion GPS. He was not only being generously compensated to help defend Kremlin cronies who had been sued by the Justice Department over a Putin regime fraud scheme, he was being generously compensated to help the Clinton campaign and the Democratic party craft the Trump–Russia collusion narrative. How convenient that he'd be able to mine the collusion script right out of his stories for the *Journal*. All he needed to do was narrow the focus myopically on Manafort, and "evolve" his theme from grubby corruption to traitorous espionage.

The Oligarchs

In that 2005 memo to Deripaska, Manafort explained that he was "offering a great service that can re-focus, both internally and externally, the policies of the Putin government." The consultant knew what he was talking about because he was already providing this same great service to Putin's ally in Ukraine, Viktor Yanukovych.

Manafort's path to Yanukovych ran through Ukrainian oligarchs who had gotten fabulously rich in the "gangster capitalism" era. The most important of these was Rinat Akhmetov, a mining oligarch who is the richest man in Ukraine. In the early 2000s, Akhmetov retained Manafort's services to improve his image and that of his sprawling conglomerate. It has been alleged that he maintained organized-crime connections when he amassed his fortune.[17] In 2005, for example, a top minister in Ukraine's economic crimes department was quoted in the Russian press asserting that Akhmetov "was the head of [an] organized crime group." Akhmetov strenuously denies the allegation. He has apparently never been charged with a crime. His wealth, he maintains, was built through careful study and a daring investment strategy. A phalanx of libel lawyers and publicists guard this assiduously cultivated reputation: Akhmetov, the self-made Ukrainian philanthropist, parliamentarian, and patriot.[18]

Following Ukraine's 1991 declaration of independence from the crumbling Soviet Union, its history has been a struggle for economic and civil liberties against a legacy of statism and endemic corruption. Ukraine is tugged by the European Union on one side and, on the other, by a regime in Moscow increasingly jealous of Russia's sphere of influence, particularly Ukraine and other former Soviet satellites. This struggle has been fought out domestically by Ukraine's political parties. In this infighting, the now-defunct Party of Regions was prominent, and, among its well-heeled sponsors, Akhmetov had the deepest pockets. He hails from the Donbas region in the east, where he holds copious coal-mining assets. The region teems with native Russians, who make up about 17 percent of Ukraine's population. Donbas was thus a Party of Regions stronghold.[19]

In a country where extraordinary wealth is concentrated in the hands of a few oligarchs, Regions claimed the loyalty of about a third of them, representing over $35 billion in assets.[20] The party has been described by Volodymyr Horbulin, a pro-West Ukrainian statesman and governmental adviser, as a motley crew of "criminal and anti-democracy figures," along with "progressive businessmen who wanted the party to become more modern and democratic."[21] Like other parties, Regions espoused Ukrainian nationalism. Its priority, though, was to forge a Ukraine that indulged and expanded the economic autonomy of its rich industrialists. That sat comfortably with the objective of cultivating friendly relations with Russia, Ukraine's far more powerful neighbor to the east. It also put Regions in robust competition with Ukrainian parties that favored economic integration and deepening political cooperation with the EU, and even military alliance with NATO—precisely to rein in the oligarchs, mitigate Russian influence, and curb corruption (at least when the pro-Europe factions weren't in power).

In this thicket, Manafort became well acquainted with Akhmetov's friend, Dmytro Firtash. That tie brought him into the orbit of former FBI Director William Session's aforementioned Russian mafia client, Semion Mogilevich. A chain-smoking, five-foot-six-inch, 300-pound fireplug of a man, Mogilevich is a regular on the FBI's list of Ten Most Wanted Fugitives.[22] "Weapons trafficking, contract murders, extortion, drug trafficking, and prostitution on an international scale": you name it, he's into it, according to the FBI. The tentacles of Mogilevich's money-laundering network are said to extend to twenty-seven countries, including the United States. In Philadelphia, he is alleged to have bilked investors out of $150 million, a scheme that resulted in the Justice Department's filing of a massive racketeering, securities-fraud, and money-laundering indictment.[23] He'll never face trial, however: Though known to trot between Kiev, Budapest, and Jerusalem, home for Mogilevich is Moscow. He is said to have cordial relations with Putin. The indictment against him was filed seventeen years ago, so the Kremlin recommends you don't hold your breath waiting for Mogilevich's extradition.[24]

Firtash, a Ukrainian, rose from service in the Soviet-era military forces to become an energy-sector billionaire, heading up RUE (Ros-UkrEnergo AG)—the Russia–Ukraine energy conglomerate. How does such a miracle take place? Well, in 2008, Firtash admitted to William Taylor, then America's ambassador to Ukraine, that "he needed Mogilevich's approval to get into business in the first place."[25] It was a highly profitable blessing. Conveniently, RUE is half-owned by the Russian government through Gazprom, the Kremlin-controlled natural-gas giant. Putin's regime thus saw fit to award RUE a monopoly on all gas trades between Russia and Ukraine. The transactions, beginning in 2003, netted billions of dollars. Firtash diverted some of the lavish proceeds to Highrock Holdings, a company based in Cyprus. Stringent privacy laws make Cyprus a favorite haven of corrupt government officials, foreign agents, money launderers, and other mobsters. You'll be shocked, I'm sure, to learn that Highrock's major shareholders included Mogilevich's wife.[26]

Like Mogilevich, Firtash is a fugitive from American justice. He is holed up in Austria, fighting extradition on an indictment by a Chicago federal grand jury. He allegedly schemed to pay Indian officials millions of dollars in bribes to approve mining rights for titanium desperately needed by the aerospace behemoth Boeing, Firtash's (unindicted) partner in an aircraft construction project.[27] As we go to press on this book, the Justice Department is still seeking Firtash's extradition, having represented to a federal judge that he is an "upper-echelon" associate of Russian organized crime.

Interesting thing about that. Firtash, along with his Ukrainian oligarch and Russian mobster associates, was long the focus of the FBI's Eurasian Organized Crime unit—the same one that handled the Bureau's relationship with Christopher Steele…who was an official FBI informant before he started working on his anti-Trump dossier. Among the Justice Department prosecutors most involved in the investigation of Firtash—friend of both consultant Manafort and crime boss Mogilevich—were Lisa Page and Andrew Weissmann. In the Trump–Russia investigation, Page was a key participant (as counsellor to FBI Deputy Director Andrew McCabe and confidant—to put it delicately—of FBI Agent Peter Strzok). Weissmann, of course, was the top prosecutor on the Mueller special counsel staff.[28]

Yup, Manafort played in a tough crowd. What ultimately put him in a special prosecutor's sights, though, was his involvement in the Trump campaign. And when that happened, it didn't help him that some of the top Obama Justice Department officials investigating Trump–Russia collusion were the same officials who, for years, had been trying to nail Mogilevich and Firtash. Like Glenn Simpson, the FBI and the Justice Department were laying the foundations for a narrative of collusion between rogues tied to Moscow and Washington. It wasn't that hard to tweak the script from suspicion of fraud schemes to suspicion of espionage.

Birth of a Manafort–Kremlin Narrative

In the Ukrainian presidential campaign of 2004, Akhmetov and Firtash ardently backed Viktor Yanukovych, Ukraine's prime minister and the Party of Regions's political leader. Of half-Russian stock, Yanukovych had a hardscrabble upbringing: orphaned young and convicted for violent robberies. Eventually, however, he was admitted to the Communist Party of the Soviet Union and later became a regional transport executive in eastern Ukraine. He developed friendships with Akhmetov and Firtash. Their friend, the Regions pro-Russian leader President Leonid Kuchma, appointed Yanukovych prime minister in 2002.

The 2004 election was a disaster for Regions. Yanukovych, advised by hard-edged Russians averse to the democratic process, was opposed by Viktor Yushchenko, who portrayed himself as the candidate seeking to move Kiev away from its shackled Soviet past and into a liberated European future. During the bitter contest, Yushchenko was poisoned by TCDD, the dioxin in Agent Orange. It had almost certainly been secreted in food he was served. Shortly before he fell ill, Yushchenko had dinner with the head of the Ukrainian security service, a man named Ihor Smeshko. Not long after the meal, Smeshko relocated to Moscow and was given Russian citizenship, insulating him from extradition. Yushchenko survived the assassination attempt, barely, but his handsome face was disfigured by lesions and blisters. "Every politician in this country and neighboring countries who turns toward the West is facing that kind of danger," he later reflected. "My poisoning took place because I had started taking steps toward the European Union. We have a neighbor who does not want this to happen."[29]

Yanukovych's subsequent election victory was so manifestly tainted by fraud that it sparked the Orange Revolution protests. In the eventual do-over, Yushchenko won decisively. Yanukovych was swept out of the prime minister's office, replaced by the woman who had become his mortal political enemy, Yulia Tymoshenko, the often—but, we shall see, not always—pro-European leftist. For a time, Manafort's pal Akhmetov left Ukraine, worried that, in the backlash against Regions, he might be detained by the new government.

In this darkest hour, Akhmetov implored Manafort to take Yanukovych on as a client and launch Regions's comeback. Manafort was reluctant, believing Yanukovych too flawed a politician and too damaged by the 2004 mischief. But Akhmetov prevailed, and the consultant proceeded to rebuild Yanukovych's image from the ground up. He also replaced the bull-in-a-china-shop strategies of Yanukovych's Russian advisers with Western-style politics—polling, micro-targeting, get-out-the-vote efforts, and the like. The metamorphosis was striking, and effective. Regions won the parliamentary elections in 2006. Unfathomably, Yanukovych was restored to the prime minister's chair.[30]

Though we are still a decade before the 2016 U.S. election, before the emergence of Donald Trump as a political figure, this is a critical juncture. It is where we begin to see the basic incoherence of the "collusion with Russia" narrative. Banking on your unfamiliarity with the nuances of Ukrainian politics, collusion peddlers would have you believe that Paul Manafort went to work for the Kremlin's guys and kept working for them while he chaired Donald Trump's campaign. Collusion with Russia, Q.E.D.

But what did Manafort actually do in Ukraine? His tutelage nudged Yanukovych in a more Euro-friendly direction, away from Putin's clutches. He pushed Yanukovych to study English. Yes, Manafort had his client play the political game—well known in American politics—of being different things to different people: speaking Ukrainian to pro-Western elements in Kiev, and sticking with Russian language and themes in the East (where Regions was especially strong). Yanukovych, however, also sounded Western themes that cannot have been music to the Kremlin's ears. Manafort had him saying he wanted Ukrainian integration into Europe, including its culture of thriving, competitive democracy. Yanukovych still expressed a desire for friendship with Russia, but did so in the geopolitical context of a country that has no choice but to court cordial relations with its stronger neighbor next door—the neighbor who is a bully, but with whom much of Ukraine shares ties of language and culture. Yanukovych would not seek to join NATO, which Russia would find provocative and which several NATO countries—not anxious to give Ukraine a joint defense pledge—mutedly opposed. But neither would Yanukovych seek a defense alliance with Russia: "We do not want to join any military bloc," he explained.[31]

This is life in Ukraine. Progress is a high-wire act, inching toward Western norms without angering the bear, appeasing the bear when he gets cranky. The tycoons try to maintain their wealth and autonomy—a little Western philanthropy here, a little kickback to Moscow there. A Ukrainian politician is not acting as a clandestine Kremlin agent when he placates Russia, which Ukraine half loves, half dreads, and fully relies on for some basic needs. The Ukrainian politician is navigating a minefield of power centers, amid rampant corruption and organized crime.

Over a decade after Manafort started working for Yanukovych and Regions, Special Counsel Robert Mueller indicted him for failing to register as a foreign agent. But notice this, so obvious it's been easy to miss: The accusation is that Manafort is an agent of *Ukraine, not of Russia*. Through two years of investigation and two extensive indictments focused on sinister international transactions, even the collusion crusaders cannot bring themselves to claim that Manafort, a foundational building block of the Trump–Russia collusion narrative, was a Russian spy. To be clear, the consultant's body of work in Kiev was not admirable. Manafort took with both his grubby hands, earning megabucks shilling for awful people. But he was not a Russian operative—not when he was in Ukraine, and not when he was in the Trump campaign. He was working, at great profit to himself, to make his clients politically viable in a Ukraine that was (and is) turbulent, deeply divided, and constantly threatened. And he wanted Ukraine to be part of the West, a notion that is anathema to Putin.

Interestingly, while Regions's comeback was strong, Yanukovych's hold on the premiership was short lived. In 2007, he was displaced by his bitter rival, Yulia Tymoshenko. Her career is worth a quick glance. Like her Party of Regions rival Dmytro Firtash, she made her fortune in the gas sector. Tymoshenko cut a deal in the 1990s that enabled her to resell gas through an arrangement with Kremlin-controlled Gazprom.[32] She became something of a national hero and Western celebrity during the Orange Revolution protests against Yanukovych. When she was in power, however, she was the emblematic Ukrainian chameleon.

And what was the main rap against Tymoshenko during her 2007–10 tenure as prime minister? *Collusion with Russia.* For all her European integration rhetoric, she worked to prevent Ukraine from taking steps to enter NATO, refused to condemn Russia's invasion of Georgia, undermined an effort to impede Russian naval vessels (making it easier for Moscow to attack Georgian forces), and, most consequentially, made a gas contract with Putin that induced Ukraine to pay higher prices than any country in Europe.[33] The deal was designed to squeeze Manafort's friend Firtash out of his sweetheart middleman role of brokering Ukraine–Russia gas deals. It enabled Putin to punish President Yushchenko (whom he didn't like any better after the poisoning plot failed) for opposing Russian aggression against Georgia and for seeking NATO membership. Si-

multaneously, Tymoshenko undercut her Regions rivals and court-
ed Putin's support (which is critical in eastern Ukraine) for the 2010
presidential run she was planning.[34] Nowadays, in their latest political
metamorphoses, Tymoshenko talks tough about Putin, while Putin
announces sanctions against Tymoshenko. But it wasn't long ago
that they were joined at the hip and he publicly sang her praises.[35]

So how come we hear only about Putin's dalliances with Manafort's
Regions clients, but never about those with their nemesis, Yulia Tymoshenko? Well, not only is she a progressive in reasonably good
standing (derided a bit these days for clothing her socialism in pop
ulism), when she decided to seek an American political consultant,
Tymoshenko had the good sense to choose Barack Obama's top campaign strategists, who cashed in when their man won the 2008 election by forming AKPD Media. [36]

Oh—you thought only gnarly Republicans play this game? Think
again. While Regions hired the Republicans' consultants, Tymoshenko's organization retained the Obama consultants, and Yushchenko's
party brought in the Clinton consultants.[37] This isn't about *collusion*.
American political consultants go to Ukraine for the same reason Wil-
lie Sutton went to the bank: *That's where the money is.* Millions of
dollars in fees for hard work in a dangerous place.

The Russian 'Intelligence Agent'

The pretense was that the dangerous place wasn't such a dangerous
place anymore. After the Soviet Union fell, the illusion was that this
was the glory of democratic transformation. The consultants did not
lead the way. They followed. Political consultants don't make money
unless there is first politics. The progressive vision entails diving into
authoritarian badlands, finding the bad guys who want to go legit (or
at least say they do), and building democratic institutions, which—
during however many decades it takes to develop actual democracy—
bring the bad-guy "reformers" together with the political consultants
in lucrative ventures.

Naturally, what was happening in Ukraine was also happening in
Russia. Long before Paul Manafort and Oleg Deripaska found each

other, there was John McCain's baby, the International Republican Institute (IRI), setting up shop in Moscow, helping shape the new politics. Of course, the Communist regime's operatives had run every sector of society. Should Washington's democracy crusaders be colluding with people tied to Soviet/Russian intelligence, military, governmental, and business sectors? Well, with whom else were they going to work? Thanks to such powerful patrons as Senator McCain, IRI is lavishly funded. You might agree with me that we could find better ways to spend tens of millions of U.S. taxpayer dollars annually than "democracy promotion" in hotbeds of gangster capitalism or sharia supremacism. But we're spending it. If you're promoting democracy in post-Soviet Russia, it's going to involve Russians.

So, to help run its democracy-promotion initiatives in the mid-nineties, IRI retained a talented linguist: a diminutive twenty-five-year-old who was born in Soviet-era Ukraine and schooled at a military language academy—trained, as was common for such students at the time, to work in support of the GRU, the military intelligence service of the Soviet Union (and now, of Russia). His name was Konstantin Kilimnik. While Kilimnik does not appear to have been a fan of the Soviet Union, he was not shy about brandishing his GRU background, which was helpful for the kind of networking he did.

As was their wont, Mueller probe investigators strained to spin Kilimnik's twenty-year-old Russian intelligence tie into suspicion that he is a current GRU operative, noting that one former associate says he was fired by IRI "because his links to Russian intelligence were too strong."[38] If that's true, one wonders why IRI kept him on *for at least eight years*, during which he helped run the institute's Moscow office. No one much cared that he had served as a translator in the Russian army and for a Russian arms exporter. Mueller concedes in passing that not all witnesses agree that Kilimnik's termination from IRI had anything to do with Russian intelligence. It appears that the institute was unhappy when Paul Manafort hired Kilimnik in 2005. Manafort, of course, was pursuing a different, financially self-interested, Party of Regions–centric agenda. But whatever the reasons for Kilimnik's parting of ways with IRI, the State Department certainly didn't see him as a problem. He became a valuable resource for the political staff at the U.S. embassy, former Deputy Assistant Secretary of State David Merkel told *The New York Times*, because he did not try to sugarcoat the financial motivations of the oligarchs who funded Regions and other parties.[39]

Kilimnik became Manafort's right-hand man, though, so there was plenty of dodgy dealing. Manafort does not speak Russian or Ukrainian. Kilimnik became his adjutant for dealing with Deripaska, as well as the Ukrainians. Manafort's previously described memo to Deripaska clearly related to potential political burnishing for the benefit of the Kremlin. Nevertheless, there has been controversy over the extent to which their business relationship entailed politics. Manafort has previously denied a political relationship, but he appeared to acknowledge it in a 2014 FBI interview; the litigious Deripaska has unsuccessfully sued the Associated Press for libel over reports that he hired Manafort for pro-Russia political work and to influence both political decisions and news coverage.[40]

In any event, Deripaska clearly did back Manafort's creation of a private equity fund, based in the Cayman Islands, a haven for tax evasion and related shenanigans. The consultant managed the fund with the help of his partner, Rick Gates, who would later become his deputy chairman on the Trump campaign (and, still later, Mueller's main accomplice witness in financial fraud cases against Manafort). Deripaska's millions were used to purchase, among other things, Chorne More (Black Sea), a Ukrainian cable and internet company. The deal was a disaster. Deripaska ultimately sued Manafort in various jurisdictions for $26 million. (*Note to self: $26 million in the hole to Putin's favorite oligarch is not a place you want to be.*) There was also a $1.5 billion deal that Manafort tried to put together with Firtash (believed to be fronting for Mogilevich) for a lavish Park Avenue skyscraper, but it fell through.[41]

There was more success on the political front. Manafort engineered the Party of Regions's return to power. Yanukovych won the presidency in 2010 and immediately announced that "integration with the EU remains our strategic aim."[42] But the triumph for the American consultant was short-lived. While Yanukovych rhapsodized about rising to Western standards, he ran his administration

in the eastern authoritarian style, enriching his allies and imprison-
ing his rivals, particularly Tymoshenko. She was prosecuted over
the gas deal with Putin she had entered into as prime minister. Russia bitterly criticized her prosecution, and when she was sentenced
to seven years' imprisonment, the Kremlin blasted Yanukovych's
government for pursuing her "exclusively for political motives."[43]

Manafort in the meantime continued to airbrush Yanukovych's
image in the West. To engage Congress on the Ukrainian government's behalf, he hired influential Washington lobbyists: Mercury
Public Affairs (a Republican-leaning outfit that does business with
Deripaska) and the Podesta Group, run by Tony Podesta (the brother
of Democratic powerbroker and eventual Clinton-campaign chairman John Podesta). Both firms were on the radar screen of Mueller's
investigators, who were determined to put some enforcement teeth
into FARA in order to nail Manafort—which meant it was no longer
business as usual for other cars on the gravy train.[44] Manafort also
steered $4 million to a politically connected New York law firm,
Skadden, Arps, Slate, Meagher & Flom. One of its partners, former
Obama White House Counsel Greg Craig, orchestrated the com-
position of a report that essentially whitewashed the Yanukovych
regime's civil-rights abuses in Tymoshenko's trial. Craig was eventually indicted by the Justice Department on a referral from Mueller's
office. Another lawyer at the firm, Alex van der Zwaan, pled guilty
in Mueller's investigation to making false statements about his consultation with Manafort's team.[45]

Yanukovych's moment of truth came in late 2013. He was poised
to sign the Association Agreement with the EU, a framework for
integration. Putin furiously turned up the heat: blocking Ukrainian
imports, drastically reducing Ukrainian exports, bleeding billions
of trade dollars from Ukraine's economy, threatening to cut off all
gas supplies and drive Ukraine into default if Kiev made its bed
with the West. Manafort pleaded with his client to stick with the
EU. Yanukovych caved, however, signing an alternative pact with
Putin to assure gas supplies and financial aid. It was over this decision that the Euromaidan protests erupted. Yanukovych fled the
country in early 2014, given sanctuary in Moscow. Subsequently,

Regions renounced Yanukovych, blaming him for the outbreak of violence and for looting the treasury.[46] The party disbanded, with many of its members reemerging as the Opposition Bloc, the party to which Manafort gravitated—along with Kilimnik and W. Samuel Patten—another political consultant protégé of Manafort's.

Foreign Money and American Politics

While Ukraine was in revolt, Manafort had had enough success that he was a viable U.S. commodity again—at least for the Trump campaign, from which the Bush-connected network of consultants and activists was shying away. Manafort was anxious to return to U.S. politics and agreed to work for free. Not that he wasn't planning to cash in—he was *always* planning to cash in, whatever he was doing and wherever he was doing it. Ever pressured by the ruinous debt he owed Deripaska, shortly after becoming Trump chairman he asked Kilimnik in an email, "How do we use [this] to get whole?" On July 7, he instructed Kilimnik to offer Deripaska information about Trump's campaign—"If he needs private briefings we can accommodate."[47] But Deripaska denies ever getting any information about Trump's campaign from the man he says swindled him, and Trump fired Manafort the next month when news broke of millions of dollars in secret payments allegedly channeled to Manafort by Yanukovych's regime.

Lots of smoke. And not the end of it. Manafort also instructed Kilimnik to pass campaign polling data to two of his Ukrainian oligarch backers, Akhmetin and Serhiy Lyovochkin. Democrats claimed that this was part of the Trump campaign's coordination with Putin—on the theory that the polling data would enable Russian propagandists to target campaign messaging at important voting districts. But there's no evidence that the oligarchs actually got any of the data, much less that they had anything to do with the Kremlin's cyberespionage—again, Trump's opposition assumes Americans hear "Ukrainian oligarch" and think "Putin operative." The likelihood is that Manafort, under increasing financial stress, was trying to impress his chief financial backers.[48]

The connections are disturbing nevertheless. Even allowing for the fact that Mueller dramatically altered the Justice Department's indulgent approach to FARA enforcement, Manafort and Gates were charged and convicted of serious tax and fraud felonies. Kilimnik has been indicted for conspiring with Manafort to tamper with a witness.[49] He is believed to be in Russia and, like other Russians Mueller indicted, he will never face an American trial, but Manafort admitted to the witness-tampering conspiracy in his prosecution. Patten, meanwhile, pled guilty for working as an unregistered agent of Ukraine. This involved scoring tickets to Trump inauguration events for Kilimnik, Lyovochkin, and an unidentified Ukrainian—tickets for which Lyovochkin, a non-American, provided the funds: a violation of campaign finance law.[50]

These actions are not "collusion with Russia." They are influence peddling. They are a snapshot of the interplay of shady foreign wealth, American officials, and the lucrative Washington political industry that brings them together. It stinks. And it is a bipartisan odor.

CHAPTER FOUR

Intel ... the Obama Way

I n 2014, it surfaced that the CIA had hacked into the computer system of the Senate Intelligence Committee. At the time, the committee's staff was investigating the agency's controversial enhanced-interrogation program, in which high-level terrorists were subjected to physically and psychologically coercive questioning, including water-boarding. John Brennan, the CIA director, indignantly denied the hacking allegation. "Nothing could be further from the truth," he insisted, shaking his head and rolling his eyes. "I mean, we wouldn't do that. I mean, that's just beyond the scope of reason in terms of what we would do."

Brennan was lying. That's what he does.

Obama's CIA had indeed spied on the Senate. And Brennan knew it. An inspector-general probe established that the hacking had occurred. While maintaining that their actions "were lawful," culpable CIA officials conceded that their actions were "in some cases done at the behest of John O. Brennan." Cornered, Brennan apologized to senior committee senators. The *mea culpa* was about as sincere as the director's original denial. Taking a page out of Hillary Clinton's Benghazi book, the CIA director handpicked an "accountability board" to investigate the matter. As I'm sure you'll be stunned to learn, Brennan exploited the pendency of the accountability board's probe as a pretext to avoid answering Congress's questions. Brennan's board then dutifully whitewashed the matter, recommending that no one be disciplined.[1]

Welcome to intel, the Obama way. It is the author of the Trump–Russia narrative.

The Benghazi Fraud

No administration in American history was more practiced in the dark arts of politicizing intelligence than President Obama's. Examples are legion. The most infamous involves the events during and after the 2012 Benghazi massacre, a jihadist attack in which four American officials were murdered: State Department employee Sean Smith, CIA security contractors Glen Doherty and Tyrone Woods, and J. Christopher Stevens, the U.S. ambassador to Libya—the first American ambassador to be killed in the line of duty since 1979.[2]

The atrocity, which occurred during the stretch-run of Obama's reelection campaign, was a blatant, coordinated terrorist strike, quite predictably carried out on the eleventh anniversary of the 9/11 attacks. The date itself is one al-Qaeda makes a habit of trying to mark by mass-murder attacks.

In this instance, the warning signs were unmistakable. After Osama bin Laden was killed in Pakistan by American special forces in 2011, his longtime deputy, Ayman al-Zawahiri, took over as al-Qaeda's emir. A little over a year later, on June 4, 2012, U.S. forces killed Abu Yahya al-Libi, the terror network's Libyan leader. Immediately afterward, Zawahiri called for vengeance, exhorting Libyan jihadists, "His blood urges you and incites you to fight and kill the crusaders."[3]

Notwithstanding such neon-flashing danger signs, the Obama State Department permitted the ambassador to travel to Benghazi, a boiling cauldron of anti-American jihadism. The U.S. government compounds there—a State Department outpost and a CIA annex, the presence of which was never explained—were left woefully under-protected, and the jihadists pounced.

The attack exposed the administration's security recklessness. It put the lie to fantasy Obama narratives that al-Qaeda had been defeated with bin Laden's death, and that Libya was trending toward democracy—rather than dystopia—thanks to Obama's war of aggression to remove Libyan strongman Muammar Qaddafi. As was customary, Obama officials conducted their actual policy (an unprovoked military intervention unauthorized by Congress) under the guise of a deceptive narrative: The administration spearheaded a U.N. Security

Council resolution permitting the use of force only to protect civilians; it then abetted decapitation bombings against the regime and the arming of anti-Qaddafi jihadist factions. On October 20, 2011, some of these "rebels" captured, tortured, and killed the Libyan dictator (theretofore supported by the Bush and Obama administrations as a key counterterrorism ally). As the famously hilarious Hillary Clinton put it afterward, "We came, we saw, he died."[4]

While Americans were still under siege in Benghazi on September 11, Secretary Clinton consulted with President Obama at about 10 p.m. Immediately afterward, she issued a public statement portraying the violence not as a terrorist attack but as an overheated response to an anti-Islamic video—an obscure trailer for a movie called *Innocence of Muslims*. Virtually no one had seen the video until the Obama administration started calling attention to it.[5] Meantime, in private conversations, Clinton confided to her daughter that al-Qaeda was behind the attack. State Department notes quote what she told Egypt's prime minister:

> We know that the attack in Libya had nothing to do with the film. It was a planned attack—not a protest. Based on the information we saw today [September 12] we believe the group that claimed responsibility for this was affiliated with al-Qaeda.[6]

In the immediate aftermath, the Obama White House and top intelligence officials—in particular, then–Acting CIA director Michael Morell, a close Clinton and Brennan ally—heavily edited the talking points originally generated by the agency. The word "attacks" was replaced by "demonstrations." References to Islam and "ties to al-Qaeda" were excised. So was mention of the involvement of Ansar al-Sharia (an al-Qaeda affiliate). Pains were taken to remove the assertion: "The wide availability of weapons and experienced fighters in Libya almost certainly contributed to the lethality of the attacks"—after all, the wide availability of weapons and fighters was directly attributable to Obama's lawless military intervention.[7] Through a spokesman, the president later described the changes to the intelligence talking points as "stylistic."[8]

The day after the attack, as survivors retrieved the dead and surveyed the wreckage, Obama proceeded with a campaign fundraiser in Las Vegas. There, he cheered supporters with the assurance that, "A day after 9/11, we are reminded that a new tower rises above the New York skyline, but al-Qaeda is on the path to defeat and bin Laden is dead."[9]

Notwithstanding that an American diplomat had been killed in Benghazi, Secretary of State Clinton—already planning her 2016 presidential bid—was unwilling to be the public face of the administration's Benghazi debacle. To make the rounds on the Sunday network television shows, then, Obama dispatched his trusted adviser, Susan Rice, at the time the U.S. ambassador to the United Nations. The spin in each of her five appearances echoed what she spun for ABC News's *This Week* (a show hosted by former Clinton White House adviser George Stephanopoulos):

> Our current best estimate, based on the information that we have at present, is that, in fact, what this began as, it was a spontaneous—not a premeditated—response to what had transpired in Cairo. In Cairo, as you know, a few hours earlier, there was a violent protest that was undertaken in reaction to this very offensive video that was disseminated.

All of this was false, including the Cairo story. In point of fact, after Egypt was taken over by an elected government run by the sharia-supremacist Muslim Brotherhood—with the demonstrable support of the Obama administration—members of jihadist organizations became a menacing fixture outside the U.S. embassy in Cairo, threatening to raid it, burn it to the ground, and take hostages. This was part of a longstanding campaign to coerce the release from U.S. custody of the "Blind Sheikh"—i.e., convicted terrorist Omar Abdel Rahman, a globally renowned, Egyptian-born jihadist icon (whom I prosecuted after the 1993 World Trade Center attack). On September 11, 2012, hours before the Benghazi attack, mobs incited by these fanatics stormed the embassy, setting fires and replacing the American flag with the infamous black jihadist banner. Although mounds of intelligence indicated that such rioting was planned, the Obama State Department put out messaging suggesting that the video, which had gotten some limited exposure in jihadist rhetoric, was the sole instigator.[10]

In her television appearances, Rice relied on politically manipulated intelligence—a staple of the Obama years. The CIA's original talking points that had been purged of terrorism references by Morell and the Obama White House. When Rice and Morell were pressed during a meeting with three Republican senators about why the talking points were altered, Morell falsely claimed that the FBI, out of concern for its ongoing investigation, had been responsible. Naturally, upon hearing that Morell was scapegoating the Bureau, FBI officials were incensed. An embarrassed CIA official fessed up to the senators that Morell "misspoke"—the Agency's acting director now suddenly remembered that he himself had led the editing process. Memory can be funny that way.

Morell had also falsely told the senators that the Obama White House did not collaborate in the editing of the talking points. As a Senate Intelligence Committee report later recounted, he "emphatically" testified that the talking points were provided to the White House "for their awareness, not for their coordination." To the contrary, an email paper trail proved consultation with the White House; there was even an email authored by Morell himself, explaining that "Everyone else has *coordinated*" on the talking points and noting "tweaks" made by both State Department and White House officials. (Emphasis added.)[11]

Although the administration knew from the start that the Benghazi siege was a terrorist attack, President Obama told CBS News in the immediate aftermath that it was "too early to know." Three days after the attack, a solemn ceremony was held at Joint Base Andrews in Maryland to mark the return home of the remains of America's dead. Secretary Clinton callously used the occasion to promote the administration's politicization of the Benghazi intelligence:

> We've seen the heavy assault on our post in Benghazi that took the lives of those brave men. We've seen rage and violence directed at American embassies over an awful Internet video that we had nothing to do with.

Soon after, the Obama State Department released commercial ads crafted for Pakistani television, condemning the video: "We absolutely reject its content and message," thundered Clinton, with Obama looking on. The president stuck to the script at his speech to the U.N. General Assembly on September 25, proclaiming, "The future must not belong to those who slander the prophet of Islam."[12]

The gaslighting did not stop there. In Los Angeles, three days after Obama's U.N. speech, his Justice Department arrested the video producer who had slandered Islam's prophet. Technically, fifty-five-year-old Nakoula Basseley Nakoula was cited for a violation of parole (what federal law refers to as "supervised release") in connection with a prior, minor fraud conviction. The usual procedure in such a case would be a summons to appear in court. But Nakoula was grabbed by police in the dead of night. This stagecraft, accompanied by the soundtrack of heated administration rhetoric, suggested to Muslims worldwide that the real Benghazi culprit—*the blasphemer*—had been apprehended. As Nakoula's family went into hiding, federal agents grilled him about his film production—running roughshod over his First Amendment free-expression rights under the guise of monitoring his computer use due to his fraud conviction. Though his "offense" was minor and nonviolent, Nakoula was detained without bail and sentenced to a year in prison. Patently aware of the constitutional improprieties, the Justice Department quietly dropped the parole "violations" related to the video.[13]

By May 20, 2013, when the CIA held a memorial service for its officers slain in Benghazi, Obama had been reelected and had named as the agency's new director John Brennan—his 2008 campaign adviser and White House counterterrorism czar.

At the memorial service, four of the CIA officers who had fought to repel the Benghazi siege were discreetly approached by an agency representative and asked for a moment of their time. They were led through a maze of offices before reaching a room remote from the ceremony site. Once the door was shut, they were presented with small packets of papers, with instructions that they review and sign the documents. It was quickly apparent that the packets contained nondisclosure agreements. It was a gratuitous brushback pitch. As intelligence officers, these surviving Benghazi heroes were covered by preexisting NDAs. The highly irregular presentation of new NDAs was the CIA's not very subtle admonition that they remain silent. Brennan being

Brennan, he first denied that anyone had been asked to sign a new NDA, then conceded that some officers may have been asked, but that this was standard procedure. Then he acknowledged that it might not have been standard procedure, but insisted that it had nothing to do with Benghazi. Finally, he admitted the connection to Benghazi but claimed the NDAs were necessary in order to process payments for the officers to attend the service.[14]

Right.

Intelligence Failure

Brennan joined the CIA four years after voting for Gus Hall, the Communist party candidate, in the 1976 presidential election. He is a notorious climber and, former colleagues say, a vindictive one.[15] Assigned to the National Security Council in President Bill Clinton's White House, Brennan latched on to George Tenet, who had worked on Clinton's transition and then been made the NSC's director of intelligence programs. In 1996, Clinton made Tenet deputy director of the CIA. By 1997, after Director John Deutsch had fallen out of favor with Clinton and other possible replacements faltered, Tenet was made director. Tenet's long tenure is best remembered for the CIA's failure to develop an effective strategy against al-Qaeda prior to 9/11, and for Tenet's own unfortunate "slam dunk" endorsement of the intelligence that Iraq had amassed prodigious quantities of weapons of mass destruction.[16]

Brennan had proved himself fiercely loyal, so when Tenet was moved to Langley he brought Brennan along as chief of staff. He eventually acceded to Brennan's desire to be made the CIA's station chief in Saudi Arabia—an unusual move because Brennan's career had been spent in the intelligence analysis side of the agency's house, not its operations directorate. Shortly after Brennan's arrival in Riyadh in 1996, al-Qaeda bombed the Khobar Towers, killing nineteen American airmen. The lack of precautions against to such an attack, the agency assessed, was the result of profound management failures, with Brennan and his staff cited for "significant shortcomings in planning, intelligence, and basic security [that] left American forces in Saudi Arabia vulnerable."[17]

Two years later, with al-Qaeda having publicly declared war against the United States, Brennan helped convince Tenet to abandon an effort to capture its leader, Osama bin Laden, in Afghanistan. Brennan preferred a Saudi gambit to negotiate with the Taliban, al-Qaeda's hosts and chief abettors, for bin Laden's expulsion. Predictably, the negotiations broke down and the CIA never got another chance. Brennan later told a congressional committee that he didn't believe the CIA's capture plan "was a worthwhile operation"—and, even if it was, that he shouldn't be blamed since "I was not in the chain-of-command at the time."[18]

In the greater scheme of things, Brennan was a bit player in what was a series of intelligence failures over several years. Under bin Laden's continued leadership, al-Qaeda bombed two American embassies in eastern Africa in August 1998, murdering over 200 people; struck and nearly sank an American destroyer, the U.S.S. *Cole*, in October 2000, killing seventeen U.S. Navy sailors; and carried out the suicide-hijacking airliner attacks of September 11, 2001, severely damaging the Pentagon, destroying the World Trade Center, and slaughtering nearly 3,000 Americans.

Tenet left the CIA in 2004, battered by failures in Iraq: weapons of mass destruction were not located (at least not in the quantities the CIA had predicted); and the ouster of Saddam Hussein, coupled with the futile cultivation of democracy in a fundamentalist Islamic society hostile to the West, enmeshed the United States in vicious civil strife, empowering Iran and triggering the rise of the Islamic State (ISIS). In the interim, Brennan had left Riyadh in 1999 and rose to the post of deputy executive director, staunchly defending the CIA's enhanced interrogations program—the controversial post-9/11 initiative that eventually prompted congressional investigations and the agency's aforementioned hacking of Senate computers on Brennan's watch. With his patron gone and the agency reeling, Brennan departed for a private intelligence gig.

Narrative: An Islam of Their Very Own

When Senator Barack Obama was campaigning for the presidency, Tenet recommended Brennan as an adviser. The two hit it off. Brennan had come to regard the "war on terror" with disdain. This disposition was appealing to the Democratic nominee, as was Brennan's positioning himself as "a strong opponent of many of the policies of the Bush administration such as the preemptive war in Iraq and coercive interrogation techniques, to include waterboarding." But Brennan's association with Bush policies he now pilloried made it politically impossible in 2009 for Obama to make him CIA director (a position requiring Senate confirmation). The newly elected president settled on a key White House post for Brennan: top adviser for counterterrorism.[19]

Obama-style counterterrorism was all about the narrative. By the alchemy of progressive piety, jihadist attacks morphed into "man-caused disasters," and war against international terrorist networks into "overseas contingency operations." The Muslim Brotherhood? *Abracadabra*! It was now a "largely secular" organization, as James Clapper, Obama's Director of National Intelligence, told a bewildered congressional panel.

Indeed, the very term *counterterrorism* was now *de trop*. The new strategy was "Countering Violent Extremism." CVE instructed that no particular brand of "violent extremism" should be singled out for special attention—jihadist terror was to be regarded as no more a threat to America than other sources of violence. What other sources of violence? In the first weeks of Obama's administration, his Department of Homeland Security provided the answer in "Rightwing Extremism: Current Economic and Political Climate Fueling Resurgence in Radicalization and Recruitment," a handy federal primer for state and local police departments. Potential perils, DHS explained, stemmed from fanatics of all religions, as well as America's purported legions of racists, and its sundry anti-abortion activists, Second Amendment proponents, immigration opponents, veterans returning from, er, overseas contingency operations, and groups "that are mainly antigovernment, rejecting federal authority in favor of state or local authority, or rejecting government authority entirely."[20]

In this fairy tale, violence was mainly catalyzed by political opposition to Barack Obama. The only thing it seemed verboten to trace terrorism to was radical Islam. The administration miniaturized the threat of "al-Qa'ida's hateful ideology," as if that ideology were not rooted in a literalist construction of Islamic scripture and centuries of fundamentalist scholarship; as if the challenges to the West were a fringe movement rather than a sharia-supremacist interpretation of Islam that is at least prevalent, if not dominant, in many countries, regions, and communities with significant Muslim populations. In sum, Obama's strategy was the apotheosis of the Bipartisan Beltway's long-standing, mulish concoction of an Islam of its very own—a belief system the only discernible tenets of which are peace and *anti*-terrorism. "Countering Violent Extremism" holds that this imaginary Islam is the only viable one. Sun Tzu's ancient maxim "know thine enemy," notwithstanding, there is no need to master sharia supremacism, to which a disturbingly sizable percentage of the *ummah* adheres, because it is a "false Islam." Drawing attention to it (did I mention that it only exists because we draw attention to it?) only makes it more alluring. The palpable mainstream status of sharia supremacism in the Middle East and elsewhere is simply not to be spoken of. After all, if we ignore it, it will go away, right?[21]

Brennan was the perfect CVE avatar. "In all my travels," he gushed in a 2010 speech, "the city I have come to love most is al-Quds," invoking the Arab name for Jerusalem—the one preferred by Hamas jihadists whose "one-state solution" is the destruction of Israel. Indeed, as Brennan well knows, an annual "al-Quds day," started by Ayatollah Ruhollah Khomeini after the 1979 Iranian revolution, is marked by anti-Israeli demonstrations by Muslim communities throughout the world, and the jihadist specialists in the Islamic Revolutionary Guard Corps of Khomeinist Iran are still known as the al-Quds forces.[22] But no need to worry: Brennan's policy plan included cultivating Iran, coupled with an initiative to "try to build up the more moderate elements" of, yes, *Hezbollah*—Iran's forward jihadist militia that menaces Israel from its perch in Lebanon and that, prior to al-Qaeda's 9/11 mass-murder attack, had killed more Americans than any terrorist organization in the world. In a 2012 policy paper, Brennan sermonized that American officials must "cease public Iran-bashing" and be willing to "tolerate, and even…encourage, greater assimilation of Hizballah into Lebanon's political system, a process that is subject to Iranian influence."[23]

Brennan opined that terrorist recidivism after release from Guantanamo Bay was "not that bad"—as if the 20 percent rate (a lowball estimate) represented a modest uptick in petty theft rather than significant reinforcement for mass murderers. Terrorists were just "a small fringe of fanatics who cloak themselves in religion, try to distort [the Islamic] faith," he twaddled in a speech at New York University. As such, the terrorists and the Americans they targeted were two sides of an "ignorance" equation—Muslims "clearly ignorant of the most fundamental teachings of Islam," and Americans who respond to terror attacks with "ignorant feelings" that could lead us "back into this fearful position that lashed out, not thinking through what was reasonable and appropriate."[24]

Speaking of ignorance about the most fundamental teachings of Islam...there is John Brennan on jihad. "President Obama [does not] see this challenge as a fight against jihadists," Brennan told the Center for Strategic and International Studies (CSIS) in the first months of the new administration. "Describing terrorists in this way, using the legitimate term 'jihad,' which means to purify oneself or to wage a holy struggle for a moral goal, risks giving these murderers the religious legitimacy they desperately seek but in no way deserve." Brennan returned to CSIS the following year to hammer the theme yet again: We must not "describe our enemy as 'jihadists,'" he admonished, because "'jihad' is a holy struggle, a legitimate tenet of Islam."

Well, there is no gainsaying that last part: Jihad is indeed a legitimate Islamic tenet. Contrary to Brennan's happy-face rendering of it, though, it is doctrinally rooted in the imperative of forcible conquest—which is how Bernard Lewis, the late, great scholar of Islam explicated it, and how untold millions of fundamentalist Muslims understand it. Thomas Patrick Hughes's venerable *Dictionary of Islam*, first published in 1885, defines *jihad* as "a religious war with those who are unbelievers in the mission of Muhammad" and "an incumbent religious duty, established in the Qur'an and in the traditions as a divine institution."

To be sure, there is a second, related understanding of jihad as an internal striving. Brennan, however, deracinates this concept—as if it were a quest for betterment in some new-age, universal sense, rather than in a strictly Islamic context. This personal "holy struggle for a moral goal," Brennan maintains, is completely benign: Jihad mere-ly "mean[s] to purify oneself or one's community." To the contrary, Islamic scholarship gives the concept of "purification" a distinctly Islamic construction: as the *Dictionary of Islam* puts it, a "striving" that is "enjoined specially for the purpose of advancing Islam and repelling evil from Muslims." The idea is to become a *more sharia-compliant* Muslim or Islamic community. Thus the vapidity of Brennan's insistence that his airbrushed jihad proves there is "nothing holy or legit-imate or Islamic about murdering innocent men, women, and chil-dren." Down here on planet earth, sharia has ideas very different from ours in the West about who is "innocent" and what uses of force are "legitimate."[25]

Nevertheless, this narrative burnished by Brennan—Islam as the solution, not the problem—became the plinth of Obama policy. In-telligence was manipulated as necessary to serve it. Brennan became the administration's liaison to Islamist activist groups demanding that U.S. military, law-enforcement, and intelligence agencies ban lecturers and purge training materials that they deemed "biased, false and high-ly offensive." Brennan promptly acceded to the Islamist agitation. An interagency task force would direct that government agencies "collect all training materials that contain cultural or religious content…relat-ed to Islam or Muslims," and consult with unidentified "subject mat-ter experts" (i.e., Islamist organizations) to "ensure that such materi-als comply with core American values" (i.e., comply with the Obama/Brennan mythology of Islam). This, Brennan assured, would be "the kind of approach that builds the partnerships that are necessary to counter violent extremism."[26]

American intelligence agencies were thus schooled. It was left to the Department of Homeland Security, from its Islamist-apologist nerve center, the Office for Civil Rights and Civil Liberties, to devel-op government-agency training programs that "bring together best Countering Violent Extremism practices." One result was a handy two-page teaching guide of CVE "Do's and Don'ts [sic]."[27] The "Don'ts" tell agents to avoid, among other things, "ventur[ing] too deep into the weeds of religious doctrine and history" or examining the "role of Islam in majority Muslim nations" (which, despite articles of CVE faith, is not so peaceful and pluralistic). The guidance further admonished American agents and analysts:

> Don't use training that equates radical thought, religious expression, freedom to protest, or other constitutionally protected activity, with criminal activity. One can have radical thoughts/ideas, including disliking the U.S. government, without being violent; for example, trainers who equate the desire for Sharia law with criminal activity violate basic tenets of the First Amendment.

One is constrained to observe that this interpretation of the First Amendment was patent rubbish. There is no free-speech protection against having one's words examined for intelligence or investigative purposes. Free-expression principles protect Americans against laws that subject speech to penalty or prosecution. That, by the way, is a protection that the Obama administration sought to deny to speech unflattering to Islam through a patently unconstitutional U.N. resolution it jointly sponsored with several Islamic nations[28]—when the administration was not busy intimidating critics into silence through such tactics as the afore-described political prosecution of Nakoula Basseley Nakoula; or when Obama's second secretary of state, John Kerry, was not busy suggesting there was a certain "legitimacy" to the *Charlie Hebdo* massacre of cartoonists and writers who had satirized the prophet Mohammed.[29]

In sum, the CVE narrative spun by Obama officials, with Brennan in the lead, expressly compelled our investigators to consider only violent or criminal *conduct*. They were told to ignore radical ideology, particularly if it had the patina of "religious expression." They were to turn a deaf ear to anti-Americanism and the desire to impose sharia, which just happens to be the principal objective of all violent jihadists, and of the Obama administration's oft-time consultants, the Muslim Brotherhood.

Selling the Iran Narrative: 'They Literally Know Nothing'

As night follows day, the narrative dictated—and thus distorted—intelligence assessments. On Brennan's watch, Obama-administration national-security officials deceptively downplayed weapons threats posed by Syria, Iran, and North Korea.[30] The president's counterterrorism adviser put his office and reputation in the service of Obama's absurdly counterfactual reelection theme that al-Qaeda was on the brink of defeat—concealing troves of classified and open-source intelligence proving that the network was both gaining territory and recruits and still killing Americans in Benghazi, Afghanistan, and elsewhere.

As extensively documented by former *Weekly Standard* editor Stephen F. Hayes and the *Long War Journal*'s Thomas Joscelyn, among the most compelling evidence of al-Qaeda's resiliency was the intelligence seized from Osama bin Laden's compound in Abbottabad, Pakistan, when U.S. forces killed him there on May 2, 2011. Yet Brennan labored mightily to keep the information from public view. The haul consisted of reams and reams of documents, including computer files, bin Laden's personal journal, and more. Brennan and Obama's other top intelligence officials selectively released just 571 of them; the Trump administration, by contrast, made 470,000 available in its first year.[31]

The political reasons for withholding and warping this intelligence are patent. The Obama narrative was that al-Qaeda had been "decimated." Therefore, the administration tirelessly depicted bin Laden as isolated and unable to control his network. The haul from the compound, however, proved that he was functioning at the time of his death as the manager of a global web of active jihadist groups, grooming new leaders to replace those being picked off by American forces and drone attacks. Similarly, Obama officials wanted the United States to withdraw from Afghanistan—both to project success in "combatting violent extremism" and to rechannel spending toward the administration's ambitious domestic priorities. Consequently, they concocted a storyline that there was growing distance between al-Qaeda and the Taliban—which fed the related fiction that the Taliban was a viable negotiating partner, rather than an incorrigibly anti-American enemy bent on conquest over the United States–backed government in Kabul. The bin Laden files put the lie to the fable: al-Qaeda and the Taliban remained close allies, fighting side by side against Americans.

Most of all, President Obama wanted his nuclear deal with Iran. For that, too, a narrative was essential to lull Americans into the illusion that the mullahs of Tehran—the regime whose proud motto is "Death to America!"—were moderating. A realistic depiction of al-Qaeda would explode that story. The truth is that jihadists traditionally put aside the internecine Sunni-versus-Shia conflict when confronting the Great Satan. Sunni al-Qaeda became a transcontinental jihadist powerhouse because it was nurtured, abetted, and harbored at key junctures by Shiite Iran and Hezbollah.[32] The bin Laden files showed that this alliance was not just a thing of the past; the Iranian regime remained a facilitator of bin Laden's network, and both sides persevered in their lethal labors against the United States. To sustain the Obama narrative, then, the files had to be suppressed. "Brennan not only fought the public release of these documents," Hayes notes. "[A]s CIA director he blocked other elements of the U.S. intelligence community from access to them."[33]

The Iran deal—formally the "Joint Comprehensive Plan of Action," an unsigned executive agreement, not a treaty—was the Obama administration's most arrogant enterprise in narrative retail. The invaluable journalist Lee Smith has closely studied the interplay between the White House, the intelligence community, and the press. President Obama and his aides have been bracingly open regarding their contempt for what they called their media "echo chamber."[34]

Obama told the public a story about preventing Iran from developing nuclear weapons, insisting that any agreement had to be verifiable, and vowing that sanctions would "snap back" into place if the mullah's cheated. At the negotiating table, meanwhile, his administration gave away the store, agreeing to the promotion of Iran's industrial nuclear capabilities (rationalized as civilian use); abiding continued centrifuge development; delegating verification duties to the U.N.'s feckless International Atomic Energy Agency; choreographing side deals between Iran and the IAEA, which would not be disclosed to Congress; tweaking the deal when Iran was out of compliance to avoid any "snap back"; and orchestrating ransom payments for the release of U.S. hostages: $400 million in untraceable cash stacked on pallets and flown to Tehran for delivery to the world's leading state sponsor of terrorism; and another $1.3 billion in thirteen furtive transfers of $99,999,999.99 each out of the Treasury Department's slushy "Judgment Fund," camouflaged as litigation settlement payments.[35]

The administration marveled at how easy it was to sculpt and sell the Iran "narrative" (that's what it was, and how they talked about it). "The average reporter we talk to is 27 years old," scoffed Ben Rhodes to *The New York Times*. "Their only reporting experience consists of being around political campaigns. That's a sea change. They literally know nothing."[36] Rhodes knows narrative. A former novelist whose brother David runs CBS News, Rhodes was Obama's deputy national security adviser (i.e., Susan Rice's deputy). The Iran deal narrative was his script to write. He is unapologetic about filling it with deceptions and misdirection when necessary. With most outlets reporting from Washington, few news organizations expend the resources needed to maintain foreign bureaus; the administration thus exploited the astonishing degree to which the press relied on a like-minded left-leaning administration for foreign affairs guidance. It crafted tales of a modernizing, moderating Iran. It deployed its ready-to-hand noble Islam narrative: Secretary Kerry telling the howler that the Iranians wouldn't dare build nukes because Ayatollah Ali Khamenei, the supreme leader, had issued a fatwa against it.[37] All these tales were fit within Rhodes's leitmotif: You either wanted the Iran deal or you wanted war.

Whether intentionally or not, the *Times*'s David Samuels gets to the Obama practice of narrative that achieved the Iran deal...and that would ultimately gin up Russia-gate:

> Like Obama, Rhodes is a storyteller who uses a writer's tools to advance an agenda that is packaged as politics but is often quite personal. He is adept at constructing overarching plotlines with heroes and villains, their conflicts and motivations supported by flurries of carefully chosen adjectives, quotations and leaks from named and unnamed senior officials. He is the master shaper and retailer of Obama's foreign-policy narratives, at a time when the killer wave of social media has washed away the sand castles of the traditional press. His abil-

ity to navigate and shape this new environment makes him a more effective and powerful extension of the president's will than any number
of policy advisers or diplomats or spies.[38]

But it was policy advisers, diplomats, and spies—their rhetoric, their
posturing, and their leaks—who propped up the carefully crafted
storylines by which the Obama administration drove its agenda.
They knew who the heroes were, so care was taken to cast the vil-
lains—the Saul Alinsky dictum that progressives must "pick the target, freeze it, personalize it, and polarize it."[39] Facts that helped were
cherry-picked; facts that hurt were contorted, misstated, or edited
out of the plot.

While these practices of processing and presenting intelligence
suited Brennan, they did not sit well with many American intelligence agents. In 2015, more than fifty analysts formally complained
that their reports on ISIS and al-Qaeda were being altered by senior
officials to support misleading Obama-administration narratives.
The whistleblowers pointed fingers, in particular, at the office of National Intelligence Director James Clapper and at the Defense Department's Central Command. The analysts complained that reports
were edited to remove unwelcome information, that candid assessments (i.e., negative assessments) of counterterrorism progress were
discouraged and sometimes rejected by their superiors, and that they
often self-censored out of concerns that their careers would otherwise flag.[40]

Three House committees (Intelligence, Armed Services, and Ap-
propriations) joined forces to investigate the allegations and found
that the Obama administration had rampantly politicized its intelligence product. Then-Rep. Mike Pompeo (R., Kansas)—now President
Trump's secretary of state after first serving as his CIA director—
helped lead the congressional inquiry. As he reported:

> After months of investigation, this much is very clear: from the middle
> of 2014 to the middle of 2015, the United States Central Command's
> most senior intelligence leaders manipulated the command's intelli-
> gence products to downplay the threat from ISIS in Iraq.

The result: Consumers of those intelligence products were provided a consistently "rosy" view of U.S. operational success against ISIS. That may well have resulted in putting American troops at risk as policymakers relied on this intelligence when formulating policy and allocating resources for the fight.

Abuse of Power in the Service of Progressive Narrative

To get the Iran deal done, the Obama administration did more—much more—than politicize intelligence to minimize Iran's commitment to building nuclear weapons and support of anti-American terrorism. Obama officials exploited their foreign-counterintelligence powers to stay a step ahead of their political opposition.

Sound familiar?

Once again, the invaluable Lee Smith provides the details.[41] Obama, Brennan, Rice, Rhodes, and the rest of the narrative-minded Obama political team realized there would be vigorous Israeli opposition to the Iran deal, just as there was ardent American opposition. Although Israel is an important democratic and regional ally, Prime Minister Benjamin Netanyahu and Ron Dermer, Israel's ambassador to the United States, became surveillance targets—agents of a foreign power, treated no differently under the law than such operatives of hostile foreign powers.

Fair enough. It is simply a fact that allies occasionally spy on each other. Obviously, their interests sometimes diverge. But there was something different about this monitoring initiative. It was not targeted merely at Israeli officials plotting their opposition strategy. *The Wall Street Journal* reported in late December 2015 that the targeting "also swept up the contents of some of [the Israeli officials'] private conversations with U.S. lawmakers and American-Jewish groups."[42] Smith elaborates:

> "At some point, the administration weaponized the NSA's legitimate monitoring of communications of foreign officials to stay one step ahead of domestic political opponents," says a pro-Israel political operative who was deeply involved in the day-to-day fight over the Iran Deal.

"The NSA's collections of foreigners became a means of gathering real-time intelligence on Americans engaged in perfectly legitimate political activism—activism, due to the nature of the issue, that naturally involved conversations with foreigners. We began to notice the White House was responding immediately, sometimes within 24 hours, to specific conversations we were having. At first, we thought it was a coincidence being amplified by our own paranoia. After a while, it simply became our working assumption that we were being spied on."

Smith elaborates:

This is what systematic abuse of foreign-intelligence collection for domestic political purposes looks like: Intelligence collected on Americans, lawmakers, and figures in the pro-Israel community was fed back to the Obama White House as part of its political operations. The administration got the drop on its opponents by using classified information, which it then used to draw up its own game plan to block and freeze those on the other side. And—with the help of certain journalists whose stories (and thus careers) depend on high-level access—terrorize them.

This is the Russia-gate scenario to a tee: political spying under the guise of legitimate national security monitoring. Subterfuge by the Kremlin is incontestably a legitimate basis for intelligence collection—a compelling one, in fact. Yet, even a compelling rationale can be used pretextually.

We know the Obama administration was not above such things.[43] Indeed, there was not even an arguable justification for Brennan's CIA to spy on the Senate Intelligence Committee—it was so beyond the pale that his initial (false) denial seemed credible. But there are many examples of politicized investigative abuse. Investigative journalist Sharyl Attkisson catalogues a number of them.[44]

For instance, Obama's IRS harassed and investigated conservative groups seeking tax-exempt status, a politicized initiative that stymied the groups' ability to contest Obama's reelection in 2012. With great indignation, President Obama, the beneficiary of the malfeasance, publicly railed that the IRS conduct was "outrageous," and that wrongdoers would "have to be held fully accountable" since there was "no place for it." Obama then held no one accountable while his handpicked IRS commissioner, John Koskinen, stonewalled congressional investigators and Lois Lerner, the official at the center of the scandal, retired with a full pension.[45]

The administration monitored journalists. Attorney General Eric Holder's approved the seizure of personal and business phone records of Associated Press reporters en masse (i.e., not a particularized search targeting a specific journalist suspected of wrongdoing). Moreover, Holder authorized a search warrant targeting the emails of reporter James Rosen, then of Fox News, in a leak investigation. To get the warrant, the Justice Department represented to a federal court that Rosen could be guilty of a felony violation of the Espionage Act for the unauthorized handling of classified information. Yes, the same Espionage Act that the Obama Justice Department chose not to invoke against Hillary Clinton—who was not a journalist with constitutional free-press rights but a public official with a sworn duty to safeguard classified information.

In 2011, President Obama loosened surveillance "minimization procedures," lowering the bar for scrutiny of the communications of American citizens incidentally swept up in foreign-intelligence gathering. Thereafter, as we shall soon see, the Obama administration systematically exploited its foreign-counterintelligence surveillance powers to spy on Americans, in flagrant violation of court-ordered surveillance procedures.

The "Fast and Furious" scandal involved a blatant Obama administration politicization of law enforcement: to wit, a "gun-walking" investigation in which thousands of firearms were allowed to be transferred illegally to Mexico. This cockamamie scheme was designed to serve a political narrative about the evils of American gun commerce, concocted to promote the progressive agenda of restricting Second Amendment rights. One of the walked guns was later used by illegal aliens who, in 2010, murdered U.S. border patrol Agent Brian Terry. After misleading lawmakers about the Justice Department's awareness of the scheme and stonewalling investigative committees, Holder became the first attorney general in American history to be held in contempt of Congress. In an apparent effort to retaliate against and undermine the credibility of ATF Agent John Dodson, a whistleblower who exposed Fast and Furious, the Obama Justice Department leaked investigative information to the media. Shortly before Holder was held in contempt, President Obama invoked executive privilege to shield Fast and Furious documents from disclosure.[46]

Holder's Justice Department also corrupted the judicial process in the service of advancing political causes and punishing political enemies and scapegoats. We have already noted the transparently political prosecution of Nakoula Basseley Nakoula, the anti-Muslim video producer the Obama administration shamefully blamed for the Benghazi massacre. The Justice Department was also heavy-handed in its indictment of Dinesh D'Souza, the writer, filmmaker, and strident Obama critic, over a trivial campaign finance violation.

It is freely conceded that D'Souza was guilty of using straw donors to contribute $15,000 to the campaign of Wendy Long, an old college friend who ran against Hillary Clinton in 2008 for one of New York's Senate seats. The comparatively small illegal contribution made no difference to the race, which Hillary Clinton won by 46 points. Such violations are routinely handled by payment of a fine to the Federal Election Commission rather than felony prosecution; indeed, the Obama Justice Department somehow summoned up the compassion needed to decline prosecution against the 2008 Obama campaign for *nearly $2 million* in illegal contributions—allowing the matter to be quietly settled over a Christmas holiday for $375,000, a record fine but still less than the $500,000 in bail prosecutors demanded that D'Souza post. And although Congress has prescribed a maximum two-year prison term when the violation is prosecuted, the Justice Department piled on a false-statements charge for the same offense so that D'Souza would face up to seven years' incarceration if convicted at trial. When he pled guilty, the Justice Department pushed for a jail sentence, which the judge declined to impose.[47]

More "appalling" and "grotesque," to borrow just some of an incensed federal district judge's description, was the Obama Justice Department's corruption of the 2010 prosecution of seven New Orleans police officers. In the anarchy that followed Hurricane Katrina in 2005, there were reports of shots fired at police on the Danziger Bridge. In the chaos, responding police shot and killed two men (one developmentally disabled), wounding four others. All the victims were African-American. Four of the seven officers involved were either African-American or Hispanic, yet the incident was predictably distorted into an episode of racial violence. After state authorities failed to win convictions, the Justice Department approved a prosecution alleging felony civil-rights and firearms offenses.

As the case was proceeding toward trial, Justice Department lawyers, using pseudonyms, posted online blog commentary in the *Times-Picayune* aimed at inflaming the jury pool against the cops— depicting the New Orleans Police Department as a fish "rotten from the head down" with racism. After some of the cops were bludgeoned into pleading guilty to obstruction charges, and others were convicted at trial, one prosecutor's role in the smear campaign came to light. District U.S. attorney Jim Letten assured Judge Kurt D. Engelhardt not to worry because, "Gospel truth," no other government lawyers were involved. But Judge Engelhardt soon realized the Justice Department was stonewalling his questions and obscuring rather than examining the misconduct. When the dust settled, it emerged that other prosecutors were also complicit in the smear campaign—a fact that was well known to the prosecutor running the "investigation." The Justice Department had also pressured witnesses with prosecution until they backed out of testifying on behalf of the police, and engaged in plea bargaining that promised "shockingly disparate" sentences for those who agreed to plead guilty rather than force the government to prove its case at trial.

Most egregiously, one of the chief culprits in the public smear campaign turned out to be Karla Dobinski, a longtime veteran of Main Justice's notoriously radical Civil Rights Division. Dobinski had been assigned to the case as part of a "taint team"—i.e., her only job was to safeguard the rights of the accused officers (making sure information they were compelled to provide to the police internal-affairs unit was not used against them). It is unclear how many inflammatory posts Dobinski published and which Obama Justice Department officials knew what she was up to because, as the Fifth Circuit U.S. Court of

Appeals later found, she was "disturbingly vague" when the district judge sought answers. What is clear is that she urged others to keep posting anti-police commentary—aptly excoriated by Judge Engelhardt as a "wanton, reckless course of action."

The Obama Civil Rights Division, it should go without saying, will be best remembered for refusing to enforce the civil-rights laws on behalf of white victims; for pushing the administration's narrative that the nation's police departments suffer from endemic racism; and for inflaming tensions in such tinderboxes as Ferguson, Missouri, after the shooting death of Michael Brown (Brown had robbed a store and attacked a police officer), and Sanford, Florida, after the shooting death of Trayvon Martin (during a fight, Martin was beating the shooter—a Hispanic man the press labeled a "white Hispanic" in order to stoke the racism storyline). As the Civil Rights Division well knew, even as it collaborated with such provocateurs as Al Sharpton's National Action Network and Black Lives Matter, its threats to bring civil-rights prosecutions in these cases were frivolous. The civil-rights laws, however, were a useful pretext for launching investigations of municipal police forces; the municipalities could not afford the prohibitive cost of litigating against the Justice Department and its nearly $30 billion per annum budget, so they typically entered consent decrees—agreeing to adopt Obama-dictated policing practices.[48]

In the New Orleans case, the Fifth Circuit U.S. Court of Appeals found that the government's purported internal probe "simply refused to follow up" on indications of press leaks by officials knowledgeable about the investigation. And, as you'll be shocked—*shocked*—to hear, the Justice Department somehow managed to "lose" data from key internet portals for the years 2010 and 2011. The Fifth Circuit found that this purge of emails and other memoranda meant Judge Engelhardt's "attempt to discover other online prosecutorial misconduct was...undermined." After considering the case for two years, the appellate court strongly affirmed Judge Engelhardt's extraordinary decision to throw out convictions and dismiss the case. Consistent with Obama-administration practice, a few officials quietly retired with their benefits intact, U.S. attorney Letten stepped down with praise from Attorney General Holder, and Karla Dobinski, safely ensconced at the Civil Rights Division, simply moved on to the next case.[49]

Skewed intelligence, abuse of process, pretextual use of intrusive investigative tactics, all in the service of politically driven narratives. This is not something the Obama administration came up with just in time for the 2016 campaign. By then, this was old hat.

CHAPTER FIVE

'An Institutional Lack of Candor'

t a Senate Intelligence Committee hearing on March 12, 2013, President Obama's Director of National Intelligence James Clapper gave false testimony. Asked whether the National Security Agency, the intelligence community's cryptology and signals intelligence powerhouse, "collect[s] any type of data on millions or hundreds of millions of Americans," he answered "Not wittingly."[1] The testimony seemed shifty at the time. It became indefensible when former NSA contractor Edward Snowden leaked thousands of documents, including some showing that the NSA was bulk-collecting the domestic phone records of millions of Americans—"metadata" about to and from whom calls were made, the time and duration, though not the actual content of the communications. But the agency was hoovering up content, too, in the form of millions of communications snatched from the internet's sinews.[2]

Clapper, the Obama administration's top intelligence official, could not keep straight why he lied to Congress. Sometimes, he claimed that the NSA's surveillance activities had just slipped his mind—i.e., the director of the nation's $50 billion per annum intelligence dynamo had forgotten about the decade's hottest of hot-button intelligence issues. Other times, he suggested that he hadn't understood the question—i.e., a seasoned military and intelligence professional who had testified in front of Congress numerous times forgot that he could have asked for clarification. And at least once he rationalized that he fully understood the question but was trying to give the "least untruthful" answer possible in a public setting—i.e., the keeper of the nation's defense secrets forgot the shopworn routine in which intelligence officials ask to move proceedings into closed session when a congressional committee's questions call for classified answers. Eventually, Clapper apologized. This was business as usual for a Washington fixture, not the Trump–Russia investigation, so the Justice Department declined to file perjury charges.[3]

Alas, the Snowden leaks did not convey the full depths of government deceit.

At a secret hearing on October 26, 2016, the Foreign Intelligence Surveillance Court (FISC) expressed stunned disbelief at what it described as the institutional "lack of candor" of the intelligence community.[4] The FISC had just been advised that the spy agencies had been illegally monitoring the communications of Americans for years. The surveillance—*spying* in common parlance—was in blatant violation of protocols, known as "minimization procedures," that had the force of law—ordered by the FISC as mandated by Congress in the Foreign Intelligence Surveillance Act (FISA).[5] Top intelligence officials had been well aware of the illegality but withheld the information from the FISC. That, too, flagrantly violated FISA rules, which require the Justice Department to inform the court "immediately" upon discovering that it has made any misstatement to the tribunal, or that the government has flouted the court's authorization orders.[6]

This is another Obama scandal that the mainstream media has refused to cover. Nevertheless, excellent reporting has been done elsewhere, especially by Jeff Carlson of the *The Epoch Times*.[7] It is a mindboggling story. Many salient details are still under the cloak of top-secret classification. As this book goes to print, it would be rash to draw final conclusions about this episode's connection to Obama-administration spying on the Trump campaign. Yet, it demonstrates beyond cavil that the administration made a habit of illegal surveillance and deception of the FISC.

The scandal, moreover, centrally involves spying on American citizens, through what's known as "incidental" surveillance—the indirect receipt of information about people who are not the specific target of an intelligence-gathering operation, including the collection of their communications. There is no doubt that incidental surveillance was key to the monitoring of Trump-campaign surrogates. That resulted in their inclusion in intelligence reports, which led to their identities being revealed ("unmasked"), in further violation of court minimization rules, which, in turn, abetted media leaks that fueled the Trump–Russia narrative.

FISA Philosophy

A little background on surveillance. Non-Americans situated outside our country do not have Fourth Amendment privacy protections. Consequently, the overseas collection of intelligence about them, including their communications, occurs with no judicial supervision. It is carried out under Executive Order 12333, which has been amended several times since being issued by President Ronald Reagan in 1981.[8]

Other foreign-intelligence collection implicates the Foreign Intelligence Surveillance Act. At its inception over forty years ago, FISA was chiefly designed to shield Americans inside the United States from such surveillance unless a court could be shown probable cause to believe they were complicit in clandestine activities on behalf of a foreign power. With congressional expansion of FISA over the last decade, the law is now also geared to mitigate the invasive consequences of sweeping global surveillance, made possible by the revolution in telecommunications technology. This latter protection is not very effective. In part, this is because the underlying concept is dubious, namely, the notion that people who interact with foreigners who are outside U.S. jurisdiction have a reasonable expectation of privacy despite being well-aware that the latter could be under surveillance—whether by U.S. or other intelligence services. There is also the problem that technological capabilities are advancing more rapidly than government's capacity to apply privacy principles rooted in the Constitution and other federal law, in particular, the tenet that there must be grounds for suspicion before communications are seized and searched).

Prior to 1978, foreign-intelligence collection was strictly a political responsibility: part of the national security duties the Constitution assigns to the political branches, with the executive carrying it out, subject to congressional oversight. It was not a judicial process. In the realm of foreign threats to American interests and security, the judiciary—the nonpolitical branch—had neither constitutional responsibility nor institutional competence.

I continue to believe this was the right way to look at the matter, and have thus always been a FISA naysayer.[9] The best articulation of this position was posited by the legendary Robert Jackson—an icon in both the political and legal arenas, who served as FDR's attorney general, Truman's chief prosecutor at Nuremburg, and a justice of the Supreme Court. Writing for the Court thirty years before FISA's enactment, Jackson opined:

> The President, both as Commander-in-Chief and as the Nation's organ for foreign affairs, has available intelligence services whose reports are not and ought not to be published to the world. It would be intolerable that courts, without the relevant information, should review and perhaps nullify actions of the Executive taken on information properly held secret. Nor can courts sit in camera in order to be taken into executive confidences. But even if courts could require full disclosure, the very nature of executive decisions as to foreign policy is political, not judicial. Such decisions are wholly confided by our Constitution to the political departments of the government, Executive and Legislative. They are delicate, complex, and involve large elements of prophecy. They are and should be undertaken only by those directly responsible to the people whose welfare they advance or imperil. They are decisions of a kind for which the Judiciary has neither aptitude, facilities nor responsibility and which has long been held to belong in the domain of political power not subject to judicial intrusion or inquiry.[10]

But then came the Vietnam-era political spying scandals and the Watergate abuses of intelligence authority. There followed an outcry for curbs on executive surveillance powers even in the realm of foreign intelligence. As usual, the Washington cure was worse than the disease: the insertion of judicial oversight, notwithstanding the issues of institutional competence and political accountability outlined by Justice Jackson.

This prescription, FISA, had been adumbrated by the Supreme Court's 1972 decision in what's known as the *Keith* case. The justices invalidated a warrantless search carried out by the executive branch for purely domestic national-security purposes—targeting three domestic terrorists who were plotting to bomb government facilities. Of course, *internal* threats to security—in America, by Americans—are entangled with dissent against government policy; they thus implicate fundamental liberties vouchsafed by the Constitution. That makes them saliently different from *threats by foreign powers*—even if those foreign powers are acting through agents situated inside the United States. The *Keith* Court recognized this distinction. So had Congress a few years earlier, when lawmakers enacted the statute that governs electronic surveillance in the context of domestic criminal investigations.[11] Nevertheless, in the post-Watergate fervor against executive power, over both proven and hypothetical abuses, a heavily Democratic Congress enacted FISA in 1978. President Jimmy Carter signed it, even though it ostensibly transferred to the judiciary significant executive authority over the monitoring of foreign threats to national security.[12]

FISA has now been the law for over forty years. It is not just a bad idea in theory; it's a bad one in practice. In the post-9/11 years, for example, the FISC went rogue, attempting—until beaten back by FISA's appellate court—to reerect the infamous Justice Department regulatory "wall" that impeded cooperation between intelligence and law-enforcement agents.[13] Nevertheless, the law is not going away; it is expanding: The judiciary is now ensconced in national-security matters.[14] Still, to my mind, this well-meaning arrangement is counterproductive. It undermines accountability: dragging the judiciary into nonjudicial matters (the execution of security policy), giving executive excesses the veneer of judicial approval, and making the abuse of surveillance authority more likely, not less

If the executive's national-security agents represent that they believe a foreign power is threatening the United States through the activities of a clandestine agent, it is only natural that a judge would be disposed to grant surveillance authority. Again, national security is principally an executive function: the courts are not responsible for it, have no expertise in it, and do not answer to the people whose lives are at stake. Would you want to be the judge who tells the FBI and the Justice Department that they lack sufficient evidence to monitor a suspected terrorist mass-murder plot? That they may not monitor a Russian cabal suspected on thin proof of undermining American elections? Of course not. It is no surprise, then, that the FISC approves government surveillance applications at an extraordinarily high rate. That does not make the FISC a rubber stamp, as ill-informed critiques deduce.[15] *The approval rate should be very high.* The court is reviewing assessments by professional intelligence analysts working for the president elected by the People to protect the nation.

Executive officials know, then, that it is highly likely the FISC will approve its applications. They also know that, unlike in criminal cases, there is never going to be a public proceeding at which their work and their representations to judges are going to be checked—counterintelligence is top secret. Naturally, this creates the temptation to present applications that are weak or even disingenuous. In the unlikely event a judge does not approve a deficient application, it is no big deal because the surveillance would not have happened anyway. But if a court does authorize surveillance, no one will ever know; and if the surveillance somehow becomes public, the agents can claim that it was legitimate *because a judge approved it*—even if the agents did a shoddy job or otherwise failed to comply with their own procedures. Recall, for example, former FBI Director James Comey's amusingly circular claim that the FBI does not engage in anything as underhanded as "spying" because its "electronic surveillance" is "court ordered."[16]

I believe we would get more diligent performance out of the executive branch if officials were held responsible for their own investigative judgments, subject to aggressive oversight by Congress. The participation of the court allows executive officials to evade accountability—as we shall see, this is what has happened with the Carter Page FISA warrants.

To be sure, mine is a minority view. Most intelligence officials and FISC judges would tell you that the FISA system is a worthy innovation that has encouraged executive intelligence officials to be more solicitous of American privacy rights. Of course, no one, myself least of all, is saying the Justice Department, FBI, and other intelligence agencies should have no one checking their work. Quite the opposite. The question is *who* should check their work, and the answer is Congress—the branch politically accountable to the self-governing people who must balance their interests in security and privacy. Note that the same FBI that told the FISA court about its Trump–Russia investigation took pains to conceal the probe's existence from the congressional Gang of Eight—which would likely have been much quicker to spot and object to political spying, and to ask hard questions about the flimsiness of the stated probable cause.

It is, nevertheless, a fair counter to say that Congress's dysfunction—its oversight muscles atrophied from decades of delegating its functions to courts and the administrative state—renders it, practically speaking, an impotent check on the executive. While lawmakers should be doing the job, courts are at least trying to do it and, many would argue, are doing it better than Congress would. Count me skeptical nonetheless. In the episode we are about to study, judicial oversight—along with conscientious fretting about it by some intelligence officials—brought Obama administration abuses to light... but it first allowed the abuses to go on for years.

Section 702

For our purposes, there are two relevant forms of FISA surveillance. More familiar is the individualized FISA warrant. It permits the FBI to monitor the communications of a specific person inside the United States. To get a warrant, the government must convince the FISC that the person is acting as a clandestine agent of a foreign power. We will discuss this category in more depth when we reach the FISA warrants issued for former Trump-campaign adviser Carter Page.

The second form is governed by FISA Section 702.[17] This is a critical provision of the FISA Amendments Act signed by President George W. Bush in 2008, following a vigorous national debate over (a) post-9/11 security needs, (b) the controversy over Bush's warrantless surveillance program, and (c) the need to grapple with the fact that the technological landscape that informed FISA's enactment in 1978 had largely been rendered obsolete by the telecom revolution.

Like operations under the aforementioned Executive Order 12333, Section 702 involves collection of intelligence about *foreigners outside the United States*, particularly their communications. Such communications used to be of no concern to U.S. courts. But modern telecom networks commonly break communications into digital "packets" that zoom through American networks even if the participants are outside the United States. This is a boon to our intelligence agencies.[18]

But it also created an anomaly: bringing within the jurisdiction of the courts foreign communications that were explicitly intended to be excluded from FISA regulation[19]—an anomaly pounced on by libertarians concerned about government spying on Americans, and transnational progressives who want to extend American legal rights to non-Americans. They successfully pressured for the formal expansion of FISA judicial supervision over surveillance of foreign communications. The rationale was that (a) these communications are physically passing through our territory (i.e., into the jurisdiction of U.S. courts), (b) the foreigners targeted for surveillance may be contacting Americans inside the United States, and (c) some American communications are unavoidably captured by the NSA's sometimes indiscriminate interception and storage of communications.

This unavoidable capture, what we've referred to as "incidental collection," is inevitable in all electronic eavesdropping—whether in counterintelligence or ordinary criminal wiretaps, whether the surveillance is done by court warrant or other lawful methods. If a mafia hitman whose phone is being tapped decides to order lunch, the local trattoria owner who answers the call will also be monitored. This unremarkable fact does not raise serious Fourth Amendment concerns.[20]

Nevertheless, FISA surveillance for foreign-counterintelligence purposes is more controversial than wiretaps in criminal investigations. The government does not have to show probable cause of a crime. Furthermore, when targeting foreigners overseas, the government need not clear *any* proof hurdle; it must simply represent that it has a legitimate foreign-intelligence purpose.

The national-security imperative to conduct surveillance against foreign threats, coupled with the low bar for its authorization, necessarily means Americans will be incidentally monitored. This is an acute concern: It is simply human nature that power is prone to abuse when its exercise is shrouded in secrecy, as it is in counterintelligence. Once we understand the rules and how the system works, it takes little imagination to realize how surveillance powers could be diverted to monitor Americans without warrants. A rogue government seeking to spy on Americans who have academic, business, or political needs to deal with foreigners (an ever-increasing number of Americans in an ever-smaller world) could just pretextually invoke these broad powers to collect intelligence about these foreigners. This would inexorably result in the monitoring of the Americans with whom the foreigners interact. Section 702 prohibits such *intentional* "incidental" surveillance (to coin an oxymoronic phrase), which civil libertarians call "reverse targeting." Such parchment prohibitions, however, are difficult to enforce when violations are kept secret from those who've been victimized.[21]

An important purpose of Section 702, then, is to provide some privacy protection—some judicial review—for Americans who are or could be subjected to incidental surveillance. Under 702, the government provides the court with certifications by the director of national intelligence and the attorney general, based on representations made by the directors of the FBI and CIA (our chief domestic and foreign-intelligence services, respectively), authorizing the intelligence community to target various foreigners. These foreigners must be reasonably believed to be situated outside the United States, and their targeting must be for foreign-intelligence purposes. There are several categories of foreign-intelligence purposes pertinent to U.S. security interests, so the government submits several certifications to the FISC; the exact number is classified, although the government estimates that these certifications resulted in 129,080 surveillance targets in 2017. (The number climbed steadily in recent years, up nearly 40 percent since 2013.) This translates into tens of millions of communications intercepted annually.[22]

The court must approve the certifications annually. Let's pause momentarily over that word, *certifications*. Remember, Section 702 surveillance is not like court-authorized, probable-cause-based monitoring of foreign agents operating inside the United States—the original purpose of FISA. Under Section 702, there is not even a requirement of individualized suspicion of a target, much less probable cause. Instead, 702 deals with foreigners outside the United States, the kind of spying American military forces and intelligence operatives have done without court participation since the Revolutionary War. When the Justice Department submits Section 702 certifications, the FISC is not asked to conclude that the contemplated surveillance is justified by evidence of potential harm to our country. The FISC is merely asked to put its imprimatur on spying that top executive national-security officials represent they have some valid foreign-intelligence reason for doing.

To be clear, I have no problem with such spying. It is essential for our security. My complaint involves the implication, created by a court process, that the foreign targets have cognizable privacy rights under American law. For the most part, the Section 702 process (as opposed to FISA's original individualized warrant process) does indeed resemble a rubber stamp: showy judicial bunting on traditional foreign-intelligence tactics. That is not to say the FISC does not work hard in scrutinizing these certifications; it does. The point is that it is not functioning as a court in signing off on these massive surveillance initiatives; it is not making evidence-based rulings, as judges do when presented with traditional search warrants.[23] Rather, to please transnational-progressives who imagine our dangerous world has been tamed by legal processes—as opposed to acknowledging that whatever stability we have owes to scary armed forces and icky intelligence operations ("spying" is such a harsh word!)—Section 702 shrouds the executive's sweeping covert interception of millions of potentially useful communications with the cover of judicial prestige. I don't think this is good for the spy agencies, because security against evil actors sometimes calls for national-defense measures of questionable legality that courts will be hesitant to endorse. Nor is it good for the courts, because their gravitas as an independent arbiter is eroded by collaboration with the executive in surveillance operations—activities that press the limits of American law and often violate the laws of the countries on whose agents we spy. One can simultaneously endorse these operations yet prefer that courts, our rule-of-law bulwark, not be involved in them.

In any event, while there are a number of certifications, the lack of need to make any evidentiary showing means all or most of them can be wrapped into a single presentation seeking FISC's Section 702 endorsement. The Justice Department, the intelligence agencies, and the FISC obviously prefer doing things this way because the certifications, which require extensive preparation and paperwork, are valid for a year; the process allows them to be reauthorized at the same time annually.

Section 702 surveillance is carried out, in the main, by what is commonly known as the National Security Agency. A hybrid, top-secret enterprise, the NSA is a Beltway alphabet soup. Part of the Defense Department but under the authority of the Director of National Intelligence, it is a civilian cryptologic bureau in a somewhat uneasy marriage with the armed forces' Cyber Command, a partnership facilitated by the Central Security Service (which is why the NSA is more formally known as "NSA/CSS").[24]

Because it is inevitable that American communications will be vacuumed up in Section 702 surveillance, Congress requires the FISC to condition surveillance on compliance by the NSA and other government agencies with "minimization" procedures.[25] These include time limits on how long information is kept in the Section 702 database, strict limits on the authority of intelligence officials to search this database for information about Americans, and rigorous recordkeeping requirements. The procedures also call for "masking" the identities of Americans who are incidentally intercepted: Before the NSA refines the raw data it collects into the reports and transcripts that are disseminated to intelligence agencies and White House security officials (such as the FBI, the CIA, and the National Security Council), it must redact information identifying U.S. persons—e.g., replacing the individual's name with a designation such as "U.S. Person #1."

It bears repeating: this is intelligence, so it is secret. Therefore—even if there is oversight by Congress and the FISC—we are to some degree at the mercy of intelligence officials. Gaping loopholes permit the unmasking of American identities if, for example, the CIA director, the FBI's counterintelligence agents, the White House national security adviser, or some other top intelligence official decides the unmasking is necessary "in order to understand the intelligence value" of the communication.[26]

The government's Section 702 surveillance program captures more than 250 million internet communications each year.[27] There are two sources. The first is "upstream" collection. This refers to the so-called "backbone" of the internet: the data routes between computer networks that make global communications possible. These routes are hosted by government, academic, commercial, and similar high-capacity network centers. They facilitate the global exchange of internet traffic. "Upstream" is distinguished from a second kind of collection, code-named "PRISM." This is the downstream gathering of information from internet service providers, such as Google, Facebook, Apple, and other firms that deal with telecom, email, texts, browsing histories, and the like.[28]

A decided minority of the total Section 702 intelligence haul is from upstream. How much of a minority is hard to say. In absolute terms, though, the overall number of communications is vast—easily in the tens of millions of communications per year.[29] Upstream collection is technologically complex. It is not possible to capture a single email related to a single target as it transits the backbone routes (or "switches") that connect networks. The NSA must instead capture packets of email data—which include lots of emails beside the targeted one. The agency sifts through these packets, finds and assembles the components of the email it is looking for, and then eventually discards the rest.[30]

Then there is the way the NSA targets. The upstream communications it collects end up in databases. When the NSA has a target about whom it seeks intelligence, it runs a search, called a "query," through the databases, using what is variously called an "identifier," a "selection term," or a "selector"—e.g., an email address, phone number, or other identifying information related to the target. Intelligence agencies may seek not only communications *to* or *from* this target; they may also seek communications *about* this target—e.g., *when the target is not a participant but is merely referred to in a communication.*

"About" queries create a heightened risk of accessing communications that may involve non-targeted Americans and have nothing to do with foreign intelligence. For example, there could be an email train involving multiple communications and participants (called a multiple communication transaction, or MCT), with no participation by the target but some fleeting allusion to the target. An "about" query to upstream data will yield the entire MCT—even though the active users may be Americans in the United States whose contacts have been seized without a warrant and have no foreign-intelligence value. "About" queries were of sufficient concern to Congress that a subsection of FISA specially addresses them and requires noncompliance incidents—material breaches of the FISC's minimization instructions—

to be reported "fully and currently" to the Judiciary Committees of the House and Senate.[31]

Obviously, a huge question is: *Under what circumstances should investigators be permitted to search the Section 702 database for Americans' information?* The law permits not only searches by intelligence agents for national security purposes; FBI agents working on criminal cases also have access. In marked contrast to the Section 702 database, information about Americans collected under EO 12333 may be accessed only for foreign-intelligence purposes, not criminal investigations.[32]

With that as background, we come to the Obama administration's flouting of FISA court minimization procedures.

Spying on Americans and Misleading the Court

In 2011, whether because minimization procedures were being transgressed or because the NSA could not technically implement them, it became clear that intelligence agents were violating both FISA and the Fourth Amendment and that they were concealing the breadth of the violations from the FISC. In a scathing opinion, Judge John D. Bates, then chief of the FISC, rebuked the government's pattern of deceiving the tribunal about "wholly domestic" communications the NSA was intercepting each year—noting that the most recent confession, involving tens of thousands of such communications, "mark[ed] the third instance in less than three years in which the government has disclosed a substantial misrepresentation regarding the scope of a major collection program."[33]

Of special concern was *the use of email addresses and phone numbers of American citizens as selectors* for database searches. Thus, the minimization procedures were ratcheted up. The most significant change was that the revised procedures *categorically prohibited NSA analysts from using U.S.-person identifiers* to query the results of upstream internet collection. This meant the NSA was not supposed to use an American's phone number, email address, or other "identifier" in running searches through its upstream database. The FISC also declined to authorize the acquisition of MCTs unless the foreign target was an active participant.[34]

In 2014, with the NSA reeling from the Snowden debacle, President Obama appointed a longtime military intelligence pro, Admiral Michael Rogers, to take over the agency in addition to commanding U.S. cyber operations (Cyber Command) at the Defense Department.[35] In the meantime, the acquisition and screening of upstream collection continued to be a perplexing challenge. For that and other reasons, including the government's poor track record of compliance and trustworthiness in dealing with the court, inspectors general of the relevant agencies began assessing the situation.

In 2012, for example, Justice Department Inspector General Michael Horowitz conducted a comprehensive study of the FBI's Section 702 procedures, issuing a lengthy report.[36] IG Horowitz found it frustrating to investigate foreign counterintelligence–related activities carried out by the FBI and the Obama Justice Department's National Security Division (which handles FISA and other counterintelligence matters). They stonewalled routinely, delaying production or simply refusing to give the IG's office relevant records.[37] Sally Yates, Obama's Deputy Attorney General who would later play a key role in the Trump–Russia investigation, had the Justice Department's Office of Legal Counsel issue a 2015 memorandum, substantially rebuffing the IG's request for access to various categories of information, including some intelligence obtained in counterintelligence investigations.[38]

At roughly the same time, the NSA's Inspector General, Dr. George Ellard, undertook a "special study" of the agency's internal controls for compliance with Section 702 targeting and minimization procedures. The snapshot on which the NSA-IG focused was the first quarter of 2015, analyzing all records of queries of the relevant database. On January 7, 2016, the NSA-IG issued its then-top-secret report. The result was eye-popping. Nearly eight years after the enactment of Section 702, the NSA had not yet "completely developed" internal "controls for monitoring query compliance."

The bottom line, the IG found, was that the NSA had "no process to reliably identify queries performed using selectors associated with" Americans outside the United States. While other types of violations were found, most prominent was that the NSA was still using U.S. person selectors to query upstream data, which, as we've seen, was strictly prohibited under the Section 702 minimization procedures. The NSA-IG concluded that 5.2 percent of the queries were noncompliant—which translates into a significant number of American communications.[39]

But that's just for starters. While the NSA was engaged in violative investigations of Americans, the FBI was giving raw FISA information, including intelligence acquired under Section 702, to private contractors. These contractors have not been publicly identified. They were not authorized to have access to the FISA information—which was even more sensitive than the materials the Justice Department and FBI were refusing to share with the DOJ-IG. Moreover, as the FISC later recounted, the contractors' access "went well beyond what was necessary to respond to the FBI's requests." The FBI and the Justice Department had no control over what the contractors did with the information. The National Security Division also did not know "whether there have been similar cases in which the FBI improperly afforded non-FBI personnel access to raw FISA-acquired information on FBI systems."[40]

On April 18, 2016, NSA Director Rogers cut off all private contractor access to raw FISA intercepts. That month, he also directed that the NSA's compliance office conduct a "fundamental baseline review of compliance associated with 702." *The Epoch Times*'s Jeff Carlson reasonably surmises that it was the NSA-IG report and the discovery of the FBI's misconduct that triggered these directives.[41]

By mid-April 2016, then, the Justice Department and its National Security Division were well aware of the NSA-IG report and the serious Section 702 noncompliance issues involving the surveillance of Americans and abusive dissemination of highly classified FISA information outside the government. Moreover, as it continued its internal investigation, NSA found that in one subset of searches, use of one of its common "tools" was leading to improper queries involving U.S. persons *85 percent of the time*. In May and June 2016, NSA reported these findings to the Justice Department's National Security Division and to the office of National Intelligence Director Clapper.[42] Yet, three months later, when the Justice Department submitted its Rule 702 certifications to the FISC so that its programs could be authorized for the next year, the National Security Division—the

Justice Department component that deals with the FISC—did not disclose these derelictions.

Of course, it was in the second half of 2016 that the Trump–Russia investigation was going full throttle, with John Brennan's CIA funneling information from foreign-intelligence services to the FBI, informants being tasked with approaching Trump-campaign figures, the Bureau opening its "Crossfire Hurricane" counterintelligence probe, the unmasking of Trump associates in intelligence reporting underway, and the FBI and Justice Department peddling the Steele dossier to the FISC. Was FISA information about Americans that had been improperly collected and accessed exploited in Russia-gate? Who were the unidentified "private contractors" to whom the FBI lawlessly provided FISA information, and were they somehow relevant to the Russia probe?[43] Did the Trump–Russia investigation factor into the Justice Department's withholding of violation information from the FISC? Was there worry, for example, that disclosure of the malfeasance might induce the court to deny a FISA warrant to monitor Carter Page? At the moment, we don't know the answers.

Here is what we do know.

In September 2016, the FBI and the Justice Department's National Security Division were compiling the FISA warrant application for former Trump-campaign adviser Carter Page.

On September 26, 2016, the Justice Department's NSD submitted to the FISC its Section 702 certifications for the following year, consistent with the requirement that they be filed a month before the deadline, October 26. The application contained supporting affidavits from the heads of the relevant intelligence agencies, including NSA Director Rogers. The government's submission withheld from the FISC anything close to a full accounting of the serious compliance issues—notwithstanding that the court should have been notified months earlier, when the issues were discovered.[44]

The following day, September 27, the head of NSD, Assistant Attorney General John Carlin, abruptly resigned, effective October 15. At the age of forty-three, Carlin had been in the critical post since mid-2013, having formerly served as chief of staff to the FBI's then-Director, Robert S. Mueller III. As chief of NSD, Carlin was among the government officials chiefly responsible for ensuring the intelligence community's compliance with court-ordered Section 702 minimization instructions, and for alerting the FISC to noncompliance issues, as required by law and court rules. Carlin had also received regular briefings on the Clinton emails and the Trump–Russia investigations. Carlin had *also* been the top national-security official who, on March 11, 2016, publicly announced the guilty plea of Evgeny Buryakov—the Russian spy against whom Carter Page had provided key assistance to the Justice Department and FBI.[45]

On October 4, the FISC held a standard follow-up hearing to discuss the government's September 26 submission. NSD Chief Carlin was reportedly present at the proceeding, which was uneventful because the government, again, failed to disclose the compliance issues the NSA's internal audits had begun uncovering ten months earlier. Carlin left the government eleven days later, replaced by his deputy, Mary McCord—who thus assumed responsibility for the NSD's oversight role in the FBI's Trump–Russia investigation. Carlin did not resurface until the public announcement that he had taken a job in the private sector in January 2017.[46] Meanwhile, the NSD and FBI obtained a FISA surveillance warrant against Carter Page on October 21, after Carlin's departure and before the FISC was alerted to the Section 702 irregularities. The Page surveillance involved an individualized warrant to monitor an American citizen alleged to be acting in the United States as an agent of a foreign power; it was not a Section 702 operation. As we shall see, however, it raises similar issues of Obama-administration withholding of salient information from the FISC.

In the interim, on October 20, with the FISC due to approve the Section 702 certifications in six days, NSA Director Rogers asked for and received a briefing from the NSA's compliance office on the fundamental baseline review of Section 702 compliance issues that he had ordered back in April. He was told that the audit turned up numerous additional violations, including "about" query infractions. Rogers ordered that "about" inquiries be shut down, and alerted the NSD of this directive.[47] Four days later, on October 24, prompted by Rogers's additional information about rampant derelictions with respect to the minimization instructions currently in place, the government finally gave the FISC an emergency oral notice that there were serious compliance issues. Rather than green-light certifications and new minimization instructions, which were due in just two days, the FISC scheduled a hearing for October 26.[48]

At the hearing, the government confessed to various irregularities, most notably that it had for years been unlawfully gathering intelligence on Americans—specifically, using U.S. person identifiers to query the upstream database, in violation of the prohibition that had been in place since 2011. The government conceded that Obama-administration national-security officials had been aware of the broad scope of the problem since at least January 2016 when the NSA's IG report was issued—a report that itself had been triggered in early 2015 by the NSA's awareness of widespread compliance issues.

The FISC found breathtaking what it described as the government's institutional "lack of candor." The judges ascribed this mendacity specifically to the NSA. Clearly, though, this was an allusion to NSA compliance problems that stretched back to the 2008 enactment of Section 702, misrepresentations about which the FISC had scalded the agency on past occasions.[49] Nevertheless, the serious violations reported in late 2016 would not have been uncovered had Rogers not pushed the issue to the fore. The internal audits that had exposed wrongdoing (including the FBI's failure to monitor private contractors with whom it improperly shared FISA information) had been known for months, not just to the NSA, but to the Justice Department's NSD, the FBI, and the Office of National Intelligence Director Clapper.

This FISC delayed certification of the next year's Section 702 collection programs until April 2017, keeping the existing programs in place on the basis of promises that "about" collections had ceased and other steps were being taken to determine the full scope of compliance issues and address them. The court issued its order approving the certifications on April 26, by which time the government agreed to abandon "about" collections and purge data that had been collected in likely violation of the Constitution under the prior, ineffective minimization instructions.

In the interim, on November 8, Donald Trump won the United States presidential election. Nine days later, on Thursday, November

17, Admiral Rogers went to visit the president-elect at Trump Tower in Manhattan. Rogers did not notify his superiors—Clapper and Obama Defense Secretary Ashton Carter—of the trip. It has been plausibly speculated that Rogers met with Trump and his transition team to discuss a position in the new administration, perhaps to replace Clapper as National Intelligence Director. Intriguingly, on the weekend that started the day after Rogers's visit, the president-elect abruptly moved the transition operation from Trump Tower to his private golf club and estate in Bedminster, New Jersey.[50]

There is surmise in pro-Trump circles that Rogers alerted the president-elect to the existence of the Obama administration's Trump–Russia investigation and the possibility that his Trump Tower offices were under various forms of surveillance. This seems highly unlikely. President Trump, who is no shrinking violet and who has access to all the nation's intelligence secrets, has never claimed that he moved his transition operation to Bedminster because of something Rogers told him. As we shall see in more detail, the president-elect was briefed on the Russia investigation and told he was not a suspect (misleadingly, I believe), on January 6, 2017. That is, two months after he met with Rogers, he does not appear to have known much about the probe—or much of anything about its focus on the Trump campaign.

Furthermore, in his now famous claim that the Obama administration had surveilled his Manhattan offices, posited in a series of tweets on March 4, 2017, Trump said he had *"just found out* that Obama had my 'wires tapped' in Trump Tower just before the victory" (emphasis added). These tweets were posted four months after Trump's meeting with Rogers.[51] There could have been many good logistical and security reasons for moving the transition operation from heavily trafficked Midtown Manhattan to a rural 600-acre setting, and for doing it on a weekend. Meanwhile, in March 2017 congressional testimony, Rogers expressly denied any knowledge—at least on the NSA's part—that the wiretapping alleged in Trump's tweet had taken place.[52]

There is, nevertheless, reason to believe that Rogers's visit to Trump caused angst in the Obama camp—angst that had been growing for weeks. Within days of the Trump–Rogers meeting, anonymous "administration and intelligence officials" leaked to *The Washington Post* and *The New York Times* that President Obama had been considering removing Rogers from his NSA perch. Elaborating, the papers reported the push for Rogers's dismissal—at a time, mind you, when Obama's term was about to expire and there was no possibility of confirming a replacement NSA chief before Trump's inauguration—was coming from Director Clapper and Secretary Carter (both of whom were also about to leave government service).[53]

In the shopworn style of Washington kneecapping, there was no coherent explanation for this deliberation over an untimely sacking—Rogers was alternatively said to be skittish about the Obama administration's purported focus on fighting ISIS (which had been such an Obama priority that ISIS had annexed a swath of Iraqi–Syrian territory that was bigger than Britain); too aloof, acerbic, and militarily wired for the sensibilities of NSA's civilian workforce; and an impediment to an organizational severance between NSA and the military's Cyber Command (which Rogers actually supported). What seems clear, however, is that the push for Rogers's ouster began in October (i.e., when Rogers was agitating over the NSA's compliance issues and the failure to reveal them to the FISA court), but that there was no media reporting about it until Rogers met with Trump and was touted as a possible replacement for Clapper.

Ultimately, President Obama did not remove Admiral Rogers. And President Trump retained him at the NSA, permitting Rogers to oversee the standing up of Cyber Command as a "unified combatant command" (a lofty military status) and endow it with more authority to combat Russian cyberattacks.[54] The admiral announced in January that he would retire in the spring, and he stepped down on May 4, 2018, an occasion marked by a ceremony honoring Rogers's leadership through the Snowden scandal and the NSA's toughest hours.[55]

Some scandals have happier endings than others.

CHAPTER SIX

Collusion: Foreign Government, the Obama Administration, and the Clinton Campaign

‘T he FBI has a very close relationship with its British counterparts."

It was February 2018 and former CIA Director John Brennan was appearing on NBC's *Meet the Press*, fielding questions about the origin of the Obama administration's investigation of the Trump campaign. Because of the U.S.–U.K. special relationship, he explained, "the FBI had visibility into a number of things that were going on involving some individuals who may have had some affiliation with the Trump campaign."[1] It was all about the Brits.

More accurate to say: It was all about Brennan.

No one did more to promote the Russia-gate narrative than Obama's transnational-progressive, hyper-political, rabidly anti-Trump spy chief. Brennan got his start in White House work on Bill Clinton's National Security Council, becoming the CIA's daily briefer to the president.[2] During the 2016 presidential campaign, he had ambitions of staying in the White House as the new Clinton administration's spymaster.

It was Brennan who peddled the conspiracy theories of his like-minded European counterparts, fearful that Trump was bent on disrupting their cherished post–World War II order (in which the United States underwrites security for the EU's social welfare state). Other officials struggled to establish Russia's responsibility for the hacking of Democratic email accounts—a high probability, but one based on equivocal evidence rendered more vulnerable by the Obama Justice Department's failure to investigate it thoroughly. Brennan, by contrast, charged ahead with all the "slam dunk" certitude of his old boss and mentor, George Tenet: Not only had the Russians done it, they had done it *because Putin wanted Trump to win*, and that was *because Putin and Trump were in cahoots*. And it was Brennan who quite publicly and proudly credited himself with spurring what ultimately became the FBI's Trump–Russia probe. We've seen that it can be risky to take Brennan at his word. On this one, though, the evidence supports him.

First, let's clear away some underbrush.

As we've already detailed, there has been a great deal of misinformation about the origination of the investigation—and even about whether there was a single investigation, as opposed to multiple threads, weaved into a Russia-gate narrative. Much of this misinformation can be blamed on President Trump himself. He could have cleared things up early on by declassifying and publishing the explanatory paper trail. Thus far (as this book goes to press), he has refrained from doing so—though the president has now delegated to Attorney General Bill Barr the authority to declassify information to facilitate Barr's investigation of the Trump–Russia investigation's genesis. Equally significantly, the president has made explosive allegations that, while in the ballpark of reality, are rife with inaccuracies. This has given intelligence officials in the United States and elsewhere the opportunity to issue denials in huffs of indignation that belie their underlying narrowness.

Let's take a notable example. As previously discussed, on March 4, 2017, the president tweeted that his predecessor had his "wires tapped" at Trump Tower. Subsequently, Fox News legal commentator Andrew Napolitano claimed that, according to his informed sources (who appear to include former CIA analyst Larry Johnson), President Obama had surveilled Trump not via American intelligence agencies but by pressing an allied intelligence service into action—specifically, Britain's Government Communications Headquarters (GCHQ).[3] GCHQ is Albion's analogue to the NSA, specializing in international signals intelligence and cryptology.

In addition to heated rebukes from Obama officials, allies, and media mouthpieces, Trump's allegation prompted pointed denials from current and former intelligence officials (Obama appointees all). James Comey, then the FBI's director, put it this way in March 2017 House

Intelligence Committee testimony:

> With respect to the president's tweets about alleged wiretapping directed at him by the prior administration, I have no information that supports those tweets and we have looked carefully inside the FBI. The Department of Justice has asked me to share with you that the answer is the same for the Department of Justice and all its components. The Department has no information that supports those tweets.[4]

Similarly, James Clapper, former Director of National Intelligence, told Meet the Press that, from the national security apparatus he oversaw, "there was no such wiretap activity mounted against…the president-elect at the time, or as a candidate, or against his campaign."[5]

Fox News (at which I am a contributor) briefly suspended "Judge Nap" and distanced itself from his reporting. GCHQ itself heatedly dismissed the explosive allegations, an extraordinary refutation from a secretive sphinx that habitually refuses to confirm, deny, or discuss its spy-ops. "Recent allegations made by media commentator Judge Andrew Napolitano about GCHQ being asked to conduct 'wiretapping' against the then president elect are nonsense," the agency declaimed. Not content to leave it at "nonsense," GCHQ added that the allegations were "utterly ridiculous and should be ignored."[6]

Now, let's say you're a normal, sober person, reasonably well-informed but with limited time and attention span for such matters. You hear vehement, sweeping disclaimers from outfits that usually tell you they can neither confirm nor deny the existence of the morning sun. Naturally, you come away thinking that the accusations about their activities—claims of political spying—must have been complete bunk.

Not so fast.

Let's examine this with care. Stripped of the high-decibel bluster, the FBI, the Justice Department, and the intelligence officials merely asserted that Trump's claim—that President Obama ordered his phones to be wiretapped—was literally wrong. But as the half-joke goes, Trump is more to be taken seriously than literally. Here, the literal denial was so thin as to be nearly meaningless. Technically, even a rogue president would never order that anyone's phones be wiretapped; a court would issue such an order, based on representations by investigators and Justice

Department lawyers. When their remarks are parsed carefully, we find that the intelligence officials did not deny that there was an investigation involving Trump and his campaign, nor even that activity at Trump Tower was scrutinized. Moreover, GCHQ's fervid denial—we were not "wiretapping" the "then president elect"—is near gibberish. GCHQ doesn't actually do much "wiretapping" (the physical placement of a listening device on a telephone circuit)—certainly not in the United States; the word is a vestige from a bygone technological era. And Trump did not claim in his tweets that he was president-elect at the time of Obama's alleged "tapping"—he said it happened "just before the victory." Plus, even if GCHQ never targeted Trump's Manhattan offices for the interception of phone calls, that hardly means it had nothing to do with any intelligence-gathering operations touching on Trump and his campaign.

Put simply, when listening to disclaimers from government officials, their indignation level should never be confused with the scope of their denial.

'Congratulations, You Will Be Defending Yourself'

It is important to understand that Donald Trump was (and remains) incredibly unpopular among Western European elites. He was the first American major party presidential candidate in three-quarters of a century to express skepticism about an unconditional U.S. commitment to the Continent's security and significance. In that vein, he took aim at NATO, particularly the lavish bureaucratic infrastructure that has outlived the alliance's original mission and, to Trump's mind, its value.

"Congratulations, you will be defending yourself," Trump warned the allies in a lengthy *New York Times* interview during the heat of the campaign. That would be the consequence, he vowed, if the United States "cannot be properly reimbursed" for the "tremendous cost" our taxpayers bear in having our armed forces protect NATO nations blessed with "massive wealth." NATO members were not "paying their bills," and if that did not change, he asserted, the alliance would have to be rethought.[7] This was a constant theme of Trump's campaign: It was time to disrupt the old order. Not necessarily trash it, but renegotiate it so that America was not taken advantage of, not on the hook to assure the security of countries that refused to pony up for their own defense. Why, he wondered, should Americans sacrifice to shield the Continent from Russian aggression while Germany, the biggest, richest NATO country, made gigantic energy deals with the Kremlin, indenturing Europe to the rogue power that, in its empirical Soviet era, was NATO's raison d'être?[8] Candidate Trump elaborated:

> We're paying disproportionately. It's too much. And frankly it's a different world than it was when we originally conceived of the idea. ... [W]e're taking care of, as an example, the Ukraine. I mean, the countries over there don't seem to be so interested. We're the ones taking the brunt of it. So I think we have to reconsider. Keep NATO, but maybe we have to pay a lot less toward the NATO itself.[9]

Trump's oft-expressed agnosticism about NATO and America's interventions around the world was coupled with blandishments toward Moscow (sweet nothings toward a despotic regime—the sort of thing progressives find seductive when uttered by an Obama or a Merkel). As I've said, Trump's Russia rhetoric sometimes crossed the line from jarring to infuriating (e.g., the drawing of moral equivalence between American and Russian intelligence operations). I feel the same dyspepsia when the president today talks about his warm friendship with the homicidal maniac Kim Jong-un. But that's Trump, and you have to take him as he is. I didn't see Abe Lincoln on the other party's ballot—the party that didn't just talk about better relations with anti-American regimes, factions, and organizations but funded, empowered, and embraced them. In any event, it is hardly unusual for an American presidential candidate to depict himself as uniquely suited to pursue the holy grail of cooperative relations with Russia—a posture taken by Obama and most of his predecessors in modern American history. But this is politics, so the Clinton camp predictably framed Trump as a threat to the post–World War II internationalist order that progressives regard as their own creation. He was, in the telling of Democrats and their Euro-chorus, bent on destroying NATO and turning the White House into an annex of the Kremlin.

If anyone could be relied on to toe this political line, it was Brennan. Even allowing that Trump can often be abrasive in a manner beneath his office, it is shocking to find a former director of the CIA upbraiding an American president as "treasonous," guilty of "high crimes and misdemeanors," and "wholly in the pocket of Putin." It is equally stunning to find this recently incumbent U.S. spy chief beginning a typical published remark with: "Just imagine if we had a President who did not live in constant fear of being exposed as a fraud"— and always in a tone that oozes *If only I could tell you what I know.*[10]

Mind you: this is how Brennan speaks *publicly*. How do you figure he conducted himself while kibitzing with like-minded European intelligence counterparts he trusted?

Foreign Interference in Our Elections Is . . . Apparently Not So Bad

In late 2015, after Trump entered the race for the Republican presidential nomination (i.e., months before anyone had ever heard of George Papadopoulos), GCHQ began taking note of suspicious "interactions" between Trump associates and "suspected Russian agents." This information was passed along to the American intelligence community as part of the allies' regular exchange of information. Other European spy services followed suit. Germany, France, the Netherlands, Estonia, and Poland were all contributors, as was Australia. In Senate Intelligence Committee testimony, Obama National Intelligence Director James Clapper later confirmed this "sensitive" stream of European intelligence, originally reported by *The Guardian*'s Luke Harding.[11] At least at the start, there was no targeted operation against Trump or his campaign; it is said to have been routine intelligence collection against Russia that was yielding "connections" of varying kinds. Again, there is nothing necessarily nefarious about "connections," and U.S. politicians across the spectrum have had them with Russia for decades. But these were *Trump* connections, so they were presumed to be dark. No, GCHQ was not "tapping" Trump's phone lines in Manhattan, but, Harding related, "both US and UK intelligence sources acknowledge that GCHQ played an early, prominent role in kickstarting the FBI's Trump–Russia investigation."

Here, it is worth noting the dismal state of U.S. intelligence on Russia under Brennan's watch. As Lee Smith catalogues, American spy agencies were caught off guard by Putin's annexation of Crimea and by the escalation of Russia's military presence in Syria—which even included the transportation of weapons and personnel through the Bosporus, a strait controlled by our NATO "ally," Islamist Turkey. Putin had taken Obama's measure. Moscow realized the president so needed its "help" on the Iran deal, as well as on the growing ISIS and humanitarian catastrophe in Syria, that the American administration would consciously ignore any provocation. In an April 2016 CNN interview, Devin Nunes (R., Calif.), then Chairman of the House Intelligence Committee, lamented that "the biggest intelligence failure we've had since 9/11 has been the inability to predict the leadership plans and intentions of the Putin regime in Russia."[12]

That was long before there was a public Russia-gate narrative, even months prior to the publication of hacked DNC emails—which first took the Obama administration by surprise, then froze it into paralysis. With an information void about Russia, and with the Obama administration both hardwired to politicize intelligence and encouraging of our allies' clear preference for the Democratic nominee, European suspicions about Trump resonated. It was the perfect storm: Even if one suspends disbelief and credits the American intelligence community's good faith, it seems clear that the paltry state of reliable information on Putin's regime rendered the intelligence community unable competently to evaluate the outlandish allegations in the Steele dossier, or to protect itself against Moscow's legendary expertise in peddling disinformation.

Carter Page

We'll soon come to the dossier. Now, let's focus on a man who would emerge as one of its main characters, Carter Page. He was first announced as a Trump-campaign foreign-policy adviser on March 21, 2016, but he had joined the campaign two months earlier.

Page is an Annapolis graduate and former naval intelligence officer who served five years in the Navy, working for a time in western

Morocco as part of a U.N. peacekeeping mission. He had been a good student, qualifying as a Trident Scholar, which enabled him to spend his senior year as a researcher on the House Armed Services Committee. Throughout his career, Page has persisted in academic work in the fields of international affairs, commerce, and security, earning an MA in national-security studies from Georgetown, an MBA from New York University, and a doctorate from London's School of Oriental and African Studies in 2011. He ran an international affairs program at Bard College, taught a course on energy and politics at NYU, and won a coveted fellowship at the Council on Foreign Relations.

Alas, Page's post-Navy career as an investment banker has been less than stellar. He joined Merrill Lynch, working first in London and then for three years in Moscow. He seems to have exaggerated his role in the firm's work. For example, when he eventually began his own investment firm after leaving Merrill in 2008, he reportedly told a U.S. State Department official in Turkmenistan that he had helped take Russia's energy giant, Gazprom, from a run-of-the-mill state-run oil company to "super major status"—a claim he had apparently also made to Turkmenistan officials.[13] In reality, Page had been a non-descript deputy office manager at Merrill, making little impression on the execs who actually handled the big accounts. "He wasn't great, and he wasn't terrible," observed Page's boss. "What can you say about a person who in no way [is] exceptional?" The private fund he started in 2008, Global Energy Capital LLC, was hoping to attract a billion dollars for investment in companies run by foreign regimes. The venture, however, has struggled since its inception. Page has continued to seek investment opportunities around the world, including in the Russian energy sector. That fact is said to have made the Obama administration suspicious—ironic, to put it mildly, given that the Obama administration encouraged energy commerce with Russia while laboring mightily to help create the Russian tech sector (see Chapter One).[14]

Page was favorably disposed toward Donald Trump from the moment the mogul launched his presidential bid at Trump Tower on June 16, 2015. What heartened Page about Trump is exactly what rankled many conservative Republicans (like me): the candidate's blandishments towards Vladimir Putin; his minimizing of Putin's monstrousness; and his vows to prioritize improved relations with Moscow—if necessary, it seemed, at the expense of important American interests. Page has not been shy about his pro-Russia views, and has a history of pro-Kremlin statements. He has blamed the deteriorating state of Russo-American relations on "misguided and provocative actions" by the United States, which he has accused of "imped[ing] potential progress" through "often hypocritical ideas such as democratization, inequality, corruption and regime change." Reasoning that aggressive responses only provoke more Russian belligerence, Page has opposed Western action (mainly sanctions) against Russia's annexation of Crimea, and has criticized the Obama State Department's purported fomenting of Ukraine's Euromaidan revolution that ousted the Kremlin-friendly government.[15]

These are noxious political positions. But they are *political* positions. In this country, Page is entitled to hold them. The Trump campaign was entitled to consider internalizing them, no matter how obtuse they may be—just as the Obama administration was entitled to posit that American national security was somehow served by lavishing billions of dollars in sanctions relief on Iran, the world's leading state sponsor of terrorism, while obliging the United States to help the jihadist regime develop an industrial-strength nuclear-energy program—*of course*, for civilian purposes only, right?

Page decided to volunteer to work on the Trump campaign. He sought and got an entrée from New York Republican Party Chairman Ed Cox, who knew Page had supported fellow Annapolis grad John McCain's 2008 presidential bid. Impressed by Page's résumé, particularly his military and intelligence service, the state party chairman forwarded Page's name to Trump's team. In January 2016, Page joined the campaign after brief meetings with its then-manager, Corey Lewandowski, and with Sam Clovis, the former Navy fighter pilot turned Iowa radio host and GOP activist, who was starting to formulate a foreign-policy shop for the candidate.[16]

Such a shop would not be easy to stock with experts. Trump's provocative positions on NATO and trade, his solicitude toward Putin, and his tirades against the Iraq war and what he framed as President Bush's ineptitude, had the Republican foreign-policy clerisy shunning his candidacy.[17]

Trump's run through the GOP primary field was already looking like Sherman's march through Georgia. Yet his advisers sensed a vulnerability as journalists peppered the campaign with questions about who was advising the would-be commander-in-chief on foreign-policy matters. Feeling the need to brandish some names, the campaign announced a handful of obscure ones—probably as much unknown to Trump as to most. They included Page, as well as young George Papadopoulos, whom we will come to in the next chapter.[18]

Suffice it to say that Page got the FBI's attention.

Politics Is Not a Predicate for a Counterintelligence Probe

Here, we come to why counterintelligence work can be so complex and difficult, compared to criminal investigations. This is not to say the latter are without their challenges. But when properly predicated, criminal investigations commence only after there is solid evidence that a penal offense has occurred or is underway. By contrast, the objective of national security is to *prevent bad things from happening*, to thwart foreign powers who might harm American interests and who do not have the legal protections of American citizens. Frequently, then, counterintelligence will involve the monitoring of people, including Americans, who may not have committed crimes, on the theory that they are serving the interests of foreign actors who may threaten us. The government is not required to wait until foreign powers have taken hostile action before engaging in countermeasures—depending on the kind of hostile action at issue, that could mean waiting until it's too late.

On the other hand (have you noticed that when we're talking law, there's always another hand?), political dissent is never—*by itself*—a legitimate basis for the government to surveil an American citizen. This principle can be easier to state than to apply. Seditious action or espionage against our country is often inextricably bound up with political dissent against our government's policies. It is not possible to separate the two entirely: To prosecute a person for criminal acts, it is necessary to prove criminal intent. *Mens rea* is often established by what a person says. Our words usually reflect the operation of our minds. The terrorism cases I prosecuted in the 1990s are a classic example: The suspects made many anti-American statements that free-speech principles entitled them to express, but when their conduct crossed the line into criminality (e.g., seditious conspiracy[19]), I was able to use their statements as *mens rea* proof. Yes, the First Amendment protected them from being *prosecuted* for making their political statements, but it did not insulate those statements from use as evidence of intent and motive for the crimes charged against them. Put another way, if a mafia don charged with murder is heard on tape telling the hitman, "*Whack him,*" you are not apt to find his lawyer mounting a free-speech defense.

But notice the salient word: *conduct.* Whether we are talking about criminal prosecution or surveillance for purposes of counterintelligence probes involving foreign powers, there must be some *purposeful action* before the government is justified in investigating an American. The PATRIOT Act, for example, stresses that First Amendment protected activity—mere speech, or mere association—is never sufficient by itself to trigger surveillance.[20] FISA also instructs that to justify surveilling an American citizen, there must be probable cause that the person is *knowingly engaged in clandestine activity* on behalf of a foreign power. The statute elaborates that such activity involves intentional subterfuge, the commission of crimes at the direction of a foreign-intelligence service, using false identities on behalf of a foreign power, or such heinous activities as sabotage and terrorism.[21] Manifestly, speech that does not cross the threshold of incitement or *unwitting* action that happens to help a foreign power is not good enough.

When we consider those principles, it is easy to understand (a) why the FBI might have had some legitimate concerns about Carter Page (remember, having "legitimate concerns" is not the same as saying he had done something wrong), and (b) why having *legitimate concerns* is not the same as having *an adequate predicate for an investigation*— or, even more, as having *an adequate predicate for the use of highly intrusive investigative techniques* that the law reserves for cases involving concrete evidence of *willful clandestine activity.*

It is not for nothing that Russia hawks derisively regarded Page as Putin's voice in Trump's campaign, while the rest of the community of international-affairs thinkers ridiculed his selection as an adviser to a major presidential candidate. In assessing Donald Trump's "baffling" array of foreign-policy advisers, *Politico* noted that Page's "discursive online blog postings about foreign policy invoke the likes of Kanye West, Oprah Winfrey, and Rhonda Byrne's self-help bestseller, *The Secret*." To be sure, Page's foreign-policy views were naïve and strangely sympathetic to a hostile foreign power. That did not make him a spy. Was he the kind of thinker we would want whispering in a presidential nominee's ear? Well, I certainly wouldn't (and didn't). That, however, is a separate question. And, on that question, it's not like the blame-America-first mindset—like its companion conceit that we should refrain from pursuing America's interests in the world—is uncommon among Washington's smart set, or among academics, such as Page, who are steeped in foreign-relations studies and have spent lots of time abroad. (Why do I think that if Page, without changing any of his Russia views, had joined, say, the Muslim Brotherhood, the Center for Constitutional Rights, or the Bernie Sanders campaign, *The New York Times* would have been fine with him?)

What else was known about Page when he joined the Trump campaign? Well, apparently through no fault of his own—i.e., not by doing anything illegal, but by traveling to Russia, by interacting professionally with Russians, as well as by seeking business opportunities and participating in academic conferences that were Russia-related (you know, the things our bipartisan political establishment told us were totally cool for the last thirty years)—Page attracted the attention of all the wrong people. The Mueller report, for example, notes that in 2008, as Page's start-up venture, Global Energy Capital, foundered, he recruited as a "senior adviser" Sergey Yatsenko, deputy chief financial officer of Gazprom (a Russian-regime-controlled global natural-gas conglomerate whose shares are publicly traded). At around the same time, he met a man named Alexander Bulatov, who worked at the Russian consulate in New York. Prosecutors say Page later learned that Bulatov was a Russian intelligence officer, but they don't allege that Page actually did anything with Bulatov—the Mueller report makes pregnant mention of the fact that they knew each other and then...the matter is dropped.[22]

In January 2013, Page did stumble into an FBI investigation of

Russian spies. At an international energy symposium in New York City, Page happened into a man he says he was led to believe was a Russian government official, attached to Moscow's United Nations mission. Unbeknownst to Page (which is how this usually works) the man was actually a Russian spy named Victor Podobnyy. By Page's own account, in the ensuing months, he and Podobnyy exchanged emails and met in person on occasion, with Page giving Podobnyy his outlook on energy-industry prospects and some documents on the subject—including parts of a lecture Page had given, which was publicly available information.

Here it gets fuzzy. In the course of its investigation, the FBI monitored conversations between Podobnyy and another spy, Igor Sporyshev. In at least one, on April 8, 2013, they discussed Page. Podobnyy described him as "an idiot," who was looking to "earn lots of money" in the Russian energy sector, perhaps with a Gazprom project. Podobnyy was trying to recruit Page as an asset—evidently, an unwitting one whom he would burn once Page had obtained whatever information he was looking for. ("I will feed him empty promises," Podobnyy told Sporyshev. "This is intelligence method to cheat, how else to work with foreigners? You promise a favor for a favor. You get the documents from him and tell him to go fuck himself.")

In June 2013, the FBI approached Page to ask about his conversations with Podobnyy. Page voluntarily cooperated with the agents, meeting with investigators several times. In fact, the Justice Department used Page's information in its arrest complaint in the criminal case against Podobnyy, Sporyshev, and another Russian spy, Evgeny Buryakov.[23]

Here, we must note, the Mueller report plays fast and loose with the facts to make Page look worse—presumably to justify the Obama administration's eventual decision to monitor him as if he and the Trump campaign were a Kremlin front operation. A reader of Mueller's report would conclude that Page, like everyone else, found out about the case against the Russian spies only in 2015, when Podobnyy was arrested. At that point, we're told, Page read the public complaint, realized he was the person described in it as "Male-1" (about whom Podobnyy and Sporyshev spoke in April 2013), spoke, and was immediately moved to tell a Russian official at the U.N. that he "didn't do anything" (under circumstances where no one was alleging otherwise). But that's not all that happened. Mueller conveniently omits that Page cooperated with the FBI in the investigation and prosecution of the spies. Don't take my word for it. Here's what Agent Gregory Monaghan said under oath in the arrest complaint:

> On or about June 13, 2013, Agent-2 and I interviewed Male-1. Male-1 stated that he first met VICTOR PODOBNYY, the defendant, in January 2013 at an energy symposium in New York City. During this initial meeting, PODOBNYY gave Male-1 PODOBNYY's business card and two email addresses. Over the following months, Male-1 and PODOB-NYY exchanged emails about the energy business and met in person on occasion, with Male-1 providing PODOBNYY with Male-1's outlook on the current [sic] and future of the energy industry. Male-1 also provided documents to PODOBNYY about the energy business.[24]

Page's interview by the FBI was not a one-off. Beginning in 2013, he was interviewed multiple times over the next three years about his interactions with Russians.[25]

Of course, even if we and Page assume that this means the government regarded Page as a cooperating witness, at least by the time the spies were arrested, that would not necessarily mean the Bureau was completely convinced Page was on Team America. Let's try to see things from the perspective of the FBI, which has the challenging responsibility of protecting our security without unduly intruding on our liberties. In 2008, Page met a Russian spy, which would reasonably have been regarded as significant, even if there was no known untoward interaction. Page was targeted for recruitment by Russian spies five year later. He provided information and documents to one of the spies. In that connection, investigating agents would probably not have known at first that (a) the information Page gave Podobnyy was public and harmless, and (b) Page thought he was dealing with a U.N. official, not a spy. The FBI may have quite reasonably worried that Page was feeding nonpublic business intelligence to clandestine Russian operatives. Until they could find out more, the Bureau may have regarded Page as a subject of the investigation.

But then they interviewed him and did enough follow-up investigation to satisfy themselves that Page was harmless—perhaps even useful. Ultimately, it appears that he was regarded as a cooperating witness. That's why the summary of his 2013 FBI interview is in the arrest complaint. Once a counterintelligence file has been opened, however, the Bureau has a habit of keeping it open. As I've stressed, counterintelligence is not prosecution-oriented; it is about information gathering— and while prosecutions end, you can never have enough information. The fact that the spies were prosecuted would not necessarily have meant the FBI was done with Carter Page for intelligence purposes— why else would agents have continued periodically interviewing him over the years?

That's a long-winded way of saying that the FBI may very well have had an open case file on Page at the time he joined Trump's campaign—i.e., the 2013 case may never have been closed, either because of bureaucratic inertia or because the matter was still considered active (perhaps because the Russian spy under indictment did not plead guilty until after Page joined the campaign).[26]

Once Page joined the Trump campaign, the Mueller report takes pains to recount, he championed the notion that Trump's ingratiating posture toward Putin could have a "game changing effect" and bring an end to what Page regarded as "the new Cold War."[27] With due respect to Page's naval service, for those of us who remember what the actual Cold War was, to have regarded Russo-American tensions— provoked by Putin's aggression—as a "new Cold War" was asinine. But it was asinine *within the bounds of political debate*. Page also made no secret of the fact that he believed the anti-Russia sanctions in place were counterproductive—a position he'd been publicly vocal about. Again, a foolish position. But being an idiot (here, Podobnyy seems perspicacious) is not being a foreign agent.

And, yes, as Mueller illustrates, Page touted that his years of experience working in Russia and its regime-dominated energy sector gave him "high-level contacts" who might be able to facilitate a meeting between Putin and Trump. He was no doubt inflating his connections, but so what? I'd be fine if the government wants to designate Russia as an adversary with which commerce should be severely restricted. (I'd rather it were done by a congressional enactment rather than a presidential proc-lamation under the International Emergency Economic Powers Act[28]—but that's a different story.) Last I checked, though, the government was *encouraging* commerce with Russia (other than with sanctioned individuals and entities). More to the point, why single out Page? In Bill Clinton, Hillary Clinton had a foreign-policy adviser who not only could (and did) arrange meetings with Putin, but could (and did) score a big payday for himself to boot. That did not make him a foreign agent. To imply that Page, who had comparatively zero influence, should nevertheless have been seen as a clandestine operative is thin camouflage for what is essentially a *political* position, namely, that a Clinton administration could be trusted to manage America's relationship with our adversary in Moscow but a Trump administration could not. Political outcomes are for voters to decide, they are not the business of prosecutors and FBI agents.

Then there was Page's trip to Moscow in July 2016. Because of the Steele dossier (which we will come to in due course), it is well known by now that Page gave a commencement speech at the New Economic School (NES). There was nothing secret about the speech. It was scheduled well in advance. Page not only made the campaign aware that he had been invited to speak; he strongly urged that Trump go in his stead. That seems presumptuous on Page's part (the candidate standing in for the adviser), except when one remembers that the NES was the same venue at which Barack Obama spoke in his first year as president—a speech that bears rereading since much of it sounds downright Carter Pagesque.[29] In any event, Page's superiors in the campaign gave him strict instructions that he was on his own, and was not to represent himself as appearing on behalf of the candidate.[30]

As we shall come to in more detail, the most indecorous aspect of the report prepared by Robert Mueller's staff of Democratic partisans is its constitutionally repugnant shifting of the burden of proof. If you are a Trump associate, the prosecutor won't leave it at "we have insufficient evidence to charge a crime, so we remain mum," as prosecutors are supposed to do. Mueller's approach is to taint with innuendo—exactly what a prosecutor is not supposed to do. Not "we don't have proof to charge a crime"; Mueller's staff says, in effect, "We can't exonerate you—there are unanswered questions here"—as if it were an

American's burden to prove his innocence rather than the prosecutor's to establish wrongdoing.

That is Mueller's approach to Page.

Page is in the collusion vortex because of Clinton-campaign operative Christopher Steele's allegation that he engaged in corrupt meetings during his Moscow trip with Putin crony Igor Sechin and Putin regime official Igor Divyekin. Page has convincingly denied these meetings. He has openly bragged for years about Russian officials he knows, but he has never claimed to know either Sechin or Divyekin. He says he does not know them, he denies meeting them, and he emphatically denies discussing a quid pro quo scheme, as alleged by Steele, in which Trump, if elected, would drop sanctions in exchange for money. The FBI has been investigating for nearly three years, and Mueller still has no proof that these things happened. Yet he won't say that. Nor will he simply say nothing, which would be appropriate. Instead, here's the end of his Page section:

> The [Special Counsel's] Office was unable to obtain additional evidence or testimony about who Page may have met or communicated with in Moscow; thus Page's activities in Russia—as described in his emails with the [Trump] Campaign—were not fully explained.[31]

In other words, Page failed to prove his innocence of the unsupported allegations lodged by a foreign spy working for the opposition political campaign.

In the emails to the campaign Mueller alludes to, Page claimed that before his NES speech, Russian Deputy Prime Minister (and NES board member) Arkady Dvorkovich made remarks expressing strong support for Trump's candidacy and hope that the two countries could "work together toward devising better solutions in response to the vast range of current international problems." Page added that this sentiment was widely shared, "based on feedback from a diverse array of other sources close to the Presidential Administration." From this jejune observation, we are evidently supposed to imagine that this "diverse array" may have included Sechin and Divyekin, who, after all, are "close to the Presidential Administration" of Putin. Therefore, the implication goes, it was up to Page to prove that he did not engage in corrupt schemes to sabotage his country, notwithstanding that the prosecutor has no proof that he did.

That is not the way American citizens are supposed to be treated by the United States government, regardless of whether the matter in question is a criminal or a counterintelligence case, and regardless of whether one thinks Carter Page and Donald Trump are fools. If you want to say there has been no shortage of Russian smoke around Carter Page over the years leading up to his time in the Trump campaign, that is obviously true. If you think that may have rated some preliminary investigative steps, such as interviewing him (as the FBI did in March 2016), that certainly makes sense. But surveillance warrants on the theory that he was a Russian agent engaged in clandestine action against our country—based on his daft belief in appeasement and the uncorroborated blather of a foreign spy who couldn't get basic facts right?

That's wrong, the prosecutor's insinuations notwithstanding.

Triangulating Manafort: Obama, Clinton, and Ukraine

It is in connection with Paul Manafort that we encounter some genuine collusion targeting the 2016 campaign: willful collaboration among foreign governments, the Obama administration, and the Clinton campaign.

Just a week after the campaign introduced Page as a Trump foreign-policy adviser, it announced that Manafort had been brought on board, too. Although the nomination was nearly in Trump's grasp, his campaign still feared that the more organized campaign of Senator Ted Cruz (R., Texas), the only viable competitor left, would succeed in cadging delegates Trump had won in state primary elections.[32] Manafort was recommended to Trump by their mutual friend Thomas Barrack. The consultant was an old political hand, experienced managing the rough-and-tumble of a convention fight. And there were added attractions: Manafort badly wanted the gig and was willing to work for free (at least "free" in terms of salary; as we previously mentioned, he had every intention of cashing in on the lofty role).[33]

As we've detailed, Manafort had longstanding, lucrative political consulting (and other business) arrangements with Ukrainian and

Russian oligarchs who had Kremlin ties. These arrangements had already been spun into a narrative of political corruption by Glenn Simpson in 2007 and 2008—when Simpson was a *Wall Street Journal* scribe, not yet the Fusion GPS impresario. (The Russia-gate tale is very much an off-the-shelf affair.)

Six years later came the Ukrainian Euromaidan uprising of February 2014, which finally forced the flight to Moscow of Manafort's client, Ukrainian President Viktor Yanukovych. With American attention intensifying as tensions boiled over in Kiev, Manafort reentered the FBI's investigative crosshairs, as did other American political consultants who did work that benefited the Party of Regions. It is difficult to say, however, what forms these investigations took.

CNN, for example, has reported that the Obama Justice Department and the FBI launched an investigation of Manafort in 2014, and that the probe included some kind of surveillance authorization from the FISC, with this monitoring finally discontinued in early 2016 "for lack of evidence."[34] This report is difficult to square with representations by prosecutors, during Special Counsel Mueller's 2018 prosecutions of Manafort, that the government was not in possession of any relevant intercepted communications by Manafort. Due-process rules would have required prosecutors to disclose such communications to the defense—or at least to acknowledge their existence, then try to convince the court that they were irrelevant to the case and should not be disclosed.[35] It is possible that that there was some kind of FISA order that did not involve monitoring of Manafort's communications. Or it could be that the FISC authorized the surveillance of a foreign associate of Manafort's—most likely, Konstantin Kilimnik—and that Manafort was neither the direct target nor a participant in any intercepted communications.[36]

At any rate, while it appears certain that Manafort's failure to register as a foreign agent of Ukraine was scrutinized after Yanukovych fled, it is unclear whether court-authorized surveillance was among the investigative techniques the government used.

Yanukovych's abdication delighted the Obama administration, which was quick to back the new administration of President Petro Poroshenko. The ensuing Obama–Clinton–Ukraine collaboration that followed has been laid bare by the dogged reporting of Peter Schweizer, Chuck Ross, Jeff Carlson, and John Solomon.[37] Kiev became so dependent on Washington for desperately needed financial support that, by threatening to withhold funds, Vice President Joe Biden pressured Poroshenko into firing Viktor Shokin, one of his top prosecutors. Shokin just happened to be investigating a natural-gas company called Burisma, which just happened to have placed Hunter Biden, the vice president's son, on its board of directors. While the Veep pushed the International Monetary Fund (IMF) to grant Ukraine a $17.5 billion loan package, Burisma lavishly compensated Hunter's law firm, to the tune of more than $3 million over an eighteen-month span. (A lot of money, but chump change compared to the Chinese government's $1.5 billion infusion in a joint investment fund with Hunter Biden while Vice President Biden, administration point man on China issues, turned a blind eye to Beijing's aggression in the South China Sea.[38])

Under the circumstances, it may seem ironic that the Obama administration prodded Ukraine to establish a National Anti-Corruption Bureau (NABU)—but the IMF, like most progressive institutions, is duly impressed by such Orwellian titles. Naturally, the fledgling NABU developed a close-knit relationship with the FBI. In 2014, NABU alerted the Bureau to a ledger said to have belonged to Yanukovych, bête noire of the new Ukrainian government. The ledger purports to show $12.7 million in cash payments to Manafort. The FBI used the information to interview Manafort, but the authenticity of the ledger has not been established. Manafort dismisses it as fake (contending that the Party of Regions paid him by wire transfer, not cash), and Ukrainian officials have conceded that they cannot prove the payments reflected in the ledger were made. The Justice Department thus reportedly closed the case with no charges. (Perhaps not coincidental to the decision not to pursue the case: Manafort had brought influential Democrats into his Ukrainian work, such as former Obama White House Counsel Greg Craig and the consulting firm started by Obama and Clinton adviser John Podesta—a firm that is still run by Podesta's brother.[39])

But then came 2016, and sudden renewed interest in the Manafort–Ukraine investigation. The interesting question is, *why?*

As we've seen, Yanukovych hightailed it to Moscow, having ignored Manafort's advice to chart Ukraine's course toward the EU rather than Russia. Afterwards, the consultant busied himself by propping up a new Ukrainian political organization, the Opposition Bloc, to supplant the Party of Regions. That put Manafort on the radar screen of Alexandra Chalupa, a Ukrainian-American and a DNC consultant who was all in for Hillary. Chalupa is said to have had an inkling that Manafort would become involved in the Trump campaign. Why she did is an interesting and thus far unanswered question. To be sure, if it was conjecture, it would have been sensible conjecture: A Ukrainian keeping tabs on Manafort would know he was a friend and former political consulting business partner of Roger Stone, who was himself vigorously supporting Trump's bid (though no longer formally part of the campaign[40]). Manafort was itching to get back into the American political arena, and Trump's steamrolling campaign would be a logical landing place; in fact, it was Manafort, not Trump, who made the first move in reaching out to Tom Barrack.

Chalupa also had good sources in Kiev who were focused on Manafort. These included Serhiy Leshchenko, a Ukrainian legislator opposed to Yanukovych's Party of Regions and the Opposition Bloc, and Artem Sytnyk, NABU's director. It was Sytnyk who took over and quietly closed the investigation of Burisma after Vice President Biden got Poroshenko to pink-slip the prosecutor. Leshchenko just happens to be a vassal of Victor Pinchuk, a Ukrainian billionaire who just happens to give millions of dollars to the Clinton Foundation. Wonder of wonders, Leshchenko took a public, strident anti-Trump position during the U.S. campaign—highly unusual for a foreign parliamentarian. "A Trump presidency would change the pro-Ukrainian agenda in American foreign policy," he told the *Financial Times*, so it was "important to show not only the corruption aspect" of the mogul, but also that Trump was "a pro-Russian candidate who can break the geopolitical balance in the world." That, he added, was why most Ukrainian politicians were "on Hillary Clinton's side." (I'm sure she was thrilled about the enthusiasm in Kiev, but enthusiasm in Wisconsin might have been more helpful.)

During the same early 2016 weeks when Chalupa was tapping her

Ukrainian sources and giving Democrats a heads-up about a potential Manafort–Trump alliance, NABU investigators and Ukrainian prosecutors journeyed to Washington. There, the Obama administration arranged for them to huddle with the FBI, the Justice Department, the State Department, and the White House's National Security Council (agencies that coordinated frequently throughout the collusion caper). Andrii Telizhenko, a political officer at Ukraine's embassy in Washington, later told John Solomon that the U.S. officials uniformly stressed "how important it was that all of our anti-corruption efforts be united." The officials also indicated to their Ukrainian counterparts that they were keen to revive the investigation of payments by Yanukovych's ousted Party of Regions government to American figures—i.e., the FBI's Paul Manafort probe. I know this may be hard to believe, but the Obama officials seem to have been less interested in Greg Craig than in Manafort.

Nazar Kholodnitskiy, Ukraine's chief anti-corruption prosecutor, told Solomon that, soon after the January 2016 Washington meetings, he found that Ukrainian officials were effectively meddling in the American presidential election. Another top Ukrainian lawman, Kostiantyn Kulyk, recalled that after the Kiev contingent's return home from the United States, there was lots of buzz about helping the Americans with the Party of Regions investigation.

Which brings us back to Serhiy Leshchenko, Ukraine's unabashed Clinton backer. And whaddya know—besides serving the government in Kiev and providing scintillating geopolitical analysis, Leshchenko had a side job: He was a source for...wait for it...*Fusion GPS*— the Clinton-campaign oppo arm that dreamed up the Steele dossier. Turns out it was Leshchenko (along with NABU Director Sytnyk) who leaked the unverified Yanukovych ledger to the media in May 2016, just after it was announced that Trump had made Manafort his campaign chairman. There is also a pending investigation into whether Leshchenko attempted to blackmail Manafort by sending text messages to the consultant and his daughter that threatened to give NABU, the FBI, and the media "bulletproof" evidence of Manafort's financial dealings with Yanukovych.[41]

The ledger's exposure, of course, is what led to Manafort's ouster from the Trump campaign. The Ukrainian payments became an important strand of the Russia-gate narrative. The wealth that Manafort's Ukrainian work generated formed the foundation of his prosecution by Special Counsel Mueller for tax, money laundering, and unregistered foreign-agent offenses.

Can anyone say *Clinton-Campaign Collusion with Ukraine?* The Ukrainian courts can: In December 2018, one such tribunal ruled that Leshchenko and Sytnyk had violated Ukrainian law by leaking the ledger. The infraction, the court added, "led to interference in the electoral processes of the United States in 2016 and harmed the interests of Ukraine as a state."

Meanwhile, CNN maintains that, sometime in 2016, the FBI "restarted" the FISA surveillance that the network says had been discontinued early in the year.[42] We will take a closer look in Chapter Eight at the claims, based on felonious intelligence leaks, that Manafort and other Trump-campaign figures were subjected to FISA surveillance beginning in autumn 2016 and continuing into the start of the Trump presidency.

When Is 'Early Spring'?

In Russia-gate, like most everything in Washington, what they don't tell you—or, especially, what they go out of their way to keep from you—is more meaningful than most information you get.

The House Intelligence Committee completed its report on Russia's interference in the 2016 campaign on March 22, 2018, but it took over a month for the report to be released to the public—festooned with blackouts insisted upon by the Justice Department, the FBI, and other intelligence agencies. Fortunately, the Committee's then-Chairman, Devin Nunes, went ballistic over the excisions. Finally, some of them were quietly un-redacted. When they were, *The Wall Street Journal*'s eagle-eyed Kimberley Strassel was keeping watch. She noticed some overlooked passages on page 54.[43]

As a result, we learned that, in what was described as the "late spring" of 2016, the FBI's then-Director James Comey briefed the principals of the National Security Council on "the Page information."

NSC principals are a presidential administration's highest-ranking national-security officials. The Obama NSC was chaired by the president. Regular attendees included Vice President Biden, National Security Adviser Rice, and National Intelligence Director Clapper. The heads of such departments and agencies as the Justice Department (Attorney General Lynch) and the CIA (Director Brennan) could also be invited to attend NSC meetings if matters of concern to them were to be discussed.

We do not know which NSC principals attended the Comey briefing about Carter Page. But how curious that the House Intelligence Committee interviewed so many Obama-administration officials who were on, or knowledgeable about, the NSC, and who had government appointment calendars that are exactingly kept, and yet none of them provided a date for this meeting more precise than "late spring" 2016. Given how mulishly the intelligence community has stonewalled questions about when and why the Trump–Russia investigation(s) originated, the haziness about a date that could easily be determined is intriguing.

Further, exactly what "Page information" was at issue? The FBI did not begin receiving Steele dossier reports about Page until July 2016. What information was so significant in the "late spring" that Director Comey needed to brief top Obama national-security officials about it? Did the FBI still have an open counterintelligence investigation on Page based on the 2013 case in which Page had cooperated with the FBI's prosecution of Russian spies (one of whom described Page as "an idiot")? Was the Page information somehow spruced up by intelligence coming over the transom from Europe? Did it seem more alarming because Page's coming on board the Trump campaign was so rapidly followed by Manafort's doing so? We don't know. We just know Page and Manafort had the attention of the Obama administration's top echelon.

At the insistence of the FBI and the Justice Department, another significant meeting was initially redacted on page 54 of the House report, purportedly out of concern for national-security secrets. When it was unredacted at Nunes's insistence, however, it became clear that national security had nothing to do with the excision. Sometime apparently before the "late spring" NSA briefing, Comey and his deputy, Andrew McCabe, met with Attorney General Lynch "about Page." Among the topics discussed was the possibility of providing the Trump campaign with a "defensive briefing." This would be a meeting with a senior campaign official to put the campaign on notice of potential Russian efforts to compromise someone—presumably Page—within the campaign.

Isn't that interesting? As we've noted, the FBI had interviewed Carter Page in March 2016.[44] Was that interview a reaction to his joining the Trump campaign? Was it an effort to gauge whether Page was still a Russian recruitment target? Was it a substitute for giving the campaign a defensive briefing, or a preparatory step in anticipation of possibly giving such a briefing? We don't know. Former Attorney General Lynch told the House Committee that a potential defensive briefing was discussed, but she could not—or, at least, did not—provide an explanation for why it never happened.

Here is what we can surmise.

It defies modern American norms for the incumbent government to investigate the opposition party's presidential campaign, and to invoke the government's extraordinary foreign-counterintelligence powers in doing so. To be sure, no sensible person would argue that the government should refrain from investigating if, *based on compelling evidence*, the FBI suspects individuals—even campaign officials, even a party's nominee—of acting as clandestine agents of a hostile foreign power. The question is, *what should trigger such an investigation*?

The Obama administration decided that the norm against exploiting government powers to investigate political opponents did not apply to the Trump campaign. The administration decided not to give the campaign a defensive briefing even though plenty of Trump-campaign officials had impeccable national-security credentials. For example, by the spring of 2016, Trump surrogates included Rudy Giuliani (a former New York City mayor, U.S. Attorney, and top Reagan Justice Department official), Chris Christie (then the New Jersey governor and a former U.S. Attorney), and Senator Jeff Sessions (then the Chairman of the Judiciary Committee and highly likely to land a top national-security position if Trump won). If all the Obama administration had been trying to do was check out a few worrisome characters who had wheedled their way into the Trump campaign despite suspicious Russia ties, the FBI could easily have alerted one or more of these former government officials.

If it was not ready or willing to do that, the Obama administration could have reacted to the news that Page and Manafort had joined the Trump campaign by interviewing them—again. As we've noted, Page was clearly available for interview. Manafort had submitted to an interview in 2014 over his Ukrainian work, and would have been hard-pressed to decline if the Justice Department (which oversees the Foreign Agent Registry) said it wanted to discuss the matter further.

Instead of treating the Trump campaign like a normal political organization, the Obama administration chose to treat it as a coconspirator collaborating with Russia. Instead of offering a defensive briefing, Obama officials made the Trump campaign the subject of a counterintelligence investigation. From the "late spring" on, it appears that every report of Trump–Russia ties, no matter how unlikely and uncorroborated, was presumed to be probative of a traitorous arrangement. Facts about Trump were viewed in the worst possible light. The mogul was never given the Obama administration's Hillary Clinton standard: the irrebuttable presumption of innocence, no matter how high the corruption evidence mounted.

CHAPTER SEVEN

A Maltese Professor, an Australian Diplomat, and a Sap . . . in London

hicanery was the force behind the formal opening of the FBI's Trump–Russia investigation. There was a false premise, namely that the Trump campaign must have known that Russia possessed emails somehow related to Hillary Clinton before WikiLeaks caused the dissemination of hacked Democratic National Committee emails to the media, beginning on July 22, 2016. Starting from that premise, the foreign ministries of the United States and Australia, through mendacity or incompetence, erected a fraudulent story that warped the Trump campaign's purported foreknowledge of Russia's perfidy into a potential espionage conspiracy.

That is what we learn from the saga of George Papadopoulos, as fleshed out by the Mueller report.[1]

The investigative theory on which the FBI formally opened the foreign-counterintelligence probe code-named "Crossfire Hurricane" on July 31, 2016, held that (a) the Trump campaign knew about, and was potentially complicit in, Russia's possession of hacked emails that would compromise Hillary Clinton; and (b) in order to help Donald Trump win the presidency, the Kremlin planned to disseminate these emails anonymously (through a third party) at a time maximally damaging to Clinton's campaign.

The theory was woefully flawed. George Papadopoulos, the young campaign adviser on whom it rests, knew nothing about the DNC emails. And there is a good chance that his claim of being told about any emails related to Clinton is false. Furthermore, even if Papadopoulos was told that Russia had "dirt" on Clinton, there is no evidence that he was informed about what Russia planned to do with it, or why.

Long before the hacked DNC emails were published, the Obama

administration was speculating—whether out of partisanship or pre-disposition about Trump—that the Republican nominee was in a corrupt conspiracy with Russia to sabotage the election. When the hacked DNC emails were published, Obama officials distorted Papa-dopoulos's gossipy statements to an Australian diplomat—which the diplomat himself had initially dismissed as nonsense—into the formal rationalization for commencing a counterintelligence investigation of the Trump campaign that they had already been conducting.

The investigation was built on a fraud.

Papadopoulos: The Origin Story 2.0

As we've seen, it has been portrayed as the Big Bang: the Magic Mo-ment that started it all...especially after the first Big Bang, the Carter Page Origin Story, faded into a withering whimper. But the George Papadopoulos Origin Story—Origin 2.0—has never added up: If the young energy-sector analyst had actually emerged in early 2016 as the key to proving Trump–Russia espionage, you would think the FBI might have gotten around to interviewing him before January 27, 2017—i.e., a week after President Trump had been inaugurated, three months after the Obama administration began FISA surveillance of Page, six months after the Bureau formally opened "Crossfire Hurri-cane," and more than eight months after Papadopoulos's meeting in a London bar with an Australian diplomat—throwing back the shots heard 'round the world.

You would probably also think Papadopoulos, Suspect One in *The Great Cyberespionage Attack on Our Democracy*, might have rated a tad more than the whopping *fourteen-day* jail sentence a federal judge eventually imposed on him. You might even suppose that he'd have been charged with some seditious felony involving clandestine opera-tions against his own country, instead of, yes, fibbing to the FBI about the date of a meeting.

That, however, does not scratch the surface. We are to believe that what led to the opening of the FBI's Trump–Russia investigation, and what therefore is the plinth of the collusion narrative, is a breakfast meeting at a London hotel on April 26, 2016, between Papadopoulos and Joseph Mifsud, a Maltese academic we are supposed to take for a clandestine Russian agent. We are to take Papadopoulos's word for it that Mifsud claimed Russia possessed "dirt" on Hillary Clinton in the form of "thousands" of "emails of Clinton." We are further to believe "the professor" elaborated that, in order to help Donald Trump's candidacy, the Kremlin would release these "emails of Clinton" at a time chosen to do maximum damage to the Democratic nominee's campaign.

The story is based on no credible evidence. If ever presented to a jury, it would be laughed out of court.

The Papadopoulos "collusion" claims (without collusion charges) are alleged in the Mueller report, which essentially repeats the grandiose "Statement of the Offense" that the special counsel included with the comparatively minor false-statement charge to which Papadopoulos pled guilty.[2] Carefully parsed, this narrative stops subtly short of alleging that the Trump adviser collaborated with *a Russian agent*. Rather, it claims that Papadopoulos engaged in a lot of twaddle with Mifsud, *whom he had reason to suspect might be a Russian agent*. The pair brainstormed endlessly about potential high-level Trump-campaign meetings with the Putin regime, including [*insert heavy breathing here*] between Trump and Putin themselves. Papadopoulos then exaggerated these meanderings in emails to Trump-campaign superiors he was hot to impress.

All this may be interesting, but it is neither nefarious nor illegal—if it were, you might have expected to find a sentence or two in the Mueller report about Bill Clinton's $500,000 payday from a Kremlin-tied bank while the Uranium One deal was under consideration.

More maddening: It is virtually certain that Mifsud was not a Russian agent. Whether he was an asset for any intelligence service, we cannot say with certainty at this point. But we can say that he had close contacts of significance with *British intelligence*, and with other Western governments. Does that mean this is a case of Western intelligence agencies entrapping the Trump campaign by first using an "asset" (Mifsud) to plant a damning "Russia helping Trump" story with Papadopoulos, and later using another "asset" (Stefan Halper) to try to get Papadopoulos to repeat that story so that "collusion" could be proved? At this point, we don't know. Here is what we do know: The United States government has never charged Joseph Mifsud. It has never accused him of being an agent of Russia. It took no steps to arrest him despite opportunities to do so. In fact, the FBI interviewed Mifsud and, when he denied Papadopoulos's claim that he had told the young Trump adviser that Russia had Hillary emails, the Bureau let him go. Special Counsel Mueller has never alleged that Mifsud's denial was a false statement.

That's a pretty curious way to treat the "Russian agent" who was the rationale for the incumbent administration's use of foreign counterintelligence powers to investigate the presidential campaign of its political opposition, no?

The Wannabes

In early 2016, Papadopoulos was an ambitious twenty-eight-year-old trying to push his way into Trump World. He had graduated from DePaul University in 2009, and a year later he received something called a "master of science degree in security studies" at University College London. Longing for a way into big-time U.S. politics, he latched on to the Ben Carson presidential campaign, after unsuccessfully seeking work on the Trump campaign. When the Carson bid cratered, Papadopoulos, who is not a lawyer, took a job at the London Centre for International Law Practice—an impressive-sounding but obscure academic institution.[3]

George's big break came in March, when the Trump campaign became anxious to show that it had some names—seemingly *any* names—advising Trump on foreign policy. Papadopoulos's résumé was passed to Sam Clovis, the campaign's cochair and top adviser. Clovis performed a Google search and found that the multilingual, ostensibly cosmopolitan Papadopoulos had done sporadic intern work for a conservative-oriented think-tank between 2011 and 2014. His curriculum vitae also touted Papadopoulos's participation in, yes, the 2012 Geneva International Model United Nations. (I confess to having thought that was a middle-school project.) Evidently, this implied to the campaign that Papadopoulos had some modicum of credibility on energy issues. Sight unseen, Clovis retained Papadopoulos over the phone as an unpaid foreign-policy adviser.

The green young man remained a fringe figure, unknown to the candidate. Indeed, before the lone time he ever met Papadopoulos, Trump characteristically bragged to *The Washington Post* that the "oil and energy consultant" was just "an excellent guy"—but he had to read it off a sheet, and he wouldn't have known Papadopoulos if he fell over him.[4] These facts underscore how farcical it is that American intelligence agencies could have suspected the chaotic Trump campaign was partnered in a sophisticated, clandestine enterprise with Russian intelligence, and that the Kremlin would conceivably have chosen Papadopoulos as its entrée to the candidate.

In Rome on March 14, Papadopoulos met Joseph Mifsud. Twice Papadopoulos's age, the Maltese professor was also affiliated with the previously noted London Centre for International Law Practice. Besides teaching there, Mifsud was an instructor at Rome's Link University. In an invaluable deep dive into the Maltese professor's background, Lee Smith explains that Link's "lecturers and professors include senior Western diplomats and intelligence officials from a number of NATO countries, especially Italy and the United Kingdom." Mifsud also taught at the University of Stirling in Scotland and the London Academy of Diplomacy, "which trained diplomats and government officials, some of them sponsored by the UK's Foreign and Commonwealth Office, the British Council, or by their own governments."[5] We'll come back to Mifsud's ties to the British government momentarily.

Like Papadopoulos, Mifsud was a shameless self-promoter (at least until Russia-gate notoriety sent him underground). He traveled frequently, including to Russia, where he participated in academic conferences and claimed acquaintance with regime officials—though how well he actually knows anyone of significance is unclear. In sum, Mifsud is the aging academic version of Papadopoulos. Thierry Pastor, a French political analyst who (with a Swiss-German lawyer named Stephan Roh) cowrote a book about l'affaire Papadopoulos, made this observation about Mifsud's brag that he knew Russian Foreign Minister Sergey Lavrov: "Yes, he met Lavrov. He met him once or twice in a large group. He knows Lavrov, but Lavrov doesn't know Joseph. [Mifsud's] contacts in Russia are with academics."[6]

The Mueller report recounts that Mifsud also maintained some

"Russian contacts" while living in London, including a "one-time employee" at the Internet Research Agency—which Mueller's prosecutors note is "the entity that carried out the Russian social media campaign." But this mention of the troll farm operation that peddled often inane 2016 campaign propaganda is bush-league innuendo: Mueller does not allege that the "one-time employee" himself had anything to do with "the Russian social media campaign," much less that Mifsud did.[7]

Nevertheless, the Trump–Russia narrative holds that Mifsud actually is a well-placed Russian agent who became interested in Papadopoulos upon discovering that he was a key (yup...) Trump adviser. According to this story, Mifsud introduced the younger man to a woman presented as Vladimir Putin's niece. The professor also hooked Papadopoulos up with Ivan Timofeev, whom prosecutors pregnantly described as "the Russian MFA connection" (as in the Russian Ministry of Foreign Affairs—Lavrov's office) when they eventually charged Papadopoulos with making false statements. Timofeev and Papadopoulos had fevered discussions about setting up a Putin–Trump meeting in Russia. Finally, at their April 26 breakfast in London, Mifsud let slip that Russia had "dirt" on Hillary Clinton in the form of "thousands" of "emails of Clinton"—which, the narrative holds, must have been a reference to the DNC emails that Russian intelligence hacked and WikiLeaks disseminated during the Democratic party's convention in July.

The story is bogus through and through. There is no proof that Mifsud is a Russian agent—Mueller never alleged such a thing, either when Papadopoulos was charged or in the special counsel's final report, which concluded that there was no Trump–Russia conspiracy. The woman in question was not Putin's niece; she was eventually identified as Olga Polonskaya, the thirty-two-year-old manager of a St. Petersburg wine company, who (the Mueller report suggests, based on a "Baby, thank you" email) may have been romantically involved with Mifsud.[8] Timofeev is actually a young academic researcher who runs a Russian think-tank, the Russian International Affairs Council. The RIAC has some sort of tie to the MFA, but no discernible connections to Russian intelligence. Like Mifsud, Timofeev is an academic; he was in an even less likely position to schedule a meeting for Putin than Papadopoulos was to do so for Trump. The hypothetical Putin–Trump summit was an inchoate idea senior Trump officials shot down even as Papadopoulos and Timofeev were dreaming it up.[9]

What about those "emails of Clinton"? Other than the word of Papadopoulos, a convicted liar and palpably unreliable raconteur, there is no evidence—*none*—that Mifsud told him about emails. The professor never showed him any emails. And in his February 2017 FBI interview, Mifsud denied saying anything to Papadopoulos about Clinton-related emails in the possession of the Kremlin. Of course, Mifsud could be lying. But there is no evidence that he would have been in a position to know the inner workings of Russian intelligence operations.

It is not enough to say that Mueller never charged Mifsud with lying to the FBI. In Mueller's report, when prosecutors have evidence that Mifsud gave inaccurate information, they say so. For example, they allege that Mifsud "falsely" recounted the last time he had seen Papadopoulos. *But Mueller never alleges that Mifsud's denial of knowledge about Russia's possession of emails is false.*[10] And if we learned anything from Mueller's investigation, it is that he knows how to make a false-statements case.

In any event, Mifsud's supposed email comment obviously made little impression on Papadopoulos. The day after he met the professor, Papadopoulos sent two emails to high-ranking Trump-campaign officials about his meeting with Mifsud. In neither did he mention emails. Papadopoulos instead focused on the possibility—farfetched, but apparently real to Papadopoulos—that Mifsud could help arrange a meeting between Trump and Putin. Prior to being interviewed by the FBI in January 2017, Papadopoulos never reported anything about Russia having emails—neither to his Trump-campaign superiors, to whom he was constantly reporting on his conversations with Mifsud, nor to Alexander Downer, the Australian diplomat whose conversation with Papadopoulos was the proximate cause for the formal opening of the FBI probe.

It was only when he was interviewed by the FBI in late January 2017, nine months after his conversation with Mifsud, that Papadopoulos is alleged to have claimed that Mifsud said the Russians had "thousands" of "emails of Clinton." There is no known recording of this FBI interview, so there is no way of knowing whether (a) Papadopoulos volunteered this claim that Mifsud mentioned emails, or (b) the email claim was suggested to Papadopoulos by his interrogators' questions. We have no way of knowing if Papadopoulos is telling the truth (and therefore hid the possibility of damaging Clinton emails from his Trump-campaign superiors for no fathomable reason) or if he was telling the FBI agents what he thought they wanted to hear (which is what he often did when reporting to the Trump campaign).

Collusion with Australia

The email component, however, is only half the concocted story that spawned "Crossfire Hurricane."

There is no evidence, including in the 448-page Mueller report, that Papadopoulos was ever told that Russia intended, through an intermediary, to disseminate damaging information about Clinton in a manner designed to hurt Clinton's candidacy and help Trump's. There is, furthermore, no evidence that Papadopoulos ever said such a thing to anyone else—including Australian High Commissioner Alexander Downer, whom he famously met at the Kensington Wine Rooms in London on May 6, 2016. The claim that Papadopoulos made such a statement is a fabrication, initially founded on what, at best, was a deeply flawed assumption by Downer.

Let's get to the curious story of the Euro-celeb High Commissioner's outreach to the unknown, unpaid Trump adviser.

Early in his candidacy, in a characteristically over-the-top reaction to jihadist terrorism, Donald Trump proposed a temporary ban on all Muslim immigration to the United States. The candidate later clarified that he wanted to explore ways to vet immigrants in order to exclude Muslims adherent to jihadism, not all Muslims.[11] But the legend of Trump the Islamophobe was born. Like most things Trumpian, it rubbed Great Britain the wrong way. England has a rambunctious fundamentalist Islamic community in its midst, and its politicians— one is tempted to say, its Tory politicians in particular—are hypersensitive to "Islamophobia" (which is not actually a phobia but an epithet developed by the Muslim Brotherhood to discourage inquiry into sharia-supremacist ideology).[12] If anything, Britain's then–Prime Minister David Cameron was the model for this Blairism of the center-right. Reflecting the distaste for Trump common among EU leaders, Cameron described Trump's remarks as "divisive, stupid and wrong," adding that a visit to England by the GOP candidate would unite Britons against him. Typically, Trump shrugged his shoulders and snorted that, if elected, he might not have a "very good relationship" with Cameron. Not unreasonably, Papadopoulos calculated that the quickest way to vault into Trump's good graces was to defend him publicly. So the tyro took it up himself to demand that Cameron apologize—which the British press ate up even if it rankled senior Trump-campaign officials.[13]

It is unknown whether Trump noticed this attention-grabbing stunt, but Downer did. Constantly networking, Papadopoulos had struck up an acquaintance with Israeli embassy official Christian Cantor, through whom he had met Downer's counselor, Erika Thompson, in April 2016. After his remarks about Cameron were reported on May 4, Downer had Thompson reach out to Papadopoulos for a sit-down with him. It was an odd request: Papadopoulos was a relative nobody working for a candidate reviled in Europe, while Downer was among Australia's top diplomats, having had a long, distinguished foreign-service career in which he dealt at the highest echelons of international relations. Plus, Papadopoulos had run off at the mouth about the *British* prime minister; of what concern was that to an *Australian* diplomat?

Well, Downer has an interesting background. He is a former foreign minister who, in that role, helped arrange a $25 million contribution by Australia to a Clinton Foundation initiative to fight HIV and AIDS—in 2006, when Hillary Clinton was a powerful U.S. senator with White House aspirations.[14] Downer also has eye-catching ties to Britain—in particular, to its intelligence services. He served on the advisory board of Hakluyt & Co., a secretive private U.K. intelligence firm founded by British spies. Top officials and advisory board members of Hakluyt include veterans of MI6 and GCHQ.[15] The board has also included such global movers and shakers as Louis Susman, a Democratic Party fundraising heavyweight who is close to the Clintons and who was Obama's American Ambassador to the Court of

St. James while Secretary Clinton ran the State Department. John Brennan appeared at an event hosted by Hakluyt's New York City office in 2018. Hakluyt's U.S. representative was Jonathan Clarke, a career British diplomat who eventually relocated to Washington. What's Clarke's relevance to this tale? Not much—except that he has coauthored two books with none other than Stefan Halper, who—we shall soon see—is a longtime asset of U.S. and British intelligence, and who was tasked to spy on Papadopoulos and other Trump-campaign surrogates. Halper and Downer travel in the same circles. In fact, they appeared together on a Cambridge University panel in 2010.[16]

Small world.

Even smaller than you think. Another traveler in British intelligence circles is, yes, Joseph Mifsud. As Lee Smith relates, Mifsud has also long been associated with Claire Smith, a prominent British diplomat who served for years on Britain's Joint Intelligence Committee, which answers directly to the Prime Minister. Ms. Smith was also a member of the United Kingdom's Security Vetting Appeals Panel, which reviews denials of security clearances to government employees. During her career in the British foreign service, Smith's postings included Beijing and Islamabad; more significantly for our purposes, she worked with Mifsud at three different academic institutions: the London Academy of Diplomacy (which trained diplomats and government officials), the University of Stirling in Scotland, and Link Campus University in Rome. Link, you may recall, is where Mifsud first met Papadopoulos. The campus is a well-known draw for diplomats and intelligence officials—the CIA holds conferences there, the FBI holds agent training sessions there, and former U.S. intelligence officials teach there. As Lee Smith observes, if Mifsud had actually been a Russian agent, he was situated to be "one of the most successful in history."[17] Not likely.

In any event, on May 6, Ms. Thompson escorted Papadopoulos to the rendezvous with Downer at the Kensington Wine Rooms. It was a pleasant conversation over drinks, though the seasoned Aussie diplomat did advise the green Trump adviser that lashing out at Cameron was strictly *de trop*. During the course of the encounter, Papadopoulos confided that he'd heard the Russians had information about Mrs. Clinton that could prove damaging. Importantly, Papadopoulos did not describe the purported information—he did not mention emails, he did not call it "dirt." Downer later described this topic as a vague reference in what was a fairly short conversation.[18]

On July 22, 2016, the eve of the Democratic National Convention in Philadelphia and two months after the Papadopoulos–Downer *tête-à-tête*, WikiLeaks began disseminating thousands of hacked DNC emails to the global press. From this occurrence, Downer suddenly drew the unfounded inference that *these hacked emails must have been what Papadopoulos was talking about* when he said Russia had damaging information about Clinton. The High Commissioner decided that, rather than just letting whatever he'd fleetingly reported to his government gather dust in the archives, he'd better raise it directly with his American counterparts—his friends at the U.S. embassy, then being run by U.S. Ambassador Matthew Barzun, the mega-fundraiser for President Obama and then–Secretary of State John Kerry, who had labored to retire the campaign debt from Hillary Clinton's first White House run, clearing the way for her to become Obama's Secretary of State.[19]

The FBI and Justice Department, as well as Australian authorities, have been suspiciously vague about how Downer's information about Papadopoulos was transmitted to the U.S. government. Special Counsel Mueller continues the obfuscation.

As *The Wall Street Journal*'s Kimberley Strassel has reported, Downer claimed, in an April 2018 interview by *The Australian*, that he reported the May 6, 2016, meeting to his government a day or two after it happened. The paper then hazily reports that after some unspecified "period of time, Australia's ambassador to the US, Joe Hockey, passed the information on to Washington." Similarly, *The New York Times* reported that "Australian officials passed the information about Mr. Papadopoulos to their American counterparts, according to four current and former American and foreign officials with direct knowledge of the Australians' role."

An unlikely story.

Rep. Devin Nunes chaired the House Intelligence Committee when it investigated Russia-gate (he is now the committee's ranking member). Nunes has reviewed the FBI case-opening document (referred to as an "EC," as in "electronic communication"), and he has told Fox

News, "We now know that there was no official intelligence that was used to start this investigation." That is, there is no indication that the investigation was commenced based on intelligence that passed through the "Five Eyes" channels (i.e., the five countries in the world's most important intelligence-sharing alliance—the United States, Britain, Australia, New Zealand, and Canada).

So, if the "Crossfire Hurricane" foreign-counterintelligence investigation was commenced by the FBI without intelligence routed through a Five-Eyes channel, what information could have started it? Of course, it was the Papadopoulos information, informally passed from High Commissioner Downer to the Obama State Department...and then on to the FBI.

On this, Australia was smoked out by Ms. Strassel's investigative reporting. Relying on "a diplomatic source," she asserted that Downer himself conveyed the information about Papadopoulos to the U.S. embassy in London. Downer subsequently confirmed that this is the case. On July 26, 2016, he personally visited the American embassy in London. With Ambassador Barzun away on vacation, Downer verbally reported the two-month-old Papadopoulos conversation to Elizabeth Dibble, the *chargée d'affaires*, in what is said to have been a brief meeting.[20]

Well, okay then, but what did Downer tell the State Department Papadopoulos said? How did the United States government describe the young Trump adviser's statements in its official documents, such as the FBI's case-opening report? We haven't been told. Although Papadopoulos is extensively quoted in the Mueller report, the prosecutors avoid attributing any quote to him based on what Downer claims he said. This mirrors Mueller's slippery false-statements charge against Papadopoulos: The prosecutors' fourteen-page "Statement of the Offense" studiously omits any reference to Papadopoulos's May 6 meeting with Downer, notwithstanding that it was the most consequential event in Papadopoulos's case. The chronology simply skips from May 4 to May 13, as if nothing significant happened in between.[21]

The government does not want us focusing on the Papadopoulos–Downer meeting because the FBI's investigation was formally opened on false pretenses—based not on what Papadopoulos actually said to

Downer, but on the untenable inference that Downer and the State Department chose to draw from Papadopoulos's blather. Mueller's report gives us not what Papadopoulos said, but *what Downer understood Papadopoulos to have "suggested,"* namely that "the Trump Campaign had received indications from the Russian government that it could assist the Campaign through the anonymous release of information that would be damaging to Hillary Clinton."

Think about that. What is called the "Trump Campaign" here is Papadopoulos, who was about as low-ranking as it got in that organization. What's preposterously referred to as the "Russian government" is Mifsud. But the Maltese professor—the source of the "indications"—was not part of the Russian government at all. More to the point, even if it were mistakenly assumed that Mifsud was a Russian-government operative (notwithstanding that the FBI could easily have established that he was not), there is no evidence that Mifsud ever told Papadopoulos that the Russian government was planning to assist the Trump campaign by anonymously releasing information damaging to Clinton.

Obviously, if Downer had actually believed Papadopoulos had information from authentic Putin-regime sources, and if Papadopoulos had told him the Kremlin was planning to release damaging information about Clinton, timed to harm her and help Trump, Downer would not have ignored these statements at the time they were made. But there was no reason to believe that Papadopoulos had such Russian contacts, and there is no basis to believe Papadopoulos made any such statement to Downer.

But we're not supposed to ask what Papadopoulos said. We're to content ourselves with what Downer thought—or, actually, with his dramatically revised thinking two months after the fact. The Mueller report repeatedly stresses the "suggestion" that Papadopoulos purportedly made—as if what matters is the operation of Downer's mind rather than the words Papadopoulos actually used. For example, prosecutors acknowledge that Papadopoulos's conversation with Downer is "contained in the FBI case-opening document and related materials."[22] But Mueller's five-line footnote—the report's passing mention of the commencement of the probe of a presidential campaign—does not quote from these materials, though it elsewhere makes quoting a habit. And here is how the Special Counsel explains why Papadopoulos was interviewed in late January 2017 (emphasis added):

> Investigators approached Papadopoulos for an interview based on his role as a foreign policy advisor to the Trump Campaign and *his suggestion to a foreign government representative that Russia had indicated it could assist the Campaign through the anonymous release of information damaging to candidate Clinton.*

The "suggestion" that Papadopoulos said such a thing is sheer invention. Plainly, it is based on the wayward deduction by Downer and the State Department that Russia's anonymous publication (via WikiLeaks) of the hacked DNC emails must have been what Papadopoulos was talking about. But that is not what Papadopoulos was talking about.

Downer claims to have deduced that Papadopoulos's barroom banter was related to the hacking and publication of DNC emails. This was specious for at least four reasons:

1) In speaking with Downer, Papadopoulos never mentioned emails. Neither Downer nor Papadopoulos has ever claimed that Papadopoulos spoke of emails.

2) There is no basis to believe Papadopoulos told Downer that Russia was planning *to publish* damaging information about Clinton through an intermediary. There is no allegation in the Mueller report that Mifsud ever told Papadopoulos any such thing, much less that Papadopoulos relayed it to Downer. Mueller's report says:

> Mifsud told Papadopoulos that he had met with high-level Russian government officials during his recent trip to Moscow. Mifsud also said that, on the trip, he learned that the Russians had obtained "dirt" on candidate Hillary Clinton. As Papadopoulos later stated to the FBI, Mifsud said that the "dirt" was in the form of "emails of Clinton," and that they "have thousands of emails."[23]

In neither the Mueller report nor in the Statement of the Offense Mueller filed in connection with Papadopoulos's plea have prosecutors claimed that Mifsud told Papadopoulos what Russia was planning to do with the "dirt," much less why. And, to repeat, Mifsud denied telling Papadopoulos anything about emails at all.

3) Papadopoulos says the emails he claims Mifsud referred to *were not the DNC emails*; they were *Clinton's own emails*. That is, when Papadopoulos claims that Mifsud told him that Russia had "dirt" in the form of "thousands" of "emails of Clinton," he understood Mifsud to be alluding to the thousands of State Department and Clinton Foundation emails that Clinton had stored on a private server.[24] To be sure, there is reason to doubt the veracity of Papadopoulos's description of Mifsud's information, but if they did in fact discuss emails, it is far more plausible that they were referring to Clinton's own emails. These were the emails that were being intensively covered in the media (including speculation that they might have been hacked by hostile foreign-intelligence services) at the time Mifsud and Papadopoulos spoke—i.e., April 2016. At that point, neither Mifsud nor Papadopoulos had any basis to know anything about hacked DNC emails.

4) The DNC emails did not damage Clinton in any material way, and it would have been ridiculous to imagine that they would. They were not Clinton's emails and she was not a correspondent in them. The emails embarrassed the DNC by showing that the national party favored Clinton over Bernie Sanders. But Clinton was already the certain nominee; nothing in the emails threatened that outcome or set her back in the race against Donald Trump.

Distorting Papadopoulos's Role to Obscure Reliance on the Steele Dossier

Immediately after taking High Commissioner Downer's information, the State Department's Elizabeth Dibble sent it though government channels to the FBI. It was exquisite timing.

As we shall soon see in more detail, in early July 2016, the FBI (and, later, the State Department) began receiving the Clinton campaign–sponsored faux-intelligence reports now infamous as the Steele dossier. Even before that, the intelligence community—particularly the CIA, under the direction of the hyper-political John Brennan—had been theorizing that the Trump campaign was in a corrupt relationship with Russia. Thus, even before Downer reported his conversation with Papadopoulos to the State Department, the Obama administration was quietly acting on the theory that Russia was planning to assist the Trump campaign through the anonymous release of information that would be damaging to Clinton.

The hacked DNC emails were a godsend for this theory. That, obviously, is why Steele—whose vaunted Russian sources had somehow failed to foretell the hacking by Russia and publication by WikiLeaks—simply folded the DNC emails into his preexisting narrative of a Trump–Russia conspiracy.[25]

Downer's report enabled the Obama administration to cover an investigative theory it was already pursuing with a report from a friendly foreign government, *as if that report had triggered the Trump–Russia investigation.* In order to pull that off, though, it was necessary to distort what Papadopoulos had told Downer.

The State Department's report to the FBI claiming that Papadopoulos had "suggested" these things to Downer was manufactured to portray a false connection between (a) what Papadopoulos told Downer, and (b) the hacking and publication of the DNC emails. That false connection then became the rationale for formally opening the FBI's Trump–Russia investigation—paper cover for an investigation of the Trump campaign that was already underway.

CHAPTER EIGHT

The Brennan Clearinghouse

D onald Trump "wants to pull us out of NATO!" So inveighed Hillary Clinton at a Milwaukee campaign rally on March 28, 2016.[1] The party conventions were still months away, but the finalists were already set: It would be Clinton versus Trump. The former secretary of state was already honing a major campaign theme. She vowed to keep Putin in check and reassure our European allies; Trump, she warned, would do Putin's bidding and abandon our European allies—ending modern history's most successful alliance in the process.

It wasn't really true: Clinton was the top foreign-policy official in an administration that had been a pushover for Putin; and Trump, despite his nauseating habit of laying the treacle on dictators, was promising policies (such as a military buildup and deregulation of the energy sector) that would be anathema to the Kremlin. But Clinton's comments were surely within the tolerable bounds of purple campaign prose—particularly between these two candidates. As we've seen, Trump believed NATO was obsolete: Its mission was complete (the Soviet Union no longer existed), and most of its members were free riding on a U.S. security guarantee that costs American taxpayers a fortune. Plus, doffing his cap to Obama/Clinton foreign policy (as practiced, rather than as Clinton described it), Trump maintained it was better to court than to provoke Russia, the shriveling rump of the Soviet empire.

In an America increasingly indifferent to the Cold War era, this posturing eight months before Election Day made scant impression. Europeans, however, paid close attention: in the chancelleries, where Clinton's progressive tilt and fawning of the "international community" (and its community banks!) were strongly preferred to the beastly Trump; and especially in the Baltic states, which feel menaced by Moscow in the best of times. For the previous decade, Latvia, Lithuania, and Estonia had fretted over the West's desultory response as Russia gobbled hunks of Georgia and Ukraine, just recently swallowing Crimea in one bite. NATO countries seemed downright meek. Economic sanctions caused the Putin regime some pain but mostly conveyed lack of resolve to push back or disturb the lucrative Euro-Russo trade in energy, raw materials, machinery, medicines, and manufactured goods.[2] The Americans seemed to be a paper tiger as long as Putin was "helping" with Iran and Syria.

At least Clinton and the Obama administration talked a good game: Unlike other countries Russia besieged in its "near abroad," the tiny Baltic states were NATO members; this, the Democrats stressed, entitled them to the alliance's Article 5 assurance of collective defense—in theory, a Russian attack on Riga should be regarded by Washington as if it were an attack on Washington itself. Whether, if the time came, Clinton would back up this chest-thumping was uncertain. But Trump, by comparison, appeared doubtful that Americans, fatigued by a decade of costly war and thankless sharia-democracy promotion, would support war with Russia over, say, Estonia. And as they hadn't taught Politesse 101 in Queens, he didn't mind saying so.

As you might imagine, that did not go over very well in Estonia.

Asked about whether the threats facing his country and the EU were existential, that country's then-President Toomas Hendrik Ilves took aim at Trump, telling a U.S. journalist, "When I sit there in Europe and read what one of your presidential candidates says, I think, 'Is the United States going to exist?'" Ilves, who grew up in New Jersey, expounded on his "good relationship" with the Obama administration and its provision of U.S. air-defense support for the Baltics. Later, he blasted prominent Trump surrogate Newt Gingrich as "geographically challenged" when the former House Speaker, in the context of discussing the wisdom of "risk[ing] nuclear war" over a conflict with Russia, dismissed Estonia as if it were a hamlet "in the suburbs of St. Petersburg."[3] When he left office in 2016, Ilves landed at Stanford, at the international-studies institute headed by Michael McFaul, who was director for Russia affairs on Obama's National Security Council before becoming the president's ambassador to Russia in 2012, under Secretary of State Clinton.[4]

Recall that Estonia was among the European countries that, beginning in the second half of 2015, passed to American intelligence agencies information about claimed "interactions" between Trump associates and suspected Russian agents. In April 2016, the BBC reported that a Baltic intelligence agency, likely Estonia's, delivered to CIA Director John Brennan what was alleged to be a recording of a conversation about Russian money being transferred into the U.S. presidential campaign.[5]

'It Served as the Basis for the FBI Investigation'

Was there such a recording? There is no mention it—or of the words "Estonia" or "Baltic"—in the voluminous Mueller report. Yet, it is said to have greatly alarmed Brennan.

Ever the partisan, Brennan was mindful that his focus on the presidential campaign could press against the legal prohibitions on domestic-intelligence activities by the agency. As he later told the House Intelligence Committee, "It was well beyond my mandate as director of CIA to follow on any of those leads that involved U.S. persons." Therefore, he "made sure that anything that was involving U.S. persons, including anything involving the individuals involved in the Trump campaign, was shared with the Bureau."[6] The vehicle for this intelligence-pooling arrangement was an interagency task force, comprised on the domestic side by the FBI, the Justice Department, and the Treasury Department, and on the foreign-intelligence side by the CIA, the NSA, and the Office of National Intelligence Director James Clapper; the Obama White House was also briefed.[7] Make no mistake, though: Brennan was the driving force. Indeed, he has bragged about his role since leaving office and commencing his political attacks on Trump.

In his House testimony, Brennan expanded on the "intelligence about interactions and contacts between U.S. persons and the Russians" that he undertook to "share...with the Bureau" (emphasis added):

I was aware of intelligence and information about contacts between Russian officials and U.S. persons that raised concerns in my mind about whether or not those individuals were cooperating with the Russians, *either in a witting or unwitting fashion*, and *it served as the basis for the FBI investigation* to determine whether such collusion—cooperation occurred.

Notice that subtle qualifier—*unwitting*. Brennan testified on May 23, 2017—over a year after instigating the FBI's Trump–Russia investigation. Yet, even then, even as he made cavalier media claims that Trump might be a Russian agent, the former CIA director was unable to point to a single willful, clandestine action on Moscow's behalf taken by people in Trump's orbit. Obama's spy chief could not even pretend that the FBI investigation he had catalyzed—a probe of the opposition party's presidential campaign—had been triggered by hard evidence.

Brennan's testimony can be summed up as follows: The Russians are insidious, and they plot to manipulate clueless Americans (e.g., George Papadopoulos, Carter Page). Putin's regime interfered with the American election by orchestrating the publication of unflattering information (mainly, Democratic emails), hoping either that Donald Trump would win, or that the likely winner, Hillary Clinton, would be badly damaged. While carrying out this plan, Russian operatives reached out to some people who were connected to the Trump campaign. Brennan supposed that the Russians must have attempted to "suborn" those people because...er...well, that's "what the Russians try to do."

But all these months later, despite an intensive, multiagency investigation, he could not say that the Russians had actually suborned anyone. At the time he left the government, Brennan conceded, "I had unresolved questions in my mind as to whether or not the Russians had been successful in getting U.S. persons involved in the [Trump] campaign or not to work on their behalf."

Do you speak political-hack? Let me translate: He's got nothing.

It wasn't for lack of trying.

By the first week in May 2016, Bill Priestap, one of the FBI's highest-ranking agents, was in London to meet with "a foreign government partner," as he grudgingly admitted to congressional investigators.[8] The admission was pried from him by Ohio Republican Jim Jordan during House Judiciary Committee testimony. FBI and the Justice Department lawyers tried frantically to deflect Jordan's questions about which foreign government Priestap had consulted, and when his relevant overseas trips—three in all—had taken place.

Evidently, the lawyers did not realize it was already public that Priestap was in Britain in early May. The cat was out of the bag thanks to the surfacing of thousands of text messages between those chatty FBI paramours—agent Peter Strzok, who worked for Priestap, and attorney Lisa Page, counselor to Deputy Director Andrew McCabe. Or perhaps the government lawyers had missed what Brennan told NBC's Chuck Todd on national television: "The FBI has a very close relationship with its British counterparts. And so the FBI had visibility into a number of things that were going on involving some individuals who may have had some affiliation with the Trump campaign."[9]

Priestap's presence in London in May is significant. The city was already the nerve center of Russia-gate. George Papadopoulos and Joseph Mifsud (he of the significant British intelligence connections) had had their now-famous breakfast meeting there on April 26, and it was in London on May 10 that Papadopoulos met with Australian Ambassador Alexander Downer. It would be in London that Stefan Halper, an old CIA hand on loan to the FBI under the watchful eye of MI6, would approach Carter Page and, later, Papadopoulos. And while it is well known that Christopher Steele, former British intelligence officer and principal author of the Clinton campaign–generated dossier, had his office in London, it is not well known that the FBI—for reasons still unexplained publicly—had retained Steele as an informant (in Bureau parlance, a "confidential human source") as early as February 2016 (i.e., months before he was contracted by Fusion GPS to write the dossier).[10]

The FBI and CIA do not run operations in Britain without clearance and often facilitation from their British counterparts. And as we've seen with Papadopoulos, the State Department is often in the mix, too.

Priestap was the Assistant Director in charge of the FBI's Counterintelligence Division. At the time, assisted by his subordinate, Strzok, he was running the Hillary Clinton–emails investigation—which the FBI was already formulating its plan to shut down despite having failed to interview key witnesses or acquire major evidence. Now, nearly three months before the "Crossfire Hurricane" was officially opened on paper, Priestap and Strzok were already steering the Bureau's Trump–Russia intelligence effort. As Brennan elaborated in his NBC interview, by the summer of 2016, the CIA "had collected a fair amount of information . . . about what the Russians were doing on multiple fronts. And we wanted to make sure that the FBI had full access to that."

Clearly, some of the information Brennan found most significant came from GCHQ. At some not-yet-specified time in the early summer, GCHQ's chief, Robert Hannigan, flew to the United States. His mission was to transfer intelligence so critical and sensitive that it was deemed necessary to exchange it face-to-face at the director level. The director Hannigan chose to deal with was Brennan. It was an intriguing choice given that GCHQ's American analogue is not the CIA, but rather the NSA, which was at this time led by Admiral Michael Rogers. As we've seen, Rogers was then investigating the intelligence community's illegal exploitation of surveillance techniques to monitor American citizens, particularly outside the United States—and, in October 2016, would reveal those abuses to the Foreign Intelligence Surveillance Court (FISC). Interestingly, just days following Donald Trump's inauguration as president, Hannigan would announce his abrupt retirement from GCHQ, for "personal reasons," after just two years on the job.[11] We don't know exactly what Hannigan told Brennan; we do know that British intelligence about Trump, filtered through Brennan, was making its way to the Bureau.

The Mythical Alfa Bank Back Channel

Did the Obama Justice Department and the FBI seek a FISA warrant in the early summer based on information they received through the

CIA from European intelligence services? There is not yet a clear answer to this question.[12]

British media sources have reported that the Justice Department sought and was denied warrants by the FISC. Citing reporting from *The Guardian*, Senators Charles Grassley and Lindsey Graham, senior Republicans on the Judiciary Committee, have pressed the question whether, in the early summer of 2016, the FBI sought a warrant to monitor four members of the Trump campaign suspected of irregular contacts with Russian officials. The FISC is said to have denied the application (which is unusual), suggesting that the government narrow its focus. Soon after *The Guardian's* story was published, the BBC reported that the Justice Department and FBI twice sought warrants to surveil two Russian banks, and that those applications were denied in June and, even when more narrowly tailored, denied again in July. The senators added that the FISC's annual statistical report, which indicated a number of applications that had been denied or modified, provided some potential support for these media claims.[13]

Additional reporting from *The New York Times* and from the now-defunct *Heat Street* (written by the conspiracy-minded Louise Mensch) indicated that the FBI had concerns about a private server in Trump Tower that was connected to Alfa Bank and SVB Bank, two major Russian financial institutions. *Heat Street* described these concerns as centering on "possible financial and banking offenses"—calling to mind Brennan's initial alarm about Russian money purportedly flowing into the campaign. FBI sources told the *Times* that the Bureau initially determined that the Trump Tower server did not have any nefarious purpose. But, according to *Heat Street*, "the FBI's counterintelligence arm, sources say, re-drew an earlier FISA court request around possible financial and banking offenses related to the server." That application was said to have "named" Donald Trump—although it was not clear whether *Heat Street* was claiming that Trump had been targeted to have his communications monitored or if he was merely alluded to in that (purported) application (as, for example, we now know he was alluded to in the Carter Page FISA application—which we'll discuss in Chapter Fifteen). Consistent with the BBC's reporting, the June application was said to have been denied.[14]

Suffice it to say that the legend of the Trump–Putin back-channel lives on in Trump-deranged circles, a technologically updated version of the storied "red telephone" arrangement.[15] It is largely based on reporting by Franklin Foer, former editor of *The New Republic*. On Halloween, just days before the 2016 election, he reported that a network of computer scientists with privileged access to internet communication logs—allowing this "Union of Concerned Nerds" to hunt down malware used by rogue states and other hackers to spy on users and steal their data—had discovered a dedicated Trump–Russia communication line. The discovery had been made in late July, after publication of the hacked DNC emails, when the scientists were reasonably theorizing that Russia-backed hackers might well have stalked other email accounts pertinent to the campaign. At first, it was thought that malware emanating from Russia had targeted a destination domain belonging to Donald Trump. Additional analysis, however, indicated that Alfa Bank, Russia's most important financial institution—and one whose oligarch executives are welcomed in Washington as Western-friendly barometers of Putin's thinking—was pinging a server registered to The Trump Organization in Manhattan. There sprung the hypothesis that "these organizations are communicating in a way designed to block other people out." The conclusion was not certain, but it was highly likely, these experts decided, that a covert hotline had been discovered.[16]

With Election Day fast approaching, some of the computer scientists tried to draw public attention to their research. Nevertheless, Alfa Bank principals Mikhail Fridman and Petr Aven vigorously denied having ever met Trump or conducted any business with his organization. Alfa Bank's investigator believed the bank's servers may have been auto-responding to spam sent by a marketing server. For Trump's part, his spokeswoman Hope Hicks told Foer that the server in question had been set up for marketing purposes, was operated by a third-party, and had not been used in six years—The Trump Organization was not using it either to send or receive messages.

Meanwhile, Trump's former lawyer, Michael Cohen, told *The Washington Times* that Trump hotels, like many hotels, collected information on guests that was later used for internet marketing pitches; he surmised that some Alfa employees had at some point stayed at a Trump hotel and gotten added to a marketing list.[17]

There is no doubt that the FBI and the Justice Department investigated the server link. Putting aside the aforementioned unconfirmed BBC report about failed attempts to obtain FISA warrants in the early summer, both the Beeb and McClatchy reported that, in mid-October, the FISC had authorized investigators' access to bank records pertaining to potential money transfers. Whether this authorization took the form of a FISA warrant (as the press accounts claim) or, as I suspect, a less intrusive form of FISA process (such as an order for disclosure of business records or a national-security letter) is unknown.[18]

In any event, Election Day was just over a week away, and Mrs. Clinton was cruising to a comfortable victory—and so brimming with confidence that she was planning a final campaign swing through Republican strongholds, hoping to run up the score on Narcissus.[19] Loose ends were being tied up all around. It was in that vein that, on October 28, FBI Director Comey infamously reopened the Clinton-emails investigation. FBI headquarters was fearful that there could be a leak that the FBI's New York field office had discovered copies of State Department emails from Clinton's private server on a laptop used by disgraced "sexter" Anthony Weiner (the former New York congressman and husband of Clinton aide Huma Abedin). Just a week later, with the FBI having purportedly reviewed all 650,000 emails, Comey made yet another public statement, reclosing the investigation and restating his conclusion that Clinton should not be charged.[20]

Nothing was going to taint or complicate Clinton's win. I believe it was in this spirit that Foer's well-researched story was subjected to immediate pushback, as he forthrightly recounts. On the same day Foer's article was published (October 31), top *New York Times* reporters Eric Lichtblau and Steven Lee Myers, who had also been chasing the story, published the report that the *Times*—in the aftermath of Trump's shocking triumph—is still kicking itself over. Under the banner headline, "Investigating Donald Trump, F.B.I. Sees No Clear Link to Russia," Lichtblau and Myers related:

> Intelligence officials have said in interviews over the last six weeks that apparent connections between some of Mr. Trump's aides and Moscow originally compelled them to open a broad investigation into possible links between the Russian government and the Republican presidential candidate. Still, they have said that Mr. Trump himself has not become a target. And no evidence has emerged that would link him or anyone else in his business or political circle directly to Russia's election operations.

On the specific matter of the suspected Trump–Alfa Bank connection that the *Times* had been examining, the reporters added that intelligence officials had

> focused particular attention on what cyberexperts said appeared to be a mysterious computer back channel between The Trump Organization and the Alfa Bank, which is one of Russia's biggest banks and whose owners have longstanding ties to Mr. Putin. F.B.I. officials spent weeks examining computer data showing an odd stream of activity to a Trump Organization server and Alfa Bank. Computer logs obtained by *The New York Times* show that two servers at Alfa Bank sent more than 2,700 "look-up" messages—a first step for one system's computers to talk to another—to a Trump-connected server beginning in the spring. But the F.B.I. ultimately concluded that there could be an innocuous explanation, like a marketing email or spam, for the computer contacts.

Given the zeal with which the CIA, the FBI, and the Obama Justice Department strained to connect Trump to Russia, cheered on by the media, this would seem fairly conclusive—though, certainly, it would likely have been written differently, or not written at all, if the tea leaves had suggested that Trump had a shot at winning.

Predictably, the election outcome brought out the Wednesday-morning quarterbacks, the recriminations, and the resuscitation gambits. The *Times*, for example, rues its overconcern for its reputation, rationalizing that even if the Trump–Alfa Bank channel angle was infirm, it could still have been wrapped into an overarching reporting package of rumored but unproven Trump–Russia interactions "with implications of treason."[21] (Query: What would the *Times* have made of invocations of "treason"—which is aiding an *enemy* of the United States, which Russia, at least formally, is not—had they been voiced by Republicans while Obama and Clinton busied themselves with the grand "reset"? After all, the *Times* and its friends still occasionally hand-wring over whether the Rosenbergs' actions had implications of treason.[22]) Heartened by Dexter Filkins's deep dive in an October 2018 edition of *The New Yorker*, Foer maintains that the Trump–Alfa Bank communication channel remains a live controversy with many questions still to be answered.[23]

And then there is the Trump–Russia narrative's chief scriptwriter, Glenn Simpson himself. In cagey congressional testimony, the Fusion GPS founder and Hillary Clinton minion distanced himself from the Alfa Bank communications channel story. The technical information behind the theory, he shrugged, "wasn't generated by us and I'm happy to say it's beyond our competence to have generated." He thus claimed, "I did not draw any conclusions from the data," which was "certainly beyond my competence."[24] In truth, Simpson had hyped the Alfa Bank story. His reluctance to say so was not due to any lack of confidence in its continued viability. Rather, he appears to have been concealing from congressional investigators the fact that he had aggressively pushed his Trump–Russia narrative on the Justice Department—including insisting to Bruce Ohr, a top official (and the husband of Simpson's contractor, Nellie Ohr), that "The New York Times story on Oct. 31 downplaying the connection between Alfa servers and the Trump campaign was incorrect. There was communication and it wasn't spam."[25] That is from Ohr's notes of his meeting with Simpson a few weeks after the election—and it sure sounds like Simpson had drawn some conclusions.

To be sure, the Alfa Bank angle was ancillary to Simpson's part in the Trump–Russia saga. His seminal contribution was the Steele dossier. And about that screed's connection to Obama-administration FISA surveillance of the Trump campaign, there is no doubt.

CHAPTER NINE

Narrative as 'Intelligence' as Disinformation: The Steele Dossier

he story of the Steele dossier is a familiar one. That is to say, the things that are wrong about it are now ingrained in conventional wisdom.

The encomia to Christopher Steele hail him as a "meticulous" British intelligence officer with a "formidable record." So highly regarded was he that MI6 put him in charge of the investigation of the Putin regime's brazen 2006 murder in London of Alexander Litvinenko, a former FSB operative who had defected to Britain. Less often mentioned is that Steele had been Litvinenko's handler when he was poisoned by the radioactive isotope polonium-210. Steele, we're further told, was so well-connected that he was chosen to run MI6's all-important Russia desk. Well, yes—but he ran it from London. In the late 1990s, through no fault of his own, his cover in Moscow was blown, along with scores of other spies. He had not been in Russia for almost twenty years when he, Glenn Simpson, and their Fusion GPS co-fabulists wrote the dossier reports. By then, Steele was a sleuth for hire, who did the bidding of such fine, upstanding clients as Oleg Deripaska, Putin's notorious aluminum oligarch.[1]

And why not? After all, Simpson, Steele's equally virulent anti-Russia, anti-Trump collaborator, had Fusion GPS doing lucrative litigation support work for Denis Katsyv—son of Pyotr Katsyv, a Putin crony and transportation minister who rose to vice president of the regime-controlled national railroad system. Simpson and Fusion labored to defend Katsyv and his company, Prevezon, from a civil forfeiture lawsuit brought by the Justice Department.

The case arose out of a massive fraud scheme orchestrated by Putin's regime, in connection with which Sergey Magnitsky, an investigator who uncovered the scheme, had been imprisoned, tortured, and murdered. The killing prompted Congress's enactment of the Magnitsky law, a bane of Putin's existence that enables the Justice Department to seize his cronies' assets. The Kremlin thus has an energetic lobbying operation against the Magnitsky law. It is led by a Russian lawyer, Natalia Veselnitskaya. Among her most influential patrons is Pyotr Katsyv; consequently, she helped represent Denis Katsyv in the Prevezon case— working arm in arm with, yes, Glenn Simpson and Fusion GPS.[2] And— *mirabile dictu*!—Ms. Veselnitskaya just happened to be the lawyer the Putin regime sent to meet Donald Trump Jr. and other top campaign officials at Trump Tower in June 2016, with the promise of campaign dirt damaging to Hillary Clinton (think of it as Russian-sourced oppo— just like the Steele dossier). It appears that the information she gave the Trump campaign—which was useless—came from Fusion GPS.

Again, such a small world.

Not Objective and Not a 'Source'

But back to Simpson's main collaborator, Chris Steele. The focus on his experience as an intelligence officer, in the media coverage of Russiagate and in the FBI's use of his so-called dossier, is a deceptive distraction. In drafting the dossier, Steele was not a meticulous intelligence agent of his country. He was a private eye marshaling information in the light most favorable to his clients. Indeed, as we'll see, State Department Russia analysts who got access to his reporting took it with a grain of salt; it was assumed that the Deripaska contractor was being spun by the Kremlin.[3]

In the 2016 election season, Steele was not a scrupulous intelligence analyst; he was a well-paid political hack, pulling together oppo for a campaign—against a candidate he despised. So was Simpson. Don't be gulled by their résumés. Yes, Simpson was a superb reporter. Steele, it is said, was a top-notch intelligence officer—I find that hard to believe based on what we've seen of his work, but let's stipulate for argument's sake that, at least at one time, it was true. It still doesn't matter: In their oppo capacity, the past lives of Simpson and Steele as an investigative journalist and an intelligence officer, respectively, are diversions, brandished to project an illusion of objectivity and professionalism.

By any objective measure, the dossier is a shoddy piece of work; the stories are preposterous. Steele gets basic facts wrong. There are undated and misdated reports. The reputed Russia expert repeatedly misspells Alfa Bank (using "Alpha"), which is among the country's most important financial institutions. In the antithesis of good spy-craft, Steele tried to corroborate his sensational claims (unsuccessfully) by using dodgy information pulled off the internet—including posts by "random individuals" (as unknown to Steele as most of Steele's vaunted sources are unknown to the rest of us).[4] No wonder Steele's former MI6 superior, Sir John Scarlett, scathingly assessed the dossier reports as falling woefully short of professional intelligence standards: They quite "visibly" were part of a "commercial" venture, unlikely ever to be corroborated, and patently suspect due to questions about who commissioned them and why they were generated.[5]

Steele and Simpson were deeply biased political actors. That is their right, of course. There's no shame in opposing Trump. He rubs many good people the wrong way—narcissistic, crass, mendacious, and with a propensity to surround himself with shady characters. There is a reason why the president's economic and policy successes have not translated into Reagan-like popularity ratings. Still, there's a problem: Steele and Simpson were themselves mendacious. They pretended to adopt just-the-facts-ma'am impartiality when, in reality, they were Hillary operatives annealed in anti-Trump derangement. Their mulish predisposition made it easy to assume the Russians must have compromised Trump—just fill in the supporting facts later.[6]

As Lee Smith notes, Simpson's journalist wife, Mary Jacoby, bragged in a Facebook post (since deleted) that Simpson was Russia-gate's impresario:

> It's come to my attention that some people still don't realize what Glenn's role was in exposing Putin's control of Donald Trump. ... Let's be clear. Glenn conducted the investigation. Glenn hired Chris Steele. Chris Steele worked for Glenn.[7]

Similarly, while he was working on the Clinton campaign's Trump–Russia project, Steele reached out to his connections in the U.S. government because, as he told Justice Department official Bruce Ohr, he was passionate in his opposition to Trump and desperate that he not be elected. In October 2016, Steele told State Department official Kathleen Kavalec that he was "keen" to push his allegations against Trump into the public record before Election Day. We know he was doing precisely that: feeding his reports to the media at the same time he was providing them to the FBI. This was no secret to the Obama administration: Steele also told Kavalec that he was managing relationships with the media and that some of his information was already in the hands of the "NYT and WP"—i.e., *The New York Times* and *The Washington Post.*[8]

To hear Simpson and Steele tell it, the Fusion team's job was to investigate Trump. Wrong. Their lavishly compensated job was to get Hillary Clinton elected. This explains the shifts in Steele's position over time. During the campaign, he hyped his anti-Trump research as critical information on which the government and the press needed to act. After the campaign, however, when Steele was sued for libel in Britain and had to answer questions under oath, he conceded that his research was "raw" reporting that had not been verified and needed to be further investigated, not published.[9] There is nothing mysterious here: When Steele's priority was for Clinton to win, he engaged in hyperbole because it seemed necessary to achieve that outcome. When Steele's priority became avoiding possible perjury charges, he conceded that his reports were little more than rank rumor.

Most significantly, Steele was not the *source* of the dossier information—no matter how many times Obama-administration officials referred to him as such. Again and again we are told that the Justice Department and the FBI presented Steele's information to the Foreign Intelligence Surveillance Court (FISC), even though it had not been corroborated, because Steele was a "credible source." He had provided solid information in the past, in particular, in the Justice Department's 2010 FIFA soccer corruption investigation.[10] As regards the dossier allegations, however, Steele was not the source; he was the *accumulator* and *purveyor* of allegations by the actual sources.

In criminal-justice parlance, when we are talking about information provided to a court in an application for some kind of warrant (e.g., a warrant to search, arrest, or wiretap a suspect), *sources* are the people who make the pertinent observations—who see the criminal conduct or hear the incriminating statements. In an application for a FISA warrant, the sources are the people who make the observations based on which federal judges are asked to find probable cause to believe a person is engaged in clandestine activity on behalf of a foreign power. Steele did not make any such observations. Instead, the observations of anonymous and sometimes unknown people were (allegedly) reported to him, and he then passed this information—multiple-hearsay levels from the original-source observations—to the FBI, which presented it to the court. Steele is assiduously referred to as a "source"; the Justice Department and the FBI figure lay people will accept this because he did pass the information to them, which sounds like what a source does. The nonspecialist in legal procedure will not spot that the court was not given any basis to credit the actual sources—the unidentified Russian witnesses on whose observations the court was being asked to rely.

Though FBI regulations and FISC rules require information to be verified before submission to a judge, Steele's information was not verified. When Person A brings you hearsay from anonymous Person B, you can't verify B's information by arguing that A is credible. Such "vicarious credibility" would be a dubious proposition in any case; it is downright laughable under circumstances where, as in the case of Steele's dossier: (1) A is not actually credible (i.e., Steele made significant errors, and the profound degree of his bias against Trump—including his research's sponsorship by the opposing candidate—was withheld from the court); and (2) anonymous B's information is hearsay even as to B (i.e., it is often second-, third-, or even fourth-hand information, derived from other anonymous sources of unknown credibility).

The Small World of Organized-Crime Buffs

There remain significant unanswered questions about Steele. For example, was he already working on the Trump–Russia investigation for the U.S. government (and/or the British government) months before he began compiling the dossier reports for Fusion GPS? As we've noted, in the Freedom of Information Act litigation that the Justice Department slow-walked, Judicial Watch finally managed to pry heavily redacted FBI reports showing that, in early February 2016, Steele was given the instructions (called "admonishments") that the Bureau routinely gives paid informants ("confidential human sources") before they begin working for the Bureau. To be sure, we don't know why this happened; it could be unrelated to Russia-gate. But the disclosure calls into question the oft-repeated version of events (articulated, for example, in Simpson's congressional testimony) that Steele felt obliged to reach out to the FBI in June 2016 because he was suddenly alarmed by the Trump "intelligence" he was hearing from his anonymous sources.

According to Simpson, Fusion GPS, which he cofounded in 2011 with another former *Wall Street Journal* reporter, Peter Fritsch, was a private intelligence firm. It performed research and litigation support for private clients, and, during campaign seasons, did research for political and media clients. Seeding stories to friendly media outlets was a significant part of Fusion's client services. In autumn 2015, *The Washington Free Beacon*, a conservative news publication, retained Fusion to delve into the backgrounds of Trump and some other GOP candidates. The *Free Beacon*'s backers were of an anti-Trump bent, and the project—which focused generally on Trump's business and finances, not specifically on Russia—wound down in spring 2016, as Trump clinched the nomination.[11] Simpson, as we've seen, has for years been interested in Russia—especially the intersection of political authority, commercial activity, and organized crime. He was particularly drawn to information Fusion had gathered on Donald Trump's business ties to Russia, including the degree to which The Trump Organization relied on Russian sources of capital when multiple bankruptcies made it difficult for the real-estate tycoon to arrange more traditional corporate financing.

Simpson obviously believed the information he had compiled, and more that might be out there if the right people did the digging, could be useful to the Democrats. Consequently, in early March 2016, he approached Marc Elias, a partner at the Perkins Coie law firm. Simpson knew Elias and his firm represented the Clinton campaign and the DNC. He pitched Elias a proposal to keep the Trump research project going and, specifically, to train it on Russia.[12]

When evaluating the collusion narrative and Simpson's pretensions to objectivity and investigative rigor, always remember that it was Simpson who made overtures to agents of the Clinton campaign; they didn't come to him. Neither the Clinton campaign nor the DNC disclosed to the FEC the work done by Fusion GPS, including the Steele dossier. Rather, the two combined to pay Perkins Coie over $12 million for "legal services" and "compliance consulting";[13] out of this amount, Perkins Coie paid Fusion $1.02 million. Fusion, in turn, paid $168,000 to Steele (who was also being paid by the FBI).[14]

Steele was brought on board in May 2016. By then, Simpson had also recruited another Russia specialist and longtime acquaintance, Nellie Ohr. When Steele was at MI6, Dr. Ohr was a researcher at Open Source Works, the CIA's in-house, multilingual division for corralling and analyzing reams of unclassified, publicly available information.[15] She graduated from Harvard in 1983 with a degree in history and Russian literature, studied in Russia in the late eighties (shortly before the U.S.S.R. fell), earned a doctorate in Russian history from Stanford in 1990, and taught Russian history at Vassar. She was also a staunch Hillary Clinton supporter.[16] Besides being Steele's collaborator on the Trump–Russia opposition research project, Dr. Ohr was (and is) married to Bruce Ohr, a Justice Department career prosecutor who by 2016 had risen to associate deputy attorney general—one of six who worked directly under then–Deputy Attorney General Sally Yates.[17]

Like his wife, as well as Simpson and Steele, Bruce Ohr specialized in international organized crime, focusing closely on Russia and Eurasia. Ohr and Steele had known each other for over a decade—since approximately 2006, when the former spy was running MI6's Russia desk and Ohr was chief of the Justice Department's Organized Crime and Racketeering Section. By 2010, Steele had left MI6 and formed Orbis Business Intelligence, his London-based firm. Through Orbis, Steele helped the FBI crack the corruption case against FIFA, international soccer's governing body.[18] It was the Obama Justice Department's most notable organized-crime triumph.

Ohr has known Simpson for many years; it is a professional rather than a social relationship, though *The Times* of London reports that Ohr may have introduced Simpson to Steele.[19] In 2010, both Ohrs and Simpson were members of an "expert working group on international organized crime," which produced a National Institute of Justice report. Back then, Simpson was at a Washington-area think-tank, having left *The Wall Street Journal*; he cofounded Fusion GPS the following year.[20]

In September 2015, while still researching Trump for the *Free Beacon*, Simpson retained Nellie Ohr as a contractor. In congressional testimony, Dr. Ohr maintained that she applied for work at Fusion because she saw an article about the firm in a newspaper and remembered Simpson's name from having read his work as a journalist covering Russian crime and corruption. She did not know Simpson well despite their collaboration in the 2010 expert working group. Simpson, however, knew she was married to Bruce Ohr, the high-ranking Justice Department official. For his part, Bruce Ohr testified that he had "seen Glenn Simpson…on various occasions over the years, and I believe my wife has as well." Interestingly, in his congressional testimony, Simpson seemed to go out of his way to avoid revealing that Dr. Ohr worked at Fusion. And Bruce Ohr failed to mention his wife's Fusion work or income during the 2016 campaign in the government disclosure form that his Justice Department position required him to complete.[21]

The Justice Department needed to be threatened with contempt of Congress before finally disclosing records of Bruce Ohr's communications, which document that he was in regular contact with Steele, including when the latter was working on Fusion's anti-Trump project with Ohr's wife and Simpson.[22] We know that Simpson testified falsely when he told lawmakers he had not been in contact with any government officials about the anti-Trump project until a meeting with Ohr after the 2016 election.[23] Simpson actually emailed Ohr to arrange a meeting with him on August 22, 2016, at the height of the presidential campaign. At the time, Fusion was wrapping up Steele's latest dossier reports, which claimed that the Trump campaign was coordinating the leaking of DNC emails hacked by Russia, and that Vladimir Putin was closely following Trump-campaign chairman Paul Manafort's ouster over secret payments from a Kremlin-backed Ukrainian political party. Moreover, as we've already seen, Simpson later beseeched Ohr to pursue the debunked suspicion of a private Trump–Putin back-channel communication system, arranged through servers connecting Alfa Bank and The Trump Organization—notwithstanding that Steele told Congress this back-channel theory was beyond his competence to assess.

It bears repeating that Simpson, Steele, and Nellie Ohr were not government agents. They were not a quasi-FBI. They worked for a private firm, retained by a political campaign. Their mission was not to make a prosecutable case on Donald Trump; *it was to get Hillary Clinton elected president*. This is why it can have come as no surprise to the FBI or Bruce Ohr that Steele was sharing details of Fusion's Trump investigation with the media. After all, *it was Fusion's investigation*—meaning, it was the *Clinton campaign's* investigation. The federal government's powers were put in that campaign's service. And if Clinton had been elected, the Trump–Russia investigation would have served its purpose; you would have never again heard a word about it.

Within the government, meanwhile, the connections of Russia-gate players to organized-crime work, and to each other, are extensive. During the FIFA soccer investigation, Steele worked with the FBI's Eurasian Organized Crime unit in New York City, which was supervised by Agent Michael Gaeta—the agent to whom Steele began bringing his dossier reports in July 2016. When Ohr was a prosecutor in New York, he worked on organized-crime cases with FBI agent Andrew McCabe, who became a supervisor of Eurasian organized-crime investigations at the FBI's New York field office. Eventually, McCabe rose to become the Bureau's deputy director. In that lofty position, his counselor was Lisa Page. She had previously been a Justice Department trial attorney, working for Ohr for five years and focusing on Eurasian organized crime. One of her most important investigations targeted Dmitro Firtash, the Ukrainian oligarch and Paul Manafort business partner we met in Chapter Three. Also focused on Firtash was Andrew Weissmann, chief of the Obama Justice Department's Criminal Fraud Section, which finally indicted the oligarch (and is still seeking his extradition). Ohr briefed Weissmann, his Justice Department colleague, on information he was receiving from Steele. Weissmann, who had been Robert Mueller's counsel when the latter was FBI Director, became Mueller's deputy when the latter was appointed Special Counsel for the Trump–Russia investigation. In that capacity,

Weissmann led the prosecution of Manafort—who had been investigated by McCabe, Page, and other FBI personnel, using information provided by Steele, which had been assembled with the help of Nellie Ohr and Simpson, and was occasionally routed to the FBI through Bruce Ohr.[24]

Again, a small world. Alas, Steele's Manafort information wasn't much use to Weissmann and Mueller since it appears to have been untrue.

Salacious, Unverified . . . and Easily Disproved

Steele began generating his reports in mid-June 2016. Cumulating to thirty-five pages, the full compilation includes seventeen reports, almost all crafted before Election Day.[25] The dossier spells out the essential collusion narrative that has been mass-marketed by Trump detractors since the 2016 election, and that the Obama administration began peddling to the FISC nearly three weeks before that. Steele may be the principal author, but the work is a Fusion GPS collaboration. Contributions were made by Simpson, Nellie Ohr, and Edward Baumgartner, a Fusion-contracted Russian translator (who happens to have majored in Russian history at Vassar College when Dr. Ohr was teaching there in the 1990s).[26] More to the point, the collusion narrative liberally borrows, thematically and substantively, from *The Wall Street Journal* reports Simpson wrote eight years earlier, examining the corrupt interplay between the Kremlin, the oligarchs, Russian organized crime, and American (mostly Republican) political consultants—such as Paul Manafort.

The dossier reports were branded "CONFIDENTIAL/SENSITIVE SOURCE" on nearly every page, the better to create the illusion of intelligence-agency rigor (rather than anonymous partisan rumor-mongering). The first report, entitled "US PRESIDENTIAL ELECTION: REPUBLICAN CANDIDATE DONALD TRUMP'S ACTIVITIES IN RUSSIA AND COMPROMISING RELATIONSHIP WITH THE KREMLIN," is dated June 20, 2016. It is the barn-burner that took the FBI's breath away two weeks later.

That is to say, a month before WikiLeaks on July 22 began leaking thousands of hacked DNC emails to the press on the eve of the Democratic National Convention, the Clinton campaign–sponsored dossier reports had already framed the collusion narrative into which all subsequent developments would be fit.

The first report sensationally claimed that, by mid-June 2016, Vladimir Putin's regime had been "cultivating, supporting and assisting TRUMP" for five years, providing the candidate "and his inner circle" with "a regular flow of intelligence from the Kremlin, including on his Democratic and other political rivals." According to Steele's star witness, described as a "former top Russian intelligence officer," the Kremlin was able to control the New York real-estate tycoon because it possessed blackmail material. This "kompromat," Steele's "several knowledgeable sources" elaborated, involved "perverted sexual acts which have been arranged/monitored by the FSB"—the KGB successor that is Russia's internal-security service.

Purportedly included in the kompromat collection was a 2013 videotape of Trump cavorting with peeing prostitutes in a luxury suite at Moscow's Ritz-Carlton hotel, what Steele described as a "golden showers (urination) show" performed on a bed in which President Obama and his wife, Michelle, were said to have slept. Trump had been in town to host the Miss Universe pageant.[27]

Would Freud ever have had a field day with Steele's unhinged abhorrence of Trump, projected through a melodramatic portrayal of Trump's supposed contempt for Obama? It's an obvious question one would have thought the FBI would ask—at least of itself, if not Steele—before presenting Steele's unverified information to a federal court. After all, the pee tape is a thing of myth, never known to have been seen. Former director Comey, now a partisan anti-Trump commentator, tells television interviewers and book-promotion audiences he cannot say for sure if his nemesis is under the thumb of Moscow's blackmail. "I honestly never thought these words would come out of my mouth," he declaimed in an ABC News interview, "but I don't know whether the current President of the United States was with prostitutes peeing on each other in Moscow in 2013. It's possible, but I don't know." In sworn testimony, though, he described the dossier's tales as "salacious and unverified."[28]

Steele claimed to be confident in the lurid story because of two sources. He described the first, "Source D," as "a close associate of

TRUMP who had organized and managed his recent trips to Moscow," and who had recently stated that "this Russian intelligence had been 'very helpful.'" Source D seemed to have claimed to be on-scene for Trump's supposed pee party—though Steele's rambling, imprecise writing style makes it unclear whether D was merely at the hotel or purports to have attended the "golden showers" performance itself.[29]

One is left to wonder: Did it not occur to the FBI that Trump had not made any "recent trips to Moscow"? Trump is a very public person, and it should not have been difficult to figure out—especially since intelligence agencies had been investigating his connections to Russia for months—that there is no record of his having been in Moscow after the brief weekend trip for the pageant in 2013. What Russian intelligence could Source D have been talking about?

In any event, Steele's belief in the episode was enhanced because of confirmation by "Source E," the half-line description of whom is blacked out in the first report. But Source E also appears at other critical junctures in the dossier and is described by Steele as "an ethnic Russian close associate of Republican US presidential candidate Donald TRUMP." (That is from a dossier report that the "meticulous" Steele forgot to date. It describes events in late July 2016.) Source E, along with "several of the staff" (it is not clear whether Steele means Trump's staff or the hotel's), were said to have been aware of the incident when it occurred in 2013, and Source E allegedly led Steele to "a female staffer at the hotel" (Source F) who purportedly confirmed the incident to another of Steele's unidentified sources (an "ethnic Russian operative" sleuthing for Steele's company).

The first notable thing here is that the FBI should have been able to find sources D and E without difficulty. It would be common sense and normal procedure to attempt to corroborate information before using it in court. If asked, Steele would have been obliged to identify his sources to investigators; he was a paid FBI informant, and he is in fact said to have identified at least some of them.[30] Even going solely on Steele's description of the sources as Trump associates with Russian backgrounds, figuring out who they were should have been a layup for the Bureau. Yet, if that sort of routine scut work was undertaken, there is no public evidence of it.

The press has identified one of Steele's sources as Sergey Millian. He was outed by both *The Wall Street Journal* and ABC News.[31] They report that Millian is referred to in various dossier reports as both Source D and Source E. Of course, in Steele's first report, he cannot be both: E is a separate source offered as corroboration of D's pee-tape story. In that report, Millian is Source D;[32] we do not know who E is, though there has been speculation as to his identity.[33] But does Millian become E in later dossier reports, as the *Journal* and ABC suggest? Probably. The best explanation for this discrepancy is Steele's slapdash style: He seems to have lost track, making Millian Source D in the pee-tape report, then making him Source E in a subsequent late July report. The *Journal* was told by "a person familiar with the matter" that Millian was the dossier source for both the "compromising video" (i.e., the pee tape) and Steele's later claim of a "conspiracy of cooperation" between Trump and the Kremlin. In the latter report, which we'll address in more detail shortly, the source for the "conspiracy of cooperation" allegation is called "Source E."[34] If both claims are attributable to Millian, then Steele designated him Source D in the first and Source E in the second.

Let's pause over Source E. After the pee-tape report, Steele identifies E as the lone source for the dossier's most critical report, written in the aftermath of WikiLeaks's publication of the hacked DNC emails. To repeat with more elaboration, Steele's undated late July report alleged:

> Speaking in confidence to a compatriot in late July 2016, Source E, an ethnic Russian close associate of Republican US presidential candidate Donald TRUMP, admitted there was a well-developed conspiracy of cooperation between them [sic] and the Russian leadership. This was managed on the Trump side by the Republican candidate's manager, Paul MANAFORT, who was using foreign policy advisor, Carter PAGE, and others as intermediaries.

Putin's regime, E added, had also "been behind the recent leak of embarrassing email messages from the [DNC] to the WikiLeaks platform."

E then goes on to allege that the "Trump campaign/Kremlin cooperation" against Clinton entails the deployment of "Russian émigré and associated offensive cyber operators based in the US." To reward these "assets" and promote "a two-way flow of intelligence and other useful information," E related that Russian diplomatic staff in key cities "were using the émigré 'pension' distribution system as cover." One of these key cities, E explained, was Miami. The success of the operation, then, depended on the local Russian émigré community, and "tens of thousands of dollars were involved." In his confusing bullet-point summary, Steele emphasized that there was an "agreed exchange of information established in both directions" (the aforementioned "two way flow"). That is, not only was Trump getting Kremlin help; he was feeding the Kremlin information from his own network of "moles within the DNC and hackers in the US as well as outside in Russia."

Steele, we must recall, urged his anti-Trump reporting not only on the FBI and the media but on the State Department. Eventually, this led to his being interviewed in Washington by Kathleen Kavalec, then the Deputy Assistant Secretary of State for Europe and Eurasian Affairs. In fleshing out his allegation about Russian émigré accomplices in Miami, Steele said that, according to his source, the Russians had constructed a "technical/human operation run out of Moscow targeting the election." Émigrés were used to "do hacking and recruiting," and "payments to those recruited are made out of the Russian consulate in Miami."[35]

Kavalec made notes of her interview with Steele—notes that the State Department withheld from congressional investigators for two years. When the notes were finally disclosed (pursuant to Freedom of Information Act claims by the conservative group Citizens United), Kavalec's assessment jumped off the page: "*It is important to note that there is no Russian consulate in Miami.*"

That's right: Source E was wrong about a fundamental element of the supposed Trump–Russia conspiracy.

The Miami émigré claim was fiction. There can have been no exchanges of mounds of intelligence and piles of money at a Russian consulate there, supporting a U.S.-based Russian émigré hacking network. It was nonsense. Equally absurd was the notion that Trump—depicted in the narrative as the bumbling-stooge beneficiary of Putin's machinations—was running his own reciprocal hacking and mole operation for Putin's benefit. It was all Trump could do to run his campaign, the most haphazard such operation in modern times (the lack of sophistication about personnel and practices lending no shortage of ammunition to the collusion arsenal).

We should note that Steele did not claim Source E provided this information directly; E supposedly spoke to someone he trusted, who then relayed the information to Steele. So here are the possibilities: E was lying, E was galactically mistaken about a major collusion allegation, or Steele's alleged source for E's meanderings got them hopelessly wrong. One way or the other, if the FBI had scrutinized Steele's sources with its usual diligence—if it had taken the minute or two it must have taken Kavalec to Google the purported Russian consulate in Miami—agents would have realized that, at a minimum, any information in the dossier from Source E was suspect. Plus, given how easy some of this information was to check out, the Bureau would also have realized that Steele's work product rated skepticism, not blind faith.

'Big Talker' and the Crème de la Kremlin

With that in mind, let's consider Sergey Millian, the apparent source of these tales about émigré hacker networks, the Trump–Putin conspiracy of cooperation, and the pee tape.

When the dossier was written, Millian was a thirty-eight-year-old native of Belarus who had immigrated to America in his early twenties. Upon arriving, he worked as a translator and used the name Siarhei Kukuts, though he was also known as "Sergey" Kukuts before settling on Millian. In 2006, to raise his profile, he started an outfit called "the Russian-American Chamber of Commerce." Sounds impressive, but it was a shell with little in the way of assets or activities—just the sort of entity, ABC News pointed out, that Russian intelligence would typically use as a front for recruitment operations, which is how the FBI is said to have suspected Millian's "Chamber" was used.[36]

Even Simpson confided to friends that he worried Millian was an unreliable "big talker."[37] No wonder. Millian has claimed in Russian and American media appearances to have a close relationship with Trump, and to have marketed Trump Organization properties as a real-estate broker. In fact, Millian barely knows Donald Trump and cannot keep straight the story of when they met. Originally, he said it was in 2007 in Moscow. When it was suggested to him that Trump had not been in Russia that year, he revised the tale, claiming to have met the mogul in Florida at a 2008 marketing meeting.

According to Trump's former lawyer, Michael Cohen, there was just one meeting, a photo op of the kind that Trump, a global celebrity, did thousands of times. Cohen denied Millian's claims of a personal and professional relationship with Trump, as well as a working relationship with Cohen, who says he never met Millian but did email him warnings to stop exaggerating his ties to The Trump Organization. No, Cohen is not the world's most reliable source, having been convicted of fraud and false statements. But he was right to contend that no publicly known evidence supports Millian's claims of close Trump ties. Further, Millian's representations have been contradictory. When challenged on his purported work as a Trump real-estate agent, he admitted never actually having represented Trump. Significantly, Millian acknowledges that he was not with Trump during the 2013 Moscow trip. And upon being exposed as an indirect Steele source, Millian dismissed the dossier as "fake news (created by sick minds)."[38]

So that's the main source.

As noted at the start of our dossier discussion, Steele also claimed that a "former top Russian intelligence officer" was his principal source for the allegation that Moscow had amassed enough embarrassing *kompromat* on Trump to blackmail him at any time of Putin's choosing. This top intelligence officer, Steele explicated, was "still active inside the Kremlin," as was a "senior Russian Foreign Ministry figure" also counted by Steele as a spy. There were supposedly other Russian sources, but these were the two Steele highlighted at the start.

We now know, thanks to the aforementioned revelation of the notes made by State Department official Kathleen Kavalec, that Steele claimed his sources included Vyacheslav Trubnikov and Vladislav Surkov. As The Daily Caller's Chuck Ross explains, Trubnikov is a regime eminence who, before Putin came to power, ran Russia's SVR (their external intelligence service, analogous to our CIA) from 1996 to 2000, and then served as first deputy for foreign affairs and Russia's ambassador to India. Surkov, most recently Russia's deputy prime minister, may be Putin's top adviser—referred to as the "Kremlin de-miurge" and "Putin's Rasputin," his special concentrations in recent years have been Georgia and Ukraine, where, you may have noticed, Russia has annexed territory and has designs on more.[39]

Really? So when Steele is not slumming with the wannabe likes of Sergey Millian, he's getting the 411 from the Crème de la Krem-lin? Count me skeptical. As Daniel Hoffman, the CIA's former sta-tion chief in Moscow, told Chuck Ross, trusted figures in Russia's national-security bureaucracy "never stop" working for the Kremlin. In Trubnikov's case, "There's no such thing as a *former* intelligence officer." And Surkov might as well be Putin's right hand. If these char-acters are Steele's "sources," it is not to spy on the Kremlin but to have the West believe what the Kremlin wants the West to believe.

Steele seems like a full-throttle hack to me. None of his information panned out, and if you're the scourge of Russia, I don't think Oleg Deripaska tops your client list. On that interpretation, it is unlikely Putin regime heavyweights would give the time of day to a British spy under whose nose the Kremlin spitefully murdered Litvinenko. The thought of Surkov and Trubnikov as Steele sources seems most implausible; it is more likely Steele was exaggerating—a habit, it ap-pears. But that is the Panglossian take on things. Surkov and Trub-nikov were sufficiently high-ranking and sophisticated to have sniffed out Steele's anti-Trump project and to have told him what he want-ed to hear. That is, it is entirely possible that Putin's regime duped Steele with disinformation about Trump—realizing that loathing of the then-candidate was unhinged in the upper echelons of U.S. intel-ligence, that much of the U.S. media was equally willing to credit any hint of corruption, and that Trump could be relied on to say outra-geous things that would add fuel to the fire.

Certainly the rest of Steele's handiwork does not fare much better than the pee tape.

The dossier, for example, accuses Carter Page of being an interme-diary between Manafort and Kremlin contacts. In July 2016, he made a trip to Moscow, during which Steele maintained that Page met with two operatives close to Putin: Igor Sechin and Igor Divyekin. Sechin heads up Rosneft, the Kremlin-controlled petroleum and natural-gas conglomerate. He and the company were (and are) under U.S. economic sanctions imposed because of Russia's aggression in Ukraine. According to Steele, Sechin proposed that if Trump were elected president and lifted the sanctions, Russia would pay Page and Trump the brokerage fee from the sale of a 19 percent privatized stake in Rosneft. Page was described as noncommittal, though he was said to have signaled that Trump would indeed lift the sanctions. Note that Rosneft is valued at nearly $60 billion. In late 2016, it finally sold a 19.5 percent stake to Qatar and the commodities trader Glencore for $11.3 billion, so the brokerage bribe would have amounted to a king's ransom.[40]

Divyekin, an official in Putin's presidential administration, is said to have informed Page that Russia had a *kompromat* file on Mrs. Clinton that it might be willing to share with the Trump campaign. He also warned that the Kremlin had such a file on Trump, too, which the tycoon should bear in mind in his dealings with Russia. The dossier also had Trump lawyer Michael Cohen getting in on the scheme—dispatched on a secret trip to Prague to meet with Putin's operatives for dark discussions about (a) damage control after public revelations about Manafort and Page ties to Russia, and (b) "deniable cash payments" for "hackers in Europe who had worked under Kremlin direction against the Clinton campaign."

Despite intense investigation (much of it after the Obama administration used Steele's information to obtain FISA warrants), none of these Steele allegations were verified. The only details that have been corroborated are ones that were readily knowable, such as the fact that Carter Page took a trip to Moscow from July 7–9 to deliver his speech at the New Economic School in Moscow. Page told numerous people he was taking the trip, the Trump campaign explicitly instructed him that he could only go in his individual capacity, not as a representative of the candidate, and the speech Page gave was public. The salient details alleged by Steele—namely, Page's supposed meetings with Sechin and Divyekin—have been vehemently denied by Page and never proved. Page, moreover, denies even knowing Paul Manafort, let alone reporting to him in an espionage conspiracy. There is no reason to believe he is lying—Special Counsel Mueller, who repeatedly referred to the dossier as "unverified" in his final report,[41] never charged Page with any crimes, and never charged Manafort with any crime having to do with Page, Trump, or Russia.

The dossier, moreover, is just as unreliable for what it does *not* say. Michael Cohen eventually pled guilty to providing misleading testimony about the extent of Trump–Russia negotiations over the potential construction of a Trump Tower in Moscow. Those dealings went on for well over a year and were widely known in Kremlin circles. Yet Steele's supposedly plugged-in Kremlin sources apparently knew nothing about it; while Trump's organization was signing a letter of intent and in serious talks to participate in a multibillion dollar transaction, Steele's sources told him Putin's regime had tried but failed to entice Trump into real-estate deals. Further, while Steele includes a report about "Alpha" Bank's relationship with Putin, his sources apparently knew nothing about strange (but ultimately inconsequential) traffic between servers for Alfa Bank and The Trump Organization—notwithstanding that it was being investigated by the FBI and several journalists prior to the election.

Folding New Events into the Partisan Narrative

Despite its jerry-built quality, efforts have been made to prop up the Clinton campaign–generated dossier by claiming that Steele's allegations have been corroborated by such events as the hacking and publication by WikiLeaks of the DNC emails. That, however, places the cart squarely in front of the horse. Steele was just following the crowd. His Russian sources clearly provided no advance warning, notwithstanding that he'd been poking around for Trump–Russia conspiracy evidence for well over a month by July 22, 2016, when publication of the DNC emails began in earnest. This is worth exploring because it highlights an insidious aspect of the dossier that has gotten too little attention: the former British spy could not foretell events; rather, after events occurred, he and Simpson wove them into the Democrats' Trump–Russia conspiracy narrative.

By autumn 2015, the FBI knew that the DNC servers had been hacked and that Russian operatives were surely the culprit.[42]

It is well known in Western intelligence circles that WikiLeaks is, at least in part, a willing agent of Russian intelligence. On June 12, 2016, over a month before WikiLeaks published the hacked DNC emails, Julian Assange gave an interview on the British television network ITV. In it, he announced, "We have upcoming leaks in relation to Hillary Clinton. ... We have emails pending publication."[43] By the time of this interview, WikiLeaks had already published a searchable index of approximately 30,000 emails from the private server on which Secretary Clinton had systematically conducted State Department business. These were the emails that she disclosed to the State Department two years after leaving office, falsely claiming they were the only ones she had that involved government business.

The natural speculation after Assange's interview was that WikiLeaks had, and was poised to release, some or all of the approximately 32,000 emails Clinton had deleted and attempted to destroy—i.e., the emails she had not surrendered to the State Department, falsely claiming none of them involved government business. But that is not what Assange said. To repeat, he coyly indicated only that the emails he was planning to publish were "in relation to Hillary Clinton." Consequently, when WikiLeaks began publishing the hacked DNC emails on July 22, 2016, it was quickly and widely concluded that the Russians were responsible for the cyberespionage operation. It was also assumed that Assange's June 12 boast about having emails "in relation to" Clinton must have been a reference to the hacked DNC emails.

Steele did not attribute the DNC hack to Russia until a few days *after* the emails started being published. He made the attribution in a dossier report entitled, "RUSSIA/US PRESIDENTIAL ELECTION: FURTHER INDICATIONS OF EXTENSIVE CONSPIRACY BETWEEN TRUMP'S CAMPAIGN TEAM AND THE KREMLIN." This is the report Steele failed to date, and in the assembled dossier published by BuzzFeed, it comes after a report the erratic spy incorrectly dated "July 26, 2015"—he meant 2016.[44] But we know Steele's report came after the publication of the hacked emails because it says so: Steele writes of "the recent appearance of DNC emails on WikiLeaks."

As we've detailed, this claim that Russia was behind the WikiLeaks DNC dump is attributable to Sergey Millian. Clearly, he was in no position to know about either end of any purported conspiracy between the Trump campaign and the Kremlin. Steele nevertheless described him as "an ethnic Russian close associate of...Donald TRUMP," and cited him (Source E) as support for the claim that "the Russian regime had been behind the recent leak of embarrassing email messages, emanating from the [DNC] to the WikiLeaks platform." Millian's multiple-hearsay meanderings are said to have been communicated to Steele through an unidentified intermediary, to whom Millian spoke in "late July." By the time Steele got this information, the fingering of Russia was old news.

Steele's claim is even less impressive in context. In the June 20 pee-tape report that begins the dossier, Steele claimed that Russia had a "dossier" of "*kompromat*" related to Hillary Clinton that had been "collated by the Russian Intelligence Services for many years and was mainly comprised of bugged conversations she'd had on various visits to Russia and intercepted phone calls rather than any embarrassing conduct."

Notice, nothing about emails. And remember: Assange's June 12 interview occurred eight days before Steele's first report, and it was widely reported in the British press. Yet, there is not even a hint in Steele's report that Russia might have emails (whether from the DNC or from Clinton herself), much less that Russia passed emails along to WikiLeaks.

On July 19, Steele completed the now-infamous report about Carter Page's purported Moscow meetings with Sechin and Divyekin. Even though this report was just three days before WikiLeaks went public with the hacked DNC emails—a time during which there must have been feverish preparatory activity that might have come to Steele's attention if his sources were actually well-placed—there is nothing in the report about Russia hacking emails and transmitting them to WikiLeaks. Even though Steele yet again took pains to allege that the Russian government possessed a "dossier of '*kompromat*'" on Clinton that it might be willing to share with the Trump campaign, the report contains no suggestion that this *kompromat* included emails.

Steele uncovered neither Russia's hacking of DNC emails, nor its use of WikiLeaks to publish them. Steele had no foreknowledge even though, right up until the moment the emails were published, he was leaning heavily on what he and Simpson portrayed as Steele's well-connected Russian sources. By the time Steele discussed the hacked emails in one of his faux "intelligence reports," days had already passed since the Clinton campaign and the DNC began publicly blaming the Kremlin. On July 24, for example, Clinton-campaign manager Robby Mook related that "experts are telling us that Russian state actors broke into the DNC, stole these emails, [and are] releasing these emails for the purpose of helping Donald Trump."[45] Steele did not discover anything. He simply echoed the narrative that the Clinton campaign was already spouting, folding it into a document that he stamped "intelligence report." The subsequent investigation by U.S. intelligence agencies, which concluded that Russia was behind the hacking, does not corroborate Steele. He was just repeating what lots of people were saying.

This is the dossier's pattern. Where Steele and Simpson made original allegations, those claims either cannot be verified or have been convincingly denied—e.g., the pee tape, Page's meetings in Russia with Putin operatives, the purported Michael Cohen trip to Prague, the nonexistent Russian consulate in Miami. But where Steele made assertions that are apparently true, they do not involve original discoveries unearthed by his network of sources. Rather, they are either (a) occurrences that were unhidden and easily knowable by anyone (e.g., Page's trip to Russia), or (b) claims that many other people were already making (e.g., that Russia hacked the DNC emails and passed them to WikiLeaks for dissemination).

Steele's project was not intelligence-gathering. It was the crafting of a campaign narrative about a traitorous Trump–Russia espionage conspiracy, into which new developments were melded as they occurred. That's why Steele and Simpson peddled the information to the media at the same time Steele was feeding it to the FBI and the Justice Department. Even Steele does not claim his reports were factual; in the British libel proceedings against him, he described them as "unverified" "raw intelligence" that "warranted further investigation."[46]

The Clinton campaign's Steele dossier was the sheer political spinning of rank rumor.

CHAPTER TEN

There's No Collusion Case...
Just Ask Julian Assange

ussia-gate is a complicated, sprawling story: multiagency and transcontinental; spanning law-enforcement and
intelligence operations; featuring top-secret redactions,
classified leaks, intricate narrative threads, and a list of
dramatis personae that would dizzy a Russian novelist. It is easy to
lose track of basic facts.

Here's the most basic one: There was never a shred of evidence
that the Trump campaign conspired with the Kremlin. Not to commit
espionage. Not to violate any law. Zip, zero, nada.

The only thing resembling evidence—i.e., made to look like authentic intelligence reporting—was the Steele dossier. A pulpy wannabe le
Carré thriller, framed by Glenn Simpson's creative theories of dark
doings at the lucrative intersection between American political operatives and a cabal of veteran Soviet spies, organized-crime chiefs,
and overnight oligarchs. The blanks were filled in by unverified tales
from the unidentified sources of Christopher Steele, a British spy who
perfectly reflected the transnational-progressive pieties of his Fusion
GPS collaborators, his Obama-administration admirers, and his global network of current and former spooks. For them, Donald Trump
was anathema: a know-nothing narcissist—as uncouth as Queens—
riding a populist-nationalist wave of fellow yahoos that threatened
their tidy, multilateral, post–World War II order.[1]

Trump had to be stopped. The rest was details.

In the summer of 2016, the details closest to hand involved the
hacking of Democratic email accounts. So that became central to
the narrative. As we've seen, once the hacked emails were published,
Simpson and Steele incorporated them into the dossier's ongoing story, after which they became the centerpiece of the purported Trump–

Russia conspiracy—with Paul Manafort managing the enterprise, his emissary Carter Page doing the legwork of messaging between the Trump campaign and the Kremlin, and Michael Cohen handling the payment arrangements (as if Guccifer 2.0 were Stormy Daniels).

As you read the story, though, you have to keep reminding yourself that it is complete fiction, and was never anything but. The only "proof" for it is Steele. Wait a second, you're thinking: What about George Papadopoulos—he of the "real" Origin Story? Well, as we've observed, there are significant reasons to doubt Papadopoulos's story. But okay, for argument's sake, let's assume that Papadopoulos is completely honest and accurate: The Maltese Professor Joseph Mifsud really did tell him that the Russians had thousands of Hillary Clinton emails. For the moment, let's ignore (a) that the British-intelligence-tied Mifsud denies telling Papadopoulos about emails, that Special Counsel Mueller has never alleged that his denial was false, and that there is no evidence Mifsud had any basis to know what Russian intelligence agencies were up to; (b) that Mifsud never mentioned emails to Australian diplomat Alexander Downer (as we've seen, like Simpson and Steele, after the hacked DNC emails were published, Downer just folded them into his story of suspicions about the Trump campaign); and (c) that Papadopoulos insists that the emails he claims Mifsud said the Russians had were Hillary Clinton's own emails from her homebrew server, not the DNC emails (which neither Mifsud nor Papadopoulos had any basis to know about when they spoke on April 26, 2016, weeks before hacked DNC emails became public).

Even if we ignore all those things, even if we assume Papadopoulos is completely truthful, *he never came close to implicating the Trump campaign in Russia's criminality.*

In fact, Papadopoulos actually exculpates the Trump campaign. Clearly, that is why Special Counsel Robert Mueller never charged him, or anyone else, with espionage. If his story is true, then this means the Trump campaign found out about Russia's hacking of Democrats from sources other than Russian officials—clearly, because the Trump campaign had nothing to do with Russia's intelligence operations. The only "evidence" that ever said the campaign was complicit in Russia's hacking—that even said Donald Trump had his own sophisticated hacking operation that was reciprocally feeding the Kremlin, unbeknownst to our $50 billion per annum intelligence community (stop chuckling!)—is the Clinton campaign–sponsored, Simpson/Steele dreamed-up, utterly uncorroborated Steele dossier.

Critically, the absence of proof was just as patent in the summer of 2016 as it is today. They had nothing. There was no evidence of a "conspiracy of cooperation" between Trump and Putin to hack Democratic emails in order to influence the election. There was only Steele's say-so that this conspiracy existed. And any competent investigator exercising professional detachment would have kept that say-so at arm's length: Steele did not come up with the hacked DNC emails angle until it was already public; there was no corroboration for his claims; his dossier reports were slipshod; a State Department official was able to spot a fundamental error instantly (the imaginary Russian consulate in Miami) and, after just moments of checking, confirm her suspicion that Steele was wrong; his sources (at least those which were identified to the FBI) were unreliable (Sergey Millian) or suggestive of disinformation-peddling (Vladislav Surkov and Vyacheslav Trubnikov); and Steele was a paid private eye working for the Clinton campaign (which should have more than outweighed any air of reliability stemming from his very different work as an officer of an intelligence agency of an allied country).

The FBI and the intelligence agencies had no indicia of *conspiracy*. They had indicia of *contacts*—of *associations*. That is night and day different. *Everyone* had Russia contacts. The Clinton campaign had not just Russia contacts; it had Bill Clinton meeting with Putin and taking a huge payment while Russia had important business before the State Department run by his wife; it had Hillary Clinton, for all her tough-on-the-Kremlin bravado, running the State Department in a manner that aligned with Russia's interests; it had Russian money pouring into the Clinton Foundation; its chairman, John Podesta, sat on the board of Joule Energy, a Massachusetts company into which Putin's venture capital firm, Rusnano, invested $35 million.[2]

The Obama administration, notoriously political in its intelligence assessments and law-enforcement actions, used Trump contacts with Russia as a rationalization for a counterintelligence investigation because it saw Trump as a Neanderthal degenerate. The Obama administration simultaneously ignored Clinton contacts with Russia, or assumed they simply must have been good-faith contacts, because it saw the Clintons as bien pensant transnational-progressives. The Obama administration bent over backward *not* to make a criminal case on Hillary Clinton—the candidate Obama heartily endorsed—despite a mountain of incriminating evidence. The Obama administration exploited every tool in its arsenal (surveillance, informants, foreign-intelligence agencies, moribund and constitutionally untenable criminal statutes) to try to make a criminal case on Trump—the candidate Obama deeply opposed—despite the absence of incriminating evidence.

What happened here is not mysterious. It is political.

Could Russia's Cyberespionage Be Proved?

The Russia-gate narrative floats the notion that the Trump campaign was complicit in Russia's *hacking* of Democratic emails, then quickly pivots to Trump–Russia *contacts*, hoping you don't notice the absence of proof that the contacts had anything to do with the hacking. But the legerdemain goes deeper than that.

The United States government's claim that Russia is responsible for the hacking, while credible and probable, cannot be proved beyond a reasonable doubt. In the absence of sufficient evidence to establish Russia's guilt in court, there was no way Special Counsel Robert Mueller could ever have proved Donald Trump, his campaign, or anyone else conspired with Russia.

Again, don't take my word for it. Instead, judge by what the government does. Or better, by what it does not do. Specifically, what it did not do to Julian Assange. The Justice Department did not indict Assange for engaging in a cyberespionage conspiracy with Russia to undermine the 2016 election. Mind you, while there is no evidence that Trump conspired with Russia, we were told for two years that Assange and his WikiLeaks organization were Putin partners, confederates in the Kremlin's hack-and-publicize scheme. Indeed, possible Trump-campaign contacts with WikiLeaks were put under the microscope, on the theory that to collaborate with Assange was to collaborate with Russia—*collusion*!

Yet, shortly after Mueller's final report was filed, we learned that the Justice Department had already indicted Assange under seal. On April 11, 2019, he was expelled from the Ecuadorian embassy in London and apprehended by British police, in large part based on American charges for which extradition was sought. But those charges do not include conspiracy with Russia. Why not?

Because the Justice Department has never been in a position to prove such a conspiracy in court.

Now, it is easy (maybe inevitable) to be taken the wrong way on this. So, to be clear, I accept, and have always accepted, the intelligence agencies' conclusion, echoed by Mueller, that Russia was behind the hacking of Democratic email accounts. There are skeptics who do not accept this conclusion, and they are not all crackpots as the media–Democrat complex would have you believe. But I do accept it. Just as I accept as true a lot of things that can't be proved in court. In twenty years as a prosecutor, I had many cases in which people I was quite confident were guilty could not be charged—not because they didn't do it, but because we couldn't prove it. And here's the thing: In a normal prosecutor's office, when it is clear a crime can't be proved, investigators move on to the next case; they don't keep a hopeless case open as a pretext for dogging people in the hope that some crime will turn up.

There is a big difference between (a) accepting an intelligence conclusion based on probabilities, and (b) proving a key fact beyond a reasonable doubt in a criminal case.

The key fact that Russia was behind the hacking of Democratic email accounts has never been proved in court. It is based, instead, on an intelligence *judgment* by three agencies, the FBI, the CIA and the NSA, announced under the auspices of a fourth, the Office of the Director of National Intelligence. My point here is not to stress that these agencies were led by Obama appointees; it is to grapple with the nature of intelligence judgments, which are executive-branch agency conclusions as opposed to judicial findings made after an adversarial contest. This dichotomy does not depend on which party is running the executive branch.

The objective of a criminal investigation is a *prosecution*, not a national-security judgment. In a prosecution, each essential element of the offense charged must be proved *beyond a reasonable doubt*. It is virtually certain that Russia's guilt could not be established under this exacting standard. Not unless the Justice Department found and corroborated an accomplice witness who was involved in the hacking, and who could be exposed in court without revealing essential intelligence operations. That apparently has not happened despite many months of investigative effort.

The intelligence agencies may have high confidence in their judgment about Russian espionage. But that does not mean this judgment could ever be proved in a criminal prosecution. In fact, the intelligence agencies' own January 6 report on "Russia's Influence Campaign Targeting the 2016 Presidential Election" flatly states: *"Judgments are not intended to imply that we have proof that shows something to be a fact."*[3]

Let that sink in.

A comparison is in order: If a prosecutor in a criminal trial were to say, "This allegation is not intended to imply that we have proof that shows the allegation to be a fact," the jury would say, "Not guilty." Indeed, the judge would dismiss the case before it ever got to jury deliberations.

Still, if you think about what intelligence agencies are for, their humility about the uncertainty of their judgments makes sense. They are protecting national security. When American lives are at stake, we do not wait to take action until the threats against us can be proved beyond a reasonable doubt. We make judgments, as the agencies' Russia report admits, based on sources of information and analytic reasoning.

The information on which these judgments are based is often fragmentary and so highly sensitive—e.g., covert agents who would be killed if revealed—that it cannot be exposed publicly without compromising top-secret intelligence operations, which would endanger the nation. The analytic reasoning gives us not courtroom proof of fact but the intelligence agencies' perceptions of probability. Intel analysts are highly trained and experts in their field. Nevertheless, their conclusions are often highly debatable or wrong—which is to be expected: The information inputs are of varying quality, so the best output they can give you is often mere probability.

Prosecutors are not in the probability biz. They are not directly responsible for national security, even if their cases promote it. The prosecutor's remit is to prove facts to a near certainty because the result of a prosecution is the removal of fundamental freedoms: liberty, property, and, in a capital case, even life. This is why evidentiary rules suppress evidence that fails the tests of authenticity and reliability (while intelligence analysts are permitted to factor in such evidence, so long as they account for its suspect nature). It is also why the "beyond a reasonable doubt" standard is imposed in criminal cases—more demanding than the "preponderance of the evidence" standard in civil cases and the "probable cause" standard that applies to arrests or search warrants, both of which are themselves more demanding than the supposition that sometimes supports intelligence judgments.

The agencies' Russia report informs us from the get-go that the full extent of their knowledge and the bases for their assessments cannot be demonstrated publicly because "the release of such information would reveal sensitive sources or methods and imperil the ability to collect critical foreign intelligence in the future." The Justice Department, therefore, is not in a position to prove what the agencies claim to know. But this limitation is not the half of it.

The most critical physical evidence of Russian cyberespionage was the DNC server system alleged to have been hacked. Yet inexplicably, in light of how Russia-gate has roiled the nation, the Justice Department never compelled the DNC to surrender this server system to the FBI so that forensic examination could be conducted. Obtaining possession of, examining, and preserving critical physical evidence is an elementary part of any investigation geared toward eventual courtroom prosecution. As one would expect, the Bureau made multiple requests, including at very high levels. But it was rebuffed. The Bureau's then-director, James Comey, affirmed the obvious: The FBI would "always prefer to have hands-on access ourselves if that's possible."[4] But why pretend that this was a voluntary cooperation situation? There was a readily available legal process—grand-jury subpoenas, or even a search warrant—that would have required the DNC, on pain of prosecution for contempt, to permit physical examination of the servers by the FBI. Yet, just as in the Clinton-emails investigation, the Justice Department of the incumbent Democratic administration refrained from forcing top Democrats to comply with basic evidence demands in an important investigation. And the FBI meekly went along. Can you imagine what Jim Comey would say if the *Republican* National Committee refused to comply with routine requests for essential information in a vital investigation and the *Trump* Justice Department declined to issue a subpoena to compel compliance?

Instead, for this critical analysis, we are expected to rely on Crowd-Strike, a private DNC contractor that had deep ties to the Clinton campaign and the Obama administration.

Think about that: We're to expect a jury in a criminal trial would simply accept non-law-enforcement conclusions paid for by the DNC, under circumstances in which (a) the DNC is invested in the storyline that Russia is the culprit in its effort to steal the election from Mrs. Clinton; (b) the DNC declined requests by the government to make its server system available for FBI examination; and (c) the incumbent Democratic administration's Justice Department unaccountably refrained from demanding—by grand-jury subpoena or search warrant—that the DNC's server system be turned over to the FBI.

Not likely.

This, of course, does not mean it was wrong for *the intelligence agencies* to accept a private contractor's analysis. CrowdStrike has a good reputation. But this state of play would not fly in a criminal prosecution—a point that is so obvious that no experienced prosecutors or investigators would be confident that they could make the case without seizing the physical evidence and conducting the government's own investigation. And you'll notice that Special Counsel Mueller, a highly experienced prosecutor who had a highly experienced, aggressive staff of prosecutors, never brought such a case.

"Attribution, as the skill of identifying a cyberattacker is known, is more art than science." This explanation—which is quite accurate—was offered by *The New York Times* in a thoroughgoing examination of the hacks on Democratic email accounts that began in late summer 2015.[5] "It is often impossible to name an attacker with absolute certainty." It is necessary to accumulate over time a reference library of hacking techniques. It becomes possible to spot repeat attackers. But once malware is used in cyberspace, it is available to any industrious hacker with the skills to copy it and reuse or refine it. These tend not to be signature attacks; there are numerous attackers and copycats. Attribution is a deductive process, not an exact science. It is a remorseless fact that forensic judgments in this area, including those rendered by intelligence agencies, are probability assessments, not definitive conclusions. And indeed, CrowdStrike is widely believed to have been wrong in a controversial 2016 judgment, when it claimed Russian operatives hacked a Ukrainian artillery app, resulting in heavy losses of howitzers in combat against separatists backed by Moscow.[6]

Moreover, there are ongoing private investigations that cast doubt on CrowdStrike's assessment of the DNC hack.

The best known of these, to date, has been produced by the left-leaning Veteran Intelligence Professionals for Sanity (VIPS), given notoriety by the left-leaning publication *The Nation*.[7] The VIPS naysayers, who are primarily former NSA officials, contend that the operation against the DNC was a not an overseas hack but an insider theft—"a download executed locally with a memory key or a similar portable data-storage device." This probability assessment is largely based on the transfer speeds of megabytes of DNC data (the speeds have been deduced from metadata in files published by the persona Guccifer 2.0).

The VIPS report is not without controversy, even within VIPS itself. Former intelligence agents associated with the group have published a spirited dissent from their colleagues' report.[8] We should note, nevertheless, that the salient objection of the dissenters is that the VIPS report *goes too far* by offering with excessive confidence the *alternative theory* of an insider theft (or "local leak"). That is, the dissenters agree with their VIPS colleagues on the matter of our concern: The government intelligence agencies' judgment, they say, is extremely suspect. And there are other examples, such as Sam Biddle at *The Intercept*, another left-leaning site, who filed an exhaustive report on the insufficiency of publicly known evidence that Russia was responsible for the hacking.[9]

To be clear, my point is not to broker the competing claims, or to contend that the U.S. intelligence agencies' judgment is wrong and those of its detractors are correct. Cyber analysis is not my area of competence, but I'm inclined to believe our agencies. The point is that *our agencies are not offering courtroom-quality proof*, as they forth-rightly acknowledge. If the Justice Department ever brought a case of espionage conspiracy, *it would have to prove the Russians guilty beyond a reasonable doubt to the unanimous satisfaction of twelve jurors*. That jury would be bombarded by defense lawyers with the government's failure to inspect the server system, the inherent uncer-tainty of intelligence judgments, the government's inability to produce intelligence sources as witnesses, and alternative theories of what hap-pened posited by competent intelligence professionals (e.g., "It was an insider job, not a hack," or "It was another hacker, not the Russians").

Couple this with the fact that everyone else in the equation has denied Russia's culpability: Putin claims the Russians did not hack; Guccifer 2.0 claims no connection to the Russians; and Julian Assange of WikiLeaks, which disseminated most of the emails for publication, claims his source was not Russia.

If upon hearing that, your response to this is to scream at me that none of these sources is credible, congratulations: You have a case of good mental health. Yes, totally correct, they are all liars. But that's not the point. There is a blackletter principle of criminal law: A pos-itive fact cannot be proved solely by a negative inference. You may believe, as I do, that Putin, Guccifer, and Assange are inveterate liars. Still, the thing they are denying is not proved by their having denied it. There has to be some solid proof that Russia did the deed. You don't get there by establishing merely that a bunch of notorious liars say Russia didn't do it.

Publicity Stunt: Mueller's Russia Indictments

"Wait a second," you're thinking. "If Russia's hacking of the Demo-cratic emails cannot be proved in court, then why did Mueller indict a dozen Russian intelligence officers for hacking crimes?"

Well, because there's no chance they will ever be tried. The indict-ment was a freebie—a publicity stunt.

Or are you prepared to take this exercise seriously? If so, I have a question: Are Russia and its intelligence operatives now presumed innocent of hacking the 2016 election? That, after all, is the rule in criminal proceedings. The indictment is proof of nothing—it's just a device to put the accused on notice of what the allegations are. The defendants are presumed innocent.

To the contrary, Russia is as guilty as the day is long. If that were not the position of the United States government, sanctions would not have been imposed. So, what is the point of indicting? It's a politicized publicity stunt, in the service of the Trump–Russia collusion narrative.

There is absolutely no chance any of the Russian officials charged will ever see the inside of an American courtroom. The indictment is an artifice by which the special counsel hoped to accomplish two objectives. First, Mueller wanted to put to rest the question of Russia's guilt, because if that is in question, many Americans will rightly demand to know why the country was put through a two-year investigation of the president on suspicion of abetting the Russians. Unfortunately, as we've just detailed, the best that can be said about the Kremlin's culpability has already been said—and not completely convincingly—in the intelligence agencies' assessment report. Mueller hoped, however, that by having a prosecutor reaffirm the intelligence assessment in a court proceeding, its conclusions would assume the gravitas of judicial findings—i.e., he hopes you won't notice that he hasn't actually proved anything, that no one has been or will be convicted. Second, the special counsel wanted to justify his superfluous investigation. It is "superfluous" in the sense that there never was evidence of a Trump–Russia conspiracy and, again, we already had a report about Russia's clandestine activities, so what did we need a prosecutor's investigation for? Answer: prosecutors are there to indict, so now we have an indictment—*woo-hoo*!

Often, no harm comes from publicity stunts. That can't be said here. Look at how farcical Russia-gate became: In announcing the indictment of Russia's intelligence officers, Deputy Attorney General Rod Rosenstein asserted, "In our justice system, everyone who is charged with a crime is presumed innocent unless proven guilty."[10]

So we have to think of the Russians as innocent?

After the president of the United States has been a suspect for two years for purportedly conspiring with them?

We are through the looking glass. Certainly, as Mueller's final report demonstrates, Russia made out better here than President Trump did: They got the benefits of our Constitution. When the Russians were charged, the prosecutor told us to presume them innocent. Charges were not recommended against the president, yet the prosecutor told us he gets no such presumption—he can't be "exonerated" until he proves his innocence.

See how politicized law enforcement works?

And still more farce. When prosecutors are serious about nabbing lawbreakers who are at large, they do not file an indictment publicly. That would just induce the offenders to flee to or remain in their safe havens. Instead, prosecutors file their indictment under seal, ask the court to issue arrest warrants, and quietly go about the business of locating and apprehending the defendants charged. But in both of Mueller's Russia cases, the hacking scheme against the intelligence officers and the so-called troll-farm scheme against other Russian operatives, the indictments were filed publicly even though the defendants are not in custody. That is because the Justice Department and the special counsel are not serious about "bringing them to justice." Everybody knows they will stay safely in Russia.

But that does not mean there are no consequences. The special counsel and the Justice Department have encouraged a new international order in which nation-states are encouraged to file criminal charges against each other's officials for actions deemed to be provocative (or, more accurately, actions that can be exploited for domestic political purposes). Understand: Our country has the most to lose in this new arrangement. Of all government officials in the world, American officials are the most active on the global stage—and, as we've seen, that includes meddling in other countries' elections. I doubt our diplomats, intelligence operatives, elected officials, and citizens will much like living in the world Robert Mueller and Rod Rosenstein have given us. If the idea was to give Vladimir Putin and his thug regime a new way to sabotage the United States, nice going.

Assange: Collusion with Impunity

Prior to the publication of the stolen DNC emails and internal documents, Julian Assange and WikiLeaks exhorted Russian government hackers to send them "new material." That is what is alleged in Mueller's indictment of the Russian intelligence officers. Assange wanted the Russians to rest assured that giving "new material" to WikiLeaks would "have a much higher impact than what you are doing"—i.e., hacking and then putting the information out through other channels.

But time was of the essence. It was early 2016. If Hillary Clinton was not stopped right there and then, WikiLeaks warned, proceedings at the imminent Democratic National Convention would "solidify bernie supporters behind her." Of course, "bernie" is Bernie Sanders, the competitor who could still get the nomination. But if Assange and the Russians couldn't raise Bernie's prospects, WikiLeaks explained, Mrs. Clinton would be a White House shoo-in: "We think trump has only a 25% chance of winning against hillary...so conflict between bernie and hillary is interesting."

In a nutshell: Knowing that Russia had the capacity to hack the DNC and perhaps Clinton herself, WikiLeaks urged it to come up with new material and vowed to help bring it maximum public attention. By necessity, this desire to hurt Clinton would inure to Sanders's benefit. And sure enough, WikiLeaks eventually published tens of thousands of the Democratic emails hacked by Russian intelligence.

A few questions. First, why was there no Sanders–Russia collusion probe? Why, when President Obama directed John Brennan, his hyper-political CIA director, to rush out a report assessing Russia's influence operations, did we not hear about the WikiLeaks–Russia objective of helping Sanders win the Democratic nomination? Brennan & Co. couldn't tell us enough about our intelligence-agency mind readers' confidence that Putin was rootin' for Trump. Why nothing about the conspirators' Feelin' the Bern?

Don't get me wrong: I don't think there is any basis for a criminal investigation of Senator Sanders. The point is: The fact that a candidate theoretically stood to benefit from a Russia–WikiLeaks cyber-espionage conspiracy was no more a criminal predicate for a "collusion" investigation of Trump than it was for such an investigation of Sanders. But there appears to have been no criminal predicate for a "collusion" investigation of Donald Trump.

A more serious question: Why wasn't Assange indicted for criminal collusion with the Kremlin— i.e., for the same hacking conspiracy for which Mueller indicted the Russian operatives with whom Mueller says Assange collaborated? The same conspiracy for which the president of the United States, though not guilty, was under the FBI's microscope for nearly three years?

Pulling Punches on Assange to Protect Mueller's Russian Hacking Indictment

The most striking thing about the Assange indictment that the Justice Department did file is how thin it is, and how tenuous.[11] Leaping years backwards, ignoring "collusion with Russia," prosecutors allege a conspiracy between Assange and then-Bradley (now Chelsea) Manning to steal U.S. defense secrets. Initially, prosecutors charged a lone conspiracy count, punishable by as little as no jail time and a maximum sentence of just five years' imprisonment (considerably less than the seven years Assange spent holed up in Ecuador's London embassy to avoid prosecution).[12]

This was very peculiar. Manning, Assange's coconspirator, has already been convicted of multiple felony violations of the Espionage Act—serious crimes that the Assange indictment says WikiLeaks helped Manning commit. This is why Manning was slammed with a thirty-five-year sentence.[13] Yet, the original indictment against Assange alleged no Espionage Act charges. After commentators (including yours truly) noted this discrepancy, the Justice Department filed a superseding indictment in May 2019, adding seventeen new Espionage Act counts. But it will prove to be a futile gesture: The reason prosecutors did not bring these charges in the first place is that they are time-barred. The statute of limitations lapsed long ago; indeed, I believe the conspiracy charge in the original Assange indictment is time-barred, too. That is, it is unlikely Assange will ever see the inside of an American courtroom.[14]

Why charge Assange with such uncertain crimes when, staring the Justice Department right in the face, is the espionage conspiracy with Russia that has been used to hound Trump? After all, unlike the president, there is no doubt Assange was complicit in encouraging the hacking scheme and agreeing to facilitate publication of the stolen emails. Mueller brought a dozen felony charges against the Russian operatives with whom, we've been told for over two years, Assange conspired. So why isn't Assange charged with at least some of these felonies?

The only sensible explanation is fear that Assange's defense would put prosecutors to their burden of proving Russia's guilt. Assange would challenge Mueller's allegation that Russian intelligence officers orchestrated the hacking and then used Assange to publicize the stolen emails. Again, the special counsel indicted the Russians on the understanding that this allegation would not be challenged, and that prosecutors would never have to try to explain to a jury why, for example, they never took possession of the DNC servers so the FBI could perform its own forensic examination rather than relying on a DNC contractor (one powerfully motivated to toe the DNC line) to determine that Russia is the culprit. Assange would exploit this vulnerability. And he would make whatever hay there is to be made from alternative analyses that cast doubt on CrowdStrike's work.

Assange has always maintained that Russia was not WikiLeaks's source. I don't believe him. I see him as a witting, anti-American tool of Moscow. But, to my chagrin, some in Trump's base—not all, but some—have made Assange their strange bedfellow, just as many libertarians and leftists embraced him when he was exposing U.S. national-security programs, intelligence methods, defense strategies, and foreign-relations information. These Trump supporters have convinced themselves that raising doubt about Russia's culpability exonerates the president—even though the special counsel has already cleared Trump of "collusion" suspicions, regardless of what Russia and Assange were up to.

In summary: If the Justice Department had indicted Assange for collusion, Mueller's Russian-hacking indictment would no longer stand unchallenged. Assange would deny that Russia is behind the hacking, and prosecutors would have to try to prove it, using hard, admissible courtroom proof—not top-secret sources who cannot be called as witnesses without blowing their cover, and not other information that might be reliable enough to support an intelligence finding but would be inadmissible under courtroom due-process standards. If the prosecutors were unable to establish Russia's guilt to a jury's satisfaction, it would be a tremendous propaganda victory for the Kremlin, even if—as I believe—Russia is actually guilty.

Meanwhile, let us remember: Despite a dearth of evidence that he was complicit in Moscow's hacking, President Trump was forced by the Justice Department and the FBI, urged on by congressional Democrats, to endure a two-year investigation and to govern under a cloud of suspicion that he was an agent of the Kremlin. Now we have Assange, as to whom there is *indisputable evidence of complicity in the hacking conspiracy*, but the Justice Department declines to charge him with it—instead, contenting itself with the dubious Manning conspiracy that may very well be time-barred.[15]

CHAPTER ELEVEN

Crossfire Hurricane

'D' amn this feels momentous. Because this matters."

It was July 31, 2016, and FBI special agent Peter Strzok was feeling downright giddy.

Strzok was one of the FBI's top national-security agents: Chief of the Counterespionage Section. He was feeling his oats on July 31 because the Bureau had just opened a counterintelligence investigation of Russian cyberespionage—the hacking attacks by which the Kremlin sought to disrupt the 2016 election. And not disrupt in some random, scattershot way. The FBI's operating theory was that the Russians were targeting the Democratic party, for the purpose of helping Donald Trump win the presidency. Strzok would be heading up one of the most significant probes in his legendary Bureau's history.

It was frisson intensified by relief and professional accomplishment. The Bureau had finally put to bed "Mid Year Exam," code name for the Hillary Clinton–emails investigation. Strzok and other FBI vets dreaded that go-through-the-motions exercise: Everyone working on the case knew that no one was going to be charged with a crime. Mrs. Clinton was going to be the next president of the United States. The FBI's goal had been to avoid being tarnished in the process of "investigating" her—to demonstrate that the Bureau had done a thorough job, without calling attention to the suffocating constraints imposed on investigators by the Obama Justice Department.

That mission had been accomplished, Strzok and his colleagues believed, by Director James Comey's July 5 press conference, outlining the evidence and recommending against charges that "no reasonable prosecutor" would bring. Now, having run the just-for-show interview of Hillary Clinton on July 2—perfunctory questioning that took place long after Comey's press statement, announcing that there would be no charges, was scripted and ready for prime time—Strzok was on the verge of a big promotion, to Deputy Assistant Director of the Counterintelligence Division—second in command of the FBI component that protects the United States from foreign threats.

But, best of all: now, he was working a *real* case, the Trump–Russia investigation. He was about to fly to London to meet with intelligence contacts and conduct secret interviews.

'We'll Stop It'

True to form, Strzok couldn't contain himself.

As was his wont, he was texting his paramour, Lisa Page, several times a day, thousands of times through the years from before the Clinton-emails caper through Russia-gate. Page, a former Justice Department attorney, had moved to the FBI and was now assigned to the heady role of counsel to the Deputy Director, Andrew McCabe. That made her one of the relative handful of Bureau officials who were in on the Trump–Russia probe—the preliminary work done by Strzok's direct boss, Bill Priestap; and now, Strzok's trip to London. Late Sunday night, as he readied for his morning flight, Strzok wrote to Page, comparing the investigations of Clinton and Trump.

> And damn this feels momentous. Because this matters. The other one did, too, but that was to ensure that we didn't F something up. This matters because this MATTERS. [Emphasis in original.]

This MATTERS. The Trump case was vital in a way the Clinton case was not. The Clinton case was a foregone conclusion. No matter how high the evidence piled, the Bureau, taking its cues from the White House and its directives from the Justice Department, would simply wave Clinton's actions off on the nonsensical ground that she lacked criminal intent. The only way the FBI could damage its zealously guarded reputation was to make an obvious mistake, one that could be spun as the Bureau having blown the case—as opposed to the well-planned spin that Clinton was exonerated at the conclusion of a diligent, professional investigation. In stark contrast, the Trump investigation mattered because the restraints were off: If FBI agents could nail Trump, they would be permitted to nail him. Indeed, they were being *encouraged* to nail him because he was seen—by the hierarchy of the Bureau and the Justice Department, by the top echelon of the intelligence community, by the Obama White House—as unfit for office and potentially a threat to their institutions.

Understand that Strzok and Page were not outliers. They were upper-echelon actors who accurately reflected the top-down ethos of their agency. Months later, when President Trump finally fired Comey, it emerged that the director had made careful notes of all his communications with Trump, even though he had never done so regarding discussions with President Obama. It was because of Trump's "nature," the former director later explained. He judged that an accurate aide-memoire was essential because of "the person I was interacting with" and the likelihood that Trump would lie about their conversations.[1]

These days, it seems as if the former FBI director is in a competition with the former CIA director over whose public commentary about the sitting president is most bracing. Comey publicly rebukes Trump as "morally unfit to be president," even penning a *New York Times* op-ed to explain how "Trump eats your soul in small bites."[2] I have known, worked with, liked, and admired Jim Comey for thirty years. I'd also note, however, that unlike the Trump appointees he has recently taken to stinging in political commentary, he actually familiarized himself closely with Trump through several months of investigation before deciding he could work for the president. And through all the awful things he says Trump did and said, the director stayed on. He didn't quit, he was fired.

The point here is not whether Comey's insights about the president are right or wrong. Even Trump supporters realize the president often says things that are not true.

I support the president when I think he is right, and though I think that is most of the time on policy, I am often put off by the president's manner. But on the subject of dishonesty, like most tepid Trump supporters, I note that Mrs. Clinton, the only viable alternative candidate on the ballot, is at least as infamous in that regard.

To my mind, the lowest moment of the Trump presidency thus far has been the day after terminating Comey, during which he insulted the former director for the consumption of Russian diplomats whom, for baffling reasons, Trump picked that moment to host at the White House. I said so at the time.[3] Within days came the lowest moment of Comey's distinguished career, his leaking to *The New York Times* of a government memo describing a confidential meeting he'd had with the president. Suffice it to say: These two guys loathe each other—and, predictably, they bring out the worst in each other.[4]

For present purposes, however, the point is that, while the Strzok and Page texts may shock us, they should not surprise us. The texts are startling because they reveal the usually exemplary FBI run amok with partisanship. By now, though, we are well aware that these messages—thousands of them, in real time, between very plugged-in officials—exhibit the culture of the Bureau's upper echelon in the last years of an administration that was tirelessly political and that abhorred Donald Trump. There is nothing in their communications that suggests Strzok and Page felt a need to shield their attitudes from colleagues, and were using private texts to blow off steam. To the contrary, their messages portray a commonality of assumptions and emotions: frustration with the futility of MYE (the Clinton-emails in-vestigation); a sense of purpose in Crossfire Hurricane (the monitoring of Trump's campaign).

By 2017, when the FBI's behavior in the MYE case was being ex-amined by the Justice Department's inspector general, Page risibly told investigators that chats with "Pete" were an outlet for her from the oh-so-apolitical Bureau: "Because I was on the Clinton investigation, I actually felt extremely constrained from talking to anyone about politics at all," she recalled, so texting her "good friend" was "like a safe place to sort of have a conversation about what was...the normal sort of news of the day because...we both knew that we weren't, it wasn't impacting anything that we were doing."

That wasn't quite how it went, though. To take just one notorious example, as Strzok prepared to interview Mrs. Clinton in early July 2016, Page explicitly warned him not to go into the session "loaded for bear" with a phalanx of agents and prosecutors who might convey the misimpression that the FBI was anxious to make the case on her. "She might be our next president," Page admonished, "You think she's going to remember or care that it was more doj than fbi?" Page thought the advice was so urgent, and was so comfortable about its reflection of Bureau thinking, that immediately after texting Strzok, she texted another colleague who was advising Deputy Director McCabe, their boss:

> Hey, if you have one opportunity to discuss further with andy, please convey the following: She might be our next president. The last thing we need is us going in there loaded for bear, when it is not operationally necessary. You think she's going to remember or care that it was more doj than fbi? This is as much about reputational protection as anything.

Was Page rebuked for infecting the FBI's investigative preparations with political calculations? Perish the thought: "I'll catch him [McCabe] before the morning briefing to give him this nugget," her colleague assured.[5]

A month later, as the FBI formally commenced its "Crossfire Hurricane" probe, Page plaintively asked her paramour, "[Trump's] not ever going to become president, right?" "No. No he won't," Strzok replied. "We'll stop it." *We'll* stop it—the "we" Strzok was talking about was the Federal Bureau of Investigation."

This was all about political calculations. Most readers are understandably stunned by the blatantly political substance of exchanges between top Bureau officials. As someone who worked closely with the FBI, including its top hierarchy, for nearly twenty years, what strikes me is their nonchalance—how offhanded Bureau officials are about political considerations and preferences...at the same time that—any objective person would notice—they were both bending over backwards *not* to make a case on Hillary Clinton and scorching the earth—on two continents—to try to make a case against Donald Trump. And now, naturally, they'd like you to believe that their politics had nothing to do with their professional judgments.

The record is what it is.

Strzok and Page recount meetings about Trump in which colleagues shared their contempt for him and were unabashed about the imperative of stopping him—or at least containing the damage they were sure he would do if elected. Here are Strzok and Page on March 3, 2016—right as Donald Trump was emerging as the near certain nominee, right as these two officials were deeply enmeshed in a criminal investigation of Clinton in which she was proved to have willfully flouted her duty to safeguard national-defense secrets and to have destroyed government records:

PAGE:	God trump is a loathsome human.
STRZOK:	Omg an idiot.
PAGE:	He's awful.
STRZOK:	God Hillary should win 100,000,000 - 0.

Again, bear in mind the level of this exchange. Page was the legal adviser to the deputy director who ran all FBI operations and was deeply enmeshed in the simultaneous Clinton and Trump probes. Strzok ran the probes hands-on, and was the Bureau's top counterespionage investigator. "Trump is a disaster," he warned on July 21. "I have no idea how destabilizing his Presidency would be." Strzok found Trump supporters equally repulsive: "Just went to a southern Virginia Walmart," he told Page on August 26. "I could SMELL the Trump support." As they watched the final presidential debate on October 19, Strzok boiled: "I am riled up. Trump is a fucking idiot, is unable to provide a coherent answer." As the polls tightened in the election run-up, Page wrote in anguish, "I'm scared for our organization," while Strzok groused that third-party candidates were "F'ing everything up" by drawing support away from Clinton. On the eve of Election Day, reading a press report entitled, "A victory by Mr. Trump remains possible," Strzok wrote, "OMG THIS IS F*CKING TERRIFYING." After Trump won, Page's thoughts turned straightaway to impeachment—she had just bought *All the President's Men*, the famous Bob Woodward and Carl Bernstein account of taking down Richard Nixon: "Figure I need to brush up on watergate."

It is important to put this in perspective. Like every American, FBI agents are entitled to their political opinions. In fact, I'd say their opinions frequently deserve more respectful attention than the average person's because they tend to be better informed and more community-minded—patriotism, fidelity to the Constitution, and service to their fellow citizens being ingrained in the FBI's DNA. But FBI agents—and Justice Department lawyers, and intelligence agents—are not entitled to allow their political opinions to affect their work.

Many well-meaning people are willing to cut the FBI slack because they share the views the agents expressed about Trump. He ran against not only establishment Washington but the system's norms. And while many of these need changing, most are prudential, particularly in the law enforcement realm. But the problem is: One can be both right and wrong. One can be right on the merits about Donald Trump's flaws, yet wrong about one's place to address them. FBI agents are entitled to their opinions, like everyone else. Then they get to vote, like everyone else. And they must accept the nation's verdict, like everyone else. They don't get to use their awesome power and their agency's hard-earned prestige to nudge the outcome in a particular direction, or to hem in the victor so that he is less than fully president, so that his hold on power won fair and square is partial, suspect, and short-lived.

Laying the Groundwork

Peter Strzok's trip to London was months in the making.

As we've seen, from the time Donald Trump announced his candidacy on June 16, 2015, CIA Director Brennan was gathering information about Trump and his associates from foreign-intelligence services. From the beginning of 2016, the Justice Department and the FBI were resuscitating investigations of Paul Manafort (involving his political consultancy for a pro-Putin Ukrainian party) and Carter Page (involving a prior effort by Russian intelligence operatives to recruit him as an asset).

At the start of February, the FBI gave Christopher Steele the admonishments (or instructions) routinely given to a confidential informant who will be doing work for the Bureau. Why? The government is not saying. We can surmise, though, that it had something to do with Oleg Deripaska, the Russian aluminum magnate, Putin confidant, and Steele client.[6] A few days after receiving FBI informant instructions, Steele emailed Bruce Ohr, his friend at the Justice Department, to note the "good news" that Deripaska had been granted an *"official* visa" to come to the United States—Steele's emphasis on the word "official" suggesting satisfaction that the purpose of Deripaska's travel was to meet with U.S. officials later that month. Steele implored Ohr to monitor the situation and keep him apprised if there were "complications." A few days later, he again contacted Ohr, noting that there was soon to be a U.S. government interagency meeting about Deripaska. Steele hoped that Ohr would be in the loop, and vowed to circulate "some recent sensitive Orbis reporting" suggesting that the oligarch was not a "tool" of the Kremlin. Steele concluded that he and his company "reckon therefore that the forthcoming OVD [i.e., Oleg V. Deripaska] contact represents a good opportunity for the USG."[7]

That's the world according to Chris Steele: the real "tool" of the Kremlin is Donald Trump, while Oleg Deripaska—a.k.a. Putin's oligarch—is a potentially invaluable Western asset.

The New York Times has reported that Steele and Ohr were both involved in a 2016 effort to turn Deripaska into a government informant—an effort that appears to have foundered when the oligarch (who had apparently been keeping Putin informed of the U.S. government's entreaties) told the FBI that their theories on organized crime and Trump–Russia collusion were off base.[8] For present purposes, though, we can glean that Steele was already an official Bureau informant throughout the time he compiled his dossier (i.e., even before providing the Bureau with his first dossier reporting in early July). We can also surmise that, at the very same time Steele was writing his allegations of a traitorous Trump–Russia conspiracy, he was zealously encouraging the intelligence community to recruit as a source a Kremlin operative who was faithful to Putin and believed Steele's collusion theory was absurd. Little wonder, as we'll see, that State Department Russia analysts familiar with Steele's private-eye work dismissed him as a shill.

In March, the FBI interviewed Carter Page. One ABC News report claims, based on "a government document" not further described, that the interview was "about contacts with Russian intelligence." The implication is that the questioning was relevant to ongoing concerns about Trump-campaign connections to the Kremlin, a theme that congressional Democrats echoed in the Schiff memo.[9] Page himself maintains, however, that the contacts with Russian intelligence discussed in the meeting involved the contacts he'd had in 2013—in the case in which he cooperated with the FBI and federal prosecutors.[10]

The evidence points in Page's favor. At the time of the interview, it appears that the Justice Department was getting ready for trial in the case of one of the Russian spies, Evgeny Buryakov. In the end, the trial did not happen because Buryakov pled guilty on March 11.[11] Had there been a trial, though, Page was a likely witness, so a pretrial preparation session would have been routine. Moreover, contrary to the ABC report, which claims that "the FBI paid him a visit in New York," Page says his interview took place at the U.S. attorney's office for the Southern District of New York and included not only FBI agents but the prosecutors on the Buryakov case. That would be standard procedure for a trial prep session. By contrast, the Trump–Russia investigation, even in its infancy, was highly classified—recall that the FBI would not even brief the congressional Gang of Eight on it because Director Comey and his advisers considered the matter "too sensitive." Thus, it is inconceivable that Page would have been interviewed on the classified matter in a prosecutor's office; the FBI would have held it in a facility secured for discussing top-secret intelligence. In addition, there is no indication that Page believed he was under FBI suspicion in March 2016, or that anyone in the Trump campaign had an inkling—Page was named a Trump foreign-policy adviser a couple of weeks after Buryakov's guilty plea.

Yet, Page clearly was under suspicion—in Washington, if not in New York. At some point that spring, Comey briefed Obama's National Security Council about Page. Comey, Deputy Director Andrew McCabe, and Attorney General Loretta Lynch also discussed the possibility of providing the Trump campaign with a defensive briefing about potential Russian infiltration—a briefing that was never given.

In April, information was reportedly passed to Brennan from the Baltics (probably Estonia's intelligence service), claiming that Russian funding was being channeled into the Trump campaign. There is no hint of such a money trail in the Mueller report; nor was there any suggestion of it in the intelligence assessment that Brennan himself led, on Obama's order, after the 2016 election. At around the same time, as we've seen, Joseph Mifsud, the Maltese professor with British intelligence ties, is alleged to have informed Papadopoulos that the Kremlin had thousands of Hillary Clinton emails.

April is also when President Obama, in a nationally televised Fox News interview, reaffirmed his endorsement of Hillary Clinton's candidacy to succeed him. In so doing, he argued that because the former secretary of state had not intended to harm national security, she had not violated the law by conducting official State Department business on her private server system and by mishandling classified information. Thereafter, having already been directed by Attorney General Loretta Lynch not to refer publicly to the Clinton probe as an "investigation," FBI Director Comey and his advisers began drafting an exoneration statement. The drafting and editing of that statement, which tracked Obama's stated "no intent to harm national security" rationale, was undertaken even though the Bureau had not yet (a) interviewed over a dozen key witnesses, including Clinton herself; and (b) obtained possession of key physical evidence.

In early May, Bill Priestap, then the head of the Bureau's Counterintelligence Division, made at least one of his trips to London—though, as we've seen, he would not even tell a congressional committee where he had traveled, much less what he was doing there. Even as a criminal investigation based on strong evidence against Hillary Clinton was being buried, Obama intelligence agencies in the United States and overseas were on the prowl for some reed—even a slender one—around which they could plausibly wrap their Trump–Russia conspiracy theory.

Then they found one.

Hack Attack

By May, the DNC realized that its computers had been hacked.[12] The realization had been a long time coming. The FBI first notified the DNC that it might be compromised in September 2015, by having a line agent contact a low-level DNC staffer by phone. Yes, if you were a top Bureau official investigating Trump, you were jetting to London from Washington or Rome at the slightest scent of collusion. Yet, though the DNC offices were just a few blocks from FBI headquarters, the agent to whom the apparently low-priority matter was assigned did not bother to visit in person. Nor, even in phoning the DNC, did the agent attempt to reach someone in a position of authority. (He obviously could not email the DNC, which would have tipped off the intruders.) Unsure they were dealing with a real FBI agent, rather than a scam artist, Democrats shrugged off the initial notification after some perfunctory checking. It would be seven months before top DNC officials learned of the potentially grave intrusion and thus stepped up security measures—just the kind of red alert you'd expect when "our democracy is under attack," right?

In the interim, it was discovered that servers of the Democratic Congressional Campaign Committee (DCCC) had also been attacked. There was, furthermore, a wave of "phishing" attacks in mid-March 2016. One of them duped Clinton-campaign chairman John Podesta, resulting in the theft of a decade's worth of emails—estimated to be 60,000 in total.[13] The extensive heists from the DNC, DCCC, and Podesta involved hundreds of thousands of emails, internal memoranda, and other sensitive files.

Two things were instantly apparent about the hacking attacks. First, though the problem was exacerbated by the FBI and DNC's collective lack of urgency in addressing it, there was never an iota of evidence that Donald Trump and his campaign had anything to do with it. No suggestion that they knew about it. No indication that they had the resources and competence to participate in it.

Second, Hillary Clinton is not much of an emailer. She was rarely an active participant in the trains of emails exchanged by Democrats—even Democrats on her own campaign. She had staff for that. Clinton later told Congress she did not even have a computer in her office at the State Department.[14] The infrequency and curtness of her communications were illustrated by the investigation of her private server: Her misconduct primarily entailed the willful installation of a nongovernment server system, in which sensitive and classified information would be exchanged and stored, and in which communications would be shielded from State Department recordkeeping. Even when using the homebrew system, Clinton was not a prodigious message writer.

Consequently, while the hacks of party email accounts were a disaster for some Democrats (such as then-DNC chief Debbie Wasserman Schultz), Clinton was essentially unscathed. And, of course, Clinton was telling the country that the reckless disregard for law and security displayed by her own email scandal was no big deal. She was thus in no position to portray hacking attacks, which highlighted the indifference of other Democrats to security, as a great blow to her campaign—which, manifestly, it was not.

No matter.

The hacking was attributed to Russia by the DNC's security experts within days of its discovery. From then on, the narrative was set: Russia was conspiring with Trump to steal the election; coconspirator Trump must be complicit; and the Democrats were victimized so Hillary must be the principal victim.

To address the hacking, the Democrats hired CrowdStrike, through one of their lawyers, Michael Sussmann, a former prosecutor and cybersecurity expert. Sussmann was a partner at Perkins Coie, the law firm through which the DNC and the Clinton campaign had hired Fusion GPS.[15] Remember the Alfa Bank yarn about a private communications channel between Trump and the Kremlin that Glenn Simpson eventually peddled to Bruce Ohr at the Justice Department (Chapter Eighteen)? Well, it is Sussmann who would steer that same story to James Baker, the FBI general counsel who signed off on FISA warrants in the Trump–Russia investigation.[16]

CrowdStrike is a deeply Democratic firm—there is a reason Sussmann chose it, and a reason the DNC allowed CrowdStrike to root around in a communications system it declined to make available to the FBI.[17] Right around the time the DNC retained CrowdStrike, President Obama appointed the firm's general counsel and chief risk officer, Steven Chabinsky, to his Commission on Enhancing National Cybersecurity. CrowdStrike's cofounder, Dmitri Alperovitch, is a senior fellow at the Atlantic Council, which is heavily funded by Victor Pinchuk—the Ukrainian billionaire and Clinton Foundation donor we met in Chapter Six, the patron of a legislator in Kiev who loudly backed Clinton's candidacy and leaked the compromising ledger that got Paul Manafort bounced from the Trump campaign. One of CrowdStrike's major investors is left-leaning Google; billionaire Eric Schmidt, the now-former chairman of Google's parent company (Alphabet Inc.), was a close Hillary adviser and provided critical tech support for her White House bid.[18]

As we've seen (Chapter Nine), Julian Assange foretold on June 12 that WikiLeaks had "emails pending publication," which would be the subject of "leaks in relation to Hillary Clinton." Educated speculation was that he might have obtained at least some of the 60,000 emails from Mrs. Clinton's private servers. Because Clinton's flimsy homebrew system had been so vulnerable to penetration, it was widely speculated that her emails had been hacked by foreign-intelligence services. FBI Director Comey conceded that this could have been the case in his July 5 exoneration remarks—which, as delivered, were toned down from an earlier draft that betrayed the FBI's conclusion: Clinton probably was hacked.[19]

Assange had already published a searchable index of the 30,000 emails Clinton had surrendered to the State Department. It was anticipated that, if he in fact had more emails related to Clinton, he might be preparing to release a trove from the thirty-two thousand emails she had withheld from the State Department—perhaps showing more interplay between the State Department and the Clinton Foundation. That speculation did not change after CrowdStrike announced, on June 14, that Democratic party accounts had been hacked.

More than likely, Assange did not yet have the DNC emails when he made his June 12 statements. Ten days later, on June 22, WikiLeaks reached out to the hacking persona Guccifer 2.0, asking for "new material." Assange obviously wanted the hackers to use his renowned WikiLeaks platform, rather than the alternatives they had recently set up—a website called DCLeaks and a WordPress blog site Guccifer 2.0 had started. WikiLeaks assured that its publication prowess would give the materials "a much higher impact." Assange despised Clinton, and he believed time was of the essence if she was to be stopped. He knew that if the Democratic National Convention, set to begin on July 26, went smoothly, support would consolidate behind Clinton, leaving Trump little chance to win in the general election. It was critical, therefore, that any new damaging material be published before the convention, to rally Senator Sanders's base. The hackers apparently agreed. After a few failed attempts, Guccifer 2.0 managed to transfer a bulging archive to WikiLeaks on July 14. On July 22, Assange released the first 20,000 for publication.[20]

Democrats were mortified, particularly by communications showing the party establishment had its thumb on the scale for Clinton—hardly a revelation, but embarrassing nonetheless. The former secretary of state was never in any danger of being derailed, however. In fact, the irrelevancy of the DNC emails to Clinton personally was a disappointment to some in Trump World, such as Roger Stone, an old friend of the magnate (and Manafort's former consultancy partner). Stone was convinced that WikiLeaks possessed devastating Clinton Foundation fodder. Though lacking an inside track to Assange, despite some characteristically self-important braggadocio suggesting otherwise, Stone schemed to reach the WikiLeaks leader and urge him on.

When WikiLeaks started publishing the hacked DNC emails, a "senior Trump campaign official" (not further identified by prosecutors) asked Stone what damaging Clinton material WikiLeaks might have. It was a natural question since Stone had disingenuously suggested he had insight into WikiLeaks's operation. In reality, Stone had no inside information; he'd heard rumors about a potential Clinton Foundation email dump, but he had no way of knowing. Though later instrumental in publishing the Podesta emails, WikiLeaks issued nothing from Clinton's own emails.[21]

The narrative, nevertheless, was set: The hacked Democratic party emails that did not actually damage Clinton—certainly not in comparison to her own, self-induced email scandal—became the "evidence" that Trump and Russia were conspiring to destroy her campaign.

The Spies, the State Department, and the FBI's Investigation

"But wait a second," you're thinking: "There was no evidence that Trump had anything to do with hacking attacks on Democrats...and even the evidence that Russia was responsible was not a lock." No problem—those narrative loose ends were already being tied up.

As we've detailed, on June 20, Christopher Steele completed his first dossier report, alleging that Putin had compromised Trump with a lubricious video, was backing Trump and feeding him intelligence to use against his political rivals, and was holding a dossier of compromising material on Hillary Clinton. Steele called his old friend Mike Gaeta, an FBI agent Steele knew from the FIFA soccer investigation, who was now the FBI's legal attaché in Rome. Steele told Gaeta he had dynamite information, but "I can't discuss it over the phone. You have to come here. Believe me, Mike, you have to come to London."[22]

To make the trip happen, the FBI needed a green light from Victoria Nuland, a high-ranking State Department official responsible for overseeing European and Eurasian affairs. Nuland had come to national prominence when then-Secretary Hillary Clinton made her the Department's spokesperson. She was also familiar with Steele. The veteran spy had befriended Jonathan Winer, a lawyer and former legislative aide to Senator John Kerry. Upon being named by Obama to replace Clinton as Secretary of State, Kerry had brought Winer to Foggy Bottom. Steele passed along to Winer some of his company's reporting on Eastern European affairs, including Russia and Ukraine. Winer showed Nuland Steele's assessments; she considered them helpful and asked that Steele continue to send them. Over time, Winer shared over a hundred of Steele's reports with the State Department's Russia experts.[23]

Not all of them shared Winer and Nuland's enthusiasm for Steele. They understood that the former intelligence officer was now a private eye, generously compensated by clients who were drawn to Steele because of his knowledge of Russia—such clients as Putin confidant Oleg Deripaska. One unidentified senior State Department official told journalist Eric Felten, "We were not aware of [Steele's] specific sources but assumed that many of them were close to Putin and were peddling information that was useful to the Kremlin." Note that Felten heard this even before we learned that, besides Deripaska, Steele counted among his sources top Putin adviser Vladislav Surkov and former SVR chief Vyacheslav Trubnikov. Felton notes that the State Department officials who saw his work most frequently and were most knowledgeable about Russia detected a "Putinesque spin" in Steele's assessments. They were not given much weight.[24]

It was as though they'd read the dossier before it was written.

Nuland approved Gaeta's trip and, on July 5 (not-so-ironically, the day of the Comey press conference exonerating Mrs. Clinton), the legal attaché winged his way from Rome to London, where he met with Steele in Orbis's offices. In the telling of Michael Isikoff and David Korn in *Russian Roulette*, the seasoned agent turned white upon reading Steele's report. After some solemn silence, Gaeta is said to have remarked, "I have to report this to headquarters."[25]

Steele was already a Bureau informant. The Gaeta meeting was the first of FBI interviews that would continue directly for nearly six months. The interviews would then continue indirectly for another few months through the Justice Department's Bruce Ohr—notwithstanding sworn representations that Steele had been terminated as an informant, made to the FISC by Bureau and Justice officials.[26] As we've detailed (Chapter Nine), immediately after WikiLeaks started publishing the hacked DNC emails on July 22, Steele incorporated this news into Fusion's Trump–Russia narrative.

It has been claimed by various FBI officials and congressional Democrats that Steele's information did not make its way to the headquarters team that was investigating Russia-gate until mid-September 2016.[27] This is simply not true.

On Saturday, July 30, 2016, Steele was in Washington, where he had breakfast at the Mayflower Hotel with Bruce and Nellie Ohr. Steele regaled the Ohrs with his allegations of a Trump–Putin conspiracy. Associate Deputy Attorney General Ohr was sufficiently stunned that he called his old friend, FBI Deputy Director Andrew McCabe. Sometime within the next few days, Ohr went to FBI headquarters to meet with McCabe and the latter's counsel, Lisa Page. He briefed them on what he had heard from Steele—both Steele's Trump–Russia allegations and the fact that Steele was working on an opposition research project connected to the Clinton campaign, along with Ohr's wife Nellie (the former CIA researcher). Even assuming the unlikely possibility that information from Gaeta's alarming debriefing of Steele had not been transmitted to headquarters immediately after their July 5 interview, Ohr ensured that the top echelon of FBI headquarters was aware no later than the beginning of August.[28]

Moreover, Nuland acknowledged in Senate Intelligence Committee testimony, "I was first shown excerpts from the dossier, I believe in mid-July of 2016. It wasn't the complete thing, which I didn't see until it was published in the U.S. press" (i.e., when the full dossier was published by BuzzFeed on January 10, 2017).[29] On *Face the Nation* in February 2018, Nuland elaborated that she was shown a synopsis Steele had passed to the State Department—"two to four pages of short points of what he was finding." Her immediate reaction, she claims, was that "this is not our purview" and that "this needs to go to the FBI, if there is any concern here that one candidate or the election as a whole might be influenced by the Russian federation."[30] Nuland's recollection is curious, to say the least. She had learned about Steele's dossier information because she had been asked to approve a trip by an FBI agent to debrief Steele; she thus had to assume the FBI already knew about the information—there was no need for her to send it to the Bureau. A more likely explanation, we shall see, is that the Obama State Department was very much a player, not a disinterested observer, in Steele's Trump–Russia project.

In that project, Steele was far from the only spy.

Or, if you prefer, "confidential human source." Or "informant." Or how about "asset"? Whatever floats your boat. Some commentators have gotten the vapors over the deployment of the word "spy" to describe covert information gathering. Regardless of what label you're comfortable putting on a person who does such work, seventy-one-year-old Stefan Halper had been one for decades by the time he was dispatched to troll Trump-campaign advisers in 2016.

"Stef" Halper is an American-born scholar who splits time between rural Virginia and toney Cambridge, where he is an eminent Life Fellow at Magdalene College. A Stanford undergrad, with doctorates from Oxford and Cambridge, Halper is the author of several books on foreign policy that both celebrate the post–World War II order and anguish over its disruption. (Sounds like a Trump guy, no?) Halper's ties to the CIA trace back decades. He was the son-in-law of the late Ray Cline, a Langley legend for his role in the 1962 Cuban Missile Crisis. Halper worked in the Nixon and Ford administrations, and on the unsuccessful 1980 primary campaign of Ford's CIA Director,

George H. W. Bush. He was even entangled in a minor agency tempest in 1980: the alleged pilfering of Carter-campaign briefing documents, claimed to have been leaked to the Reagan campaign in advance of the candidates' only debate. (This was in the era before Mrs. Clinton showed the best debate prep is advance knowledge of the media's questions, not the opponent's answers.[31])

For decades, Halper has been close to Sir Richard Billing Dearlove, a British intelligence fixture who served as director of MI6 for five years, through 2004. Sir Richard is a mentor and adviser to none other than Christopher Steele. Halper and Dearlove were among a small group of eminences who ran the Cambridge Intelligence Seminars—until they jointly and messily stepped down in December 2016, with Halper claiming the enterprise was coming under "unacceptable Russian influence." Odd, given that Halper is an old friend of Vyacheslav Trubnikov—the former Kremlin spy chief...and claimed key source of Chris Steele. (Again, such a small world.) Anyway, before that contretemps, in the late spring and quite out of the blue, Carter Page was invited to attend one of the Halper/Dearlove seminars. Having recently been named as a Trump foreign-policy adviser, Page eagerly accepted. The seminar, called "2016's Race to Change the World," was scheduled for the second week in July—what a coincidence: right after Page's trip to Russia. Though he was not asked to speak, Halper's group paid Page's airfare. He traveled to Cambridge directly from his speech at the New Economic School in Moscow. Halper was a gracious, gregarious host. The only discussion of Trump's candidacy was Halper's passing mention that he knew Paul Manafort—which put him one up on Page, who had never met the then-manager of Trump's campaign. But Halper enticed Page into a cordial relationship—they spoke frequently over the next fourteen months (during most of which Page was under FISA surveillance), with Page sometimes visiting Halper's Virginia farm.[32]

It was shortly after Page's trip to Cambridge, via Moscow, that Steele wrote his explosive July 19 dossier report, claiming that while in Russia, Page had met with (a) Putin crony and Rosneft CEO Igor Sechin, to discuss a corrupt quid pro quo exchange of future energy cooperation for anti-Russia sanctions relief (which Steele eventually refined into a staggering multimillion dollar bribe offer to Trump); and (b) Putin's presidential administration official Igor Divyekin, to discuss *kompromat* files—the one on Hillary Clinton that the Kremlin might be willing to share with the Trump campaign, and the one on Donald Trump that the Kremlin was warning his campaign to bear in mind. This was information Steele was most keen to impart to Bruce on July 30, and which Ohr promptly passed along to FBI Deputy Director McCabe and his counselor Lisa Page.

Palpably, the FBI's insistence (echoed by House Democrats) that its investigative team at headquarters did not have access to Steele's reporting until mid-September is an effort to disconnect the farcical, unverified dossier allegations from the Bureau's formal opening of the "Crossfire Hurricane" investigation on July 31. This position cannot be squared with the facts that (a) Gaeta, the agent who obtained Steele's information on July 5, needed prior approval from headquarters to meet Steele, and reportedly found the information so startling he blurted out that headquarters would need to be notified right away; (b) Halper, the FBI informant, met with Page at the Cambridge Seminar, three weeks before the investigation was formally opened; (c) Nuland, the State Department official who approved Gaeta's trip, was given a synopsis of Steele's information in mid-July (we're to believe the State Department's front office had the information from the FBI informant who had been interviewed by the FBI agent, but that the FBI's own front office didn't?); (d) Nuland says she instantly directed that the FBI be notified (presumably, if it had not already been alerted by its own agent); and (e) Ohr, upon being briefed by Steele himself in Washington on July 30, promptly notified McCabe and, within no more than a few days, met with McCabe and Lisa Page.

Here, a commonsense observation bears making. In the FBI and the Justice Department, it is a far more consequential matter to seek a wiretap warrant from a federal court, under oath and with top-level approvals, than to take the ministerial step of opening a case file—which does not obligate investigators to do anything. It is simply not credible to suggest that the Steele information, which was coming into the Bureau from several channels starting in early July, would not have been considered in merely opening a case, yet would soon afterward be relied on in a sworn FISA warrant application. And note: When the Bureau and the Obama Justice Department took the critical step of seeking a FISA warrant, the chosen target was Carter Page—in reliance on the Steele dossier—not Papadopoulos, Mifsud, or some other target.

That is not to say the Steele dossier was the only game in town in these frenetic early summer days. Recall that this is when GCHQ chief Robert Hannigan transmitted intelligence thought to be so sensitive that he was impelled to fly to Washington and deliver it to CIA Director John Brennan, face-to-face (as we noted in Chapter Eight).

And then there was Alexander Downer—who just happens to be another acquaintance of Stef Halper and Sir Richard Dearlove. As we've detailed (Chapter Seven), when news of the hacked DNC emails went global on July 22, the Australian diplomat suddenly decided that this must have been what George Papadopoulos had been talking about when they met in the London bar two months earlier. Downer deduced this from Papadopoulos's passing mention that Russia might have damaging information on Mrs. Clinton, notwithstanding that Papadopoulos had not said anything about emails; he had no reason to know about DNC emails; he had no information about what Russia might be planning to do with any damaging information it might have; Mrs. Clinton was not damaged by the DNC emails; and Russia's responsibility for the hacking, though suspected, had not been established.[33] (But other than that . . .) On July 26, Downer moseyed over to the American embassy in London, where Chargée d'Affaires Elizabeth Dibble took his "suggestion" about what Papadopoulos must have meant and transmitted it through government channels to the FBI.

It was this notification that is said to have triggered the formal opening of the FBI's Trump–Russia investigation. Clearly, the most benefit of the doubt we can give that claim is this: Downer's exaggeration of Papadopoulos's remarks may have been the proximate cause for Crossfire Hurricane, but it was very far from being the only cause.

CHAPTER TWELVE

I Spy

I n the wee hours of Thursday morning, July 28, from their separate homes among their separate families, Lisa Page and Peter Strzok texted each other while watching the Democratic National Convention. Unable to coo over each other, the lovers cooed over Vice President Joe Biden ("he's just a really sincere guy") before grousing over those "stupid *ss Bernie supporters" who were making life difficult for Hillary Clinton. A more telling window into their thinking was what they were jointly reading off the left-leaning website Talking Points Memo. The Josh Marshall post was entitled "Trump & Putin. Yes, It's Really a Thing."[1]

It's an interesting article, like a road map an anti-Trump journalist can only dream two of the country's top FBI officials might pore over—especially officials working counterintelligence, where the probative value of evidence often seems secondary to its potential for intrigue. Marshall observed that Donald Trump was deeply dependent on Russian financing. In just the last year, his debt load had increased by $280 million (to a staggering $630 million). Trump had trouble finding financing because of prior bankruptcies, so he'd relied heavily on Russian capital to rebuild his business. "Russians make up a pretty disproportionate cross-section of a lot of our assets," Trump's son Don Jr. had told a real-estate conference in 2008.

Marshall stressed that shady Russian oligarchs were involved in Trump development ventures. He speculated that Trump's tax returns might reveal the depth of financial ties to Moscow, but noted Trump's reneging on the promise to disclose them. He observed that Trump had brought into his campaign both Paul Manafort, who had worked for years for a Kremlin-backed Ukrainian party, and Carter Page, a

Putin apologist with financial ties to Gazprom, the Kremlin-controlled energy behemoth. He explained that Putin had "aligned all Russian state controlled media behind Trump." And Marshall maintained that the Trump campaign, though otherwise indifferent to the party platform during the Republican convention, had intervened to water down an amendment on providing assistance to Ukraine against Russian aggression.[2]

After reading Marshall's post, Strzok said it highlighted something he and Page had been discussing, and that he hoped his boss, Bill Priestap, had taken up with "the 7th floor"—where the FBI's top officials have their offices. Underscoring how reflective the Page–Strzok running dialogue was of the mood at headquarters, Strzok said he would send the Marshall post to Priestap.

There was more discussion, but the Justice Department and FBI excised it from the copy of the texts disclosed to the public. Just a hunch, but I'm betting the redacted portions do not agitate over Russian money lining the Clintons' pockets while the Uranium One transaction was pending Obama-administration approval, or over Secretary Clinton's role in promoting the development of Russia's tech sector— to the delight of some Clinton Foundation donors, and the dismay of the Defense Department, and at least some sentient officials at the FBI.

'The White House Is Running This'

By late Friday afternoon, Strzok and Page were buzzing about the "new case." Strzok was hoping to get thinking on it from Deputy Director "Andy" McCabe before making strategic plans with Priestap. Page was busy finishing up the "lhm"—the "letterhead memo" the FBI prepares when investigative information is to be shared outside the Bureau. It was already clear that the Crossfire Hurricane loop would include Justice Department lawyers and State Department officials. Strzok was getting set for his Sunday-night flight to London.

He had been talking with a State Department counterpart there, who was keeping "Main State" (Foggy Bottom) informed. That was critical because Strzok's trip was extraordinarily sensitive. Breaking with diplomatic protocol after tense negotiations, the American and

Australian governments had agreed that Strzok and another agent would be permitted to interview High Commissioner Alexander Downer, Canberra's top emissary to London. Naturally, the British government, too, was involved. Downer had informed the American embassy that he believed Trump-campaign adviser George Papado-poulos had tipped him off to a Russian scheme to swing the presiden-tial election to Trump—mainly by hacking and releasing information that could damage Clinton, such as the tens of thousands of Demo-cratic party emails now in circulation.[3]

Soon after bursting at the seams over how "momentous" it was to be working finally on a case that "MATTERS," Strzok was crossing the Atlantic, arriving in London on Monday morning, August 1. The en-suing texts show that events in Britain were nerve-wracking. McCabe was hands-on and wanted to be briefed immediately after Strzok inter-viewed Downer—which was apt to irritate Strzok's direct boss, Pries-tap. Sliding into her role as McCabe's counselor, Page instructed Strzok to be careful of what he signed so the FBI could "lawfully protect" the information—meaning, *conceal it*. As she put it, "Just thinking about Congress, foia [the Freedom of Information Act], etc." A much tighter circle of government lawyers than usual was in the loop—a group that included Trisha Anderson, who had served in the Justice Department's prestigious Office of Legal Counsel (and is married to Charles New-man, a lawyer on Obama's National Security Council). Anderson was acting in the stead of James Baker, the Bureau's general counsel, who was out. Strzok was agitating that holdup by the lawyers could derail his shot at interviewing Downer.

Ultimately, Strzok cryptically reported that the session with the diplomat was a success. As he headed back home on August 3, he agreed with Page: keep a tight ship. For that, the Bureau had to prior-itize "control" over the "information flow."

But the Bureau was not in control, not ultimately.

Strzok was back in Washington by the next evening, heading straight to the office from the airport to prepare to brief the bosses. On the afternoon of August 5, he and Page had a tense conversation about an imminent meeting involving "agency people"—apparently, the CIA. Later, there was an interagency meeting of some kind. Afterwards, Strzok told Page the meeting had been the "best we could have expected"...other than when one official—whose name has been redacted—told him, "The White House is running this."

For that, he could thank John Brennan.

Brennan's Steele Trap

He's so "relieved"!

That's what the former CIA director had to say for himself after the Mueller report's findings became public in late March 2019. "I am relieved that it's been determined there was not a criminal conspiracy with Russia over our election," said the man who had tweeted the last two years away, telling the nation that its president was a traitor. "I think that's good news for the country."[4]

Sure is. But, gee, Mr. Director, why did you say all those awful things?

"I don't know if I received bad information," Brennan spluttered from his comfy new MSNBC digs. "I think I suspected there was more than there actually was?"

Ya think?

What Brennan "suspected there was" was the disinformation in the Steele dossier. He has been trying to distance himself from it for months—telling anyone who would listen that he made sure not to use any unverified information that was not an official U.S. intelligence product in his postelection assessment of Russia's election meddling.[5] But that is not the tune he was singing during the 2016 election season.

The Washington Post is Collusion Central, and Brennan is the hero lionized in its epic report, "Obama's secret struggle to punish Russia for Putin's election assault."[6] Other officials were paralyzed by misgivings, unsure of what was happening, and why, after the hacked DNC emails were released. "I feel like we sort of choked," a "former senior Obama administration official involved in White House deliberations on Russia," told the paper. But not Brennan. Nope. He was ripe dead certain when others were skeptical: Putin was backing Trump to the hilt; he had Trump compromised and he was trying to get him into the Oval Office to govern America in alignment with the Kremlin's wishes. *That* was the explanation.

But how did he know?

He knew, the *Post* tells us, because he possessed "an intelligence bombshell." It was "a report drawn from sourcing deep inside the Russian government that detailed Russian President Vladimir Putin's direct involvement in a cyber campaign to disrupt and discredit the U.S. presidential race." Obtaining such deep-cover intel, the *Post* marvels, was an astonishing feat of spycraft. How did ol' John do it? How did he manage to flip Putin's top guys and—

Uh...wait a second.

Didn't Brennan testify that he made sure the FBI knew everything that he knew from outside sources—you know, because he would never want the CIA accused of illegally spying on Americans? Brennan just wanted to be a facilitator, right? He was going to leave all the big investigative decisions up the Bureau. His only role, he tells us, was to make sure the FBI had all the information he could give them.

FBI officials told Congress, however, that—try as they might—they just weren't able to verify Steele's information. How is that possible if Brennan was showing them what he had, and what he had was "sourcing deep inside the Russian government" that implicated Putin himself in the hacking scheme?

That's exactly the information that Steele claimed to have. So, if Brennan had the same information, doesn't that mean Brennan's information must have corroborated Steele's information?

No. It means Brennan's information *must have been* Steele's information.

We now know that Steele bragged to the State Department that his sources included two of Putin's top guys, Vyacheslav Trubnikov and Vladislav Surkov. It is confirmed beyond question that Steele shared that information with State Department official Kathleen Kavalec, and it has been reported that Steele identified at least some of his sources for the FBI. There is thus no reason to believe the head of the CIA would not have known this. Brennan was dealing regularly with his British counterparts. Steele, an FBI informant, remained deeply wired into British intelligence and into the U.S. State Department—which has an intimate global working relationship with the CIA. It is inconceivable that Brennan did not know Steele's sources.

But we don't really have to speculate.

John Brennan's CIA and Jim Comey's FBI took very different approaches to their congressional disclosure obligations. Comey is a shrewd political actor (and he has become overtly partisan in his post-Bureau life—which no one should begrudge him as long as he's honest about it). But in his high-minded top-cop incarnation, Comey was ostentatiously disdainful of politics—the personification of progressive theory that the Justice Department and FBI should be so insulated from their political superiors in the executive branch, and their political oversight in Congress, that they effectively become an independent, unaccountable fourth branch of government.

Brennan, in stark contrast, is a political animal. He did not swim against the tide of his political masters. He went with the flow. He made sure his subordinates followed suit. He gave the White House and its congressional allies the narratives they demanded. Politicized intelligence.

Observe how this contrast played out in Russia-gate.

The FBI defied the Constitution's grant to the people's representatives of the power to monitor the activities—particularly, activities under the guise of national security—of agencies such as the FBI, which Congress created, regulates by law, and funds with taxpayer dollars.

To resolve the obvious tension between the needs for investigative secrecy and political accountability, Congress created the so-called "Gang of Eight." It is comprised of the bipartisan leaders of the Senate and House, as well as the chairperson and ranking member of each chamber's intelligence committee.[7] This way, the FBI and the CIA are able to disclose their most sensitive operations to Congress confident that these matters will not leak.

Under Comey's direction, the FBI decided not to inform Congress about the Crossfire Hurricane probe in its quarterly Gang of Eight briefings. The usually unflappable director seemed to be caught flatfooted when asked about this decision in March 2017. At a public hearing of the House Intelligence Committee, Comey mentioned *en passant* that the Bureau had just recently told Congress about the investigation. He was then questioned by a very young backbencher from upstate New York, Republican Congresswoman Elise Stefanik:

STEFANIK: ... If the open investigation began in July and the briefing of congressional leadership only occurred recently, why was there no notification prior to... the past month?

COMEY: I think our decision was it was a matter of such sensitivity that we wouldn't include it in the quarterly briefings.

STEFANIK: So when you state "our decision" is that your decision? Is that usually your decision what gets briefed in those quarterly updates?

COMEY: No, it's usually the decision of the head of our counterintelligence division

STEFANIK: Why was the decision made not to brief senior congressional leadership until recently when the investigation had been open since July? A very serious investigation—why was that decision to wait months?

COMEY: Because of the sensitivity of the matter.

This series of answers is specious. Comey is an exceptional witness, so I can't help but think he'd have had better answers, and avoided the wormy appearance of throwing his counterintelligence chief (Priestap) under the proverbial bus, if he'd anticipated the questions. Of course, he may not have had satisfying answers because what the FBI did is simply indefensible. The Gang of Eight was established precisely to deal with the situation presented here: making extremely "sensitive" operations known to Congress while they are being undertaken. By definition, there cannot be a matter that is too sensitive to disclose. If there were, then the unelected bureaucrats, rather than the sovereign—i.e., the People, through their elected officials—would decide what the sovereign gets to know. That's not how American constitutional democracy works.

More to the point, there is nothing decorous about this protection of "sensitivity." It is classic Washington swaddling of sharp politics in euphemism. The problem here was not that information was sensitive. It is that eight political leaders, including four senior Republicans, would need to be told that the FBI, under the incumbent Democratic administration and in the stretch-run of a presidential election, was investigating the Republican candidate and his campaign, using counterintelligence authorities authorized by Congress.

That was against our constitutional and historical norms. Norms, of course, are meant for normal times—and we hope that adhering to them reinforces normalcy and stability. But sometimes there are crises, and they have to give way. It is hard for me to believe Jim Comey thought this might not be grasped by, say, Mitch McConnell. I don't think Republicans (or seasoned Democrats who understand that what goes around comes around) would have dismissed out of hand the possibility that the Obama administration's investigation was appropriate—despite how notoriously political the Obama administration was. But there would not have been uncritical acceptance. The Gang of Eight would have asked tough questions: What was the predicate for this investigation? Was it serious enough to merit not only a preliminary inquiry but such intrusive measure as FISA warrants and the use of confidential informants to infiltrate a political campaign? And since anyone can make a serious allegation, what was the corroboration for the claim that the Trump campaign was conspiring with the Kremlin?

These are precisely the questions that the FBI and the Justice Department still have not answered three years later. It is one thing to say, as the government does, that these matters are classified and cannot be spoken of publicly. It is quite another thing to withhold information from the congressional entity that has been created to deal with that very complication.

The only sensible conclusion is that the FBI did not disclose what it was doing because it did not want to be put in a position of answering the question: *What is your evidence?*

CIA Director Brennan took the opposite approach. He embraced the Gang of Eight process, albeit in his own political way. It was a way to get explosive information into the hands of hardball politicians—such as Senator Harry Reid, a brass-knuckles pol in the best of times. Recall Reid's false claim that 2012 GOP presidential candidate Mitt Romney had not paid his taxes, then his "justification" of the slander: the observation that Romney lost.[8] Well, in this instance, the now-retired lawmaker was...about to retire—meaning he was untroubled by the usual concerns about blowback for playing political hardball.

And as an artful operator in his own right, Brennan followed the practice of briefing the eight members separately, over nearly a month's time—between August 11 and September 6. With a straight face, he maintains that he "provided the same briefing to each of the Gang of Eight members."[9] We're evidently to believe he gave exactly the same briefing to Reid as he gave to, say, Devin Nunes. We're also to believe that, in a complex, transcontinental investigation, there were no new developments throughout that critical four-week period that would have called for tweaking the briefing. You'll just have to take his word for it.

Let's consider what had to have been communicated to Senator Reid in that briefing.

Shortly after speaking with Brennan, Reid fired off a letter to FBI Director Comey that was bristling with anger.[10] It was now clear to Reid not only that Russia was "tampering in our presidential election," but that "the evidence of a direct connection between the Russian government and Donald Trump's presidential campaign continue[d] to mount." Trump was an "unwitting agent" of the Kremlin, Reid thundered, quoting former Acting CIA Director Michael Morell, a Clinton supporter and Brennan ally (whom we met in Chapter Four's discussion of the administration's Benghazi cover-up). After venting his spleen about the hacked DNC emails, Reid came to the point:

> Further, [t]here have been a *series of disturbing reports* suggesting other methods Russia is using to influence the Trump campaign and manipulate it as a vehicle for advancing the interests of Russian President Vladimir Putin. For example, questions have been raised about whether *a Trump advisor* who has been highly critical of U.S. and European economic sanctions on Russia, and who has conflicts of interest due to investments in Russian energy conglomerate Gazprom, *met with high-ranking sanctioned individuals while in Moscow in July 2016.* [Emphasis added.]

Undoubtedly, the "series of disturbing reports" in question refers to *the dossier reports* then being compiled by Christopher Steele. And among the main allegations Steele was pushing at the time—the same allegation that he stressed in his breakfast meeting with Bruce Ohr and that Ohr, in turn, stressed to FBI officials McCabe and Lisa Page—was Carter Page's purported meetings with "high-ranking sanctioned individuals." Igor Sechin, with whom Steele alleged Carter Page met, was under U.S. sanctions; Igor Divyekin is not known to have been under sanctions, but he was an important (if little known) official in Putin's administration—and Steele had reported, in any event, that Page was surely meeting with other figures in the widely sanctioned regime, too.

This is the information that Brennan was running with. He clearly thought the FBI was being overly cautious—a function of the fact that the Bureau uses court processes and must therefore vet information more carefully than the CIA before using it. Brennan was using pressure from Reid to light a fire under Comey.[11]

The salient point is that Steele's information is what Brennan had. It is the information the CIA director used to brief Congress. There is no reason to believe he had or used different information to brief President Obama, along with other top administration national-security officials, in early August. If Brennan had lines of information from deep inside the Kremlin that were different from the ones Steele purported to have, then the FBI would have used them to verify Steele's information. The Bureau was never able to do that.

Targeting Trump

That is not to say the Bureau didn't try.

The relationship informant Stefan Halper struck up with Carter Page paid quick dividends. Halper was able to monitor Page—not that anyone ever established that Page was doing anything worth monitoring. Plus, Halper induced Page to give him an introduction to Sam Clovis, the Navy vet and GOP activist from the critical presidential primary battleground state of Iowa. Clovis had been quick to hop on the Trump Train, was the campaign's national cochairman, and had been given the influential task of arming the candidate with foreign-policy advisers. As you'll recall by now, his performance was erratic—see, e.g., Page...Papadopoulos...

Given the caliber of help he'd assembled, Clovis had to figure the estimable Dr. Halper was manna from heaven. To be sure, most anyone who browsed his *Silence of the Rational Center* for just a few minutes would pause to wonder what interest Halper would have in advising a populist-nationalist rabble-rouser.[12] Still, Clovis no doubt realized that Trump's political shtick, the wild style and jock-shock rhetoric, belie the brass-tacks fact that he is a fairly conventional, nonideological centrist—more right-of-center now than the New York limousine liberal he was for most of his life. Until recent years, when Trump seized on immigration enforcement as his defining issue, many—myself included—would have pegged him as a Clinton Democrat (indeed, in 2008, Trump pronounced: "I think Bill Clinton was a great president"[13]). If Henry Kissinger finds Donald Trump worth advising, why wouldn't Stef Halper?[14]

After getting Clovis's contact information from Page, Halper sent him a cloying email him in late August 2016:

I am a professor at Cambridge University lecturing on US politics and foreign policy. I am what is called a "scholar practitioner," having served in the White House and four presidential campaigns—two as policy director. Over the past month I have been in conversation with Carter Page who attended our conference in Cambridge on US elections. Carter mentioned in Cambridge, and when visiting here in Virginia, that you and I should meet. I have enjoyed your comments and appearances in the media; you hit the sweet spot focusing Trump's appeal to working America. May I suggest that we set a time to meet when you are next in Washington. Meanwhile, all the best, Stef an Halper.[15]

Within days, the two met up in Virginia. As in his initial contact with Page, the experienced informant ingratiated himself without making any mention of Russia. As Clovis recalls, "There was no indication or no inclination that this was anything other than just wanting to offer up his help to the campaign if I needed it."[16] The Clovis connection gave Halper an entrée into real Trump policy-making circles. In fact, even after Trump won (and the Crossfire Hurricane investigation continued), Halper was invited to advise the White House on China issues—eventually meeting with Peter Navarro, President Trump's chief trade negotiator (who knew Halper from having interviewed him while making a documentary years earlier).[17]

The ill-conceived defense of the Obama administration's deployment of confidential informants (spies) holds that the investigation did not really target Donald Trump or his campaign (and, later, the Trump administration). Rather, the government merely probed a few suspect actors in Trump's orbit (principally, Page, Manafort, Papadopoulos, and Michael Flynn). In this vein, it has been pointed out that the FBI does not appear to have specifically instructed Halper to target Clovis—though it is conceded that the informant alerted his handlers that he was doing so.[18]

This critique misunderstands both informant work and the nature of the investigation. In long-term investigations (as opposed to brief, transactional assignments, such as an undercover drug buy), informants are given general instructions about the objectives of their part of the operation, and then turned loose. In a counterintelligence investigation, where the objective is to gather information about the nature of relationships between people and foreign powers, rather than to collect evidence of crimes, this can be very broad, loose guidance. That is especially so when dealing with an old hand like Halper (who, no doubt, has been at the game much longer than the agents who were handling him). The informant's task is to progress from the initial target (e.g., Page or Papadopoulos) to that target's associates—preferably his superiors (e.g., Clovis and beyond). That is how the probe comes to grasp exactly what is going on, who is involved, what each person's role is, etc. Halper would not have notified the FBI that Page had gotten him to Clovis, and so on, if that progression were not germane to the operation. That is how investigations are supposed to work.

Crossfire Hurricane was an investigation, principally, of Trump. As the Steele dossier so heavily relied on by the Obama administration elucidates, the operating assumption was that Trump personally was enmeshed with the Kremlin. That was the theory pushed by Brennan, whose postelection commentary illustrates that he understood Trump to be a willful, corrupt actor. Whether this was the case, or whether Trump was an unwitting target of Russian-controlled operatives (or whether the suspicions of him were baseless all together), would have been questions the investigation was seeking to answer. Such questions could not have been answered by confining the inquiry to the doings of, say, Carter Page.

Furthermore, as we shall see presently, the FBI viewed the investigation as an "insurance policy." That is, in the unlikely event Trump won the election, the investigation would give the Bureau a vehicle to monitor the new president and limit the damage FBI officers claimed to fear he would otherwise do to their institution and to the country. Clearly, this was not just an investigation of Page or Papadopoulos. It was to be expected that a skilled informant such as Halper would start with them and then go wherever the trail took him—working toward Trump. That is why he pressed Papadopoulos about the Trump campaign, not just about Papadopoulos himself.

Let's consider Halper's interaction with Papadopoulos. It is not difficult to grasp what happened—nor why the FBI, the Justice Department, the CIA, the State Department, and British and Australian authorities are not anxious to discuss the matter or reveal its paper trail.

As we've seen, Alexander Downer, the Australian diplomat, runs in the same British intelligence circles as Halper and Dearlove, which held Trump in the same disdain as did their friends in establishment Washington, such as Senator McCain and the Clintons. After Papadopoulos, in the capacity of a green, young Trump adviser situated in London, intemperately rebuked Prime Minister Cameron in public, Downer arranged to meet him. Trying to impress Downer during their discussion, Papadopoulos made a passing remark that Russia might have damaging information about Clinton. Downer believed Papadopoulos was an airhead and took no action because he thought so little of the remark.

Two months later, when the hacked DNC emails were released by WikiLeaks—which was controlled by Assange from the Ecuadorian embassy in London, to the great dismay of British intelligence—Downer perceived an opportunity to implicate Trump. So he twisted Papadopoulos's remark into something Papadopoulos had not said—a "suggestion" that the Kremlin possessed emails related to Clinton that it would release to help Trump defeat her, possibly with Trump's knowledge. Did Downer distort Papadopoulos's remark based on Assange's public statement in June that WikiLeaks had Clinton-related emails? Did Downer have any way of knowing that Mifsud, also friendly with British intelligence, may have told Papadopoulos Russia had emails? We don't know. We do know that Downer decided to take his distorted version of Papadopoulos's remark to the American embassy in London—an ardently pro-Clinton branch of a State Department that was already receiving reports from

London-based Christopher Steele that Trump and Putin were in a corrupt conspiracy involving the publication of hacked DNC emails.

The State Department routed Downer's information to the FBI, whose headquarters was inclined to believe the worst about Trump. The Bureau was also receiving Steele's reporting, and it was being pushed hard by the CIA (which had the ear of the president) on the theory that the publication of the hacked DNC emails was Exhibit A of Putin's scheme to get Trump elected—a scheme in which, by Brennan's lights," Trump was probably complicit. The Bureau immediately opened a formal investigation of Trump's campaign. Negotiations quickly ensued between the Obama State Department and the Australian government to allow the FBI to breach diplomatic protocol and interview Downer as a witness—with the cooperation of the British government, the host country for the interview. The Bureau dispatched its top counterintelligence agent, the virulently anti-Trump Peter Strzok, to interview Downer. The diplomat related his exaggerated "what Papadopoulos's comments suggested to me" version, which Strzok—having studied his Josh Marshall—was ripe to internalize as evidence of a Trump–Russia conspiracy involving stolen Democratic emails.

Strzok brought this information back to his superiors, including Deputy Director Andrew McCabe, who assumed hands-on control of the case, and who was now being briefed by Justice Department official Bruce Ohr about Steele's allegations. With the cooperation of the British government and the CIA, the Bureau decided to use the Cambridge-based, longtime CIA and FBI informant Halper, who had already made contact with Page and Clovis, to run an operation at Papadopoulos. The objective would be to get Papadopoulos to implicate the Trump campaign—and perhaps even Trump himself—in the scheme to influence the election by illegally hacking and disseminating Democratic emails, a scheme in which Trump's coconspirators were imagined to be the Putin regime and WikiLeaks.

This was an ambitious investigation, so the FBI did not leave it to Halper alone. Another operative was assigned: an attractive woman who goes by the name Azra Turk. This is probably a pseudonym, but because she is a covert asset who may well be involved in other undercover operations (past and/or ongoing), we have confirmation at this time neither of her name nor her status—she has been publicly described as "a government investigator," but it is not known whether the "government" in question is the U.S. government, or for what agency she is an investigator.[19]

The FBI and other government intelligence agencies have tried to keep the name and any photographs of "Azra Turk" out of news reporting. They were similarly protective of Halper when his role emerged. This is entirely appropriate. We need people willing to do the often dangerous work of covert intelligence operations in order to protect the United States. We will not find willing people if the government becomes notorious for failing to safeguard their identities, endangering them and their loved ones. Nevertheless, the indignant anger over questions about the Crossfire Hurricane undercover operations displayed by current and former government officials is misplaced.

There are many crucial public interests at stake in this controversy, including the right of the American people to govern themselves through election processes kept free of tampering by the incumbent government. It is remarkable that commentators who rightly worry about external interference in our campaigns by foreign powers are insouciant regarding the dire threat of internal interference by government officials. The latter threat is more insidious: Foreign meddling is apt to be presumed adversarial, so we are on guard. U.S. officials, by contrast, act under the color of legal authority and we generally presume their good faith. They are in a position to do more damage (which, by the way, is exactly the reasoning of critics who argue that Trump's transgressions against presidential norms are dangerously destabilizing).

This insouciance, moreover, is blatantly partisan. The media–Democrat complex is quick to assume that Republican administrations will abuse their intelligence and law-enforcement powers for partisan ends. When it comes, however, to the potentially abusive actions of Democratic administrations, any questioning or call for examination of patently suspect decisions, such as the decision to investigate the opposition political campaign, is limned as a reckless attack on our institutions and the rule of law itself.

With the charge of recklessness, the shoe should be on the other foot. If our law-enforcement and intelligence agencies do not want inquiries into their use of informants and other spying tactics, *then they need to use them judiciously.*

As a former prosecutor, I can assure you that there are many things prosecutors are permitted by law to do but which are not done in the vast majority of cases because, if applied, they would be seen as overkill. In most cases, it is not necessary, for example, to break a company with subpoenas and indictments; to charge trifling crimes against the wives or children of a suspect; to demand fee information or other testimony from a suspect's lawyer; to subpoena a journalist in order to identify a source. The law might allow such things to be done, but in most situations, the public would rightly see them as abuses of power. The authority to take extreme measures exists because there is the rare, extraordinary case in which doing so might be appropriate and necessary—in which a factual predicate justifies drastic investigative tactics. But before such tactics are used, good investigators have a thoughtful discussion along the lines of "Are we going to be able to defend this?"

In this country, it is the public's right (and a properly functioning media's responsibility) to question government officials' use of the powers we entrust to them. That means the onus is on government investigators to consider beforehand whether the tactics they contemplate using are appropriate. They should not be heard, after the fact, to complain, "How dare you ask me that?" And obviously: If they had a sound reason, grounded in real evidence, for suspecting a presidential candidate was in a corrupt conspiracy with a foreign power, they should not only be able to tell us what it is; they should be *anxious* to tell us what it is.

Papadopoulos: Carrots and Sticks

Pursuant to the FBI's direction, Halper on September 2, 2016, sent Papadopoulos an unsolicited email, offering him a $3,000 honorarium to write a policy paper on a Mediterranean natural-gas project involving Turkey, Israel, and Cyprus—ingratiatingly pitched as Papadopoulos's area of expertise. The young Trump adviser was then in the United States, but the Cambridge professor offered to fly him to London and lodge him, all at Halper's expense, for academic discussions on the subject. Papadopoulos accepted the offer.

As this book goes to press, the Obama administration's decision to use informants is under scrutiny by the Justice Department's inspector general and prosecutors. Trying to get out in front of those inquiries, unidentified "people familiar with the F.B.I. activities of Mr. Halper, Ms. Turk, and the inspector general's investigation" described those activities to *The New York Times*. Tellingly, they explained that Ms. Turk, a well-trained investigator, was assigned to provide "a layer of oversight" for Halper, and because she would be able to "*serve as a credible witness in any potential prosecution that emerged from the case*" (emphasis added). This underscores a major and abusive flaw of the Trump–Russia investigation: In the absence of a solid factual predicate for a criminal investigation, foreign-counterintelligence powers were used as a pretext to dig for criminal evidence that would support a hoped-for prosecution.

Just as telling is what Turk said to Papadopoulos when they first met in a London bar on September 15. Posing as Halper's research assistant, Turk buzzed the adviser with a direct question: Was *the Trump campaign* working with Russia? Not "Was Papadopoulos working with Russia?" Not "Do you know whether your fellow Trump adviser Carter Page is working with Russia?" The investigative theory here was the theory of the Steele dossier, the theory of John Brennan, the theory that Downer and the State Department conveyed to the FBI: *The campaign run by Donald Trump was scheming with Russia.*

Turk texted Papadopoulos as soon as he arrived in London, to invite him for drinks. Clearly, the fact that Turk is alluring and was quick to be social was meant to beguile Papadopoulos—to put him at ease to discuss incriminating topics he might otherwise be unwilling to touch on. In the end, Turk sent Papadopoulos emails saying that meeting him had been the "highlight of my trip" and gushing, "I am excited about what the future holds for us :)"—the smiley-face symbol accentuating the point. An unidentified source told The Daily Caller's Chuck Ross that Turk flirted heavily with Papadopoulos and later attempted (apparently unsuccessfully) to meet Papadopoulos in Chicago, where he lives.[20]

Papadopoulos, however, had nothing to give Turk and Halper. His first London meeting, in the cozy bar, was with Turk alone. Her bracing questions about the Trump campaign and Russia got nowhere. The following day, Papadopoulos met Halper at a private club in London, with Turk joining the conversation. It appears that this was just a get-to-know-each-other session. But Papadopoulos and Halper agreed to meet again the next day for drinks at the Sofitel hotel on the West End, sans Turk. This time, Halper jumped right in, asking Papadopoulos loaded questions about the hacked emails and how exactly Russia was helping the Trump campaign. As later described by Papadopoulos, they were the inculpatory questions an informant would typically ask a suspect he was covertly recording, along the lines of: "So George, hacking is in the interest of your campaign. Of course the Russians are helping you…and of course you're probably involved in it, too. That's correct, right George?" Papadopoulos says he was livid at Halper's insinuations, telling him, "I have no idea what you're talking about." Papadopoulos recalls it as an unpleasant conversation, with the older man sweating in the role of aggressive interrogator. The Trump adviser claims to have ended the meeting abruptly and angrily.

I have my doubts about how angry he could have been: Papadopoulos did write the paper for Halper, deliver it as requested in October, and collect the $3,000.[21]

It is worth observing here that the FBI would not undertake such an undercover operation in London without the blessing of British authorities. The *Times* suggestively notes that "British intelligence officials were also notified about the operation, the people familiar with the operation said, but it was unclear whether they provided assistance." What is clear is that the venture was a bust. The paper's sources conceded, "The London operation yielded no fruitful information."[22] If I may translate, in the Obama administration's Trump–Russia parlance, "fruitful" only means "incriminating."

Were Halper and Turk the only covert operatives the government deployed against Papadopoulos? We don't know. Papadopoulos recounts that, "out of the blue," he was contacted on LinkedIn by none other than Sergey Millian. The outreach occurred on July 22, the day the hacked DNC emails started being published and about a week before the FBI opened the Crossfire Hurricane probe.

As we've seen, Millian has a history of overhyping his ties to Donald Trump. He struck up a relationship with Papadopoulos, online and in a few in-person meetings. Millian claimed to be working with Trump on real-estate ventures, and to have a professional tie to Bashneft, a Russian energy company. In October, the two met at the bar in the

Trump International Hotel in Chicago. Papadopoulos says Millian made "some sort of shady business proposal," in which Papadopoulos would be paid $30,000 per month as a media consultant for the energy firm, but he would be required, simultaneously, to continue working for Trump. Papadopoulos says he smelled a rat and rejected the offer.

Yet he continued to email and meet with Millian. In October, Papadopoulos was booted from the campaign for making ill-advised comments to the Russian press.[23] But at the inauguration festivities after Trump was elected, Papadopoulos ran into Millian, who was accompanied by his music producer friend, Aziz Choukri. According to Papadopoulos, Millian had been meeting with Senator John McCain and other lawmakers. When they met later for cocktails, Papadopoulos claims Choukri blurted out, "Oh, you know, Sergey is working for the FBI," as Millian looked on sheepishly. Choukri denies the story. While Papadopoulos now says he suspected Millian was an informant, two unidentified sources said to be "familiar with the FBI's Russia investigation" told *The Washington Post* that Millian was not working for the Bureau—at least during his interactions with Papadopoulos.[24]

Millian, meanwhile, is apparently out of the country, and Special Counsel Mueller's staff claimed to be unable to interview him.[25] This leads to another unseemly episode of prosecutorial innuendo: As with Trump and Page, Mueller claims Papadopoulos cannot be exonerated because his behavior could not be fully evaluated—Mueller was frustrated by Millian's unavailability. To repeat, it is not an American's burden to establish his innocence; it is the prosecutor's burden to prove guilt or, if the prosecutor cannot, to remain silent rather than to smear. Here, the fact is that Mueller had as much access to Papadopoulos as he could have wanted, in addition to two years to investigate him, during which numerous witnesses were interviewed. All Mueller could come up with was a false statement about the date of a meeting.

Papadopoulos is not a straight shooter. You may have noticed that this book takes his assertions with a grain of salt, and there are a few allusions in the endnotes to his "Deep State" memoir. That said, the heavy-handedness of his prosecution is something to behold.

The FBI formally began interviewing Papadopoulos in January 2017. They never had evidence of a serious crime. Mueller's staff knew Papadopoulos was represented by counsel, and they could thus have arranged to meet with him at their offices at any point. Instead, they waited until the night of July 27, 2017, when Papadopoulos, then twenty-nine years old, landed in the United States on a flight from Germany. If there was an arrest warrant for Papadopoulos at the time, it has never been publicly released. Of course, police do not need a warrant if they have probable cause to make an arrest, but that generally applies to a situation in which they observe a crime being committed and need to intervene lest the suspect flees. Here, the probable cause involved a false statement made months before. There was no legitimate reason to arrest Papadopoulos in this manner. Mueller could have contacted his attorneys and had him surrender at court for processing and a bail hearing. If the point was to get Papadopoulos's attention, that would have more than done the trick.

By arresting him at the airport at night—i.e., after the court was closed—prosecutors ensured that Papadopoulos would be shocked, scared, and imprisoned for the night. FBI agents grabbed him as soon as he stepped off his flight in Virginia at about 7 p.m. He could not lawfully have been questioned since prosecutors knew he had retained lawyers. But they also knew those lawyers were in Chicago, so Papadopoulos would not be able to see them—he was permitted to speak to them by phone that night. Records indicate he was not booked at the city detention center in Alexandria until about seven hours later, at 1:45 a.m. That this was a blatant intimidation tactic is shown by what happened in court the next day: Papadopoulos was released on his own recognizance—no posting of bail required. If there was no need for prosecutors to seek a bail package as a hedge against flight, then there was no reason to arrest Papadopoulos in the first place. They did it because they could. They did it as a message that this was just a taste of what was in store for Papadopoulos if he refused to cooperate—which, of course, he did, though to what good end is not clear since there appears to have been no conspiracy his cooperation would have helped uncover.[26]

That's worth keeping in mind when investigators and their backers become indignant at the suggestion that they might occasionally use their awesome powers abusively.

CHAPTER THIRTEEN

Amateur Hour

s the FBI and intelligence agencies feverishly hunted down Trump–Russia connections, the Trump campaign made sure they would eventually have some to find— and made matters worse by acting guilty. The Trump campaign's actions were legal, even if their revelation could have been politically damaging. The president's dissembling was a gift to his detractors.

Shortly before being inaugurated, President-elect Trump tweeted, "I HAVE NOTHING TO DO WITH RUSSIA—NO DEALS, NO LOANS, NOTH-ING!" He was more expansive at a press conference, claiming that his business dealings with Russians were limited to "selling condos" and one big real-estate deal in Florida, in which he sold to a Russian oligarch for about $100 million a mansion he'd purchased for about $40 million.[1]

The president-elect seemed oblivious to the fact that his foes would not accept this as further evidence of his "art of the deal" savvy, but as a $60 million Russian payoff. But that would be the least of the problem. More consequential was the adamant claim of no business dealings with Russia.

It wasn't true.

Trump Tower Moscow

For years, Trump and his organization had been enticed by the concept of a Trump Tower in Moscow. The idea picked up steam in 2013, when Trump hosted the Miss Universe pageant in the Russian capital. By late 2015, as Trump emerged as a serious candidate for the presidency, the negotiations were gaining traction. Trump's point man on the project was Michael Cohen, a Trump Organization attorney notable not so much for legal acumen but for his brass-knuckles style and loyalty to the boss.[2]

On January 20, 2016, Cohen had an extensive telephone conversation with the personal assistant of Vladimir Putin's press secretary, Dmitry Peskov. As the eventual criminal charges against Cohen would spell out, the presidential candidate's lawyer outlined the Moscow project, including a description of "the Russian development company with which the [Trump] company had partnered." Cohen asked for the Kremlin's help "in moving the project forward, both in securing land to build the proposed tower and financing the construction."[3]

Cohen had been referred to Peskov by Donald Trump's friend Felix Sater, who is an interesting character to say the least. Born in Moscow, Sater is a former business partner of Trump's, having been the managing director of Bayrock Group, a real-estate conglomerate involved in the construction of the Trump SoHo building in Manhattan. Sater is also a convicted racketeer and a former (we assume it's former) government informant.[4] He often boasted of ties to Putin. For example, referring to the Trump Tower Moscow project, Sater told Cohen in a November 3, 2015, email:

> Michael[,] I arranged for [Donald Trump's daughter] Ivanka to sit in Putins [sic] private chair at his desk and office in the Kremlin. I will get Putin on this program and we will get Donald elected. We both know no one else knows how to pull this off without stupidity or greed getting in the way. I know how to play it and we will get this done. Buddy our boy can become President of the USA and we can engineer it. I will get all of Putins [sic] team to buy in on this.

Sater served as an intermediary between The Trump Organization and the Kremlin on the Moscow project. On January 21, the day after Cohen spoke with the Kremlin press official, Sater sent Cohen a message asking him to call: "It's about Putin. They called today."

In the ensuing months, the Moscow project was discussed several times within the Trump company. Cohen separately talked with Trump and

Sater about the likelihood that Trump would travel to Russia in connection with the project, potentially to meet in person with Putin. On May 4, Sater sent a message to Cohen explaining that he "had a chat with Moscow," and that while Cohen could come to Russia for a "pre-meeting trip" at any time, they needed to address whether a potential Trump trip—for a meeting of "the 2 big guys"—would happen "before or after the [Republican] convention" in Cleveland. Cohen responded, "My trip before Cleveland. [Trump's trip] once he becomes the nominee after the convention."

The next day, Sater told Cohen that Putin's press secretary was extending an invitation for Cohen to be his personal guest at "the St. Petersburg Forum which is Russia's Davos," from June 16–19. There was also this carrot: Cohen would get to meet with one or both of Putin and Dmitry Medvedev.[5] Sater emphasized that such meetings would not be limited in scope to the Moscow project— "anything you want to discuss including dates and subjects are on the table."

Cohen quickly agreed to come to St. Petersburg. But on June 14, just two days before the forum, he abruptly told Sater he was pulling out.

This timing, along with Cohen's gruff manner in aborting the trip to Russia for a potential meeting with Putin, is fascinating. On June 14, Cohen met with Sater "in the lobby" of Trump Tower—i.e., he wouldn't even bring Sater up to the office. Succinctly, Cohen told his friend that he would not be making the trip to Russia "at that time." Notably, the brush-off had actually started on June 9. That's when Sater began sending "numerous messages to Cohen about the trip, including travel forms for Cohen to complete." But beginning June 9, Cohen cut Sater off, wanting nothing to do with Russia.

So what was going on that so abruptly suspended Trump Tower Moscow? I suspect it had a lot to do with what was going on in Trump Tower Manhattan.

The Trump Tower Meeting

June 9, 2016, was the day the hurtling Trump campaign's amateurish ways caught up with it, the day its top officials allowed Donald

Trump to be had by Vladimir Putin. The campaign was duped into participating in a Russian lobbying session—with the potential that Donald Trump could be compromised if Putin decided to publicize the meeting and spin it as he saw fit.

The Trumps were neither political people nor old intel hands schooled in the wiles of Russian influence operations. They were winging this. The New York real-estate world from which they come is cutthroat and mobbed up, but it is a world where personal relationships count. Donald Trump supposed that he had struck up such a relationship with Aras Agalarov, a Russian real-estate tycoon sometimes referred to as the "Trump of Russia" because he self-brands his buildings. In 2013, he was Trump's partner and host when the New York magnate brought the Miss Universe pageant to Moscow. Back then, Agalarov was already being quoted in state-run media about his Crocus Group conglomerate's negotiations to become Trump's partner in developing a Trump Tower in the Russian capital.[6]

You'll not be surprised to hear that Agalarov has close ties to Putin and the regime—having such ties being how you get to become and remain a billionaire in the industries of a ruthless dictatorship that poses as a free-market democracy. Russia's oligarchs no doubt have some close personal relationships with colleagues and peers, but they never forget where their loyalties lie.

Agalarov has a pop-star son, Emin, whose British publicist, Rob Goldstone, was also friendly with the Trump family. On June 3, 2016, Goldstone emailed Donald Trump's oldest son with a proposition from the Agalarovs. Don Jr., then thirty-eight, had been groomed to lead the family business; now he was trying his hand at politics in a national presidential campaign—a feat akin to promoting your high school's second-line starter to triple-A so he can get ready to pitch for the Yankees next week. Goldstone claimed that Russia's chief prosecutor had just met with Aras Agalarov and "offered to provide the Trump campaign with some official documents and information that would incriminate Hillary and her dealings with Russia and would be very useful to your father." Goldstone stressed that this was "obviously very high level and sensitive information but is part of Russia and its government's support for Mr. Trump—helped along by Aras and Emin."

Minutes later, Don Jr. emailed back, telling Goldstone, "if it's what you say I love it especially later in the summer." By the late summer, of course, the campaign stretch-run would be on. An explosive revelation against Mrs. Clinton at that point could tilt the race in Trump's favor. Don Jr. agreed to speak directly with Emin Agalarov to work out the logistics of transferring the information.

It turns out that this information was not actually a file from the chief Russian prosecutor. We might think of it, instead, as the second Fusion GPS dossier.[7]

As we've already observed, while Glenn Simpson, Chris Steele, and the Fusion gang were (as they'd have you believe) heroically working against the Putin regime's plot to install a Kremlin stooge in the White House, they were also not so heroically working *for* Putin's regime by scheming to undermine whistleblowers who were risking their lives to expose Moscow's corruption. Naturally, Simpson wouldn't want to look at it that way. He'd tell you Fusion was merely doing litigation research for a law firm that was defending a client. But that client was Prevezon Holdings, a Cyprus-based investment company controlled by Denis Katsyv, the son of Pyotr Katsyv, a powerful Putin crony who runs the regime's national railroad system.

In 2013, Prevezon was sued by the Justice Department in an asset-forfeiture action focused on breathtaking Kremlin fraud and brutality.[8] It arose out of a $230 million swindle orchestrated by the Putin regime, which later involved the detention, torture, and murder of Sergey Magnitsky, who exposed the scheme. The Justice Department's lawsuit dealt specifically with the regime's fleecing of an investment fund called Hermitage. Years earlier, Hermitage's chief executive officer, Bill Browder, retained Magnitsky, an auditor at a Moscow law firm, to investigate the Russian government's role in the fraud. It was this investigative accounting that led to Magnitsky's brutal killing. Outrage over that atrocity induced Congress to pass the 2012 Magnitsky Act—reluctantly signed by President Obama, after his administration tried to derail its passage, which threatened to complicate the Russia Reset then being steered by Secretary of State Clinton.[9] The act enables the federal government to seize and forfeit fraud proceeds. That hits Putin's kleptocracy where it lives, and thus has provoked a furious Kremlin campaign to get the Magnitsky Act repealed. A key component of that campaign is the smearing of Bill Browder.

The repeal effort has been spearheaded by the Russian lawyer Natalia Veselnitskaya, with Glenn Simpson and Fusion providing valuable assistance on the Browder front.

It was the Magnitsky Act that the Justice Department used to sue Prevezon. Veselnitskaya is Prevezon's lawyer in Moscow, and she helped the company retain American counsel to defend them in the suit—a lawyer ironically named John Moscow and his firm, Baker Hostetler. These lawyers, in turn, hired Fusion GPS to do research on Browder and Hermitage for litigation purposes. Veselnitskaya was ultimately indicted for obstructing justice in the case, based on her collaboration with the Russian government in providing the court an official document purporting to exonerate Putin-regime operatives and Prevezon.[10]

As became painfully evident during Simpson's congressional testimony, while he poses as the gold standard of objectivity, his outrage is selective and powerfully influenced by whoever happens to be paying him. He made it his business, in the Prevezon case and various other forums, to abominate Browder. But what about the Kremlin that has a target on Browder's back?[11] What about Putin's pals the Katsyvs? What about the shady regime-tied lawyer Veselnitskaya? All Simpson could say in his testimony was that he assumed his paying clients were good upstanding people since they were being represented by a respected U.S. law firm, and that Veselnitskaya seemed like a smart, ambitious lawyer. But, gee whiz, Simpson wouldn't be able to tell you more than that because she only speaks Russian, and Simpson doesn't—the Russia expert helping represent a Russian business says he has no idea what the Russian lawyer might have been jabbering about at their meetings.[12]

Fusion was doing the anti-Browder research for Putin's cronies at the same time it was doing the Trump–Putin research for the Clinton campaign.[13] Unfortunately, such projects have a way of crashing into each other. The Browder examination turned up the nugget that the billionaire Ziff family invests with Browder. Ziff Brothers Investments also backs the Clinton Global Initiative (a project of the Clinton Foundation), the Democratic party, and various Democratic candidates. Because of their ties to Browder (and the low bar for accusing those who cross the regime), Russia decided that the Ziff brothers' income involves Russian tax and fraud violations.[14]

Laughably, this was the "very high level and sensitive information" that was hyped to Don Trump Jr. as certain to "incriminate Hillary Clinton."

Even as Putin's regime steers its country into steep decline, we tend to imagine the Russians are both ten feet tall and ten moves ahead on the chessboard. They're not. It is surely possible that, with no experience in the electoral politics of a free society, the Russians did not grasp American campaigns well enough to appreciate that alleged misconduct by donors, even if the allegation were colorable, would not damage a candidate as long as the candidate was not complicit. Maybe someone in the regime really believed this Ziff–Browder stuff was dynamite campaign dirt.

Far more likely, though, was that the offer of information to Don Trump Jr. was a pretext and a lure. The Kremlin is fixated on Browder and on reversing the Magnitsky Act. By conning Don Jr. into taking a meeting, the Russians could kill two birds with one stone. First, they could lobby the Trump campaign's top echelon against the Magnitsky Act (just as they have been lobbying anyone in Washington who would listen). Second, Putin would gain leverage over Trump: By agreeing to meet a Kremlin emissary on the promise of receiving damaging information about Clinton, the Trump campaign made its principal vulnerable—at a time advantageous to Russia, Putin could threaten to expose the meeting, which would damage Trump politically. (Indeed, the exposure of the meeting—not by Putin but by *The New York Times*'s impressive investigative journalism—has done exactly that.[15])

'Waste of Time'

Veselnitskaya was chosen to be the regime's emissary to meet with Don Jr. on June 9. She was coming to the United States from Moscow for a hearing in the Prevezon case that morning, in the Second Circuit U.S. Court of Appeals in Manhattan. And wouldn't you know it: She met with Glenn Simpson both before and after the Trump Tower meeting—which meetings, Simpson is certain, had absolutely nothing to do with the Trump Tower session at which Veselnitskaya used Fusion's anti-Browder research... although Simpson did concede that he understood from Denis Katsyv's U.S. lawyers that the information he'd unearthed would be provided to Veselnitskaya if "it was useful and interesting to her."[16]

For its part, the Russian side seems to have understood that the Browder–Ziff information (i.e., the Hillary dirt) was useless. Despite the signals sent to Don Jr. about the purpose of the meeting, Aras Agalarov called his United States–based Crocus employee, Ike Kavaladze, on June 6, instructing him to attend a meeting with The Trump Organization that would concern the Magnitsky Act. Kavaladze was to act as Veselnitskaya's translator. To prepare him, Agalarov quizzed him about the Magnitsky Act and sent him a short synopsis for the meeting, as well as Veselnitskaya's business card.[17]

After the Second Circuit hearing on the morning of June 9, Veselnitskaya convened a lunch in Manhattan to get ready for the Trump Tower meeting that afternoon. She invited Rinat Akhmetshin, a slick, Soviet-born American biochemist and lobbyist with longstanding ties to the Russian military and intelligence services. Akhmetshin had worked on behalf of Putin cronies; in fact, he was working for the Katsyvs in the Prevezon case, just like Veselnitskaya and Simpson. He had also helped Veselnitskaya with anti–Magnitsky Act lobbying initiatives.[18] There has also been plausible hypothesizing (mainly by Lee Smith) that Akhmetshin is one of Christopher Steele's sources, but this is no more confirmed than most anything else about the Steele dossier.[19] In any event, Veselnitskaya also invited Kavaladze to the lunch, as well as Anatoli Samochornov, another Russian translator who worked on both the Prevezon case and the anti-Magnitsky lobbying. At the lunch, Veselnitskaya showed Akhmetshin a document alleging that Browder and the Ziff brothers had engaged in financial misconduct and later made donations to the DNC.[20]

From lunch, this group of four Russians (Veselnitskaya, Akhmetshin, Kavaladze, and Samochornov), along with Rob Goldstone, made their way to Trump Tower. There, they met in the Trump offices with Don Trump Jr., Jared Kushner (the now-president's son-in-law and adviser), and Paul Manafort, then the campaign manager. The meeting was a dud. After Don Jr. invited Veselnitskaya to begin her presentation, she alleged that the Ziff brothers had violated Russian law, earning profits which had then been donated to the DNC or the Clinton campaign, suggesting they could be convicted of tax evasion and money laundering under American and Russian law. But when Don Jr. asked a few basic questions, such as how any of these funds could be traced to the Clinton campaign, Veselnitskaya replied that she had no idea, since she could not say what became of the money once it entered the United States.

Kushner became visibly irritated, asking, "What are we doing here?" He texted Manafort that the meeting was a "waste of time" and emailed his Kushner Companies subordinates to ring him so he'd have an excuse to leave—which he did on cue. Meantime, Akhmetshin and Veselnitskaya pivoted to their opposition to Russia's Magnitsky Act, which had prompted Putin, in retaliation, to ban U.S. adoptions of Russian children. Apparently realizing that the promise of campaign dirt had just been a way for Russian lobbyists to get in the door, Trump Jr. curtly explained that his father, as a private citizen, was in no position to address the Magnitsky issue; perhaps, they could revisit it if Trump was elected. The meeting broke up after just twenty minutes, with Goldstone apologizing to Don Jr. for its futility.[21]

Again, it was on the date of this failed confab that then–Trump Organization lawyer Michael Cohen began blowing off Felix Sater's requests that Cohen complete the final preparations for the Russia trip. Despite Cohen's patent enthusiasm for it just a few days earlier, the trip was canceled. Surely, it had dawned on the campaign that the Kremlin could be working to compromise Donald Trump.

As Special Counsel Mueller concluded, there is insufficient evidence to conclude that Donald Trump was informed about the
Trump Tower meeting.[22] To my mind, this is largely beside the
point; it would be ridiculous to suggest that Don Jr. would have
gone forward with plan to get campaign dirt on Clinton from
Russia unless he believed his father would approve. Like many
things in electoral politics, this was icky but there was nothing
illegal about it. The hysteria over the fact that Trump would take
oppo from foreign sources, including adversary governments, is
especially rich given that, at that very moment, Hillary Clinton's
campaign was paying for a foreign former spy to obtain oppo
on Trump from Kremlin sources—while simultaneously tapping
Ukrainian government sources for oppo, which was deployed to
rock the Trump campaign and force Manafort's ouster.

By the late spring of 2016, Trump's favorable comments about Putin
and his selection of Russia sympathizer Carter Page as a foreign-
policy adviser were already turning Russia into a campaign issue,
exploited by Hillary Clinton and fretted over by Trump skeptics
and opponents in Republican circles. Obviously, it would have
been politically damaging had it been publicly revealed that the
Trump campaign, at its top level, met with a Kremlin-tied lawyer
in hopes of scoring campaign dirt. Moreover, it would have been
politically damaging had it been revealed that Trump's organization was in serious negotiations to build Trump Tower Moscow.
Not only would that have put the lie to the candidate's insistence
that he had no business of consequence in Russia; it would have
suggested that Trump expected to lose the election and was laying
the groundwork to dive back into his real-estate business.

Ironically, these episodes were unknown to the FBI when they
occurred. The Bureau, busy scouring Britain for Trump–Russia
evidence, missed what was happening under its nose in New York
City—even though Veselnitskaya was deeply involved in a Justice Department lawsuit, was working for the Putin regime and
meeting with likely regime operatives, and needed the federal government's permission to travel to the United States. Nevertheless,
Trump Tower Moscow and the Trump Tower meeting in Manhat-

tan would become major staples of the collusion narrative. They dogged Trump for two years of his presidency and gave the special counsel a rationale to continue the investigation—despite the dearth of evidence that Trump was in an espionage conspiracy with Putin—because Trump and his subordinates made matters incalculably worse by lying about them.

Michael Cohen perjured himself before Congress, telling lawmakers the Trump Tower Moscow deal had petered out in January 2016, when in fact negotiations continued throughout that year, while Trump ran for the presidency.

When *The New York Times* discovered the Trump Tower meeting, President Trump directed the release of a statement, attributed to Don Jr., which created the false impression that the meeting had been about an issue concerning "the adoption of Russian children"—i.e., the fallout of the Magnitsky Act. The president overruled his advisers, particularly Hope Hicks, who had implored him to permit the release of the emails and get out in front of the potential eruption. Only when Don Jr. learned that the *Times* had and was about to publish his emails, showing that he took the meeting on the expectation of getting damaging information against Mrs. Clinton, did he admit that this was a purpose of his sit-down with Veselnitskaya.[23] At that point, the president changed his tune, rationalizing that there was nothing wrong with a campaign's accepting opposition research (which was true, but a little late in the day). The president, his lawyers, and his advisers also hemmed and hawed about whether he had dictated the misleading statement that had been put out in his son's name—until the president waived off the question as "irrelevant" because lying to the media (and, by extension, to the public) is not a crime. As he put it, "It's a statement to *The New York Times.* ... That's not a statement to a high tribunal of judges."[24] In the interim, some Trump apologists veered between claiming that Veselnitskaya was not a Kremlin emissary and claiming that she had been steered to Trump Tower by the Obama Justice Department—both absurd contentions.[25]

These missteps were part of a larger pattern. Donald Trump was the main target of the fraudulent collusion narrative, but his instinct to issue false denials was reliable fuel for the collusion fire. Not for nothing is he often called his own worst enemy—which, for a guy with lots of enemies, is saying something.

CHAPTER FOURTEEN

Insurance Policy

"OMG I CANNOT BELIEVE WE ARE SERIOUSLY LOOKING AT THESE ALLEGATIONS AND THE PERVASIVE CONNEC-TIONS." Peter Strzok was aghast, and this hysterical text he sent to Lisa Page on August 11, 2016, showed it. Like John Brennan, Victoria Nuland, and Bruce Ohr, they were dumbfounded by Chris Steele's allegations. And fully inclined to believe them.

And the pressure was on not just to believe them *but to do something about them.* The 2016 election was just three months away.

There was never a Russia-gate moment when the electoral clock was not ticking, loudly enough to have everyone's attention. How badly had Clinton been damaged by one investigation, and could Trump be stopped by the other? That was implicitly clear on July 5, when Director Comey publicly exonerated Hillary Clinton in Washington while, on the same day in London, Agent Michael Gaeta conducted the FBI's first Russia-gate interview of Steele. It had been explicitly clear two months earlier, on May 4, when Page alerted Strzok that Senator Ted Cruz had just dropped out of the Republican primary race, ensuring that Donald Trump would be the nominee. After digitally blurting out "What?!?!??[,]" Strzok's very first reaction was: "Now the pressure really starts to finish MYE"—Mid Year Exam...the Clinton-emails investigation.

The political calendar always hovered, and the cases were always two sides of the same coin—which came up Clinton every time.

In hindsight, from the Trump perspective at least, the fact that Clinton was going to be elected president—and it was a *fact* as far as the investigators were concerned—had a salutary effect on the FBI. The Bureau did not *want* to be thrust into the politics of the 2016 election. Don't confound any objections to the way the FBI handled things with an FBI *desire to handle things.* Out of 330 million Americans, the public narrowed the contest for the nation's highest office to two extraordinarily flawed candidates. That was not the Bureau's call. To be sure, it certainly seems that whenever there was a choice to be made between quietly going about its business or thrusting itself into the limelight, Jim Comey's FBI jumped out front. Still, this was not prearranged: with Clinton in particular, a no-win investigation was the hand that was dealt, and the FBI had to play it. As for Trump, while it is manifest that headquarters believed him unfit for office, this did not mean—as the caricature has it—that FBI officials were Hillary devotees, except in the default sense that an election is a binary choice and somebody has to win.[1]

Undeniably, there was bias against Trump. Just three days before Strzok's "OMG" outburst about the supposedly "pervasive connections" between Trump and the Kremlin, Page was the hysterical one:

> "He's not ever going to become president, right? Right?!"
> "No. No he won't," Strzok replied. "We'll stop it."

It cannot have been lost on these experienced investigators how paltry was the evidence against Trump. But they were out of practice: the criminal case against Clinton was not going to be charged no matter how much evidence there was; and the Trump probe was shoved into the shadows of counterintelligence, where corners are cut because everyone knows there will be no adversarial court proceedings. That made it easy to believe Chris Steele, a well-regarded, heart-in-the-right-place former colleague, who saw Trump as they saw Trump. Who needs more corroboration than that? That is what Comey told the Senate Judiciary Committee when pressed on this point:

> When asked at the March 2017 briefing why the FBI relied on the dossier in FISA applications absent meaningful corroboration—and in light of the highly political motives surrounding its creation—then-Director Comey stated that the FBI included the dossier allegations about Carter Page in the FISA applications because Mr. Steele himself was considered reliable due to his past work.[2]

They believed Steele, so they believed the Russians had finally reeled in Carter Page after years of trying. They believed Alexander Downer's subjective impressions of what George Papadopoulos's barroom comments "suggested." It sounded consistent with Steele's claims, so who cared that Downer's suggestion did not accurately reflect what Papadopoulos had actually said, or that Steele's claims couldn't be proved? Everything was classified, the Gang of Eight was not going to be told about any Trump investigation until after the election—which Clinton was going to win anyway.

People do not think this way when they know they have to be able to prove things to a jury. When I was a prosecutor, I believed a lot of bad things that investigators and sources I trusted told me. But professionally, you never, ever forget that there are legal burdens of proof and rules of admissible evidence. You get judged by whether you've met them. And if for some reason you do forget, your headquarters is there to remind you.

Unless, of course, you *are* headquarters and there is no backstop to save you from what happens to all institutions, no matter how venerable, when there are no rules and no supervision.

The unabashed blatancy of the bias against Trump is why I believe the Justice Department Inspector General was wrong to conclude that this bias could not be deemed causative of any particular investigative decision in the Clinton-emails case.[3] Still, the practical effects of FBI bias against Trump were more in evidence after the election than before. Everyone was extremely confident that Mrs. Clinton would win, so before November 8, they exhibited a circumspection that disappeared afterwards.

Public Criminal Investigation v. Classified Counterintelligence Probe

It is this conceit that Clinton was a shoo-in, and not anti-Clinton bias, that explains why the FBI was appropriately mum regarding the Trump probe, despite being very public in many of its Clinton probe actions. Democrats and their media allies ceaselessly snark about this disparity, and the complaint has a surface appeal.[4] But, as the sage maxim teaches, there is real iniquity in treating fundamentally different things as if they were the same.

The Trump and Clinton investigations were fundamentally different. The former was counterintelligence, which is classified. Silence is required not only for national-security reasons but because counterintelligence probes are not premised on proving violations of the criminal law. The mandate that criminal violations be proved in open court, where the accused has a right to mount a defense, is the main reason why criminal investigations become public. Preelection, no prosecutor or investigator ever had the nerve to claim, formally, that Trump had violated the criminal law—notwithstanding the Obama administration's fever dreams about a grand Trump–Putin conspiracy.

In stark contrast, the Clinton probe was a criminal investigation. Most criminal investigations are eventually publicized, and some are unavoidably public because of the nature of the suspected criminal activity, or because of the suspect's public position, or both. Here, Clinton was a former secretary of state who had flouted her public trust—her legal obligations to maintain government records and safeguard classified information. It was inevitable that her misconduct would become public, because its objective was to defeat transparency laws. That can't stay secret forever. The State Department grapples constantly with a flood of Freedom of Information Act disclosure demands (from the media and indefatigable outfits like Judicial Watch). When public controversies involving international affairs occur, such as the Obama administration's handling of the Benghazi massacre, there are certain to be years of congressional hearings and court proceedings that pose document demands. Clinton's malfeasance was revealed in a referral to the Justice Department by the intelligence community's inspector general. This was well known when the FBI caught the case. While classified information was pertinent to the Clinton caper, the investigation itself was not classified.

The effort to draw equivalence between the two investigations, demonstrable in Senator Harry Reid's August 27 letter pressuring Comey to investigate Trump in the campaign stretch-run, is ill-conceived. To be sure, most of the Democrats' ire stems from Director Comey's decisions to go public with the evidence against Secretary Clinton and to notify Congress, just days before the election, that the investigation against her was still pending. These were, indeed, inappropriate actions because Clinton was not charged with a crime. Of course, to stress this is to glide past the inconvenient fact that most Americans who tried what Clinton pulled would have been indicted. But even if we ignore that little detail, it remains true that the FBI is simply not in the cosmic justice business. It is in the rule-of-law business. Mistakes happen in all human endeavor, but in law enforcement, we are always obliged to follow regulations, not emotions. We do not rationalize that because Mistake A has been made, fairness dictates that Mistake B must follow. The improper leaking of nonpublic law enforcement information (the evidence against Clinton) was never a legitimate basis to demand what would have been the criminal leaking of classified information (the existence of and intelligence related to a counterintelligence investigation against Trump).

Now let's move from airy principle to real-world facts. *The Trump–Russia investigation was leaked.* As we'll see in more detail shortly, the Clinton campaign not only choreographed the investigation (and not just through Fusion GPS); it also attempted to exploit the existence of the investigation in the campaign's final weeks. CIA Director Brennan armed influential congressional Democrats with Trump–Russia intelligence, and they proceeded to make public statements. Jennifer Palmieri and Jake Sullivan, respectively Clinton's chief spokesperson and national-security adviser, aggressively directed the media's attention to the collusion story. Many media outlets picked it up. When news broke of the Alfa Bank allegation—the claim that Trump and Putin had a back channel for private email (see Chapter Eight)—Sullivan was quick to issue a statement: "This could be the most direct link yet between Donald Trump and Moscow. ... This secret hotline may be the key to unlocking the mystery of Trump's ties to Russia."[5]

What gnaws at Camp Clinton is that the FBI did not join the public spectacle. Under the radar, the Bureau may have been taking aggressive investigative measures that were unjustifiable under the circumstances (deploying informants, applying for FISA warrants), but it respected the laws and procedures that make counterintelligence probes secret. This was not because FBI officials were just better people than everyone else. As we'll see, after Trump's election, discretion largely went out the window. Before the election, though, practical considerations drove FBI decision-making. Mrs. Clinton was the heavy favorite. The FBI is not supposed to factor political calculations into investigative judgments, but it did. Comey was candid on that point in trying to explain his controversial October 28 letter informing Congress that the emails case was still under review—the letter over which the inspector general rightly censured Comey, and which Mrs. Clinton blames for her defeat (when she is not blaming Putin, collusion, the DNC emails, deplorable Trump voters, the Electoral College, Fox News, climate change, the Lindbergh kidnapping, and anything imaginable besides a lackluster campaign in which she got outworked).[6]

Once again illustrating the inextricable interrelatedness of the Clinton and Trump probes, October 28 is the same day "intelligence officials" leaked to the *Times* that the Bureau, after extensive investigation, had not found any actionable ties between the Trump campaign and the Kremlin. None of this Machiavellian narrative-shaping is ever a good idea, but the FBI's point was not to lift Trump and sink Clinton. The objective was to give Clinton a clean slate: When she was inevitably elected, nobody would be able to say that the Bureau had sat on damning evidence against her, and there would be no Trump–Russia contrails. President Hillary Clinton would be able to begin her administration with the upbeat message that the voters had rendered their judgment fully aware of all relevant information, and therefore it was time to turn the page and govern—not spend two years with her subordinates lawyering up while her political opponents pined for a special counsel.

It was a sensible strategy, but sensible strategies don't always work. The problem with playing this game of crafting narratives instead of just following rules is that there are no sure things. Games are made to be lost.

Preelection, Brennan had to pressure Comey because the Bureau, already charred by the Clinton-emails debacle, did not want to be perceived as overly anxious to jump into a campaign-season probe of Trump. But Democrats were agitating, and a Trump win, while highly unlikely, was not so impossible that it could be dismissed out of hand. At every turn, the FBI, and the Obama administration broadly, had to weigh (a) the ability to hurt Trump by openly exercising their awesome powers, against (b) the implausibility of his election. Clinton was going to win, but she was unpopular and might not pull away. The polls might tighten. There was always the possibility that overt investigative activity, especially in the absence of solid evidence, would outrage enough of the public that Trump's chances could actually improve. When you ignore the little angel on your shoulders whispering, "Just follow the rules and don't try to predict the politics," the world gets very complicated.

Hope for the Best, Prepare for the Worst

On August 15, a number of FBI officials including Strzok and Page gathered in Deputy Director McCabe's office. We do not know everything that was said and planned at that meeting. We do know, however, that Page counseled caution. As she and Strzok recounted the meeting while texting the next day, Page had opined, "There's no way he gets elected." Strzok, however, believed that even if a Trump victory was the longest of long shots, the FBI could not "take that risk." He insisted that the Bureau had no choice but to proceed with a plan to contain the damage that would be wrought by a Trump presidency: "It's like an insurance policy in the unlikely event you die before you're 40."

This is such a damning comment—a shocking one for those of us who revere the FBI—that, naturally, there have been attempts to explain it away, some of which would be hilarious but for the situation's gravity. Strzok and his apologists, for example, have offered the straw man that the agent "didn't intend to suggest a secret plan to harm the candidate"—as if any responsible person ever suggested that the FBI was plotting Trump's assassination.[7]

Motivated by blatant anti-Trump animus (and outrage at Russia that was outsize given how historically routine and practically inconsequential its campaign meddling was), solid investigators got swept into the herd mentality. They credited shoddy information, rather than attempting to verify it as their duty demanded. They would have been delighted to derail Trump's candidacy if they could, but it is not the objective of an insurance policy to prevent a disaster. Insurance is a hedge against the fallout of a disaster. That's a big reason why, even though espionage and hacking conspiracies are very serious crimes if proved, the Trump probe was designated as counterintelligence, not criminal. The idea was not to arrest Trump. It was to keep him under monitoring. It was to limit the damage he would be able to do, if elected president, in the event he really was a Kremlin plant. If he was not elected, the matter could be dropped and no one would be any the wiser. If he won, investigators could paralyze him—the threat of an obstruction allegation would hem him in—while they looked for provable misconduct that could predicate a prosecution, trigger his impeachment, or at the very least render him too damaged politically to be reelected.

The main thrust of the insurance policy would be the Steele dossier. As we've seen, informants were deployed to attempt to obtain incriminating evidence. Papadopoulos, in particular, was pressed to admit that the campaign was collaborating with Russia in the hacking and dissemination of emails. There, as we've seen, the FBI even slipped "Azra Turk" into the equation so, on the off chance that Papadopoulos confessed, there would be a government operative available to testify while Stefan Halper quietly disappeared into the top-secret mist. (By the way, anybody want to bet against me that there are tapes we haven't yet heard?) Most of the premiums, though, were paid toward the dossier. It was the long-term plan.

By mid-August, Steele had reported that Putin was directing the hacking plot on Trump's behalf. Carter Page, said to be supervised by Manafort, had supposedly met with Putin's operatives while in Moscow, discussing not only Clinton *kompromat* but a corrupt quid pro quo on Russia sanctions that Steele eventually inflated into a bribe scheme potentially involving tens of millions of dollars. Trump lawyer Michael Cohen was purportedly in Eastern Europe (Steele eventually settled on Prague as the site), meeting with Kremlin agents and paying off the hackers (for DNC emails that even Steele, speaking through his regime sources in a later report, had to concede had no real impact on Clinton).

In Trumpian excess, the GOP nominee asserted at a July 27 press conference, "Russia, if you're listening, I hope you're able to find the 30,000 emails that are missing. I think you will probably be rewarded mightily by our press."[8]

I confess to being amused by it at the time, the sort of thing that you know shouldn't make you snicker, but does—just as Democrats would feel about some partly jocular, mostly savage remark by, say, Joe Biden or James Carville. The contention, made by Democrats ever since, that Trump was calling on Russia to hack Clinton is so overwrought one doesn't know where to begin. The theory of the Trump–Russia conspiracy was that *Trump took the orders from Putin*; he didn't give them. Trump had clearly been referring to the State Department emails improperly stored on Clinton's private server and destroyed at Clinton's direction, not the DNC emails the Kremlin had caused to be hacked. And as everyone believed at the time, Clinton's servers and all devices known to contain copies of her existing emails were in the off-line possession of the FBI—Russia may have hacked Clinton's emails long ago, but those emails were no longer available to be hacked.

Palpably, Trump did not and could not direct a Russian hacking. This was an attention-grabbing gambit, in the stretch-run of the contest and in Trump's outrageous style, to call voters' attention to one of his rival's greatest vulnerabilities: the lawlessness and national-security recklessness of her private server system and destruction of government records.[9]

Of course the statement was injudicious, but only because it was not an isolated incident. As we've seen, a number of Trump's public statements about Putin had been jaw-dropping: praising him as a "strong leader" and "far more [of a leader] than our president [Obama] has been a leader"; defending Putin after the British government found that he'd approved the poisoning of a defector ("Have they found him guilty? I don't think they've found him guilty"); drawing a moral equivalence between Russian-regime murders of dissenters and covert operations by U.S. intelligence (to an interviewer's description of Putin as a "killer," Trump responded: "There are a lot of killers. Do you think our country is so innocent?").[10]

Disturbing? Yes. Many of Trump's statements are disturbing. The trend has not ceased during his presidency. As this book goes to press, the president has just tweeted that he is confident the sociopathic North Korean dictator Kim Jong-un ("Chairman Kim") "will keep his promise" to Trump to refrain from long-range missile tests. The context: Kim had just directed short-range missile tests in violation of international sanctions the United States is supposed to enforce. The president not only laughed off this provocation; for good measure, he added that he "smiled" upon hearing that Kim "called Swampman Joe Biden a low IQ individual."[11] If Trump's Putin treacle upsets you (as it upsets me), try reading his blubber about how he and Kim "fell in love."[12] This is Donald Trump's way. Do you find it nauseating? Me too. I make an effort (often, it takes extraordinary effort) to tune out the blather and focus on important policies with which I emphatically agree, but it is absurd to suggest that what a president *says* does not matter. It matters a great deal. Trump's shock-jock shtick would have constituted a fine reason in 2016 for Americans to campaign vigorously against him, especially if there had been a tolerable alternative. All that said, though, none of this claptrap is close to being espionage—even if one thinks, as John Brennan maintains, that there is such a thing as "unwitting" espionage.

'Corroboration': Circular Reporting and Another Dossier

As summer 2016 dwindled, Fusion GPS stepped up the Clinton-campaign effort to leverage government investigative power with media influence. Glenn Simpson arranged to meet with Bruce Ohr on August 22, providing the Justice Department official with more details from Steele's reporting about Trump–Russia connections. For professional reasons, Simpson, a self-described "journalist for rent,"[13] preferred to pretend that he was not a government informant—you never know when they might want to subpoena, say, your "research" on behalf of Putin's "Destroy Bill Browder" project, so you want to be able to claim full free-press protections. Simpson thus resisted contact with the FBI, using Ohr to transmit campaign dirt. He would later tell congressional investigators that he did not have contact with Ohr until after the election—and that, of course, it was Ohr's idea, not his.[14]

Fusion's real blitz occurred in mid-September. On Friday the 16th, Steele emailed Ohr to say he would soon be in Washington "on business of mutual interest." Steele was in town by Wednesday the 21st. He and Ohr agreed to meet for breakfast on Friday, since by then Steele said he'd have gotten through a series of "scheduled meetings."[15] As it turned out, Simpson had set up meetings for Steele with a number of prominent journalists: Michael Isikoff of Yahoo News, *The New Yorker's* Jane Mayer, Tom Hamburger and Rosalind Helderman of *The Washington Post*, and *The New York Times's* Steven Lee and Eric Lichtblau, as well as a session with CNN.[16]

On September 23, right after these press briefings, Isikoff filed his bombshell story, "U.S. intel officials probe ties between Trump adviser and Kremlin."[17] The account, featuring a picture of Carter Page, related that the U.S. government was conducting an intelligence investigation to determine whether Page, a Trump adviser, had opened up a private communications channel with such "senior Russian officials" as Igor Sechin and Igor Divyekin to discuss lifting economic sanctions if Trump became president. Isikoff's dispatch was rife with allegations, from what were portrayed as "intelligence reports," that "U.S. officials" were actively investigating. These were actually *Steele's* reports, paid for by the Clinton campaign, but framed in a way that would lead readers to assume they were *official U.S. intelligence reports.*

That is not to say there was a lack of official American government involvement. Isikoff's story asserted that U.S. intelligence agents were briefing members of Congress about these "intelligence reports." And they were: Brennan had briefed the Gang of Eight. The story described the reaction of three Gang members—all Democrats. Senator Dianne Feinstein and Congressman Adam Schiff (both of California), issued a joint statement explaining that, according to what they'd been told, "very senior levels" of the Russian government were making "a serious and concerted effort to influence the U.S. election." The letter Senator Reid had written to FBI Director Comey was also emphasized, with reference to Page's purported meetings with Sechin and Divyekin. Isikoff's story elaborated that "questions about Page come amid mounting concerns within the U.S. intelligence community about Russian cyberattacks on the Democratic National Committee." Those would be the cyberattacks that Fusion GPS had conjured into a Trump–Russia conspiracy, in which Page was the foot soldier for Trump and his campaign manager, Paul Manafort.

Isikoff obviously checked with his government sources to verify what Steele and Simpson had told him about the ongoing government investigation. His story recounts that "a senior U.S. law enforcement official" confirmed that Page's alleged contacts with Russian officials were "on our radar screen. ... It's being looked at."

It was more than being looked at. Notwithstanding the lack of support by independent evidence, Steele's reporting was being elevated to grist for a FISA warrant on Page. The Obama administration would try to paper over the deficiencies by presenting Isikoff's article to the court as if it were verification of Steele's reporting—media reporting substituting for gumshoe investigating, and Steele offered as corroboration for Steele (with an audacious government representation that Steele had not been Isikoff's source—at least not "directly").

By then, Steele's reporting to the FBI would also include rank rumor supplied by the State Department, courtesy of two other longtime Clinton hatchet men, Sidney Blumenthal and Cody Shearer, who had been peddling their own anti-Trump dossier since the spring.

In Washington, Steele, who was toting his reports, let his State Department friend Jonathan Winer read them, but not keep a copy. Like others who perused Steele's work, Winer was stunned by the bottomless depths of Trumpian depravity depicted therein. He prepared a two-page summary, which he shared with Assistant Secretary Victoria Nuland, and which both of them agreed simply had to be brought to the attention of Secretary of State Kerry.

Then, later in September, Winer says he spoke with his "old friend" Blumenthal. In a self-defensive op-ed he was later invited to publish at *The Washington Post*, Winer recalled that Blumenthal's emails had been hacked in 2013—though Winer managed to avoid mentioning that some of those emails, exchanged with then–Secretary of State Clinton through her private server, dealt with the 2012 Benghazi terrorist attack and contained classified information (Blumenthal did not have a security clearance and did not work for the government, Clinton having been forbidden by the president from hiring him after Blumenthal's Blumenthally work against Obama in the 2008 campaign).[18] Winer decided to discuss Steele's confidential anti-Trump reporting with Blumenthal—strictly for academic purposes, of course. Now, try not to be too stunned when I tell you that Ol' Sid just happened to bring along a copy of the notes assembled by his running buddy, Cody Shearer—whose ties to the Clintons run deep and, natch, unseemly.[19]

Shearer's meanderings "alleged that the Russians had compromising information on Trump of a sexual and financial nature." Imagine that!

The invaluable Lee Smith obtained a copy of this Blumenthal–Shearer dossier, a collection of two undated reports, each four pages long.[20] Shearer—a one-time journalist who specialized in gossip and has no intelligence background—based his reports on interviews with "journalists and various media personalities, as well as [an] unnamed Turkish businessman," who allegedly had "excellent contacts with the FSB" (Russia's internal security service). The "reports" were entitled "Donald Trump—Background Notes—The Compromised Candidate" and "FSB Interview."

Uncannily similar to Steele's reports, Shearer's memos related that Trump and Paul "Manniford" were involved in a corrupt conspiracy with Russia. Shearer also rehashed the left-wing media theme that Trump, in desperate need of financing after his bankruptcies, laundered money for Russian oligarchs in return for capital. From his tentacles in the FSB, Shearer had learned "that Trump...had been flipped [to the Kremlin side] in a honeypot operation in Moscow." The mogul, he added, had been "filmed twice in Moscow in November 2013, during the Miss Universe Pageant," including "[o]nce in the presidential suite of the Ritz Carlton Hotel," with "a copy of the sex videos" stashed in "Bulgaria, Israel and FSB political unit vaults in Moscow." Sure seems like a lot of copies of a video no one reports having seen, but I digress. Shearer concluded that the Kremlin was pushing hard to get its compromised candidate elected president of the United States, through the theft of emails and even tampering with voting machines. The mysterious Turkish businessman chimed in that his unidentified Russian source knew of a "cut out," through whom Trump, once elected, would communicate "into President Putin's office."

Winer could not help but be "struck" by "how some of the [Shearer] material echoed Steele's but appeared to involve different sources." Though he did not know Shearer, Winer assumed—what, with Blumenthal vouching for him—that these reports constituted assiduously researched, impeccably sourced intelligence that should promptly be brought to the attention of the master himself, Chris Steele. Winer shared a copy with the former spy, "to ask for his professional reaction." Yes, indeed, Steele replied, this could well be "collateral" information—similar to his own reporting but separately sourced. Knowing Steele was generating reports, Winer let him keep a copy of Shearer's notes. Naturally, in his quest to give the FBI every stitch of anti-Trump rumor he could locate, Steele incorporated Shearer's information as part of his research, transmitted to the FBI's intelligence database.[21] According to former Representative Trey Gowdy (R., S.C.), who saw some of the relevant documentation as a congressional investigator, the FBI listed information from Blumenthal as part of its purported corroboration of Steele.[22]

When they later referred Steele to the Justice Department for a possible false-statements prosecution, Judiciary Committee Senators Charles Grassley and Lindsey Graham recounted that, in a memo dated October 19 (but not published by BuzzFeed), Steele had outlined Shearer's information as a report from the "US State Department," traceable to "a foreign subsource" (the unidentified Turk with the purported but unidentified FSC source), and then routed through Shearer, Blumenthal, and Winer.

The Obama State Department, which hoped and expected to become the Clinton State Department, remained invested in Steele's anti-Trump project through the end of the campaign. These days, former Assistant Secretary Victoria Nuland (who left State within days of Trump's inauguration), poses as a pillar of rectitude: Immediately upon hearing about the dossier in July 2016, she says, she admonished her subordinates.

> [T]his is about U.S. politics, and not the work of—not the business of the State Department, and certainly not the business of a career employee who is subject to the Hatch Act, which requires that you stay out of politics. So, my advice to those who were interfacing with [Steele] was that he should get this information to the FBI, and that they could evaluate whether they thought it was credible.[23]

That, however, is not what happened. Nuland, of course, had approved Agent Gaeta's July 5 trip to London to interview Steele, so she knew the FBI already had Steele's information. The State Department, meanwhile, hosted Steele at Foggy Bottom in October 2016 to brief select officials on his dossier allegations about Donald Trump. Nuland incoherently claims both not to have known about the briefing and to have consciously cho-

sen not to attend it. As Eric Felten observes, how odd that State Department officials could see dabbling in the dossier as a potential Hatch
Act problem but be untroubled by having Steele himself presenting his
information "to State Department officials in State Department offices
on State Department time"—the same information he and Fusion were
presenting to the media in the waning days before the election.[24]

Fellow Agent or Source?

How surprised should we be that the State Department gave Steele the
Cody Shearer/Sid Blumenthal dossier? After all, the FBI was feeding
Steele information, too. In late September, following his return from
Washington meetings with select Obama-administration officials and
favored journalists, Gaeta summoned Steele to Rome to meet with
agents who had flown in from the United States to debrief him. It
wasn't a normal witness debriefing, though. It was more like a conference among law-enforcement peers conducting a common investigation. The agents shared some of their information and sought reciprocal contribution from Steele.[25]

This was a huge part of the problem with the former British intelligence officer: U.S. investigators could never seem to make up their
minds whether he was a source (as indicated to the court) or a fellow
investigator (as suggested in their meetings). The distinction is sig
nificant: A source or witness is someone from whom agents adduce
information; it is essential to keep this a one-way street, since the investigator is always trying to evaluate credibility and the reliability of
information. You have to be able to keep straight what the witness is
telling you based on his unique information, versus what he is telling
you based on what you have told him—or based on what he infers
that you want to hear from what your questions suggest.

That wall was never maintained with Steele, for two reasons. First,
he was not really a source; he was an informant relying on hearsay from
sources. That is, his role in the investigation was analogous to an FBI
case agent, who aggregates other people's information. Second, while
Steele technically was not a government agent, he had been one (for
an allied government). And he was still in the investigations business—

though now in search of income, not truth. Plainly, if Steele hadn't been a former agent who seemed like a current agent, no one would have given him the time of day. Normally, a good investigator puts little or no stock in an informant whose sources are far away, sometimes anonymous, multiple-hearsay layers removed, and unverifiable.

In Rome, the Bureau shared details of their investigation as if Steele were another FBI agent. Investigators told him about George Papadopoulos, whom Steele did not know. And they held out the possibility of paying him $50,000 if he could corroborate his claims. (*Hint*: That means they knew his claims were not corroborated, and that this was a big problem—Steele's own personal credibility was irrelevant if the sources, who had purportedly made the pertinent observations, could not be verified.) As things worked out, his dossier was soon made public; according to Steele, he not only wasn't paid for his information, he didn't even get reimbursed for traveling to Rome for the meeting.[26]

The FBI's inability to verify Steele's information remains a sticking point to this day. Rather than admit failure, top Bureau officials expatiate about corroboration as an organic process that never really ends unless information is outright refuted...conveniently flipping the constitutional burden of proof, under which the government must prove its suspicions, not treat them as proven until disproved.[27] To take the position, *years after information has been acted on*, that although not yet verified it may someday be is an appalling abuse of investigative power. That, however, is Russia-gate in a nutshell: No rumor is ever dismissed because, when it comes to Trump, it is no longer the FBI's obligation to verify information; it is somehow the suspect's burden to show that the suspicions are wrong. And no one is ever exonerated because, when it comes to Trump, it is no longer the prosecution's burden to prove guilt; the accused must establish his innocence.

Despite the pining about how asking questions about the conduct of this investigation imperils the very foundations of the republic, I am going to go out on a limb and say: that's not very American.

CHAPTER FIFTEEN

FISA Warrants: Targeting Trump, Not Page

n the eight years between the 1993 World Trade Center bombing and 9/11, al-Qaeda repeatedly attacked the United States. The government struggled to decide whether international terrorism was strictly a criminal matter, to be investigated with such techniques as criminal wiretaps, or a national-security matter, to be investigated under FISA and other intelligence-gathering procedures. Obviously, it was both. But that caused the Clinton Justice Department sleepless nights over what seemed—to me, among other terrorism prosecutors and investigators—to be overwrought fears of hypothetical abuses, remote from real-world experience.

I guess I owe Jamie Gorelick an apology.[1]

The then–deputy attorney general and other Clinton DOJ officials were worried about FISA. What if you had rogue agents who were predisposed to believe a group of suspects was guilty, but couldn't prove it? The rogues did not have enough evidence to seek a regular wiretap or search warrant. Mightn't they be tempted to use FISA? They'd just need to claim that there was some vague national-security aspect to the case; to pretend that their investigation was connected to a broader counterintelligence investigation of a foreign power. The rogues could then seek FISA warrants to surveil the suspects. The agents would call it "counterintelligence," but in reality they'd be conducting a criminal investigation—eavesdropping and conducting other surreptitious searches—even though they did not have probable cause to believe a crime had been committed.

See, if the government is conducting a criminal investigation, it is supposed to proceed under criminal-law authorities. In the statutes and rules governing those authorities, Congress has incorporated significant due-process protections for those under suspicion. Criminal investigations implicate our fundamental rights to liberty and property—some-times, even life. The Constitution thus safeguards us with presumptions of innocence and privacy. The government can overcome them only by proving to a court, and ultimately a jury, that we have committed serious offenses. Counterintelligence law circumvents these protections. We indulge that circumvention for three reasons: (1) national security is potentially threatened; (2) the main target of suspicion is a foreign power with no constitutional rights, not an American citizen; and (3) the objective of the investigation is to collect intelligence to protect our nation from the foreign power, not to build a criminal case in which the liberty and property of American citizens are imperiled.

But what if counterintelligence were invoked pretextually? What if the foreign power were just a guise for investigators, in effect, to end-run our constitutional protections—to conduct a criminal investi-gation without a predicate crime, without just cause?

Based on this fear that FISA could be used pretextually to con-duct criminal investigations, the Clinton Justice Department imposed "the Wall." Unlike the Wall of President Trump's imagining, President Clinton's was metaphorical. To prevent investigators from exploiting FISA to steer criminal investigations, a regulatory barrier was imposed between the FBI's counterintelligence agents on one side, and criminal investigators and prosecutors on the other. It became practically im-possible for the two sides to cooperate and share information.

One result was the desired clamping down on potential FISA abuse. But the cure proved worse than the disease. With counterintelligence and criminal investigators unable to compare notes and build an intel-ligence mosaic, the left hand no longer knew what the right hand was doing. This enabled terrorists to escape detection. Inevitably, catastro-phes would occur, such as 9/11.

After 9/11, the Wall was razed. Your humble correspondent was among the loudest celebrants, but that celebration seems unbecoming now. Back then, it seemed ridiculous to believe the FBI and the Justice Department would resort to FISA pretextually. I posited that, even if we assume a rogue agent who was determined to conduct a criminal investigation despite the absence of a factual predicate (i.e., evidence connecting the suspect to a crime), it would be far easier for the rogue to fabricate the evidence needed to get a criminal wiretap than to fabricate a national-security angle so he could use FISA. I insisted that if the rogue tried to go the FISA route, he'd never get away with it. FISA is a whole different FBI/DOJ chain of command. It has too many levels of scrutiny in the upper ranks of the bureaucracy—responsible superiors who would stop the rogue agent in his tracks before that agent ever got near FISA's specialized court.

I was wrong.

What I didn't factor in was the possibility that, for political reasons, the upper ranks of the FDI and the Justice Department might decide to do an investigation by themselves. That should never happen. The Justice Department and the FBI generally ensure that each investigation is conducted by the Bureau's field office located in the district where the crime occurred or the threat emanates. As a matter of law, this satisfies constitutional requirements.[2] As a matter of prudence, it insulates investigations from the intense political pressure of Washington, home to Main Justice and FBI headquarters. Moreover, it clarifies the role of headquarters, improving its capacity to supervise and enforce policy in a detached, effective manner.

In almost every investigation, and particularly in high-profile, high-stakes investigations, investigators are motivated to be aggressive, to press the margins of their authority. It happens to the best prosecutors and agents. You become convinced that your bad guys are the worst bad guys in the history of bad guys. You rationalize the expedience of corner-cutting and rule-bending as promoting what seems to you to be the higher public interest of neutralizing bad actors. After all, the bad actors are *your* problem, the *immediate* problem. You understandably see your main job as stopping them. Somewhere in the back of your mind, you know you should be mindful of lofty concerns about the system of justice, the presumption of innocence, and the Bill of Rights. But right now, they are not your focus—someone above your pay-grade worries about that stuff.

Well, that someone is headquarters. The bosses are supposed to be the cooler heads, elevated from on-the-ground investigation. They are there to protect the system, to prevent abuse—to police the police, not conduct the investigations.

Nevertheless, in Russia-gate, headquarters became the investigator. And headquarters may be headquarters, but when it is handling an investigation, its prestige and wealth of experience does not make it any more immune from the temptation to run roughshod over the rules than any other set of aggressive investigators. The only difference is that when headquarters starts to run roughshod, there is no one there to say, "No, we don't do that."

Just as ordinary field-office investigators are tempted to keep their supervisors in the dark when they are ignoring a norm or blowing out a guideline, top rungs of the Obama Justice Department and the FBI convinced themselves that they needed to work outside the system in order to safeguard the system. They decided that one presidential candidate posed a grave threat. They forgot who the sovereign is. They persuaded themselves that they were not engaging in politics but instead shielding vital institutions. They decided that because their hearts were pure, the rules needn't hold them back. They withheld information from Congress—declining to brief the Gang of Eight, rationalizing that the "sensitivity" of investigating the incumbent administration's political opponents in a presidential campaign justified a defiance of oversight—concealing what they were doing from those sure to object. They withheld essential information from the FISC about the source of their information (the Clinton campaign), and about the apparent unreliability and deep bias of their main witness (Christopher Steele), even as their presentation of unverified allegations flouted FBI guidelines.

Headquarters exists to prevent investigators from such abuses. But here, headquarters became its own supervisor. Such arrangements tend not to end well.

Final FISA Warrant Preparations

As Election Day neared, the Clinton campaign stepped up efforts to call voters' attention to the Trump–Russia narrative, which Steele—simultaneously the campaign's agent and the Obama administration's informant—was vigorously thrusting on the FBI and the State Department.

On September 19, James Baker, the Bureau's general counsel, rendezvoused with Michael Sussmann, the lawyer for Perkins Coie—the firm representing the Clinton campaign and DNC, which were then pushing the anti-Trump dossier on FBI investigators, through Steele.[3] It was an extraordinary meeting in the campaign stretch-run. Sussmann, a former prosecutor, was obviously well aware that FBI counsel are advisers who avoid becoming entangled in the physical handling of evidence. Yet, he initiated contact with Baker and supplied him with documentation, including some on computer storage devices—transparently calculating that evidence passed on to agents by the Bureau's general counsel would get prompt attention. The information related to, among other things, the purported Alfa Bank scheme—the claim that Donald Trump had established a communications back channel with the Kremlin.[4] Recall that the Alfa Bank claim was also pressed by Glenn Simpson on the Justice Department's Bruce Ohr, and Clinton-campaign adviser Jake Sullivan touted it as potentially "the most direct link yet between Donald Trump and Moscow." Baker knew that Sussmann was peddling the same information to *The New York Times*.[5]

Baker, who would soon review and green-light the FBI's application for a FISA warrant to surveil Carter Page, accepted the documentation, even though he later told Congress, "I was very uncomfortable handling evidence." He got over his discomfort, though, not only taking Sussmann's submission (and follow-up calls), but also accepting Steele's dossier reports from his longtime friend, David Corn, the reporter from left-leaning *Mother Jones*.[6] It was through Corn that Steele went public with his role in the FBI's Trump–Russia investigation, a week before the 2016 election (in a fit of pique that the FBI had publicly reopened the Hillary Clinton-emails investigation while it was remaining mum about the Trump–Russia investigation that depended on Steele's corruption allegations).[7] Baker's meetings, like Justice Department official Bruce Ohr's earlier meeting with FBI Deputy Director McCabe and his counsel Lisa Page, illustrate what the House Intelligence Committee later found: Senior Justice Department and FBI officials were aware that the political origins of the Steele dossier traced to the Clinton campaign and the DNC.[8]

Meanwhile, Michael Isikoff's September 23 Yahoo News article was followed like clockwork by a Clinton-campaign statement bewailing Trump adviser Carter Page's "chilling" ties to the Kremlin. Echoing

Isikoff's reliance on the Steele dossier information it had sponsored, the campaign expressed shock that Page would meet with Igor Divyekin, "who is believed by U.S. officials 'to have responsibility for intelligence collected by Russian agencies about the U.S. election.'" After all, Clinton's flack added, "Russian hackers continue their attempts to influence the outcome of our elections, something Trump openly invited" (an apparent but detail-free reference to Trump's press conference quip that he hoped Russia would find the 30,000-plus emails Mrs. Clinton had withheld from the State Department).[9]

The bad publicity prompted the Trump campaign to distance itself from Page. Apoplectic, he fired off a letter to FBI Director Comey, requesting that the Bureau promptly end its reported inquiry regarding his July trip to Russia.[10] Page emphasized that the report (based on Steele's signal allegations) was false: "[F]or the record, I have not met this year with any sanctioned official in Russia," even though doing so would not have violated the law. He further informed the director that he no longer had an investment stake in Gazprom, having divested "a de minimis equity investment" by selling it "at a loss." Page expressed bewilderment that his holdings and transactions were of any relevance, since they, too, were lawful. After belittling the media reporting about his trip as "preposterous," Page closed with this:

> Having interacted with members of the U.S. intelligence community including the FBI and CIA for many decades, I appreciate the limitations on your staff's time and assets. Although I have not been contacted by any member of your team in recent months, I would eagerly await their call to discuss any final questions they might possibly have in the interest of helping them put these outrageous allegations to rest while allowing each of us to shift our attention to relevant matters. Thank you in advance for your consideration.

Page was not done. In speaking with a plethora of journalists who'd contacted him after the Isikoff article, he'd been told that the Clinton campaign was pushing the narrative of his central role in a Trump–Russia espionage conspiracy. In a subsequent letter to the Organization for Security and Co-operation in Europe, he related that he had learned, from what he described as a "reliable source," that "a law firm close to the Clinton campaign has hired a London-based private investigator to investigate my trip to Russia."[11] Even before Steele went public, the Clinton campaign's use of Perkins Coie to retain him (through Fusion) for a project aimed at attacking Mrs. Clinton's political opposition was so widely known that even Page had heard about it. Yet, Democrats would have us believe neither Steele nor FBI headquarters were aware of it.

There was disquiet at the FBI, too. Although Peter Strzok would later disclaim any involvement in FISA warrant applications, an October 11, 2016, text was later found in which he reported to Lisa Page that he was "currently fighting with Stu for this FISA." "Stu" appears to be a reference to Stuart Evans, a deputy assistant attorney general for the Justice Department's National Security Division. Clearly, Justice was concerned about the Carter Page FISA—specifically, about Steele: Did the application being drafted adequately disclose the extent and nature of his bias? Did his flagrant bias undermine the required probable cause showing that Page was a clandestine agent of Russia?

Tellingly, when the FBI was first forced to disclose the texts, the words "Stu for this FISA" were redacted. Congress and the public were told only that Strzok was "currently fighting with"...and the rest was blacked out.

The following day, Lisa Page texted her boss, Deputy Director McCabe, to report that the Justice Department had now been given "a robust explanation re any possible bias of the chs [the confidential human source—Steele]" but that there was still a "holdup" due to "Stu's continuing concerns." We will soon come to the likely subject of those "concerns"—a laborious footnote about Steele in the FISA warrant application, which hid more than it explained about the former spy's anti-Trump bias. Page told McCabe that there was a "strong operational need to have in place before Monday if at all possible"—i.e., that Strzok had investigative reasons to push for court approval of the FISA warrant prior to Monday, October 17 (for "insurance policy" purposes—note that if the ninety-day warrant were approved before October 20, it could be renewed for another ninety days right before Trump and his new Justice Department team took office, in the unlikely event he won the election).

Page had told Stu that McCabe and "boss" (presumably, Director Comey) had given the "green light." She lamented, though, that her own voice was not enough: "a high-level push"—i.e., direct contact by McCabe to Evans—would be needed to get the warrant application approved by the Justice Department. Later that day, Page told McCabe, "If I have not heard back from Stu in an hour, I will invoke your name to say you want to know where things are." Page appears to have spoken with Evans that evening, but the issue was not resolved. On October 14, Strzok told Lisa Page they still needed some "hurry the F up pressure" from FBI higher-ups.[12]

At this delicate juncture, the last thing Strzok would have needed was more damaging evidence of Steele's bias. Yet that is what he got. Recall that it was on October 11 that the State Department's Kathleen Kavalec interviewed Steele. She shared with the FBI the notes she had taken, indicating that (a) Steele's report of the Trump–Russia conspiracy's use of a Russian consulate in Miami had to be false because there was no such consulate; (b) Steele said he was managing the relationship with media outlets (including *The New York Times* and *The Washington Post*), which were in possession of some of his information; and (c) Steele was anxious for his anti-Trump allegations to be made public before Election Day. It is highly unlikely that these assertions, so patently germane to Steele's competence, credibility, and bias, were shared with any of the Justice Department officials who were troubled by Steele. They certainly do not appear to have been shared with the FISC.

FISA Warrants: Probing Trump Ties to Russia

On Halloween, Donald Trump got a treat. *The New York Times* reported that, despite much investigation, the FBI had not been able to link his campaign and his associates to Russia's cyberespionage operations aimed at influencing the 2016 campaign. Unbeknownst to the candidate, though, the trick had come ten days earlier: On October 21, the Obama Justice Department and the FBI obtained a FISA warrant from the FISC. Election Day was less than three weeks away.

The warrant, targeting Carter Page, was the first of four ninety-day warrants. For nearly a year, the FBI would monitor Carter Page's communications with whomever he was, *or had been*, in contact.

When the warrant was first sought, and each time it was reauthorized, the FBI first described the Kremlin's hacking of Democratic emails and other cyber tactics to the court. Then, an agent asserted under oath:

> [T]the FBI believes that the Russian Government's efforts [to influence the 2016 election] were being coordinated with Page and perhaps *other individuals associated with Candidate #1's campaign.*

"Candidate #1" was Donald Trump. Candidate #1's campaign was being run by Donald Trump. This is the critical fact that must always be borne in mind in any consideration of the Obama administration's use of the unverified Steele dossier as the predominant basis for seeking warrants to surveil an American citizen and an American political campaign.

The investigation was about Donald Trump.

He was never referred to by name as a "subject of the investigation." Indeed, technically speaking, it is a misnomer to speak of "subjects" of a counterintelligence investigation. *Subject* is a term of art in *criminal investigations*, referring to a person whose conduct is being evaluated by the grand jury for possible indictment. The purpose of a counterintelligence investigation is not to build a criminal case; it is to detect and thwart the threatening designs of foreign powers. The only real subject of a counterintelligence investigation is the foreign power—here, Russia.

Such legal niceties, however, are of little relevance when the exercise is pretextual. The Trump–Russia investigation was conducted under the guise of counterintelligence, but it was always a criminal investigation—a probe of a suspected espionage conspiracy—for which investigators lacked an adequate factual predicate.

To obscure this reality, the Obama administration's defenders posit two arguments: (1) Carter Page was not actually a member of the Trump campaign at the time the FISA surveillance began; and (2) the investigation was not really about Trump but about people in the orbit of the campaign (Page, Manafort, Gates, Papadopoulos, Flynn) who might have been infiltrating it on behalf of Russia.[13] Collectively, these claims are contradictory; individually, they are laughable.

First the contradictions. If the surveillance of Page was justifiable because he was no longer formally a campaign adviser (i.e., if the surveillance was consistent with the American norm against using government surveillance powers to monitor a political campaign), then how can it have helped the Bureau determine whether people who were in the campaign's orbit were acting as agents of Russia? If the FBI was worried about Russian infiltration of the Trump campaign, why monitor a guy who was no longer in a position to infiltrate? And why tell the court, in no uncertain terms, that Page was "coordinating" in Russia's cyberespionage in conjunction with *other individuals associated with the Trump campaign*? Absent seeing Page as "associated with the campaign," the warrant makes no sense. FBI agents had been dealing with Carter Page and his Russian contacts for years; they didn't accuse him of being a clandestine agent of the Kremlin until he joined the Trump campaign.

Now, let's take the claims separately. Page and the campaign parted ways when the September 23 Isikoff article and resulting Clinton-campaign statement stoked negative publicity. Yet, as we've seen, the Trump campaign was not a regimented enterprise. Page continued to have contacts with Trump officials—not only during the campaign but, post-election, during the transition and into the new administration.[14]

More significantly, investigators were at least as interested in *Page's prior communications* as they were in his prospective ones. Nearly always ignored in all defenses of the FISA warrants is the fact that such surveillance authorizations enable the FBI to intercept not only forward-going communications but also *any stored communications* (such as emails and text messages) the target might possess.[15] Indeed, Justice Department Inspector General Michael Horowitz, who is investigating potential abuse in the acquisition and use of FISA surveillance authority, has reportedly asked those involved in the investigation why, if they were not scrutinizing the campaign, they did not use a filter team to screen out messages related to campaign activity.[16] Of course, there is no good answer. Remember, Steele had claimed that Page met in July with Putin-regime operatives Sechin and Divyekin. Page is adamant that he did not, and the FBI had nothing to corroborate Steele's allegation. Clearly, investigators were seeking the mother lode of stored communications and documents tracing back to Page's Moscow trip. Putting aside that warrant allegations are supposed to be verified before presentation to the court, not by execution of the warrant; plainly, the FBI hoped to corroborate Steele's allegations by seizing Page's communications from back when he was undeniably a Trump-campaign adviser.

Even more to the point, Page was merely a *vehicle* for surveillance; the *objective* was to probe *Trump* ties to Russia. Trump was the only reason the Obama administration cared about such relative nonentities as Page and Papadopoulos (as well as Manafort, who had also been severed from the campaign by the time of the first Page FISA warrant). Steele's allegation was that Trump and Putin conceived the conspiracy; the others were just functionaries. That was the theory of the FISA warrant application. Again, the investigation was about Donald Trump. If it hadn't been, the FBI would have given his campaign a defensive briefing, counseling it to be wary of agents of Russian influence who might be trying to penetrate and influence the candidate. Instead, the Obama administration launched a full-fledged FISA investigation because Trump himself was portrayed as the agent of Russian influence.

'VERIFIED'?

In July of 2018, after the Justice Department and the FBI stonewalled congressional committees for over a year, President Trump finally pressured them into the public release of the four Carter Page FISA warrants.[17] While relevant dates have (weirdly) been redacted, the first is known to have been issued by the FISC on October 21, 2016,[18] with reauthorizations following in January (while Obama was still in office), April, and June of 2017—the final one lapsing in September. FISA information is highly classified; the president's disclosure of the warrant packages, even in heavily redacted form, was unprecedented.

Each FISA application is labeled "VERIFIED APPLICATION" (bold caps in original). Each one makes this representation, breathtaking under the circumstances:

> The FBI has reviewed this verified application for accuracy in accordance with its April 5, 2001 procedures, which include sending a copy of the draft to the appropriate field office(s).

In reality, the applications were never *verified for accuracy*—not in any commonsense understanding of that phrase.

The Bureau's "April 5, 2001 procedures" are usually referred to as the "Woods procedures," named for Michael Woods, the agent who developed them. They were firmly implemented during the tenure of FBI Director Robert Mueller, designed to address the quality-control problem of erroneous allegations in FISA submissions due to the wide variety of source information. As Mueller explained to the Senate Judiciary Committee in 2003, "the goal of the procedures is to ensure accuracy with regard to...the facts supporting probable cause[,]" among other things. Because FISA proceedings are not adversarial, an American gets only as much due process as the exchange of information between the government and the FISC entails. If followed, the procedures force a searching analysis of each factual assertion. There is an elaborate chain of required approvals, and the Bureau even formed a FISA unit to track the verification process, all to ensure that only reliable information is provided to the court. The FBI's Domestic Investigations and Operations Guide (DIOG) mandates that the Bureau "ensure that information appearing in a FISA application that is presented to the [FISC] has been thoroughly vetted and confirmed."[19]

Patently, the procedures aim to instill a culture of rectitude. The standard libertarian critique of FISA is that the executive branch cannot be trusted to police itself without an adversarial process. The court, try as it might, is not equipped or incentivized to challenge the government the way a defense lawyer would; the judges do not have the investigative facilities to determine whether they are being misled. The procedures address this deficiency (unavoidable in classified national-security matters), but they work only if they are internalized, rather than gamed—if compliance means not only verifying information but being forthright with the tribunal in disclosing facts that bear on the credibility of information providers.

Plainly, in the Trump–Russia counterintelligence investigation, the process broke down.

It is challenging to describe the FISA warrants and the issues that surround them. Though upward of 400 pages were disseminated publicly, the documents have been very heavily redacted. The president has often indicated that he would direct additional disclosure, but that has not happened as this book goes to press.[20] Inevitably, the excision of most of the documentation has resulted in claims by Obama-administration apologists that the warrant applications were not overly reliant on the Steele dossier: all the really damning stuff, we're to believe, must be in the redactions, we just can't see it because it's too top-secret. Of course, we know this is not so because congressional investigators, who *have* seen the unredacted documents, report that the Steele dossier was substantially relied upon as the predicate.[21]

More to the point, the significance of the redactions is patently overblown. The vast majority of what is blacked out has nothing to do with the probable-cause showing against Carter Page. In fact, while the probable-cause showing is the most significant part of any FISA-application package, it is a comparatively small part. The term "package" is appropriate because a government submission to the FISC includes much more than the application signed by the investigative agent; there is also a lengthy certification by a top-ranking national-security official (here, the FBI's director or deputy director), a short approval declaration by the Justice Department (here, the deputy attorney general), and the proposed warrant itself to be signed by the judge.

In congressional testimony, former FBI Director Comey claimed that FISA submissions are often thicker than his wrists.[22] Besides being a bit of an exaggeration, this description failed to convey that most of the documentation is unrelated to probable cause. Lots of paperwork does not equal mountainous evidence.[23] For example, the first Page submission was just eighty-three pages, which my unscientific supposition says is not as thick as the average toddler's wrist. Of these, the package's last twenty-nine pages are not part of the warrant application at all. They consist of certifications and approvals redacted because they set forth, among other things, secret authorities the government is granted in order to carry out the surveillance, the manner in which the surveillance is to be conducted, the communications facilities the FBI is permitted to monitor, the methods by which the Bureau is permitted to gain access to those facilities, the minimization instructions that must be followed to avoid unauthorized monitoring, and so on—all heavily redacted for obvious reasons.

While a great deal of the remaining fifty-four pages is blacked out, that hardly means we are clueless about what most of the redacted information conveys. To the contrary, the so-called "VERIFIED APPLICATION" has numbered paragraphs that, for the most part, correspond to the sections of the FISA statute that governs such applications, Section 1804.[24] Having a format in which the application's paragraphs conform to the statutory requirements makes it easier for the reviewing judge to see that all legally mandated information is included. The requirements are set forth in nine subsections of the statute; the paragraphs of the Page application match up with these nine subsections.

Only one of these subsections pertains to the all-important probable-cause showing. It directs the FBI to provide the court with "a statement of the facts and circumstances relied upon" to justify the Bureau's beliefs that (a) the proposed target is an agent of a foreign power, and (b) the facilities or places the Bureau wants to monitor are being used for the target's clandestine activities.[25] In the end, just thirty-three pages of the first Page application relate to probable cause—and, mind you, these are double-spaced pages often containing fewer than twenty lines, with many lines consisting of a subheading or just a word or two of text. We are not talking *War and Peace* here.[26]

A goodly chunk of these thirty-three pages does not address Carter Page at all. It's all about Russia: the FBI explains that the regime in Moscow is a foreign power, that it has been fiddling in our elections since the Cold War, and that it meddled in them in 2016 by cyberespionage (with the help of WikiLeaks). We are eight pages into the factual recitation before we get to Page. The section related to him—the gravamen of the application—covers two topics: the Russian attempt to recruit Page as a source in 2013, and the Steele dossier. The latter makes up the bulk of the probable-cause showing, pages 15–27, and includes the allegation the FBI patently hung its hat on: Steele's claim that, while in Russia in July 2016, Page met with the two Putin-regime heavyweights, Sechin and Divyekin.

Even parts of what the application labels as the Page section have nothing to do with Page. There is a long footnote on Steele, which we will come to. And there is an excursion, based on media reports, into how Trump may be soft on Putin, how he may meekly accept the annexation of Crimea, and how the Trump campaign's supposed intervention in Republican-platform-writing at the GOP convention weakened a plank on arming Ukraine (which we discussed in Chapter Twelve). There is also a five-page section largely based on Michael Isikoff's September 23, 2016, Yahoo News article about Page's purported meetings with Sechin and Divyekin. Notably, even though the Bureau continued going back to the FISC for nine months, and thus had more than ample time to do its own investigation into these matters, the Justice Department and the FBI simply regurgitated this press-generated reporting in every application. The FISC judges apparently never questioned this peculiar species of "proof"—which makes you wonder if cut-and-paste from the newspapers is standard operating procedure in top-secret, national-security surveillance.

The concluding pages of the probable-cause section do not even pretend to add to the probable-cause showing. Essentially, they pose a summary of what the foregoing pages have established. There is then apparently a description of criminal statutes Page had allegedly violated. We have to say "apparently" because these pages are all blacked out—and, of course, because Page has never been charged with a crime, even though the Justice Department and the FBI four times represented to the court that there was probable cause to believe he was a clandestine agent of Russia engaged in espionage against the United States that involved complicity in the hacking of email accounts.

So much attention has been lavished on the redactions that not nearly enough has been paid to the ramifications of what has been disclosed. The warrant applications are stunning in their concealment from the FISC of the Steele dossier's Clinton-campaign provenance and Steele's extensive credibility problems. The applications are also unabashed about using counterintelligence authorities to conduct a criminal investigation in the absence of a predicate crime.

Concealing the Dossier's Clinton-Campaign Origins

The FBI and the Justice Department withheld from the FISC the fact that Steele's work was a project of the Clinton campaign and the DNC. Unlike most concealments, this one is not accomplished by simply omitting the relevant facts; it is an exercise in obfuscation, played out in a footnote that runs well over a page—the sort of farce as to which a diligent supervisor would admonish a shifty underling that if it takes this much effort to avoid disclosing something, that's a sure sign that it needs to be disclosed.[27]

Congressional Democrats have nonetheless claimed that these dense paragraphs prove the Justice Department "was transparent with the Court about Steele's sourcing."[28] Really? The FISA warrant application says that Steele, referred to as "Source #1," was "approached by" Fusion GPS founder Glenn Simpson, referred to as "an identified U.S. person," who

> indicated to Source #1 that a U.S.-based law firm had hired the identified U.S. Person to conduct research regarding Candidate #1's [i.e., Trump's] ties to Russia. (The identified U.S. Person and Source #1 have a longstanding business relationship.) The identified U.S. Person hired Source #1 to conduct this research. The identified U.S. Person never advised Source #1 as to the motivation behind the research into Candidate #1's ties to Russia. The FBI speculates that the identified U.S. Person was likely looking for information that could be used to discredit Candidate #1's campaign.

Five things are worth noticing here.

First, behold the epistemological contortions by which the Justice Department and FBI rationalized concealing that the Clinton campaign and the DNC paid for Steele's reporting. They ooze underhandedness.

Second, Christopher Steele was not just someone brought into the equation by Glenn Simpson; he was a paid FBI informant before he was recruited by Fusion for the anti-Trump project. It is inconceivable—or at least it ought to be—that the FBI would use information from a paid FBI informant, who was simultaneously being paid by third parties for the same information, without getting to the bottom of exactly who the third parties were.

Third, the "U.S.-based law firm" is Perkins Coie, counsel to the Clinton campaign and the DNC, for whose campaign purposes it retained Fusion GPS (meaning, Simpson and Steele). Remarkably, Perkins Coie's clients go unmentioned. That is, the Clinton campaign and the DNC used a law firm as a cutout to conceal their roles in generating anti-Trump research (possibly in violation of campaign finance disclosure requirements). Aiding and abetting the scam, the Justice Department and the FBI—which are supposed to uphold the imperatives of verification and transparency, and are responsible for enforcing campaign-disclosure laws—take pains to tell the court only about the law firm, as if the clients were unknown or irrelevant to the court's consideration of Steele and Simpson's credibility.

Fourth, the FISA warrant application asserted: "The identified U.S. Person never advised Source #1 as to the motivation behind the research into Candidate #1's ties to Russia." You are to believe that Simpson did not tell Steele the Clinton campaign and the DNC were sponsoring their project, and that—even though the Justice Department's Bruce Ohr and the FBI were aware of the Clinton/DNC connection—the omniscient former British spy, who supposedly knows the deepest secrets of the Kremlin, was somehow in the dark about whom he was working for.

Sure. In any event, there was only one reason to include a statement about the "motivation behind the research" in the application: The FBI and the Justice Department fully realized that implied biases in the process of compiling the dossier's allegations, including Steele's implied biases, *were material to the FISC's evaluation.* Prosecutors and federal agents do not get to tell a judge reasons that a source's reports should be thought free of bias while withholding the reasons why bias should be inferred. If you know it is necessary to disclose that the "identified U.S. person" (Simpson) was being paid by "a U.S.-based law firm" (Perkins Coie), then it is at least equally necessary to disclose that, in turn, *the law firm was being paid by its clients*: the Clinton campaign and the DNC. To tell half the story is patently misleading.

It is inconceivable that Steele did not know the Clinton campaign and the DNC had sponsored the Fusion research he was conducting. It was not a secret at Fusion: Nellie Ohr knew enough about whom she was working for to tell her husband, Bruce, that the project was connected to the Clinton campaign. Bruce Ohr told Congress he communicated this fact to the Bureau precisely because he knew it was a salient indication of potential bias. Simpson and Steele briefed experienced journalists, and Carter Page recalled that some reporters who contacted him after the Isikoff article was published said the Clinton campaign was behind the allegations against him. Page, upon doing his own research, learned that "a law firm close to the Clinton campaign had hired a London-based private investigator to investigate my Russia trip." In addition, the State Department's Jonathan Winer had shared with Steele a second dossier compiled by Cody Shearer and Sidney Blumenthal. It asserted that Fusion GPS had been hired by the DNC to "rack [sic] down Trump compromised story."[29] The House Intelligence Committee found that the Justice Department and the FBI were well aware of the dossier's Clinton campaign and DNC origins. How could all these people know, but Steele himself be kept in the dark?

Fifth, Democrats who have tried to defend the FISA warrant application comically highlight a damning assertion as if it were his home run: *"The FBI speculates that the identified U.S. Person was likely looking for information that could be used to discredit Candidate #1's campaign."* This vague statement, they claim, was adequate disclosure of the dossier's political motivation. But the statement is patently deceptive. It was simply not true that the FBI had to "speculate" that a political motive was "likely" involved; *the FBI knew to a certainty that a very specific political motive was involved.* Nearly three months before the warrant application was submitted, Justice Department official Ohr told the FBI that Simpson was working for Fusion on an anti-Trump research project for the Clinton campaign and the DNC. Ohr had also met personally with Simpson in August, and then passed his allegations about Trump to the FBI. When you know X is true for a specific reason, it is misleading to speculate that X may be true for some potential reason.

Steele's Credibility

The dense footnote, in which the Justice Department and the FBI obscured the dossier's Clinton-campaign and DNC origins, also undertook to dismiss significant issues related to Steele's personal credibility and reliability—mainly by the more traditional subterfuge of omitting material information, though there was plenty of circumlocution, too. These problems got more acute over time, and thus later iterations of the footnote became more farcical.

It is truly astonishing that Democrats and other defenders of the FISA warrants contend with a straight face that Steele's contempt for Donald Trump was sufficiently disclosed because the footnote conveys a political motivation "to discredit [Trump's] campaign." But even that drastically watered-down description is not attributed to Steele; *it is attributed to Simpson ("identified U.S. person"*—not "Source #1"—"was likely looking for information that could be used to discredit Candidate #1's campaign"). There is no description of *Steele's* personal motivation. The footnote refers to Steele's "reason for conducting the research into [Trump's] ties to Russia," but the only reason described is Simpson's "likely" political motivation. There is no discussion of Steele's own political or personal biases. Rather, the footnote merely assures the court that Steele's reporting has "been corroborated and used in criminal proceedings" and that the FBI has "compensated" him, assesses him to be "reliable," and "is unaware of any derogatory information pertaining to" him. The footnote then moves on to Steele's methodology for collecting information.

This is another indication of a flaw we've previously noted: The FBI regarded Steele as a fellow investigator, whose biases were suppressed by his professionalism. He was not treated as an informant whose biases had to be factored in and accounted for. There is no disclosure that he despised Trump, professed desperation that Trump not be elected, and was unabashedly hopeful that all his allegations would be disclosed by Election Day—under circumstances where it was evident that, as a political partisan working for the opposition campaign, he had begun disclosing these allegations through the media.

The footnote's assertion that Steele's "reporting has been corroborated" did not make clear that the FBI meant *only his reporting done in the past*. To be sure, Steele's "previous [reliable] reporting history" and the prior use of his information in criminal proceedings (apparently, the FIFA soccer case) were referenced. But it was not made clear that his Trump–Russia information had not been corroborated.

The disclosure that Steele had been "compensated" by the Bureau does not appear to explain that he was formally signed and indoctrinated as an FBI informant (there are redactions, so it is not possible to say for sure). That is a minor matter. What's major are the assertions that Steele was reliable and unsullied by "derogatory information." By October 21, the FBI had been receiving Steele's reports for nearly four full months, and his major allegations remained unverified. Just days earlier, it had been brought to the FBI's attention that Steele had identified a nonexistent entity (the Russian consulate in Miami) as a hub of the purported Trump–Russia conspiracy—a foundational error that the dossier indicates Steele had been reporting for weeks. The Bureau, meanwhile, had had months to run down Steele's sources and learn that some of the most critical ones either were not positioned to know the information sourced to them (e.g., Millian) or could be peddling disinformation (e.g., Surkov and Trubnikov). Plus, Steele was advocating for, apparently doing paid work for, and getting information about Russia from Oleg Deripaska—an oligarch and Putin confidant (and one whose connection to Paul Manafort was among the reasons the Bureau had made Manafort a suspect in the collusion caper).

The footnote's description of Steele's methodology makes one wonder what the FISC was thinking about. The judges were told that Steele tasked his "sub-sources" to collect information, which they transmitted to him for forwarding to Simpson. It is the observations of these "sub-sources" that are offered to the court to show probable cause, but the sub-sources are not identified, nor is the court given any reason to credit them—or even told how many hearsay links stretch between the alleged fact, a sub-source's acquisition of it, and the communication of it to Steele. Everything rests on Steele's purported reliability—even though he did not make a single relevant observation.

Finally, it was blatantly obvious that Steele was leaking to the media. For those of us who admire the FBI, the legerdemain on this score is truly embarrassing.

First, we must note that the application relies heavily on Isikoff's Yahoo News article while denying that Steele is the source for the article—at least the "direct" source. This appears to be a blatant case of circular reporting: Unable to verify Steele's information, the government tries to have Steele corroborate Steele, through a media account, as to which the obvious sourcing to Steele is kinda sorta denied. It would be easier to contend that the Justice Department would not engage in such a practice if media reports were not cited elsewhere in the submission (and if we had not since learned that Steele and the FBI used media reports in the futile effort to verify Steele's information).

In attempting to defend the FISA warrant, Democrats argued that the lengthy discussion of Isikoff's article was not circular reporting; rather, it was offered "to inform the Court of Page's public denial of his suspected meetings in Russia" (with Sechin and Divyekin).[30] But this makes no sense. It was not necessary to supply a lengthy, substantive summary of the article for that purpose (a citation would have done the trick). More to the point, Isikoff's article did not even include a denial by Page; it said that he declined requests for comment, and that he "declined to say whether he was meeting with Russian officials during his trip." Furthermore, the Grassley–Graham memo includes this passage, which is redacted from the FISA warrant application as publicly disclosed: "[T]he information contained in the September 23rd news article generally matches the information about Page that [Steele] discovered during his/her research[.]" To be sure, there are other redactions which make it hard to draw a firm conclusion; but it is difficult to imagine why the Justice Department would make this assertion except to imply that Isikoff's article—purportedly not sourced directly to Steele—bolstered Steele's research.

Let's put the circular reporting issue aside and focus on the sleight of hand regarding whether Steele was Isikoff's source, and regarding his media contacts generally.

It is palpable that Steele is the probable source, but the application drops another footnote, rationalizing that the "FBI does not believe that [Steele] *directly* provided this information to the press" (emphasis added).[31] The implication is that Simpson must have been Isikoff's source because, the court is told, Steele has represented to the Bureau that he "only provided this information to [Simpson] and the FBI." Yet the FBI knew that Steele had also shared information with both the Justice Department's Ohr and the State Department's Kavalec, both of whom knew he'd had contacts with the media. More significantly, the application does not say whether the FBI asked Steele if he was Isikoff's source; and he is not described as denying it. It looks, instead, like the FBI didn't ask the question—probably because it didn't want to know the answer.

Why do I say that? Just ten days after the FISA warrant was granted, Steele went public with his cooperation in the Trump–Russia investigation, through David Corn's October 31 *Mother Jones* article. At that point, the Bureau had no choice but to remove Steele from the investigation—at least ostensibly—for violating its press contacts rule, which forbids informants from discussing the substance of their investigative work and covert relationship with the FBI. Three months later, just before President Trump's inauguration, the FBI disclosed in its application to reauthorize the Page FISA warrant that it had "suspended its relationship with" Steele back in October due to his "unauthorized disclosure of information to the press."[32]

We do not know if, at some point earlier point, the Justice Department notified the FISC about this suspension in some form that has not been disclosed. If not, then this footnote in the January 2017 renewal application marks the first time the court was notified. That, in itself, would be a violation of the FISC's rules, which require that the court be promptly informed if the government learns it has provided misinformation.[33] Clearly, Steele's violation of the press contacts rule strongly suggested that he had previously transgressed it—particularly in connection with the Isikoff article.

But that's not the half of it. The Justice Department and the FBI do not claim in the footnote that Steele *lied about* his contacts with the press; they say he was suspended *because he had* press contacts. Note that months later, when the FISA packages were finally disclosed to Congress, Judiciary Committee Senators Grassley and Graham referred Steele to the Justice Department for a possible false-statements prosecution for lying about his media communications. Subsequently, Justice quietly closed the matter without charges.[34] I believe that this is because Steele did not lie. There is no reason to think he would have hidden press contacts from the FBI when (a) he was open about them in speaking with other government officials; (b) it was well known that feeding leads to journalists was a core part of Fusion's modus operandi; and (c) getting Hillary Clinton elected, not investigating Trump, was Fusion's objective.

It is more likely, then, that the Justice Department and the FBI knew what Steele was doing (at least tacitly), but refrained from asking him about it. The Obama administration was leveraging its counterintelligence investigation with media leaks. The Isikoff report had been a perfect example—a melding of leaks from intelligence sources, congressional Democrats, and the Steele dossier. On April 10, 2017, the day before the news broke that Carter Page was under FISA surveillance, Strzok texted that he needed to speak with Lisa Page "about [a] media leak strategy with DOJ." The inspector general's report lamented a culture of media leaking at the FBI.[35]

The FBI never represented to the court that it had asked Steele point blank whether he was chirping to the media. And when Corn's article made the obvious explicit—Steele was talking to the press—the FBI never claimed that Steele had lied about what he was up to. I'm betting that's because he didn't lie. Remember, though Steele was an FBI informant, his Trump–Russia reporting did not start as an FBI investigation; it was a Fusion–Clinton campaign opposition-research venture, in which transmitting damaging information about Trump to the press and the electorate was the whole point. The FBI and the Justice Department wanted Fusion to succeed on that score—they wanted Trump to lose; the FISA investigation was just an insurance policy. Consequently, though FBI informants are not supposed to communicate information to the media, in this instance the informant's job was to communicate information to the media, and it was in connection with that job that he came to the FBI in the first place.

The Bureau danced around this awkward arrangement by not pressing him hard about his media contacts, and then making vaporous representations to the FISC about how they "believed" (fingers crossed behind back) he probably wasn't leaking.

Just as indecorously, the FBI maintained that Steele's information continued to be reliable despite his violations of the rules—even as the months went by and his information continued to go unverified. In fact, by the time of the January renewal, the intelligence community was distancing itself from the dossier: the information was dismissed as "pseudo-intelligence" (Clapper's term) that was "salacious and unverified" (Comey). Yet, the FISC was never told this, nor that Steele had invented the "Russian consulate in Miami"—nor that the sources of Steele's that had been identified were unreliable.

Worse, the disclosure that Steele had been suspended from the investigation was indefensibly misleading. Even after the FBI purported to banish Steele as an informant, it used Bruce Ohr as a back channel. Steele passed his information to Ohr, who forwarded it to the Bureau. And by May 2017, after the president fired Director Comey and Acting Director McCabe opened an obstruction investigation against Trump, the FBI was asking Ohr to reach out to Steele so they could attempt a formal reengagement.

It was never true that Steele was suspended from the investigation. And it was never true that his information was reliable.

Pretextual Use of Counterintelligence to Conduct a Criminal Investigation

Every one of the four Page warrant applications made the following assertion (emphasis added):

The Purpose of the Authorities Requested

The FBI's foreign intelligence goals for this investigation are set forth in the certification of the Executive Branch official contained herein. However, the authorities requested in this application *may produce information and material which might, when evaluated by prosecutive authorities, constitute evidence of a violation of United States law, and this investigation may result in an eventual criminal prosecution of the target.* Nevertheless, as discussed in the certification, at least a significant purpose of this request for [REDACTED] is to collect foreign intelligence information as part of the FBI's investigation of this target.

This is so matter-of-factly brazen, buried on page 41 of the fifty-four-page application, that we can easily miss its significance. *FISA authorities are not criminal-law authorities.* It is not just that FISA is not *designed* to ferret out evidence of crime; it is not *permitted* to be used for that purpose. FISA's objective is the collection of foreign intelligence, the gathering of information about the actions and intentions of foreign powers that may threaten American interests.

The Page warrant applications imply that it is a standard part of the process that "prosecutive authorities"—i.e., prosecutors, criminal investigators, grand juries—peruse FISA evidence to determine whether crimes have been committed. Not true. Prosecutors normally have nothing to do with FISA. Counterintelligence is not "prosecutive"; it aims to gather information about other countries and their operatives, not make criminal cases.

There is an exception, but it is not unique to FISA. It is a common-sense exception that applies across the board in federal law: If investigators are conducting a legitimate investigation, and they unexpectedly stumble upon evidence of a crime, they are not required to ignore it even if it wasn't what they were looking for in the first place. If, for example, a federal agency is soliciting contract bids and a patently fraudulent bid comes in, it can be referred to criminal investigators. If the FBI is doing a background check for a woman who has applied for a federal job, and agents discover she has committed bank fraud, the Bureau will refer that for prosecution. If an FBI agent is executing a search warrant that permits the seizure of guns with obliterated serial numbers, and the agent happens to find a bag of cocaine on the premises, the drugs may be seized and the culprit prosecuted on narcotics charges. Similarly, if the FBI is conducting a lawful FISA surveillance and thus learns that suspected agents of a foreign power are plotting to blow up a building, that evidence may be handed over to criminal investigators for a terrorism prosecution.

There is nothing remarkable about this exception. Everybody knows about it. It would never be spelled out in a normal search warrant. Prosecutors and agents do not write in their warrant applications, "If the premises contain incriminating materials other than that which the court has authorized agents to seize, the FBI may seize those materials." Were they to include such a provision, it would be suggestive of an unconstitutional "general warrant"; it would intimate that the government's real agenda was to hunt for evidence beyond what the warrant specifies.

Just the same, it is not necessary in a FISA warrant application to spell out the exception for good-faith, unintended discovery of criminal evidence. Doing so strongly suggests the FBI and the DOJ realize that they are conducting a de facto criminal investigation. It suggests that they are pretextually using FISA, because they either lack grounds to justify a criminal wiretap application (which requires probable cause of a crime), or they desire to conceal their criminal probe under the cover of classified intelligence. It suggests that the overarching objective is *to make a criminal case*, not to collect foreign intelligence.

As we shall see, this exploitation of counterintelligence authority to assess whether crimes were committed also sings aloud in the breathtaking March 2017 testimony in which then-Director Comey announced the existence of the Trump–Russia investigation. Its echo is heard in then-Deputy Attorney General Rod Rosenstein's appointment of Robert Mueller as special counsel.

This raises a question that should gnaw at those of us (such as your humble correspondent) who have championed robust national-security powers in an era dominated by international terrorism: Is this pretextual use of FISA something that the Justice Department and the FBI designed specifically for the Trump–Russia investigation, or is it standard operating procedure in all counterintelligence cases?

Alternative Investigative Techniques

Whenever the Justice Department and the FBI apply for a surveillance warrant, whether under FISA or the criminal law, they must convince the court that surveillance—a highly intrusive tactic by which the government monitors all of the target's electronic communications—is necessary because the information the government seeks "cannot reasonably be obtained by normal investigative techniques." This is not a box that the government can check with some boilerplate blather. Justice Department guidance instructs that, "when drafting this section of the affidavit" in support of surveillance authority, the Justice Department must include "facts particular to the specific investigation and subjects," and that "general declarations and conclusory statements about the exhaustion of alternative techniques will not suffice."[36]

Normal investigative techniques include interviewing the subject. There are, of course, situations in which such alternative investigative techniques would inevitably fail—a mafia don or a jihadist is not likely to sit down with FBI agents and tell them everything he knows. But Carter Page was not only likely to do so, *he had a documented history of providing information to the FBI*—information sufficiently reliable that the Justice Department used it in an arrest complaint and was prepared to call him as a government witness until a guilty plea obviated the need to do so.

This is a particularly disturbing aspect of the FISA episode. There appears to have been a conscious effort to provide the FISC with a skewed portrait of Page's background—in particular, his prior dealings with the government. Much is made of the fact that Russian spies attempted to recruit Page. Understated are the facts that (a) Page cooperated with the FBI and the Justice Department in a prior investigation; (b) the Russian spies in that case explicitly regarded him as "an idiot" whom they were trying to dupe; (c) since the Kremlin can be as diabolical and sophisticated as the FBI suggests, there is not much chance it would use as a foreign agent in a delicate operation a person regarded as incompetent—much less an Annapolis grad and former U.S. naval intelligence officer who had recently helped the U.S. government convict a Russian intelligence operative; and (d) the Kremlin and its agents would have known that Page—*who had never in his life met Donald Trump* (and apparently still hasn't)—did not have the kind of relationship with Trump that would have made Page a suitable conduit for proposing traitorous deals.[37]

Frustratingly, we do not know what the Justice Department and the FBI represented to the FISC about why interviewing Page would not have sufficed. For some reason, the Justice Department redacted this portion when the application was disclosed to the public. FBI agents had not only extensively interviewed Page over the years; they had done so as late as March 2016 when preparing for trial in the Russian spy case. Moreover, in Page's September 25 letter, penned right after the Isikoff article was published two days earlier, Page implored Director Comey to dispatch agents to interview him, offering to tell them the details of his Russia trip and insisting that—contrary to Steele's allegation—he had not met with any sanctioned Russians while in Moscow. The FBI evidently never responded to the letter.

Furthermore, by the time the Justice Department and the FBI submitted the FISA warrant application in October, their informant Stefan Halper had been in regular communication with Page for nearly four months. Use of a confidential informant is yet another alternative investigative technique that can make electronic surveillance unnecessary. Halper remained in contact with Page into September 2017 (when, not coincidentally, the FISA coverage lapsed and was not reauthorized). With Page both available for formal interviews by the Bureau, and subjected to covert interviews by the Bureau's informant, what could be the justification for arguing that there were no alternatives to monitoring all of Page's emails, texts, and phone calls?

A constant theme of the Carter Page FISA misadventure: There appear to be no good answers.

CHAPTER SIXTEEN
'Flood Is Coming'

O n her way out the door and out of her job as national-security adviser, Susan Rice wrote an email-to-self.[1] Except it was not really an email-to-self. It was quite consciously an email *for the record*.

As she stroked her White House keyboard fifteen minutes after noon on January 20, 2017, Rice was technically back in private life, back where private people have private email accounts—even notepads if they want to scratch out a reminder the old-fashioned way. Yet, for a little bit longer, Rice still had access to her government email account. She was, as ever, the aide-de-camp—the confidant President Obama had trusted in 2012 to peddle the anti-Muslim video fable to the Sunday shows just days after the Benghazi jihadist attack. Now, though no longer a government official, she was still in a position to generate an official record. With a foot-and-a-half out the door, it was time.

It was the memo born in a crossfire hurricane. Rice was attempting to sculpt the dispositive historical account of a meeting the Obama White House was fretting over, along with its Justice Department, FBI, and intelligence agencies. The email would masquerade as the contemporaneous account of a powwow that had happened over two weeks earlier, when everything was finally in place to trigger the insurance policy: the plan to envelop the Trump presidency in an investigation the president would be powerless to end; the plan to portray Trump publicly as exactly the compromised tool of the Kremlin the Obama administration had been secretly telling the FISC he was. The plan would subject the new administration to close monitoring by unaccountable bureaucrats, while politically devastating intelligence leaks made Donald Trump a one-term president, if not less.

"*By the book.*" Rice was emphatic on that. President Obama, we're told, insisted that the top national-security officials of what he hilariously describes as his "scandal-free" administration must do everything in the Trump–Russia investigation "by the book."[2] Of course, the Book of Common Sense tells you that people who've been doing things by the book for years don't need to be told that. Just as it tells you that a memo like the one Rice hastily planted on January 20, purporting to summarize decisions made fifteen tumultuous days earlier, is not written to preserve an accurate, real-time record of what was decided. It is written to rationalize those decisions in the wake of cataclysmic events—and the storm sure to follow.

Obama's Counterintelligence Probe

Recall that the Obama White House had been involved in the Trump–Russia investigation from the first. That is not a dig. That is the way it is supposed to be. Trump–Russia was a counterintelligence investigation, and such investigations are done *for the president*.

Note the contrast. As we've observed, criminal investigations are done to build indictments. Prosecution after a criminal investigation is the vindication of the rule of law in judicial proceedings. To be sure, it is constitutionally permissible for presidents to insinuate themselves in such investigations. In our system, investigation and prosecution are innately executive powers, exercises of the president's authority. Yet, presidents know the integrity of the justice system hinges on the perception, as well as the reality, that criminal cases are controlled by law, not politics. They thus customarily limit their active role to the setting of overall enforcement priorities (e.g., more resources for counterterrorism, less for border security), intervening in individual cases only rarely—most commonly, to invoke the pardon power if an injustice has arguably been done. Otherwise, the White House is passive. The Justice Department and its component agencies (principally, the FBI) administer criminal justice under the watchful eye of the courts, which protect citizens by applying the Constitution and congressional law.

Counterintelligence investigations are different in kind. They are not done to build prosecutions or uphold the rule of law. They are conducted strictly to support the president's constitutional duty to protect the United States against threats from foreign powers.³ Internationally, this mission is supported by the CIA and other intelligence agencies that engage in the often dangerous business of collecting information outside the United States, and thus outside the jurisdiction of our law and the writ of our courts. Domestically, however, the FBI functions as the nation's security service. That is because domestic intelligence collection directly affects Americans. It is conducted within the jurisdiction of American law, so we want it done by a federal agency that is always subject to constitutional and other U.S. legal restraints.

Because the FBI is also the nation's premier law-enforcement agency, this means domestic policing and security from foreign threats are housed under the same bureaucratic roof. This distinguishes our system from that of, for example, England, where these functions are handled by separate agencies. The FBI's dual role can be an advantage: If done within guidelines that protect the rights of Americans, leveraging law enforcement and intelligence-gathering can improve the performance of both, making us safer. On the other hand, as we've seen, the combination has great potential for abuse: Due-process and privacy protections can be eroded if the FBI uses counterintelligence powers pretextually to conduct criminal investigations—an abuse I used to insist would never happen, but which, alas, was the signature feature of Russia-gate.

Moreover, the conjoining of police and intelligence functions can cause confusion, not just for the public but for FBI and Justice Department officials. Many of high rank piously obsess over the "independence" of these agencies, as if they composed a separate fourth branch of government, insulated from political accountability. Such talk is constitutional illiteracy. The separation between political authority and law enforcement is prudential, not mandatory. And there is no separation at all between political authority and counterintelligence. To repeat, *counterintelligence is not law enforcement.* It is a mission carried out by the national-security divisions of the Justice Department and the FBI, solely to assist the president. In our constitutional system, the responsibilities of protecting the nation from the likes of Russia and determining what intelligence is necessary to do so are entrusted to the elected president. It is the president who is politically accountable to those whose lives are at stake. Unelected bureaucrats play a vital role, but it is a support role, in which they are accountable to the president, and thus to We the People. The history of regimes whose police powers are insulated from political accountability is not a happy one.

Counterintelligence investigations are done *by* the FBI but they are done *for* the president. The Trump–Russia counterintelligence investigation belonged to President Obama, and he was not a passive principal. Remember that when Agent Peter Strzok, fresh back from his secret early August 2016 London interviews, attended the first big hush-hush interagency meeting about the investigation, he was told, "The White House is running this."[4] So it was. Had it not been, there would have been no reason for the White House national-security adviser to be writing an eleventh-hour CYA memo—or, rather, a *C the Boss's A* memo.

Obama Knew All About Russia's Espionage in Real Time

Rice's memo concerns a White House meeting on January 5, 2017, when President Obama huddled with national-security officials regarding their assessment of Russia's interference in the election. Of course, Russia had not actually interfered *in the election*; it interfered *in the campaign* by publicizing stolen emails and peddling propaganda, most of which was too ridiculous to influence anyone (except, I suppose, the rare voter who decided based on the depiction of Hillary, in Satan's horns and boxing gloves, squaring off against Jesus).[5] No ballots or voting processes were manipulated.

But let's not quibble over a good story, which was then being composed. The president had ordered this intelligence assessment to be rushed to completion while he was still in office. By the time of the January 5 Oval Office confab, Obama had already started taking theatrical action based on it. So, let's pause over the president's sudden, postelection decision to treat Russia's provocation as if it were a national-security emergency, if not an act of war.

In reality, Obama and U.S. intelligence agencies had been intimately aware of the Kremlin's cyber operations *while they were taking place during the campaign.* Indeed, on August 4, 2016, CIA Director John Brennan cawed about it to his Russian counterpart, FSB chief Alexander Bortnikov. Subsequently, in early September 2016, on the sidelines of the G-20 summit in China, Obama himself delivered directly to Putin what we're assured was a stern warning to cease and desist. The administration knew exactly what Russia did, in real time and well in advance of the election. In fact, on October 6, Obama's Office of the National Intelligence Director (James Clapper) and Department of Homeland Security (under Secretary Jeh Johnson) issued a joint statement expressing "confiden[ce] that the Russian Government directed the recent compromises of emails from US persons and institutions, including from US political organizations," such as the DNC.[6]

Yet, the president refrained from any meaningful response. Not only that. When White House National Security Council staffers urged that Moscow be hit with countermeasures that had actual teeth, rather than stern warnings, Rice issued a stand-down order.[7] In the meantime, both President Obama and Secretary Clinton, just days before the election, lambasted candidate Trump for daring to question the integrity and legitimacy of the election. At that moment, everything of importance we now know about Russia's cyber hijinks was already known to the incumbent Democratic administration.

The chief executive, who had the power to expose and punish Putin's perfidy, knew all about it and did nothing. In fact, in the immediate aftermath of the election, before a transparently political pivot to the collusion narrative, Obama himself conceded that Russia makes a habit of interfering in American elections, and that its mischief-making is always futile. He acknowledged that 2016 had been no different, neither the nuisance nor its futility. The Kremlin's "manipulations were not particularly sophisticated," he opined. "This was not some elaborate, complicated espionage scheme." Instead, the Russians had merely "hacked into some Democratic party emails that contained pretty routine stuff"—sure, any of us would find that "embarrassing or uncomfortable" if it were our own emails, but "there was not anything particularly illegal or controversial about" the emails at issue here.[8]

Just so.

The blunt fact is that the officials best informed about Russia's provocation fully understood that it was par for a course played many times over. In the greater scheme of things, it was trivial—as campaign spending and messaging, it was a drop in the ocean. And Democrats, who had spent the entire campaign insisting that Hillary Clinton's own emails were immaterial to voters, were in no position to claim that the exposure of forgettable emails written by nondescript Democrats was even relevant, much less decisive.

No one—not Obama, not Clinton, not Putin, and probably not Trump himself—believed Trump was going to win the election. Because Clinton was the certain victor, Democrats made a calculated decision that nothing said or done would even hint that her coronation reflected anything other than the will of the people. Since Russia's shenanigans had no effect on the election, there would be no retaliation. No escalation would prevent the new Clinton administration from persisting in the Obama legacy of risibly weak responses to Russian aggression. No action would be taken that might inhibit Clinton from entering deals with Putin—maybe more nuclear-arms treaties like Obama's New Start debacle, the kind that get progressives swooning while Moscow builds up its arsenal (and we cut ours).[9]

Ten Weeks . . . and a Choice to Make

Once Clinton lost, however, all bets were off. Now, in a mere ten weeks, President Trump would take charge of the government's intelligence agencies and files.

What did that mean? In just ten weeks, the new president would be positioned to discover that the Obama administration had exploited its foreign-counterintelligence powers to spy on the opposition party's presidential campaign. Donald Trump would learn of the embarrassment, now being kept under wraps, that rampant abuses of surveillance authorities during Obama's tenure, and energetic efforts to conceal them, had prompted the FISC, during a secret October 2016 hearing, to scold the intelligence agencies' "institutional lack of candor."[10]

It would become apparent to Trump that the Obama administration had been telling the FISC that his campaign was traitorously complicit in Russia's hacking of Democratic email accounts. Trump would be poised to find out that the FBI, in coordination with the CIA, the State Department, and friendly foreign governments, had for months been running informants at Trump-campaign advisers, aggressively asking them loaded questions designed to implicate the campaign in Russia's hacking operations. He would hear of the "unmasking" of Trump associates in intelligence reporting so that Obama officials, such as Rice and Brennan, could monitor them. It would become clear to Trump that these steps were taken in stealth, withheld even from the Gang of Eight that was created precisely to prevent such audacious executive action in the absence of high-level congressional oversight.

Most significantly, Trump would grasp that he, as the Republican nominee and now the president, was the target of the investigation. Not the campaign; *Trump himself.*

It would inevitably dawn on the new president that, had he not been the target, Obama national-security officials would have given him or one of his surrogates with strong national-security credentials (Rudy Giuliani, Chris Christie, Jeff Sessions, etc.) a defensive briefing to warn that the campaign might be infiltrated by agents of Russia. As Obama Attorney General Loretta Lynch later admitted to congressional investigators, giving such a briefing "is not an uncommon thing to do…in intelligence matters."[11] But instead, Obama officials made a conscious decision to use against their political opposition the counterintelligence powers entrusted in them for the protection of national security against foreign threats. That is, although Obama officials fully realized that *providing a defensive debriefing to the campaign* would be the standard practice to address concerns about some campaign participants (such as Paul Manafort, Carter Page, and George Papadopoulos), they rejected that option and made a willful decision *to investigate the campaign as a corrupt enterprise.* Donald Trump's corrupt enterprise.

Given the scandalous modern American legacy of domestic political spying, the Obama administration had to know this was an extremely controversial choice to make. The choice made perfect sense, though, if it was *the candidate himself,* not just sundry campaign hangers-on, whom intelligence agents suspected of being a foreign agent. What defensive brief could possibly eradicate a rival foreign power's infiltration of the Trump campaign *if the Obama administration had made up its mind that Trump himself was the problem?* The Trump campaign wasn't going to remove Trump.

Donald Trump is nothing if not shrewd. He would realize all of this. Furthermore, Trump would know that Obama's Justice Department and the FBI largely based their suspicions—suspicions they took to a secret federal court—on unverified, multiple-hearsay rumor-mongering generated by the Clinton campaign. Simultaneously, it would be clear to Trump, these same officials were burying a criminal case against Clinton, one supported by such daunting evidence of guilt that the plain language of criminal statutes had to be distorted to avoid enforcing them.

Ten weeks. That is when Trump would inherit the keys to the intelligence kingdom. President Obama and his top advisers thus had a stark choice.

They could sit back passively and hope Trump would be content with the power and trappings of the nation's highest office, willing to excuse his opponents' excesses after a heated campaign, quietly convinced to look forward rather than backward. There were even some indications he could be reasoned with: In the days following his election victory, Trump took pains to say he was not actually hot to have Hillary Clinton prosecuted for mishandling classified information and destroying government records—even though he'd spent the campaign whipping up his base's "lock her up" fervor.[12] Maybe Trump would see the sense in keeping a top-secret shroud over the Russia investigation's targeting of the Trump campaign. Maybe the Obama administration should refrain from any anticipatory damage control.

Or, instead, Obama officials could assume that Trump would be Trump, that he'd be enraged, and that he'd be too mercurial to keep the investigation concealed, even if disclosure was not necessarily in his interests (after all, because of the FBI's excellent reputation, many Americans would believe that if there was smoke, there must have been fire—that maybe Trump really was a Putin stooge). The Obama administration had to figure that the new president, who reveled in his "punch back twice as hard" image, would be inclined to reveal everything and then go on offense. Consequently, if the investigation was going to be disclosed anyway, Obama officials had to figure it would be better for them if they orchestrated the disclosure themselves, rather than leaving it to Trump. That way, instead of a political liability, the investigation would be a political weapon—an *insurance policy*.

Through a campaign of government action and stealthy intelligence leaks, the public could be convinced that there truly was a sinister Trump–Russia conspiracy. The media could be depended on to play along. As the investigation of the Trump campaign was gradually revealed, the public might be increasingly convinced that Obama officials had simply done what duty demanded. The president and his minions could use their waning days of control over the levers of power to cement the Trump–Russia collusion narrative into conventional wisdom. If done methodically enough, the new president and his staff, Washington novices, might even be intimidated into allowing the investigation to continue—for fear of being seen as obstructing it.

For Obama officials, the latter course was the only choice. You want to say it's the choice that came naturally to an administration run by an Alinskyite progressive schooled in the extortionate use of power, process, and the press against political foes? I'm in no position to say you're wrong.[13] But there was more to it than that. There was the adamantine conviction of Obama officials that Trump was deeply corrupt.

The portrayal of Trump and his minions as compromised by the Kremlin was more than just political posturing. For many Obama officials, it was an article of faith. Never forget: In making the Obama administration's application for a FISA surveillance warrant, the FBI represented to the FISC that Trump's campaign was likely complicit in Russia's cyberespionage. This representation continued to be made through the first nine months of Trump's presidency. Of course, when Obama officials first posited this allegation, they never expected it to see the light of day. Still, no such asseveration would have been made unless some of these officials believed it in their bones. That they could not prove it was seen, in the moment, as a temporary inconvenience that time would overcome.

They believed it. In their obdurate disdain for Trump—not disdain for a mere political adversary but for a man they'd internalized as an irredeemable villain, a white supremacist nationalist bent on disrupting social progress and the international community—they abandoned the cool professional's detached objectivity. They convinced themselves that Christopher Steele was a reliable British intelligence pro, rather than a well-paid partisan hack. They were confident that Steele's claim of an elaborate Trump–Russia conspiracy must be true...they just hadn't been able to corroborate it yet. Surely that would happen any day now...if they could just keep the investigation alive.

Just as in the Clinton's email scandal, the key decision—this time to project a case against Trump rather than bury a case against Clinton—traces directly back to President Obama.

Orchestrating Collusion

On December 6, less than a month after Clinton's defeat and despite having pooh-poohed both the Kremlin's meddling and the very notion that American national elections can be stolen, the president ordered CIA Director Brennan to assess the impact of Russia's activities.[14] Brennan was to coordinate a review of intelligence by the relevant agencies—in particular, the CIA, the FBI, and the NSA—and compose a nonclassified summary for public consumption.

Think about that.

This is the federal government we're talking about. Completion of a multiagency report after a public controversy typically takes months, if not longer. Here, the matter was far more challenging. It involved classified information of the highest order, the tapping of the intelligence community's most sensitive sources of information about the deliberations and actions of the Putin regime, our most intelligence-savvy competitor. It routinely takes professional investigators at the Justice Department and the FBI well over a year to finish probes of far less complex matters, even though they have subpoena power to compel the production of relevant documents and the testimony of knowledgeable witnesses. In stark contrast, most of the witnesses and evidence relevant to Russia's 2016 espionage operations were either beyond the grasp of American investigators, or too highly classified to be exposed in court. And, though some critical proof, such as the hacked servers, was easily accessible, the Democrat-controlled Justice Department had curiously chosen not to subpoena or otherwise seize it from the Democratic National Committee. Nevertheless, the president demanded that the intelligence community's major investigative arms complete the investigation in a matter of days.

There were only two rational reasons for doing this. First, it ensured that the report would be completed by Obama's own intelligence chiefs, in particular, the hyper-partisan Brennan, not Trump appointees. Second, it meant the report would be submitted to Obama himself, not to the new president. The Obama administration would orchestrate the rollout.

Naturally, as we saw with the exoneration of Mrs. Clinton, summary reports are not that difficult to pull together quickly when the outcome is predetermined. On December 28, with the public rollout of the report imminent, the president signed an executive order, effective the next day, announcing "Additional Steps to Address the National Emergency With Respect to Significant Malicious Cyber-Enabled Activities" by Russia.[15] Having thus elevated to a "national emergency" these activities that Obama had deemed too petty to address when they were actually happening, the chief executive made a point of noting an ongoing multi-departmental investigation which could very well find that there had been "tampering with, altering, or causing a misappropriation of information with the purpose or effect of interfering with or undermining election processes or institutions."[16] In reality, as the president had publicly stated, there had been peddling of irrelevant emails and moronic propaganda — which is why he had ignored it.

By the order, Obama expelled thirty-five people described as Russian "intelligence operatives." He slapped sanctions on two Russian intelligence agencies—the military and civilian spy services, respectively, the GRU and FSB, as well as four "cyber officials" and three companies said to support Russian cyber operations. Further, he shuttered Russian-owned buildings on Long Island and Maryland's eastern shoreline, which were suddenly branded as intelligence operations. Mind you, these facilities and operatives had been up and running throughout Obama's presidency. No meaningful action was taken against them throughout the 2016 campaign, while Obama was being extensively briefed about Russia's hacking and propaganda operations. Nor when Russia annexed Crimea, consolidated its de facto seizure of eastern Ukraine, propped up Assad, armed Iran, buzzed U.S. naval vessels, and saber-rattled in the Baltics. Only now, to prop up a postelection emphasis on the Trump–Russia narrative.

'We Cannot Share Information Fully as It Relates to Russia'

As a new year was ushered in, another clock was ticking. The ninety-day surveillance warrant on Carter Page had been issued on October 21, meaning it was scheduled to lapse right as the new president was being inaugurated on January 20. If the Obama administration wanted to ensure its renewal, that would have to be done while Obama was still in office. Consequently, a reauthorization application—an elaborate process that calls for a thoroughgoing review at the top echelons of the FBI and the Justice Department—was underway.

To continue the investigation would be tricky, requiring both that the Steele dossier be revisited (since it would be reaffirmed in the new surveillance application), and that careful consideration be given to how the investigation would be explained to the incoming president. After all, if it were forthrightly explained to Trump that he was the focus of an investigation in which the Justice Department and FBI had already told a federal court that he might be a Russian agent, how could they be sure that he would allow the probe to continue? That he would retain for a nanosecond the Obama appointees who had orchestrated it?

There was thus a lot on the Obama administration's plate on January 5, when the president convened his national-security team at the White House. The administration's top political officials in the national-security sphere—the president, along with Rice and Vice President Biden—were joined by the heads of the four top intelligence agencies: Clapper, Comey, Brennan, and Rogers, along with Deputy Attorney General Sally Yates.[17] Topping the agenda was "Assessing Russian Activities and Intentions in the Recent US Elections," the report Obama had ordered Brennan and his colleagues to complete, along with a nonclassified summary for public consumption.[18] Significantly, the four intelligence chiefs were scheduled to brief President-elect Trump on the same report the very next day, at Trump Tower in Manhattan.

According to Rice's memo, immediately after discussion of the report, Obama directed Yates and Comey to join him for "a brief follow-on conversation," along with Biden and Rice. Unlike most others at the meeting, the DAG and the FBI director would be staying on in their jobs after Trump took office. If the Russia investigation were to be sustained after Trump's inauguration, it would be up to them to persevere in it.

So, what instructions did the president give them—aside, *of course*, from the admonition that everything must be done "by the book"? This is how Rice recalled it in her last-second email (emphasis added):

> President Obama said he wants to be sure that, as we engage with the incoming team, we are mindful to ascertain *if there is any reason that we cannot share information fully as it relates to Russia.*

Remember, Rice wrote this fifteen days after the meeting. She knew quite well that the administration had not "shared information fully as it relates to Russia"—such as the information that Yates and Comey had signed off on FISA warrant applications alleging that the Trump campaign was complicit in Russia's espionage.

Rice's email continued with a blacked-out paragraph—almost surely referring to some of the information that the Obama administration had decided "we cannot share" with the new administration. Obama's key aide then closed by reciting the president's final instruction to Director Comey: Obama was to be informed "if anything changes in the next few weeks that should affect *how we share classified information* with the incoming team."

You have to keep reminding yourself: Rice was not writing a contemporaneous memo; "the next few weeks" *had already happened.* As Trump was about to take the reins, Rice was writing a post-facto rationalization for withholding information from him. While the Obama administration had promised cooperation with the Trump transition, the events of the two weeks before Trump's inauguration had been indicative of concealment and deceit. Rice was painting a happy face on them: Not Obama's fault, you see; it was just what "the book" required.

So what happened in those two weeks?

Politicized Intelligence

On January 6, the intelligence community assessment (ICA) was publicly released. Given how hastily it was slapped together, we should not be surprised that it was less than convincing in its titillating conclusion that Russia's interference was intended to help Trump win.

Brennan's CIA and Comey's FBI solemnly expressed high confidence in this conclusion (the NSA just had "moderate confidence"). Why? They couldn't tell us. The agencies maintained that the secretive nature of their work, the need to preserve intelligence methods and sources, forbade them from describing all of the information that enabled them to read Vladimir Putin's mind.

Sure.

The problem, of course, is that if you're essentially going to say, "Trust us," you have to have proven yourself trustworthy over time. Here, we are talking about an intelligence community whose own analysts have complained that their superiors distort their reports for political purposes. In just the past few years, they have preposterously told us that they had "high confidence" that Iran suspended its nuclear-weapons programs in 2003; that the NSA was not collecting metadata on millions of Americans; and that the Muslim Brotherhood is a moderate, "largely secular" organization. We have learned that the Obama administration intentionally used a compliant media "echo chamber" to sell the public on the Iran nuclear deal (and the fiction that the jihadist mullahs of Tehran were moderating). We saw U.S. intelligence and law-enforcement agencies back the Obama administration's political claim that "violent extremism," not radical Islam, is the explanation for terrorist strikes; that a jihadist mass-murder attack targeting soldiers about to deploy to Afghanistan was "workplace violence"; that al-Qaeda had been "decimated"; that the threat of the ISIS "JV" team was exaggerated; and that the Benghazi massacre was not really a terrorist attack but a "protest" gone awry, incited by an anti-Muslim video.

And that was before the FBI asserted with confidence that Trump-campaign officials were complicit in Russia's cyberespionage attacks against Democrats—a representation the Bureau made to the FISC at the same time intelligence community chiefs were belittling the Steele dossier as uncorroborated rumor that could not be included in the ICA.

To be sure, our intelligence agencies overflow with patriotic Americans who do the quiet, perilous work that saves American lives. *As an institution*, however, "Trust us" is not going to get them very far.

The three agencies based their conclusion that Putin was rooting for Trump on speculation ("Putin *most likely* wanted to discredit Secretary Clinton because" he blames her for protests against his regime), along with heavy doses of hypothesis (Putin is said to have: liked "Trump's stated policy to work with Russia"; seen Trump's election as a potential pathway "to achieve an international coalition against the Islamic State", "had many positive experiences working with Western political leaders whose business interests made them more disposed to deal with Russia"; etc.). This guesswork, it is worth noting, was based on publicly available press reports. It didn't tell us anything we couldn't have surmised on our own, even without intelligence training and access to classified information.

There is no doubt that Putin meddles in Western political campaigns, as Russia traditionally has. And we can readily assume that he, like everyone else, has his favored candidates. But Putin is a cold, calculating man, one who would not permit his eccentric preferences to intrude on his real-world objectives. His realistic hope for us is destabilization: raising hot-button issues, exploiting racial divisions and economic anxieties, inciting tensions between rivals but not necessarily picking one over the other. Putin knows Russia is not going to take over the United States; but if factions are alienated against Washington and the cultural mainstream, it makes governance and social cohesion difficult. That is his goal for us. Internal strife makes it hard for an American administration to pursue American interests, opening opportunities for Moscow. This counsels in favor of supporting *the likely losers*, not the expected winners.

Our intelligence community knows this. After all the huffing and puffing about Russia's "espionage" and "covert ops" to try to "denigrate" Mrs. Clinton, our agencies acknowledged that the Russians assumed Clinton was going to win. Mainly, Putin was trying to fire up dissenters who might undermine the effectiveness of her anticipated presidency. Even if we accept that the Russians wanted Trump to win, they were not daft enough to believe they could actually swing the election to him.

The agencies' report, however, was conceived as a political document. It makes boldly suggestive declarations, conjuring visions of a Kremlin-orchestrated coup, ballast for the Democrats' election-theft narrative. The agencies, for example, tossed in an inchoate conclusion that Russian intelligence has "researched US electoral processes and related technology and equipment," and even "accessed elements of multiple state or local electoral boards." Wait a second, you're thinking, does that mean they fiddled with the actual votes? No. If you read on, you learn that the Department of Homeland Security "assesses that the types of systems we observed Russian actors targeting or compromising are not involved in vote tallying."

So why mention this at all? It wouldn't be because Trump supporters were highlighting the fact that Russia's hacking had no impact on the *electoral process*, would it? Would John Brennan do something like that? No way, right?

"We did not make an assessment of the impact that Russian activities had on the outcome of the 2016 election." That is what the report says, though you wouldn't know it to hear a Democrat discuss the matter. Yes, the report breathlessly attests that Russia wanted to "influence" the election, but the agencies admit that the Kremlin's desire was to "undermine the U.S.-led democratic order" and "faith in the US democratic process." Did anyone need an intelligence report to know that?

The Trump Tower Dossier Briefing . . . and CNN Is There!

The intelligence chiefs met the president-elect on January 6 at Trump Tower. The main topic was the ICA. It was FBI Director James Comey's first-ever encounter with Donald Trump. As he later recounted in lawyerly Senate testimony, he had a plan for this session and executed it to a tee.

First, the intelligence chiefs explained the report to the incoming president. Notice the distinction: They briefed Trump on *the report about Russia's interference in the campaign*, not *the ongoing investigation of Trump campaign coordination in Russia's cyberespionage*. The latter was hinted at in a two-page synopsis of some Steele dossier information that Clapper and the other intel chiefs decided to incorporate in the stack of top-secret briefing materials (though it is unknown if Trump ever saw it). It included the information that was already publicly known because of Senator Reid's letter to Director Comey after being briefed by Brennan in the late summer—focusing on Carter Page's alleged meetings with Sechin and Divyekin.

The chiefs told Trump about the findings that Russia had interfered in the election, that Putin wanted to hurt Clinton and help Trump. They did not tell him about the suspicions confided to the FISC: that they suspected Trump himself was compromised, that his campaign was complicit in Putin's scheme.

Comey elaborated that the chiefs had also decided to brief Trump "on some personally sensitive aspects of the information assembled during the assessment." That would, of course, be the Steele dossier. Except...not *all* of the Steele dossier. Comey was clearly referring to the part that would soon be the most notorious, but least consequential: the claims that, in 2013, Trump had cavorted with micturating prostitutes at the Ritz-Carlton Hotel in Moscow, and that Russian intelligence recorded the escapade.

In his later testimony, Comey explained that he had been asked by Clapper to handle this part of the briefing alone. The stated rationale was that the presence of fewer people would "minimize potential embarrassment to the President-Elect." That is laughable. Trump would not be more or less embarrassed depending on whether this information were conveyed by one or more than one intelligence official he barely knew. Comey, moreover, was quick to assure Trump that this scandalous allegation was "salacious and unverified"—suggesting that it was yet another in a long line of tabloid-style Trump stories, so why would he have anything to be embarrassed about?

If the information was salacious and unverified, why waste the president-elect's time with it? Comey's testimonial explanation was not very persuasive. The rationalization involved blackmail. There was apparently a lot of blackmail on the brain in the last days of Obama's administration. As we'll see shortly, an incoherent fear-of-blackmail rationale would also be offered by Acting Attorney General Yates for placing General Flynn under investigation.

With respect to the pee-tape allegation, Director Comey reasoned that "to the extent there was some effort to compromise an incoming President, we could blunt any such effort with a defensive brief-ing." But if the story was nonsense, there was nothing to be concerned about. And the intelligence community had already concluded that the Steele dossier was too unreliable to include in the ICA.[19]

By so solemnly briefing such rank rumor, the director succeeded only in persuading the president-elect that a J. Edgar Hoover move was being pulled on him: a not so subtle warning that Comey could leak this compromising information at any time if Trump crossed him, which is how senior FBI officials feared the new president would take it.[20]

Comey also told the Senate, "We knew the media was about to publicly report the material and we believed the [intelligence commu-nity] should not keep knowledge of the material and its imminent re-lease from the President-Elect."[21] Well that's…intriguing. The dossier had long been an open secret, circulating among media and political people. How exactly did the agency chiefs know that press outlets were suddenly about to leak it? And why did the director specifically mention CNN as among the outlets that possessed the dossier and was "looking for a news hook"?

Few journalists have followed the Russia-gate saga with the tenac-ity and attention to detail of Mollie Hemingway.[22] As she notes, it was Clapper, Obama's National Intelligence Director, who prevailed on Comey to do the one-on-one briefing with Trump. As we've seen, Clapper has a history of misleading Congress. In later House Intelli-gence Committee testimony, Clapper first flatly denied discussing the Steele dossier with any journalist. But then, when confronted about whether he'd discussed it with CNN's Jake Tapper, Clapper changed his tune, admitting that he'd spoken about it with Tapper as well as other journalists. Clapper recalled that his conversation with Tap-per occurred around the time the intelligence chiefs briefed President Obama and President-elect Trump—i.e., January 5 and 6.[23]

Interestingly, the FBI's Deputy Director Andrew McCabe also had a line on CNN's deliberations. Around noon on January 8, he emailed senior FBI leadership, with the tart subject line, "Flood is coming."

It sure was.

"The sensitive story." That is what McCabe related that "CNN is close to going forward with." The network's "trigger" for running with "the sensitive story" was the fact that, somehow, "they know the material was discussed in the brief and presented in an attachment"—a reference to the intelligence chiefs' briefing of the president-elect and the two-page synopsis of the dossier they had decided to include in the briefing materials. Minutes later, McCabe emailed Deputy Attorney General Sally Yates to alert her on this latest news about "the sensitive reporting." "[A]s expected," he elaborated, "it seems CNN is close to running a story about" it. Yates, who had met with President Obama three days earlier at the Oval Office confab Rice would later memorialize on her way out the door, clearly needed no further explanation about what "the sensitive reporting" was.[24]

On January 10, 2017, CNN published its blockbuster story, based on leaks from "multiple US officials with direct knowledge of the briefings," that the intelligence chiefs had told President-elect Trump about the dossier—at least some of it. The story, under the byline of Jake Tapper and three other journalists, noted that a two-page synopsis of the dossier had been included in the briefing materials. Within minutes of the CNN report, BuzzFeed published the full dossier—which, Tapper later lamented, had undermined the impact of CNN's reporting.[25]

Did I mention that Clapper inked a deal in August 2017 to become a CNN commentator?[26]

From the Brits to McCain to the FBI

Incidentally, BuzzFeed's acquisition and publication of the dossier is an interesting story of Trump–Russia collusion—i.e., coordination in crafting of narrative between journalists, current and former government officials, our good friends the Brits, and their good friend (and Trump nemesis), John McCain.

The late senator had an aide named David Kramer, a former State Department Russia expert, whom he had recruited to the McCain Institute.[27] On November 19, 2016, days after Trump had been elected president, McCain and Kramer attended the Halifax International Security Forum. There, Kramer was pulled aside by Sir Andrew Wood, Britain's former ambassador to Moscow and a confidant of Christopher Steele's. Wood had been consulted by Steele regarding the sensational dossier allegations. Alarmed, he told Kramer that his former British spy friend had gathered intelligence indicating "possible collusion" between Trump and Russia, and that the Kremlin might even have "compromising" information about the president-elect.

These revelations seemed so troubling that Kramer agreed they must be shared, pronto, with Senator McCain. He proceeded to introduce McCain and his top staffer, Christopher Brose, to Wood, who walked the senator through Steele's story. Wood said Steele would be willing to meet with the senator or his emissary. McCain turned to Kramer and asked him to fly straightaway to London.

On November 28, Kramer traveled overnight across the Atlantic. At Heathrow Airport, he met up with Steele, who, in furtive spy-novel style, had texted him to look for the man in the blue coat clutching a copy of the *Financial Times*. The former spook drove Kramer to his flat. After a quick shower, McCain's aide was given the dossier reports to read, along with a scrap of paper on which were scribbled the identities of some of Steele's sources. Kramer recognized some of the names from his Russian work.[28]

Steele acknowledged that the data was raw and unverified, in need of follow-up investigation. He said he had given the materials to an FBI agent in Europe (Gaeta) and "was hopeful that the FBI would take a serious look at this." He apparently did not mention that the Bureau had been looking at it for over four months, and had recently terminated him as an official informant for exposing their investigation in his *Mother Jones* interview (which Kramer had not yet read). Steele said he was worried about the portents for the U.S.–U.K. alliance, and thought "having Senator McCain weigh in would be hopeful in terms of giving the FBI additional prod to take this seriously."

After a brief lunch, Steele drove Kramer back to the airport for the quick-turnaround flight home. He did not give Kramer a copy of the dossier—it was, after all, sensitive reporting. Rather, he arranged for Simpson to contact Kramer in Washington the next day. At Fusion's Dupont Circle office, Simpson gave the dossier to the McCain aide, explaining that *The New York Times* was already aware of some its allegations. Simpson agreed to remain in touch with Kramer regarding the dossier's delivery to Senator McCain and any next steps. The following afternoon, December 1, Kramer gave the dossier to McCain and Brose at the senator's Capitol Hill office, advising the senator to alert the directors of the FBI and the CIA about the material. Though Steele had told Kramer the FBI already had his reports, McCain indicated that he would personally share the dossier with Director Comey. He visited the FBI director on December 9, delivering the dossier. (The senator, who was already quite ill by then, died in August 2018.)

In the meantime, Kramer kept a copy. After he met with Simpson, a series of journalists began contacting him. Obviously, Simpson and Steele calculated that the dossier would be more newsworthy if reporters heard about it from the McCain camp than if they heard about it from Fusion. In his dealings with the media, Kramer says he stressed that Steele's jaw-dropping allegations were unverified, and that it was vital to maintain discretion while the matter was under investigation. He discussed the dossier with David Corn, the *Mother Jones* reporter who had interviewed Steele and given some of the dossier to the FBI's general counsel, Jim Baker. He talked about it with ABC News producer Matt Mosk and correspondent Brian Ross, who appeared to have at least some of the dossier already. He spoke about it with *The Washington Post*'s Tom Hamburger and Rosalind Helderman.

The McCain aide also took it on himself—with all due discretion, of course—to provide copies of the dossier to McClatchy's Peter Stone and Greg Gordon, to Fred Hiatt of *The Washington Post*'s editorial page, to *The Wall Street Journal*'s Alan Cullison, and to NPR's Bob Little. In addition, at Steele's request, Kramer met with CNN's Carl Bernstein (of Watergate fame), first in New York City on around January 3 or 4, then in Washington a few days later (i.e., during the period when CNN was also speaking with Clapper about Steele's allegations). During those discussions, Kramer decided to give Bernstein a copy.

Finally, at Steele's urging, the McCain aide met with BuzzFeed's Ken Bensinger. Steele vouched for Bensinger as a "very trustworthy and professional" journalist whom Steele had "worked with" during the FBI's FIFA soccer investigation. Bensinger called Kramer from Los Angeles and said he would soon fly cross-country to see the dossier. They met at the McCain Institute in Washington on December 29—Christmas season, when the office was mostly vacant. After rehearsing his connection with the sensitive matter through Sir Andrew Wood and Senator McCain, Kramer allowed Bensinger to read the document. Explaining that he was a slow reader, Bensinger asked if he could take pictures of the document, but Kramer asked him not to do that...before leaving him alone in a room with the dossier for about twenty minutes.

On January 10, Kramer met in Washington with the *The Guardian*'s Julian Borger about Steele's anti-Trump research. As they sat in a lounge, a large television was tuned in to CNN, which suddenly broke the news about the dossier. The pair traded "Holy shit!" exclamations. Kramer quickly returned to his office, where a distraught Simpson called to say that BuzzFeed had published the dossier—each page photographed by Bensinger in Kramer's office. The McCain aide replied that he would "ask them to take it down." He immediately phoned Bensinger, and "the first words out of [Kramer's] mouth were, 'You are gonna get people killed,'" Bensinger would not agree to remove the dossier from Buzz-Feed's website, though he promised to consider some redactions and to keep Kramer's name out of the coverage. Simpson subsequently told Kramer that the publicity (which Steele and Simpson had instigated) was causing him and Fusion considerable problems. Steele told Kramer he was going into hiding because *The Wall Street Journal* was about to identify him as the author. Kramer pleaded with the *Journal*'s news editors not to do that, but they had already made up their minds.

The president-elect flew into a rage over the coverage. The CNN report about the briefing had obviously come from the intelligence agencies, and, he observed in Trumpian hyperbole, the machinations of these officials were reminiscent of Nazi Germany's tactics.[29] The intelligence agencies expected news coverage about the dossier because some of their officials were talking to the media. They used that expectation as their rationalization for briefing Trump on the "sensitive reporting." The intelligence chiefs' decision to brief Trump on it became CNN's rationalization for breaking news about the dossier. In turn, CNN's breaking of the news became BuzzFeed's rationalization for publishing the dossier.

The Russia-gate narrative now had a fitting public script: raw, unverifiable innuendo, given the presumption of trustworthiness because it was about Trump.

CHAPTER SEVENTEEN

Not a Suspect?

What would make the Obama administration think Trump would allow the Russia investigation to contin ue if he was the main suspect? Of course, the adminis- tration thought no such thing.

The urgent need to keep investigating "Russia's attack on our de- mocracy" would be stressed to the public. Obama had already taken care of this. First his ballyhooed "national emergency" executive order announced Russian sanctions, the expulsion of Russian operatives, and the seizure of Russian properties. Next, he rolled out the intelligence agencies' assessment, which addressed Moscow's provocation in stark terms and emphasized that Trump was the *intended* beneficiary—just a short hop from the portrayal of Trump as the *complicit* beneficiary.

From a political standpoint, this would ratchet up the pressure on the new president to let the investigation proceed. Then, to put Trump at ease, he would be told he was not a suspect, even though the pub- lic would surely assume he was the main suspect. This news would be delivered to him by Director Comey—who would repeatedly tell the new president that they needed to guard against creating a public narrative that the FBI was investigating him—even as the FBI repeated Steele dossier allegations in FISA warrant applications, and even as, we shall see, the director himself made the stunning public revelation that the Bureau was investigating Trump-campaign coordination in Russia's cyberespionage.[1]

The FBI director is given a ten-year term of office. Director Comey sometimes suggested this was Congress's way of ensuring the inde- pendence of the nation's top federal law-enforcement agent. Not so. The tenure provision was enacted in 1976,[2] after J. Edgar Hoover's death four years earlier. What Congress and President Gerald R. Ford wanted to ensure was that there would never again be a director who reigned for nearly a half-century with Washington cowering in fear of the deep dark secrets in his files. The ten-year term was conceived as a limit, not a license. It subjected the Bureau to more political control, not less. More importantly, as Director Comey rightly recognized in his conversations with President Trump, the ten-year term is merely nominal. As a matter of constitutional law, all executive power is reposed in the president; therefore, subordinate executive officials, including the FBI director, are delegates who are permitted to exercise the president's power at the president's pleasure. They may be removed without cause.[3]

Donald Trump prizes personal loyalty (to him) above all else. He did not know the FBI director. It would not have been difficult to figure out, though, that they were not personalities that would coexist easily. The new president's circle of advisers was not exactly the Jim Comey Fan Club—Rudy Giuliani, who had hired Comey as a young prosecutor in the 1980s, had become disenchanted. So why did Trump retain Comey when he could easily have dismissed him?

It is a confounding question. But Comey is one of several Justice Department officials appointed by Obama and kept on by Trump. Perhaps mindful of how difficult Democrats would make it for his nominees to be confirmed, the new White House hoped to minimize the sense of disarray in its early days. Comey can also be a singularly charming, impressive fellow in a one-on-one setting—smart and funny, without the condescension sometimes on display in public settings. He exudes confidence and competence. He surely swept the new boss off his feet. Plus Trump, for all his *Apprentice* bravado, has a real-life aversion to firing people. With the Russia frenzy rising, however, the most significant thing Comey could do simultaneously to keep his job and preserve the investigation was to assure Trump that he was not a suspect—that the FBI, that Comey himself, did not have the new president under investigation and did not suspect him of wrongdoing.

The best way to do that was to highlight the lewd aspects of Steele's reporting while downplaying the rest. In Senate testimony after his May 2017 dismissal, Comey explained that his plan at the January 6 briefing of Trump was to alert the president-elect to "personally sensitive aspects of the information assembled during" the ICA—to let him know of "the existence of this material even though it was salacious and unverified"; to let Trump know that they were trying "to minimize potential embarrassment to" him.

This was a very crimped depiction of Steele's allegations. And even though the full dossier was published just four days after Comey spoke with Trump, that did not reveal the full story behind the dossier's genesis and the extent of reliance on it by the Obama Justice Department and the FBI. That is why, when Trump hosted Comey for dinner at the White House on January 27, and when they spoke on other occasions, Trump kept coming back to the purported pee tape, expressing disgust and ruminating over whether he should direct the FBI to investigate it so he could prove it did not happen. Because of the way he was briefed, the president was focused only on the salacious material, not the more significant, traitorous allegations that Steele had made and that the FBI was acting on.

A thought experiment. What do you suppose we'd have heard from the president if, at the briefing, Director Comey had said something along these lines:

> Mr. President-Elect, that salacious story about prostitutes in Moscow is part of a set of reports by a former British intelligence officer, compiled during the 2016 race and paid for by the Clinton campaign. It alleges that you and your campaign engaged in a "conspiracy of co-operation" with the Russian government, in which your point man was Paul Manafort, who used your adviser Carter Page as an intermediary. Page is said to have met with two top Putin operatives in July while in Moscow, where they discussed (a) the possibility that you'd drop sanctions in return for significant financial considerations, (b) their willingness to share compromising information about Hillary Clinton with you, and (c) compromising information about you that they possessed and could use against you if you were not accommodating toward Russia. Later, the reports state, your lawyer, Michael Cohen, was dispatched to Prague for a secret meeting with Russian officials to work out paying the hackers of the DNC emails. It is further alleged that Putin's regime had your full knowledge and support in leaking the DNC emails to WikiLeaks; in fact, we've been

told you were running your own reciprocal operation and sending information to the Kremlin.

There is much more in the reports, but that is the gist. Although the intelligence community has not been able to verify these allegations, the FBI has great confidence in the former British intelligence officer who provided the information to us. Therefore, in October, just three weeks before Election Day, we and the Justice Department incorporated these allegations in an application to the Foreign Intelligence Surveillance Court for a warrant to monitor all of Carter Page's communications—including from when he was in Moscow in July, allegedly meeting with Kremlin operatives on your behalf. As a matter of fact, in the next few days, we're planning to reaffirm these same allegations about your campaign and the Kremlin in another warrant application so the court can renew the surveillance for ninety more days. Come to think of it, that would be the first ninety days of your presidency, so congratulations on that.

Suffice it to say that, if President-elect Trump had been given a briefing of this breadth, his reaction would have been comparable to Mount Vesuvius circa 79 A.D. He would have figured out in short order, from competent advisers, that this investigation had proceeded largely at the urging of his political opponents, in the absence of corroboration. The chance that he would have retained any official who had had a hand in approving or conducting the investigation would be closer to "are you kidding me?" than slim.

To sustain the investigation by minimizing Trump's relevance to it, the FBI and the Justice Department had to redefine the concept of being "under investigation." For purposes of the Trump–Russia probe, a person was deemed "under investigation" only if he was *the formal target of a FISA warrant*—as if the warrant application were the totality of the investigation, as if the person formally targeted for surveillance were the *only* person of interest to the FBI. By thus bowdlerizing what it means to be a suspect, Comey could repeatedly assure Trump that he (Trump) was not "*personally* under investigation." After all, Trump himself was not the target of the surveillance—he was not alleged in the FISA warrant application to be an "agent of a foreign power"; only Page was...*for clandestine activities allegedly undertaken on Trump's behalf.*

This is a distorted understanding of how investigations work. Whether eavesdropping is done in criminal or national-security cases, the objective is always the same: *to uncover the full scope of a conspiratorial enterprise.* The point is to identify all of the conspirators, to demonstrate how the scheme operates, and to show the complicity of the most insulated leaders. Carter Page may have been the *surveillance target* named in the FISA warrant, but he was of low rank in the suspected conspiracy. The point of monitoring Page was to determine exactly what he was doing and, just as crucial, *who was directing him.* In the conspiracy outlined by Steele, Page was a virtual nobody. *His only relevance was vis-à-vis Trump.*

The investigation was about suspected Kremlin complicity *with Trump*; it was about the possibility that an adversary regime was in a position to blackmail *the president of the United States.* It was never about Carter Page.

From the FBI's perspective, there was no downside to telling Trump he was not a suspect. As Comey acknowledged in his testimony, any assurances that Trump was not under investigation were only "as of that moment."[4] Trump's status could change instantaneously if the investigation of other people, such as Page, turned up any evidence implicating Trump. In a normal investigation, to be in that status is to be a *subject* of the investigation, not a person who is not a suspect.

This dissonance was not lost on the FBI. Before meeting with Trump on January 6, Comey met with his own FBI "leadership team" of advisers and discussed the plan to tell Trump he was not a suspect. At the Senate hearing, the former director was asked whether all of his advisers agreed with the plan. Comey's answer was telling:

> Was it unanimous? One of the members of the leadership team had a view that, although it was technically true [that] we did not have a counterintelligence file case open on then-President-elect Trump[,]...because we're looking at the potential...coordination between the campaign and Russia, because it was...President-elect Trump's campaign,

this person's view was, inevitably, [Trump's] behavior, [Trump's] conduct will fall within the scope of that work.

Comey's unidentified adviser was clearly right: The fact that there was not a formal case file open on Trump just meant that he was not the express target of a FISA warrant. Trump was still the most central figure in the investigation.

The former director overruled his adviser, but he elaborated that their difference was over words, not substance:

I thought it was fair to say what was literally true: There is not a counterintelligence investigation of Mr. Trump. And I decided, in the moment, to say it, given the nature of our conversation.

Comey thus went ahead with the plan to tell Trump he was not under investigation. But his adviser was not swayed by the director's insistence that *being under investigation* required *having a formal file open as a FISA surveillance target*. Comey recalled that this adviser's position

didn't change. His view was still that it was probably—although literally true, his concern was it could be misleading, because the nature of the investigation was such that it might well touch—obviously, it would touch the campaign, and the person at the head of the campaign would be the candidate.

Right. The Obama administration's investigation was about the candidate: Donald Trump.

Criminalizing Politics: The Investigation of General Flynn

Could anything have made the Obama administration giddier than the prospect of making a criminal case on Michael Flynn?

Flynn is a retired army lieutenant general, who made his mark on modern insurgent warfare by helping revolutionize the rapid dissemination of battlefield intelligence. He was promoted by President Obama to lead the Defense Intelligence Agency (DIA). He is also a headstrong man who got himself on Obama's bad side by questioning counterterrorism strategy, particularly the administration's weakness on Iran. He was detested by Obama political and national-security officials for calling them out on politicizing intelligence. The FBI was not a fan, least of all Deputy Director Andy McCabe, because Flynn had supported an agent who claimed the Bureau had subjected her to sex discrimination.[5]

After Obama fired him from the DIA post, Flynn became an important Trump-campaign surrogate, which gave him a national media platform from which to rip Obama's foreign policy. When Trump won the election, Obama counseled him against tapping Flynn for a top administration job. Trump ignored the advice, naming Flynn his national-security adviser.[6] Flynn worked on the Trump transition and incensed Obama officials by lobbying against a U.N. resolution against Israel that the administration, in its profiles-in-courage style, orchestrated then abstained from voting on. The collusion narrative notwithstanding, Russia rebuffed Trump's entreaties on the Israel resolution.[7]

Obama's late-December imposition of sanctions on Russia got the attention of Sergey Kislyak, the Kremlin's ambassador to the United States, just as the administration figured it would. Kislyak, who has a wide, bipartisan circle of Washington contacts, got in touch with Flynn, who was dealing with a variety of foreign counterparts as a member of Trump's transition team.

The next day, December 29, Flynn called the president-elect's Mar-a-Lago resort in Palm Beach, where senior transition officials were cobbling together a new administration for the candidate no one had expected to win. Flynn and his colleagues discussed the Russia sanctions and their potential effect on Trump's foreign policy. Flynn was advised to convey the message that Russia should resist any urge to escalate the situation. Immediately afterward, Flynn called Kislyak. The topic of sanctions was discussed, but not a deal on sanctions. Rather, Flynn simply urged that Russia limit itself to no more than a reciprocal response, rather than escalate matters.[8] This, obviously, is what we should hope any responsible American official, regardless of party, would propose.

As an overt agent of Russia, Kislyak was subject to FISA monitoring; one would think Flynn, a former DIA director, would have suspected as much.[9] In any event, the FBI counterintelligence agents were not only eavesdropping on Kislyak's discussion with Flynn; they were doing so in consultation with "Obama advisers," as *The New York Times* gently described them.[10] The *Times* elaborated:

> Obama officials asked the FBI if a quid pro quo had been discussed on the call, and the answer came back no, according to one of the officials, who like others asked not to be named discussing delicate communications. The topic of sanctions came up, they were told, but there was no deal.

Asked not to be named discussing delicate communications. That's a good one. Let me translate. The officials did not want to identify themselves because they were committing a felony: FISA intercepts are classified, and disclosing them to unauthorized people, including the media, is a crime.

Two things, in any event, should be observed. First, the Flynn investigation was a vindictive farce: Even if there had been a substantive discussion of sanctions, there would have been no law violation, but there was no such discussion—just the mere mention of sanctions, prompting Flynn's proper response: don't escalate. Second, the Flynn–Kislyak communication became the grist for an outrageous classified leak for which, to this day, no one has ever been prosecuted.

As we've seen, the FBI and the Justice Department were forced to disclose portions of the House Intelligence Committee Report that they had initially redacted. We thus learned that, for some period of time during 2016, the FBI was conducting a counterintelligence investigation of General Flynn. There are still relevant redactions, so the basis for this investigation remains unclear. It apparently took place during the campaign, but whether it was related to Moscow's cyberespionage activity is unclear (though it seems unlikely). It is quite possible, though, that the FBI opened an investigation on the decorated thirty-three-year combat veteran of the U.S. Army on suspicion that, yes, he was an agent of Russia engaged in clandestine activity against the United States.

It was Director Comey's recollection that he had "authorized the closure" of that investigation "by late December 2016."[11] It is unclear whether the investigation was actually closed. In the meantime, the Obama administration took the position that Flynn's conversation with Kislyak could be a criminal offense. This was absurd. There was no illegality in Flynn's communications with officials of foreign governments. Of course, Trump was not yet president and there was postelection fervor over Russia, so if Flynn had engaged in negotiations with Kislyak, it would have been *politically* boneheaded. But not illegal. President Trump eventually dismissed Flynn as national-security adviser on February 13, 2017 (after only three weeks on the job), and Flynn was later prosecuted by Special Counsel Mueller (we'll come to that). But Flynn's firing and prosecution were not due to his discussion of sanctions with Kislyak, as tirelessly portrayed by the narrative. Flynn was fired for inaccurately describing his Kislyak conversation to Vice President Pence and other administration officials, and he was prosecuted for summarizing that conversation inaccurately to FBI agents.

On January 12, 2017, *The Washington Post*'s David Ignatius published a leak from an unidentified "senior U.S. government official," describing Flynn's communications with Kislyak after Obama announced the anti-Russia sanctions.[12] Naturally, the classified leak was not the crime that interested the journalist; Ignatius instead focused on an imaginary crime—one which just happens to have been under consideration at that very time in the top tier of the Obama Justice Department: Flynn's flouting of the Logan Act.[13]

Deputy Attorney General Yates was theorizing that it might be possible to prosecute Flynn under this vestige of the John Adams administration, a dark time for free-speech rights. The statute purports to criminalize "any correspondence or intercourse" with agents of a foreign sovereign conducted "without authority of the United States"— an impossibly vague term that probably means permission from the executive branch. No court has had an opportunity to rule that the Logan Act is unconstitutional because, realizing its infirmity, the Justice Department never invokes it. In its 219-year history, the Logan Act has not resulted in a single conviction; indeed, there have been only two indictments, the last one in 1852.[14]

Yet, the Logan Act is what Yates had in mind. In later Senate testimony, she recounted that, in the first days of the new administration, she and Mary McCord (who had replaced John Carlin in Justice's National Security Division) brought their ongoing concerns about Flynn to the attention of Trump White House Counsel Don McGahn. According to Yates, "the first thing we did was to explain to Mr. McGahn that *the underlying conduct* that General Flynn engaged in was *problematic in and of itself.*"[15] The "underlying conduct," of course, was Flynn's communication with Kislyak—his temerity to engage in talks with foreign officials without approval from the Obama administration.

Since this Logan Act theory does not pass the laugh test, Yates also had a fallback rationale: "blackmail." This may have been even more ludicrous.

It turned out that the Obama administration had not only been surveilling Flynn's communications with Kislyak; it had been monitoring the Trump transition team's political commentary. (Once you've been surveilling your political opposition for a few months, it's apparently hard to stop.) Obama officials had thus heard Vice President Pence (among other Trump spokesmen) deny that Flynn had discussed sanctions with Kislyak. They deduced that Flynn must have misled his superiors. This was preposterous. The Justice Department would have been very busy indeed if every untrue statement made publicly by an Obama official had been grounds for investigation. It was no business of federal prosecutors whether Pence had inaccurately reported Flynn's conversation in a press statement, or whether Flynn had inaccurately informed Pence. Yet, Yates surmised that Russia now had "leverage" over Trump's national-security adviser: The Kremlin knew Flynn had discussed sanctions with Kislyak and, hence, must have lied to Pence. So, the—um—reasoning went, Putin could secretly threaten to expose this lie, which would intimidate Flynn into doing his bidding.

Got that? Me neither.

That's because its silliness is palpable. First, Flynn and Russia also knew that *the U.S. intelligence services had a recording of Flynn's conversation with Kislyak.* Blackmail only works if the compromising information is secret. The very fact that Yates knew what was on the recording illustrates that Russia had no unique knowledge it could hope to exploit against Flynn. In fact, as the Kremlin had to know, so many American officials were aware of the Flynn–Kislyak conversation that one of them had leaked it to David Ignatius. Second, Russia would not have concluded that Flynn necessarily misled Pence just because Pence repeated an inaccuracy. Broadcasting misinformation about diplomatic contacts is common—it was the story of Obama's Iran deal. The Kremlin would probably have assumed that the fledgling Trump administration was telling a politically useful lie: The media–Democrat complex was so agitated about Obama's Russia sanctions that, if they admitted discussing them, Trump officials risked cries of "Treason!"

And before you throw this book at me, I didn't say political or diplomatic lies are admirable. I said they're not prosecutable—and we don't want the Justice Department monitoring our politics or diplomacy.

The investigation of Flynn was baseless. So much so that Obama officials could not provide Congress with a coherent rationale for why FBI agents were dispatched to interview him as if he were a criminal suspect. When the House Intelligence Committee Report's redactions were revealed, we finally got to see this portion that the Justice Department had concealed ("EN" refers to endnotes):

> The Committee received conflicting testimony from Deputy Attorney General (DAG) Yates, Director Comey, Principal Deputy Assistant Attorney General [Mary] McCord, and Deputy Director McCabe about whether the primary purpose of the interview was investigating potentially misleading statements to the Vice President, which the Vice President echoed publicly[,] about the content of those calls [EN 94, citing Yates]; a possible violation of the Logan Act [EN 95, citing Yates]; or a desire to obtain more information as part of the counterintelligence investigation into General Flynn. [EN 96, citing McCabe, who did not recall that Comey had authorized closing the counterintelligence investigation a month earlier.]

Not only was there no good legal reason to interview Flynn. There was no good factual reason. The Justice Department and the FBI already had a recording of the Flynn–Kislyak conversation. They knew what had been said—that's why an intelligence official was able to leak to the *Times* that there had been no corrupt quid pro quo. Nor was Flynn needed to interpret the call. When agents want a witness to explain unclear or coded parts of a recorded conversation, they play it for the witness and then ask, "What did this mean? What did that mean?" That's not what happened in Flynn's interview. Without the recording being played for him, he was instead asked to narrate from unaided memory what had been said four weeks earlier—an eternity for a busy official engaged in hundreds of conversations. This kind of interrogation makes sense only if the agents are hoping to nail the interrogee by finding inconsistencies. It's called a perjury trap.[16]

This is why lawyers do not let their clients sit for interviews by investigators until they have had an opportunity to review the relevant material and prepare the clients for questioning. But Flynn did not have a lawyer. The president's national-security adviser was quite intentionally braced at the White House by the FBI. Former Director Comey has been glibly brazen about it.

It was January 24, Flynn's second full day as national-security adviser to a president with no national-security experience. He was crazed. Yet, pursuant to an instruction by Director Comey, Deputy Director McCabe called Flynn to say two agents—Peter Strzok and Joe Pientka—would be coming by to see him. He was discouraged from seeking counsel. As the FBI well knew, an interview of a member of the president's staff is supposed to be sought by the Attorney General through the White House Counsel. That way, there's nothing sneaky: the White House Counsel has an opportunity to be present, and the official sought for an interview can be advised—including advised whether he should have counsel.

Asked in a book-tour interview how the agents managed to get into the White House and grill Flynn, Comey quipped, "I sent them." His left-leaning New York City audience loved it. He continued, weirdly bragging that this was something "I probably wouldn't have done or maybe gotten away with in…a more organized administration." Normally, he said, there is a "process," so that

> if the FBI wanted to send agents into the White House itself to interview a senior official, you would work through the White House counsel and there would be discussions and approvals and it would be there. I thought, "It's early enough, let's just send a couple of guys over."[17]

What is it President Obama likes to say? Oh yeah, "Everything by the book."

Flynn, to repeat, was eventually charged by the Special Counsel with lying to the agents—months after the FBI had reportedly closed the case upon concluding that he hadn't lied; there had just been innocent failures of recollection.[18] House Intelligence Committee Republicans contended that Comey himself had indicated Flynn did not lie. In media interviews, the former director expressed bewilderment over this. In one, Comey told ABC host and Clinton pal George Stephanopoulos: "I don't know where that's coming from. ... That—unless I'm—I said something that people misunderstood, I don't remember even intending to say that. So, my recollection is I never said that to anybody."

Yet, when the Justice Department was pressured to reveal passages that had been redacted from the Intelligence Committee's report, there was this testimony from Comey: "[T]he agents...discerned no physical indications of deception. They didn't see any change in posture, in tone, in inflection, in eye contact. They saw nothing that indicated to them that he knew he was lying to them."[19]

Of course, it is always possible that there is some undisclosed testimony that would put this apparent contradiction in a more favorable light. It is worth noting, though, that as long as Comey was the FBI director, Flynn was never charged with lying or any other crime. And, if anything, the snippets of McCabe's testimony thus far disclosed are even more favorable to Flynn:

> [The] conundrum that we faced on their return from the interview is that although [the agents] didn't detect deception in the statements that [Flynn] made in the interview...the statements were inconsistent with our understanding of the conversation he had actually had with the [Russian] ambassador.

McCabe added: "The two people who interviewed [Flynn] didn't think he was lying, [which] was not [a] great beginning of a false statement case."

Only when Robert Mueller and his very aggressive team of prosecutors took over the case was Flynn charged with lying. Flynn's apologists argue that he was railroaded. Yet, he pled guilty, voluntarily admitting he had lied. When his defenders insisted that he had done this under pressure—broken financially by legal fees, distraught that prosecutors might turn their sights on his son—the judge in his case offered him the opportunity to withdraw his guilty plea and argue that his rights had been violated. He declined, reaffirming that he had misled his interrogators.

For that, Flynn has no one to blame but himself. He should never, however, have been put in that position. What the FBI and the Justice Department did to Flynn, what the Obama administration did to Flynn, was not illegal. But like most everything else in Russia-gate, it was not right.

CHAPTER EIGHTEEN

Nine Days in May

he insurance policy was transferred to a new carrier—
Special Counsel Robert Mueller—in May 2017, over the
course of nine dizzying days that had the nation reeling.
It was on March 20, though, that the tectonic plates
shifted.

March 20, 2017, was the beginning of the end of Russia-gate. Not
of the investigation. President Trump would remain under a cloud of
suspicion for two more years. In fact, it would become more clear than
ever that he was the target of a criminal investigation. The media–
Democrat zeal to remove him from office would become unbridled.
Trump–Russia, though, would be over. It would no longer be a collusion case. It would be an obstruction case. And, perforce, that would
make it an impeachment case.

It was FBI Director James Comey's overreach on March 20 that set
the chain of events in motion. To understand why, we have to retrace
some steps.

Unmasking and Leaking

On January 6, after meeting with President Obama and his administration's national-security team the preceding day, Director Comey briefed President-elect Trump on the salacious sliver of the Steele
dossier. Trump was not told that the dossier was a Clinton-campaign
opposition-research project. He was not told that Christopher Steele
was a rabid anti-Trumper. He was not told about the ongoing FISA surveillance, based on the FBI's representation to the FISC that Trump's
campaign may have been complicit in Russia's cyberespionage plot to
influence the 2016 campaign.

The briefing was leaked to CNN, which led to the publication of the dossier and a torrent of media coverage portraying a Trump–Russia conspiracy.

The dam had burst; the flood was on. But the pressure had been building for weeks after Trump won the election. There had been a steady stream of classified leaks. It emerged that top administration officials—including CIA Director John Brennan, National Security Adviser Susan Rice, and, most oddly, Samantha Power, Obama's ambassador to the U.N.—had caused a surge in the "unmasking" of American citizens in U.S. intelligence reporting.

Ordinarily, unmasking is a rare phenomenon in foreign-intelligence collection. As we've seen, our main intelligence agencies—the FBI, the CIA, and the NSA—gather immense streams of information about foreign actors through various programs, such as Rule 702 collection. These collection efforts incidentally sweep up communications by and about Americans. Under minimization procedures required by law, the identities of the Americans are "masked"—concealed in the refined intelligence reports generated from the raw information collected. But if there is a valid foreign-intelligence purpose—i.e., if a high-ranking government official claims an American's identity must be revealed in order for the national-security significance of the information to be understood—then that official may ask for the American's identity to be disclosed, i.e., *unmasked.*

As you can see, the technical legal threshold for unmasking is low. Whether that means, as a practical matter, that masking is illusory as a due-process protection for Americans depends on how the minimization rules are respected and enforced. It depends on whether intelligence community leaders breed a culture of constitutional fidelity or political expedience.

Director Comey told Congress that the FBI is "obsessive" about concealing the identities of Americans.[1] That is why unmasking is a big deal. When an American is intercepted, the collecting agencies (the FBI, the CIA, and the NSA) don't shrug their shoulders and say, "Well, we could provide a marginally better understanding of the meaning of this communication if we revealed the name of the American." Their practice, we're to understand, is more along the lines of: "We don't reveal the names unless it is absolutely necessary to understanding a communication of real significance, and even then, we prefer to use some substitute (e.g. 'American Diplomat No. 1') rather than the actual name." The agencies take this position not because they are good, honorable people (though most of them are). They take it because it is in their interest. If they fail to protect the identities and privacy of Americans, and the inevitable scandal arises, an irate public will demand that Congress curtail their spying powers. Without these powers, national security cannot be protected adequately. Disasters will happen, and the agencies will be blamed for failing to stop them

To be sure, there is a great deal of room for abuse. There can be reverse targeting: foreigners surveilled not because they are of particular intelligence interest but because they interact with Americans; due to the monitoring of the foreigners, the Americans are "incidentally" shadowed. National-security officials can claim a foreign-intelligence reason to unmask, when, in fact, their real purpose is political.

There is reason to be suspicious about political motivation when unmasking is sought by either intelligence officials who are notoriously political (e.g., Brennan) or White House officials whose roles as political advisers bleed into their national-security portfolios (e.g., Rice). After all, the three main collecting agencies—again, the FBI, the CIA, and the NSA—are the intelligence entities that do the actual investigations. Presumably, if there is legitimate unmasking to be done, those three agencies are in the best position to make that judgment (and, as Comey explained, they lean heavily *against* unmasking). It should not be necessary for other consumers of intelligence (e.g., White House National Security Council members working on defense policy) to seek unmasking. But they are permitted to do so, and if the NSA gets an unmasking request from, say, Susan Rice—known to be the president's confidant— would you want to be the underling who tells her she can't have it?

Toward the end of the Obama administration, unmaskings spiked.

In February, *The New York Times* ran a page-one extravaganza, based on leaks from "four current and former American officials." "Trump Campaign Aides Had Repeated Contact With Russian Intelligence" screamed the headline.[2] Spy agencies were said to be scouring "phone records and intercepted calls" from various streams of intelligence collection, showing that "members of Donald Trump's 2016 presidential campaign and other Trump associates had repeated contacts with senior Russian intelligence officials in the year before the election." At the time, the account continued, "Russia was trying to disrupt the presidential election by hacking" Democrats, while Trump was "speaking glowingly about" Putin and saying "he hoped Russian intelligence services had stolen Hillary Clinton's emails and would make them public." Consequently, the FBI was sifting through mounds of call logs and intercepted communications, as well as banking and travel records. Much of this involved "routine electronic surveillance of the communications of foreign officials." Instead of concentrating on these proper surveillance targets, intelligence officials were shifting their focus to Americans—specifically, Americans connected to Trump—who had been monitored incidentally.

Devin Nunes, then-chairman of the House Intelligence Committee, proceeded to disclose that, after the election, the identities of Trump-campaign and -transition figures had been unmasked by Obama national-security officials. When he implicated Rice, she initially denied knowing what he was talking about. As tends to happen with Rice, though, it was soon confirmed that her original story was misleading. True to form, she revised the story a few times before finally admitting that, well, yes, she had indeed directed the unmasking of Trump-campaign officials. At least for now, the story is that the Obama administration was trying to understand why the crown prince of the United Arab Emirates was in New York City shortly after Donald Trump was elected. The prince was meeting with Trump advisers. I'm betting that Team Obama was thinking: *Logan Act*!

Meanwhile, we learned that Ambassador Power, whose U.N. diplomatic post was not one in which the need to unmask American identities for intelligence purposes is apparent, sought unmaskings *hundreds* of times. Alarmingly, Power claims she is not responsible for most of the requests made in her name. So, who did it? We don't know—all we know is that, if she is telling the truth, something went very wrong here. As we've seen, there was a dramatic increase in the number of queries by government officials seeking information about American citizens from NSA databases. Nunes concluded that "the total requests for Americans' names by Obama political aides numbered in the hundreds during Obama's last year in office, and often lacked a specific intelligence community justification."[3]

Questions about unmasking have been shunted aside since first arising in 2017. Part of that is due to lack of disclosure. As the defense to unmasking charges shifted from "it didn't happen" to "there's nothing inappropriate about it," Republicans meekly accepted the Democratic argument that there is almost certainly no *crime* involved. That is probably true: No blatant penal offense arises out of noncompliance with minimization instructions or when an official who has the lawful discretion to act exercises that discretion for political purposes. That, however, misses the point. Many government abuses of power are not courtroom-prosecutable felonies. They can be much more serious than that because they are not merely private transgressions; *they pervert the system of governance.*[4] That is why the Framers did not require impeachable offenses to be indictable crimes: The fact that a government official cannot be prosecuted in criminal court for some abusive action does not mean that the action was proper or that the official is fit to wield power.

It is also worth posing the obvious rhetorical question: If a Republican administration had unmasked the identities of Democratic political officials, is there any chance that we would not by now know the whole story—and that heads would long ago have rolled?[5]

The unmasking controversy has a context. So does Obama's curious executive order, issued at the very end of his presidency, suddenly expanding the scope of intelligence officials who would have access to raw intelligence. The context is the transparent effort to craft a public narrative that Donald Trump could be a pawn of the Kremlin, that he could be the beneficiary of an election rigged by a hostile foreign power.

That's why you have the leaking.

Those are not the words of your humble correspondent. They are the words of Evelyn Farkas, a former deputy defense secretary, one of the Obama administration's most senior policy officers on Russia. She left the administration in 2015, subsequently joining the Clinton presidential campaign. In March 2017, letting her guard down among friends during an MSNBC interview, Farkas let slip that current and former Obama-administration officials had been encouraging Congress to demand disclosure of classified information:

I was urging my former colleagues and, frankly speaking, the people on the Hill, it was more actually aimed at telling the Hill people, get as much information as you can, get as much intelligence as you can, before President Obama leaves the administration. ... Because I had a fear that somehow that information would disappear with the senior people who left, so it would be hidden away in the bureaucracy...that the Trump folks—if they found out how we knew what we knew about their—the Trump staff dealing with the Russians—that they would try to compromise those sources and methods, meaning we no longer have access to the intelligence.

On a roll about all the "good intelligence on Russia" the Obama administration had, Farkas just came right out and said it:

That's why you have the leaking.[6]

It wasn't random leaking. It was leaking with a purpose. It was leaking in the service of a collusion narrative that, on close scrutiny, was based on no credible evidence—the Trump campaign had nothing to do with Russia's hacking operations, and those operations had no effect on the outcome of the election. On close scrutiny, this narrative was driven by proof of Russia "connections" of the kind that were not unique to Trump associates, and by the self-interested, multiple-hearsay reporting of Christopher Steele. Naturally, President Trump was inordinately frustrated. He was trying to govern, trying to get a new administration up and running. But the public was being told, by seemingly reliable top intelligence insiders, that Trump was in cahoots with the Kremlin. Any day now, we were led to believe, the smoking-gun proof would come to light and he would be driven from office.

Private Assurances, Public Scandalizing

The FBI's investigation pressed on, seeking evidence that the campaign Trump ran had engaged in a conspiracy with Russia in which Trump was the willful beneficiary. To sustain it, Director Comey tried to put the president at ease. Regardless of what the government leaks told the public,

Comey told Trump not to worry, he was not a suspect. The director delivered that soothing message to Trump the first time they met on January 6. He did it again at their dinner on January 27, even discouraging Trump from ordering the FBI to investigate the pee-tape allegation. His reasoning now seems amazing: The FBI would not want to help create a public narrative that it was investigating the president. At the time, that very narrative was inundating the public through classified leaks about the state of the investigation, repeated, hour after hour, by the mass media.

Trump decided to fight back, with the Trumpian penchant for attention-grabbing overstatement. It wasn't enough for the president to say it now appeared to him that the Obama administration had used the government's foreign-intelligence surveillance powers to spy on his campaign—which would have been true. Trump had to make it personal, and inaccurate: *President Obama had tapped Trump's wires.* Trump might have been the wronged party, but the hyperbole undermined his case. Everyone chimed in with outrage—former Obama officials, current intelligence officials, congressional Democrats and some of their embarrassed Republican colleagues, media pundits.

This is the problem with the president. Even when he is right, his exaggerations and erratic outbursts, his "take me seriously but not literally" style, his proclivity to distinguish friend from foe in intensely personal (indeed, self-absorbed) terms, make it exhausting to plead his case. Concededly, to my mind, this is better than having a president who gets rolled over because he won't fight back when it's time to fight back—either because it's beneath his dignity, or because the press will say mean things. Still, no one likes to be on the defensive all the time, including when it should be time to play offense.

In this instance, there is no doubt that President Obama was informed and approving of the counterintelligence measures. I suspect he was probably the maestro, mainly through Brennan. Instead of focusing on that—on whether there had been sufficient grounds to override the American norm against an incumbent administration's use of counterintelligence powers against its political opposition—we were talking nonsense about wiretaps at Trump Tower (for which there was no evidence) and whether the president was lying (as opposed to misfiring while in the general vicinity of the truth).

To be sure, the new president's allegation against his predecessor was factually inaccurate. Yet, it was not "baseless" as the incessant ridicule put it. Trump had gotten close enough to the truth that he needed to be squelched.

On March 20, Director Comey did the squelching.

The director had been called to testify before the House Intelligence Committee. At the start of the hearing, he made this breathtaking opening statement (emphasis added):

> I have been authorized by the Department of Justice to confirm that the FBI, as part of our counterintelligence mission, is investigating the Russian government's efforts to interfere in the 2016 presidential election and *that includes investigating the nature of any links between individuals associated with the Trump campaign and the Russian government and whether there was any coordination between the campaign and Russia's efforts.* As with any counterintelligence investigation, *this will also include an assessment of whether any crimes were committed.*

It is against Justice Department policy to confirm the existence of *any* investigation. The Trump–Russia investigation was not just any investigation. It was a classified counterintelligence investigation. That was why, despite great pressure from Democrats and the Clinton campaign, the FBI had refused to discuss it publicly prior to the election—i.e., when it was certain Mrs. Clinton would win. Comey said he had been "authorized by the Justice Department" to make his stunning disclosure, but Trump appointees were not running the Justice Department. Attorney General Sessions had recused himself, and Rod Rosenstein, nominated to become Deputy AG, had not yet been confirmed. Comey's "authorization" had come from Obama Justice Department holdovers (the same people who had advised Sessions that he needed to recuse himself in a manner that was rash and more sweeping than dictated by the circumstances[7]).

Even in the exceedingly rare instances when the FBI might publicly refer to an ongoing investigation (because, like investigation of the Russian regime, it has been referred to in a public government document, such as the ICA), the Bureau never names the subjects of those investigations. Doing so patently prejudices those subjects. Lay people generally do not appreciate the distinction between a counterintelligence and a criminal probe. All the public knows, upon hearing remarks such as Comey's, is that someone is under investigation by the FBI—which often means someone is guilty of a serious crime.

The director's additional comments only exacerbated the problem: "*As with any counterintelligence investigation, this will also include an assessment of whether any crimes were committed.*" No, as we've discussed, criminal assessments are not a standard part of counterintelligence probes. Counterintelligence is not geared to investigate crimes or build prosecutions; it collects information about foreign powers that may threaten American interests. It is not regular FBI procedure to scour foreign intelligence for criminal evidence. To the contrary, criminal prosecutions are often resisted because due-process discovery rules could require disclosure of top-secret intelligence. There is simply an unremarkable, commonsense principle that always applies in any situation: If agents happen to find criminal evidence while they are legitimately conducting some other kind of investigation, they need not ignore that evidence; it may be (but not need be) turned over to criminal investigators and prosecutors.

By phrasing his testimony this way, Comey had to know that the average person would believe President Trump himself was under investigation by the FBI for complicity in Russia's espionage operations to influence the campaign. And that is exactly what many Americans did believe. Comey's testimony appeared to validate the explosive *Times* story from February about Trump-campaign contacts with Russia—notwithstanding that Comey would later dismiss that report as "almost entirely wrong."[8] Indeed, the *Times* reported on the director's bombshell March 20 testimony under the page-one headline "F.B.I. Is Investigating Trump's Russia Ties, Comey Confirms." Even as Comey was giving his testimony, Neera Tanden, president of the Center for American Progress, which heavily influences Democratic-party messaging, tweeted (next to her "Resist" avatar), "The FBI is investigating a sitting President. Been a long time since that happened." On the internet and throughout the country, the director's stunning announcement was understandably and predictably interpreted as confirmation that Trump himself was under FBI investigation.[9]

Tellingly, the director later noted that he had "briefed the leadership of Congress on exactly which individuals we were investigating and . . . told those Congressional leaders that we were not personally investigating President Trump."[10] He had done that, however, in the closed-session part of the Intelligence Committee hearing, out of public earshot. Members were obliged to keep that part of the proceedings secret. In the open hearing, with all of the media covering and all Americans as the intended audience, the impression unmistakably conveyed was that the president was personally under suspicion of involvement in a traitorous scheme.

Think about this from Trump's perspective. He knew he had not conspired with Putin. After months of investigation, there was no evidence that he had done so. Whatever threads the FBI was following were sufficiently remote from Trump that the FBI director had told him, repeatedly, he was not a suspect. Yet, a monumental decision, in which the president was not consulted, had been made by Comey—in consultation with officials Trump had not appointed, at a Justice Department that had been a thorn in Trump's side from Day One. The director would proclaim to the nation not only that there was an ongoing FBI probe focused on Trump's campaign, but also that criminal prosecutions were a distinct possibility. Trump had to wonder: *What conceivable point could there have been in that announcement other than to cast suspicion on me?*

Ten days later, on March 30, Trump called Comey to complain about the "cloud" over his presidency. Naturally, suspicions had intensified since the director's testimony, impairing the president's capacity to govern. Was this a significant problem for the president? Consider this: In 2019, even after Special Counsel Mueller's investigation grudgingly concluded that there had been no Trump–Russia conspiracy, public polling showed that nearly half of all Americans nevertheless believed that Trump worked with the Kremlin to interfere in the 2016 presidential election.[11] In their March 30 conversation, the president pressed the director on what the FBI could do to help "lift the cloud." Comey yet again privately confirmed that the president was not personally under investigation; but he was recalcitrant in the face of Trump's insistence that "We have to get that fact out."

The director had gone public with the powerful suggestion that Trump was the principal subject of the FBI's investigation, but would not go public with his assertion that Trump was not personally under investigation. That is indefensible. The latter position is justifiable only if the former disclosure is never made—either say nothing (always the best approach, and the one the rules counsel), or say everything, but you can't create and foment a misimpression. In later testimony, the former director recalled that he and Justice Department officials (again, not Trump appointees) were "reluctant to make public statements that we did not have an open case on President Trump." Comey rationalized that if such an announcement were made, and some evidence against Trump were to materialize, he (Comey) would be obliged to correct the record, causing even greater uproar and suspicion. Of course, this is what had happened when the director mishandled the Hillary Clinton investigation—first by going public with the evidence against an uncharged person, and then by very publicly reopening the investigation just days before the election, in order to correct the record.

Again, though, think about this from Trump's perspective. It was not his fault that Comey's handling of the Clinton situation—the decision to make improper, prejudicial statements, that spawned a perceived need to make damaging clarifying statements—had imploded. More to the point, Trump was president and Comey was his subordinate. It was the president's call, not the FBI director's, to decide what the public should be told about a counterintelligence investigation being done in support of the president's national-security responsibilities. If Trump was willing to run the risk—a slight risk after so many months of investigation—that new evidence of Trump's guilt might someday emerge, calling for a politically damaging correction of the record, how was it Comey's place to countermand the chief executive?

Trump had to figure that Comey was not being straight with him: privately assuring him he was not a suspect, but insinuating otherwise in public. Was Comey lying to him? Was Comey's reluctance to state publicly that Trump was not a suspect because the director hoped and expected that damning evidence would come to light? Did Comey believe Trump actually had conspired with Putin?

May 3 was the last straw. Comey again appeared at a congressional oversight hearing. He refused to comment on the Russia investigation beyond acknowledging the confirmation of its existence in his earlier testimony. When pointedly asked whether he had ruled out anyone connected to the Trump campaign, including the president, from potential criminal charges, the director declined to answer. This refusal to budge had the effect of reaffirming what he had said on March 20. In the public mind, Trump would remain a suspect who could eventually face prosecution for conspiring with Russia.[12] Naturally, the president reacted angrily, lashing out against Attorney General Sessions over his recusal from the Russia investigation, which had rendered him unable to supervise Comey.[13]

How Not to Fire an FBI Director

The situation had become untenable. Trump decided that Comey had to go. That weekend, at his manse in Bedminster, New Jersey, the president dictated an angry letter to his staffer Stephen Miller. Never finalized or sent, the letter emphasized Comey's assurances to Trump on three occasions that Trump was not a suspect; described the Trump–Russia allegations as "fabricated and politically-motivated"; rebuked Comey's handling of the Clinton-emails investigation and failure to hold leakers accountable; and insisted that Republicans, Democrats, and the public had lost trust in the director. The president also suggested that Comey had pleaded to keep his job at their January 28 dinner but that Trump had given him no guarantees—a strange bit of revisionist history: Trump was empowered to fire the director regardless of any previous assurances, and there had been no indication that Comey was on some sort of probation.

White House Counsel Don McGahn persuaded the president to hold off on his letter and let the Justice Department explain Comey's termination. McGahn had met with Sessions and the newly confirmed Deputy AG, Rod Rosenstein, and knew they were supportive of Comey's removal. Trump agreed, but in directing Rosenstein on May 8 to write an explanatory memo, he told the new DAG to include Comey's refusal publicly to affirm private assurances that Trump was not under investigation. Rosenstein did not argue with the president, but he did not do as instructed, either.

Rod Rosenstein was a Trump appointee, but he was not of Trump World. The president did not know him. Trump likes résumés, and Rosenstein's is impressive—Wharton School, Harvard Law, *cum laude*, editor of the *Law Review*, prestigious D.C. Circuit judicial clerkship, adviser to top officials in the Clinton Justice Department, work on Ken Starr's Whitewater investigation. It was President Bush 43 who made him U.S. attorney for Maryland, but he proceeded to win over the blue state's two Democratic senators, and President Obama retained him. For that reason, he was among the forty-six Obama-appointed U.S. attorneys who were still in their jobs when, toward the start of the new administration, they were directed to submit their resignations and make way for Trump appointees. Somewhat awkwardly, Trump then declined to accept Rosenstein's resignation because, it turned out, his advisers had already settled on Rosenstein to be Sessions's deputy at the Justice Department.

Rosenstein had well and carefully cultivated his reputation as an apolitical lawman. I am not a Rosenstein fan, but I don't mean that as a dig—the country works much better when law enforcement is seen as a profession rather than a political calling. For purposes of understanding what follows, though, because Rosenstein's reputational motivations cannot be divorced from his consequential decisions and sometimes erratic actions, it is important to grasp that he saw himself (with justification) as beloved by both parties, and he aimed to keep it that way. At a time when Trump nominees for top executive offices were extraordinarily difficult to move through the Senate with Republicans holding a razor-thin 51/49 majority, Rosenstein breezed to confirmation by a margin of 94 to 6.

Rosenstein is a deliberate Washington creature. He agreed with the firing of Comey, but when controversy set in, he wanted it known that the firing was not his idea. And his agreement in Comey's dismissal was rooted in the director's unapologetic flouting of Justice Department guidelines in the Clinton-emails case; it had nothing to do with

Russia. Beltway Democrats and Republicans brayed that Russia's interference in the campaign was very serious business, so Rosenstein wanted no doubt that he, too, thought it was very serious business.

Yes, he would write a memo in support of Comey's dismissal, but he would do it based on his own rationale—not Trump's. Of course, if the boss tells you to do something, and you decide it's a bad idea, you're supposed to let the boss know that ahead of time, not just do it your way. But the Trump administration is, shall we say, untraditional in that regard. Rosenstein hadn't been around long, but it was long enough to see that White House and Justice Department lawyers sometimes ignore the president's suggestions—directives are taken as suggestions. Trump seems to prefer it that way: he is a nonlawyer who realizes his impulses need tweaking, the courts are hostile to him, and his subordinates are trying to steer him away from trouble; plus, proceeding by tweet and suggestion, rather than formal orders, gives him maneuvering room to blame subordinates when things go awry, as they tend to do.

So, Rosenstein would write the memo his way and hope Trump would come around once he read Rod's paean to bipartisanship: celebrating the Republican and Democratic consensus (so wonderful! so rare in today's Washington!) that Director Comey had wronged Hillary Clinton. The DAG inveighed: "The Director was wrong to usurp the Attorney General's authority" and "to release derogatory information" about an uncharged person (Mrs. Clinton). Rosenstein being Rosenstein, his memo's conclusion is slippery. He wouldn't just come out and say that Comey should be fired. He pointed out that "the President has the power to remove an FBI director" and that the FBI under Comey had lost "public and congressional trust," which it was "unlikely to regain" unless it had a director who "understands the gravity of [Comey's] mistakes and pledges never to repeat them." Then, Rosenstein pointedly noted, Comey refused to do this.[14]

The president liked Rosenstein's memo as far as it went, but he balked at its failure to include what he'd told Rosenstein to include— *what was important to Trump*. He directed Miller to write a short cover letter. In it, Trump accepted what was spun as the Justice Department's recommendation that Comey be removed, but he pointedly stressed what Rosenstein had omitted: before the cock crowed, Comey had three times denied the president was under investigation.[15]

I have met Donald Trump once. At the urging of his friend Rudy Giuliani (who hired me as a prosecutor all those years ago—a little before he hired Jim Comey), I attended a meeting with candidate Trump to discuss radical Islam, terrorism prosecutions, immigration enforcement, and border security. Mr. Trump could not have been more gracious to me. It was a good meeting, he asked very good questions, and—in that small group—he was charming, solicitous, funny, and unpretentious. I could see why people like him. Whatever "it" is, he's got it.

Of course, I was there to try to help him. Unfortunately, the president has another side, often an unsightly display toward people he has decided are enemies. In many ways, this is understandable. Many of Trump's opponents are *enemies*. They self-identify that way. They want to be understood that way because it endears them to legions of Trump enemies for whom Trump opposition is less a substantive position than a tribal affiliation or cultural aesthetic. TDS—Trump Derangement Syndrome—is not a quip, at least not always. It's a real thing. If massive numbers of people reacted to me that way, I hope I'd keep Christian compassion at the front of my mind, but I'm sure I'd be bitter about it.

The president gets worse than bitter. He can be vindictive and cruel. That's how he treated Jim Comey. I've always liked Comey even while often disagreeing with him, so you could say I'm biased. You might also figure: Comey was trying to take the president down; his behavior since he was fired is that of a woke anti-Trump partisan; and if Trump stuck it to him, he deserved it. Moreover, Trump has been Trump for seventy-three years and it got him to the White House, so who the hell am I to say how he should conduct himself? Nevertheless, how you treat someone—including, and maybe especially, someone who has crossed you—says more about you than it does about the someone. In his understandable exasperation over Comey's machinations, Trump lost perspective. He decided it wasn't enough to fire Comey; he needed to humiliate Comey. The re-sult resulting moves made the president look awful, spooked Rosenstein, and resulted in the appointment of a special counsel. In other words, Trump's political enemies got exactly the monitor and impeachment investigation that the insurance-policy concept was designed to achieve.

The president rejected a subordinate's plea that Comey be permitted to resign rather than be fired. The director was given no notice of his immediate termination. Trump did not address him man-to-man, superior-to-subordinate. The White House waited to pull the trigger until after the director had flown across the country, where he was scheduled to speak to agents at the Los Angeles field office about the FBI's mission—a part of the director's job at which Comey was peerless. While there, in front of other people, Comey learned he'd been terminated from television news reports. It was so surreal, he thought it was a gag. There was not even the courtesy of a curt phone call. It was an indecent way to remove a subordinate, particularly one who, regardless of the president's righteous frustration, had served the United States well in many capacities over many years.

Unfathomably, the president picked May 10, the day after firing Comey, to host top Russian diplomats at the White House—Ambassador Kislyak and Putin's longtime Foreign Minister Sergey Lavrov. For the consumption of these officials—operatives of an anti-American regime that persecutes dissenters—Trump gloated: "I just fired the head of the FBI. He was crazy, a real nut job. I faced great pressure because of Russia. That's taken off."[16]

Thus did the president not merely fail to grasp that, as between the Russians and Jim Comey, Comey is not the enemy. Trump also created evidence that could be used against him in an obstruction investigation: asserting that, by firing Comey, he had relieved the pressure of the Russia investigation. To be clear, I am not claiming the president actually meant what these remarks have been portrayed by Trump's opposition as meaning; namely, that he fired Comey because he was afraid the director was about to nail him for colluding with Russia in an espionage conspiracy. Trump clearly meant he had been under a cloud of suspicion due to the disingenuous way in which Comey was publicly framing him as the culprit in what Trump saw as a hoax. But if I may go lawyer on you for a moment: If you don't want to be accused of obstructing an investigation of your alleged collusion with Russia, don't invite Russia's top operatives over to the White House to gloat over firing the FBI director who is investigating Russia, and then add for good measure that you booted him to take the heat off.

See, not that hard: If you don't want a meritless investigation against you to continue, then don't giftwrap reasons to continue it.

On Comey's firing, the president, his advisers, and especially Rosenstein had badly misdiagnosed the Democrats. They figured that Rosenstein's memo—so solicitous of Mrs. Clinton, so respectful of Democratic as well as Republican rebukes of Comey—would be applauded by Democrats, who blamed the former director for Clinton's defeat. It had apparently escaped their notice that Democrats had moved on from Hillary. Inciting anti-Trump derangement was now the order of the day. After Trump was elected, Comey had made himself useful in that effort, particularly in his March 20 testimony. Whatever contempt Democrats might silently harbor for Comey, the president's firing of him presented a political opportunity to accuse Trump of obstructing the Russia probe—a tack that seemed a lot more promising than the Russia probe itself. The president, Democrats said, must've feared that the FBI director was about to expose a corrupt Trump–Putin conspiracy.

The fierce Democratic reaction sent Rod a-reeling, anguished by such taunts as this one by Senator Christopher Murphy (D., Conn.): "You wrote a memo you knew would be used to perpetuate a lie. You own this debacle." Meanwhile, thrown by the unanticipated blowback, Trump White House officials publicly shifted all blame to Rosenstein. Vice President Pence was insistent that Trump had simply "accept[ed] the recommendation of the deputy attorney general and the attorney general to remove Director Comey."[17]

This administration ploy simply whetted the opposition's appetite. Democrats and their media allies goaded Trump: not only was the administration misrepresenting the true reasons for Comey's dismissal, the big bully himself was hiding behind the Justice Department. Never one to leave a bait behind, the president proceeded to tell NBC's Lester Holt that the decision was wholly his own, not one for which he relied on his subordinates. Comey was a "showboat" and a "grandstander" who had plunged the FBI into "turmoil," the president said, so Trump decided to replace him with "somebody that's competent." Upon deciding "to just do it," Trump added, "I said to myself, I said, 'You know, this Russia thing with Trump and Russia is a made-up story, it's an excuse by the Democrats for having lost an election that they should have won.'"

Could it possibly have been worse for Rosenstein? He had put himself out there by writing a memo that was not his idea—before our eyes, he seemed to be shifting with the wind from proud volunteer Comey executioner to reluctant draftee. Now, the president was pulling the rug out from under him, saying the memo for which he was being filleted didn't matter anyway. It had all been for naught.

Leaking and Obstruction

The president continued careening. In the early morning of May 12, he tweeted, "James Comey better hope that there are no 'tapes' of our conversations before he starts leaking to the press."[18] You have to hand it to Donald Trump: Not many presidents, while being stridently accused of obstructing an investigation, would flip right to the Watergate page in the playbook. Weeks later, the president would finally concede that there were no White House recordings. But Trump being Trump, he could not bring himself to say he was just lashing out in a fit of pique; he stressed that *he* did not have any recordings—implying that maybe Comey was secretly recording him. (So, I guess his original tweet was to warn Comey about…Comey—or something.[19])

As it happened, the former director *was* recording the president, but not electronically. He had done it the old-fashioned way. Comey did not trust Trump and thought the president would lie about their conversations (which, in the way of the jilted, he became bolder about telling everyone once he'd been cashiered). Thus, each time Comey had any meeting with Trump, he wrote a memorandum immediately afterward—to serve as his aide-memoire, as well as potential evidence against Trump if there were ever a criminal charge or an impeachment process.[20]

The president's suggestion that Comey would start "leaking to the press" soon had Comey responding…with a leak to the press. At an Oval Office meeting on February 14, the day after Trump fired his friend and ardent supporter General Flynn, the remorseful president told the director, "I hope you can see your way clear to letting this go, to letting Flynn go." Comey immediately wrote a memo documenting the statement. Now, knowing that Trump was being accused of obstructing the Russia investigation, Comey poured fuel on that fire by leaking his memo, which he realized would be reported as an attempt by the president to obstruct the Flynn investigation. He hoped that the leak would prompt the appointment of a special counsel. To investigate exactly what is unclear.[21] But a special counsel would be the new iteration of the insurance policy: a watchdog overseeing the man Comey saw as the unfit president so regrettably elected by the benighted voters—a prosecutor who would dig up enough dirt to make Trump un-reelectable in 2020, and maybe get him impeached before that, even if there was no prosecutable crime. Comey shared the memo of his conversation with his friend (and mine) Columbia Law School Professor Dan Richman, who provided it to *The New York Times* at Comey's direction.

This was unseemly conduct on Comey's part. Ironically, in the section of the then-director's two-page memo right before he quotes Trump asking him to go easy on Flynn, Comey describes a discussion in which he quotes himself emphatically agreeing with the president that the leaking of sensitive government information is malignant. ("I said I was eager to find leakers and would like to nail one to the door as a message.")

Put aside that the FBI does not appear to have done much to address the tidal wave of classified leaks in the first months of the Trump administration. Leak cases, after all, are tough to make: too many people in government are cleared for access to sensitive information, and the Justice Department appropriately resists pressuring journalists to reveal their sources. The point is that no one knows better than Jim Comey that it is indefensible to leak a private exchange between the FBI director and the president of the United States. It does not matter how poorly the director feels he has been treated. Nor does it matter that the director thinks he has a higher calling—that the rules against leaking must yield to the purportedly greater good of exposing roguish presidential behavior, in the hope of securing a special counsel appointment (just like the Justice Department rules against public comment on the evidence against uncharged people must yield to the former director's subjective sense of the public's right to know). If everyone is a law unto himself, then there is no law; there is anarchy.

I don't see why anyone is offended that Comey made notes of his conversations with Trump. Trump has made a number of explosive allegations about Comey; Comey sensed that the president might do that, and of course he wanted to protect himself. And since he was under no duty to make any notes, there is no merit in the complaint that he chose to make notes of his conversations with Trump but not Obama. He trusted Obama but not Trump. That was his prerogative. It is a problem, though, that the director thought of the notes as his own property. This was *government* property. The information he had access to and conversations he was privileged to participate in flowed from his position of public trust, and nothing else. He was not merely a private citizen sharing his personal thoughts with the Paper of Record. Even after an official leaves government service, fiduciary duties continue to obtain.

It was obvious that some of the information in the memos could be classified—and, in fact, after Comey left the government, the Bureau assessed that a number of his memos did contain classified information. During the former director's tenure, the Justice Department prosecuted General David Petraeus for mishandling classified intelligence. Among the species of information described in the indictments were notes of Petraeus's conversations with President Obama. When a high-ranking national-security official is having a business-related conversation with the president, the specter of classified information always hovers. Many of the topics that naturally come up in such conversations are presumptively classified by executive order. All that said, the summary of the Trump–Comey meeting about Flynn is not classified.[22] That does not mean it was appropriate for Comey to disseminate it outside the government. Less than a week before he was fired, Comey told a Senate committee that there would be "severe consequences" if he found out FBI agents had leaked investigative information.[23] I don't think an agent caught sending *The New York Times* interview notes from a conversation with a witness would have lasted very long in Comey's FBI. Moreover, even when information is not deemed classified, all executive officers know that the president has a legally recognized confidentiality privilege covering communications with subordinates. It is the president's privilege to invoke. It was wrong for Comey to share a privileged conversation without the president's approval—even if Donald Trump's many detractors laud him for doing so.

It is also wrong knowingly to create a misimpression. The patent point of leaking the memo was to suggest that Trump had already obstructed the Flynn investigation, and therefore the firing of Comey ought to be seen, through that lens, as an obstruction of the Russia investigation—or, at least, as reasonable enough grounds to suspect obstruction that a special counsel should be appointed to investigate. Comey, however, knew full well that Trump had not obstructed the Flynn investigation.

Put aside that Trump had the power to shut down the Flynn investigation, that he never did, and that Flynn was eventually convicted of making false statements. On their face, Trump's statements to Comey were not obstruction—he did not order Comey to take any action; he said he hoped Comey would let the Flynn matter go. The director obviously did not feel pressured; he said he ignored Trump. If there was an ongoing investigation of Flynn, Trump's statements had no effect on it. Furthermore, the president has the constitutional authority to weigh in on the merits of an investigation. Again, all executive power in our system is vested in the president. Every day, in federal districts all across the country, agents and prosecutors weigh whether investigations should be continued. When they do that, they are exercising the president's power. It is nonsensical to suggest that the president himself cannot exercise that power.

In addition, if Comey had believed he witnessed a crime, he would have been obliged to report that fact. He did not. In the three months between February 14, when Comey spoke with Trump about Flynn, and May 9, when Comey was fired, the director assured the president that he (Trump) was not under investigation. Plus, in his May 3 testimony (again, nearly three months after the Flynn conversation), the director told a Senate committee that he had never had an experience in which he had been ordered (at least by the Justice Department) to shut a case down for political reasons.[24]

Rod Rosenstein's Resistance

Such gripping pathos. Rod Rosenstein grousing that Trump had used him. Rosenstein remorsefully wishing that Comey, whom he'd just portrayed as mutinous and incorrigible, was still running the FBI so the admiring Rod "could bounce ideas off him." The distraught deputy attorney general unsure of what to do: maybe wire up against the president? Maybe try to round up enough cabinet officials willing to say Trump was loony to the point of incapacity, for purposes of invoking the 25th amendment?

Maybe appoint a special counsel?

After over a year of Justice Department stonewalling, *The New York Times* had the story last September.[25] Dazed by the harsh partisan reaction to his admirably clement bipartisan memo in support of the firing-of-Comey-that-was-absolutely-not-my-idea, a "conflicted, regretful and emotional" Rod Rosenstein spent the days that followed grappling with the matter of most urgency to the United States of America: how to restore the reputation of Rod Rosenstein. In the end, he decided to appoint as special counsel a Beltway eminence, Robert Mueller, as has been exhaustively documented. (Trust me, I'm exhausted.) But not before Rosenstein flirted with some ideas that were...I think the technical term is...bonkers. When this was revealed, he issued a weaselly non-denial denial repudiating his weasel moves:

> The *New York Times*'s story is inaccurate and factually incorrect. ... I will not further comment on a story based on anonymous sources who are obviously biased against the department and are advancing their own personal agenda. But let me be clear about this: Based on my personal dealings with the president, there is no basis to invoke the 25th Amendment.[26]

Let's parse this.

The *Times* story "is inaccurate and factually incorrect." Rosenstein wouldn't say exactly what was wrong in the report. He was careful not to say that the gist of the report was wrong—he just figured you'd hear it that way if he sounded indignant enough.

You can't trust "anonymous sources": *this* from the guy who, in approving the final Carter Page FISA warrant application, endorsed asking a court to rely on anonymous sources—some of them Russian operatives—who were channeling information through a foreign spy from whom the Justice Department continued to take information even after telling a federal court that the spy had been cut out of the investigation for leaking to the media.

And my favorite: Rosenstein knows "there *is* no basis to invoke the 25th Amendment" against President Trump. Of course, that does not respond to what the *Times* report actually says, which is that *back in May 2017*, when he was an emotional wreck because Democrats were being mean to him, Rosenstein urged that there *might at that time be* a basis to remove the president under the 25th Amendment if he could get enough top officials to agree that Trump was unfit to discharge his duties.

The *Times* tells us that Rosenstein "grew concerned that his reputation had suffered harm" and that he "became angry at Mr. Trump." Sensing which way the wind was blowing, desperate to get back in the Democrats' good graces, the deputy AG started singing from the #Resistance hymnal: Trump is unfit. Of course, Trump was neither more nor less unfit than he'd been at any other time. Rosenstein's sudden concern about the president's suitability was about Rosenstein, not Trump. The deputy AG now felt the need to show his former admirers, as emphatically as circumstances would allow, that he was on the right side of this question. Let's look at the steps he took.

1) Wiretapping the President

Rosenstein seized on the most current agenda item: Trump's interviews of candidates to replace Comey.[27] He began badmouthing the president as dangerously unserious. He allegedly urged that he or a top FBI official, such as then–Acting Director McCabe, should covertly record conversations with Trump to amass evidence of the president's derelictions and incapacity.

Regarding this eye-popping *Times* claim that he proposed wiretapping Trump, Rosenstein's allies insisted he was just kidding. Clearly, enough people heard the deputy AG talk about covertly recording the president that he could not credibly deny doing so. Thus, Rosenstein issued a non-denial denial: "I never pursued or authorized the recording of the President." Notice: No one said he gave a *directive*; the allegation was that he floated the *idea*. In fact, Rosenstein may not have been totally serious about wiring up. But rest assured he was dead serious about *appearing ready to monitor the president*—i.e., about assuring anti-Trump bureaucrats that he was with them, especially those who had good relations with Democrats, such as McCabe.

2) Invoking the 25th Amendment

Rosenstein also broached the possibility of invoking the 25th Amendment.[28] This overwrought suggestion appears never to have advanced beyond the larval stage. The amendment contemplates removal of a president who is incapacitated in the *medical* sense. It is not a substitute for impeachment, which is the remedy for unfitness in the sense of *maladministration*, about which Rosenstein was talking.

Furthermore, the 25th Amendment calls for a written declaration by the vice president and a majority of the cabinet. Rosenstein, by contrast, is said to have told McCabe that he might be able to get a grand total of two cabinet officials on board: then–Attorney General Sessions and John Kelly, who was then the homeland-security secretary (he later served as White House chief of staff). There is no indication that Rosenstein ever actually raised the possibility of a 25th Amendment coup with either of them. Still, this was more than idle chatter: Rosenstein's "joking" about secretly recording Trump came in this context of exploring whether a case for removing the president from office could be built. The idea would have been to capture some outrageous statements by the president, then use those statements to persuade cabinet members that he was unfit.

Hence, the non-denial denials from Rosenstein: "I never pursued or authorized recording the President and any suggestion that I have ever advocated for the removal of the President is absolutely false." Right. As already noted, Rosenstein's assertion in September 2018 that the president was *at that point* fit to serve did not actually respond to the *Times* report—which said that Rosenstein, while in an agitated state *in May 2017*, intimated that Trump might *at that time* be unfit and removable. Equally unresponsive was the deputy AG's vehement denial that he "advocated for the removal of the President." The *Times* did not allege that Rosenstein *advocated* for Trump's removal; it says he *raised but did not seriously pursue* the harebrained notion that Trump could be removable under the 25th Amendment.

Tellingly, Rosenstein avoided claiming that he never *discussed* the 25th Amendment at all, with anyone. Again, the evidence he did so is overwhelming. Unable credibly to deny it, he deflected it. The deputy

AG was more serious about being perceived as favoring Trump's removal than about putting his neck on the line in an actual removal effort.

3) Appeasing Democratic Demands for a Special Counsel

The most consequential step Rosenstein took to appease Democrats was his appointment of Robert Mueller as special counsel.

As we've detailed, the president's performance after Comey's dismissal was bizarre. It intensified the already heated Democratic calls for the
appointment of a special counsel for the Russia investigation, notwithstanding the absence of any factual evidence that the president, for all
his missteps and Twitter twaddle, had actually committed a crime.

No one was more affected by this pressure cooker than the deputy
AG. By May 12, 2017, the *Times* recounts, an "upset and emotional"
Rosenstein was longing for Comey's return to the Bureau's helm. By
May 14, Rosenstein was asking FBI officials whether he ought to call
Comey directly to seek the former director's advice about appointing a
special counsel—a suggestion the officials are said to have shot down as
a "bad idea." At that very time, the just-ousted Comey was leaking his
Flynn memo to the *Times*, hoping it would spur appointment of a spe-
cial counsel. Implicitly, this was an appeal to Rosenstein; by regulation,
the decision whether to name a special counsel was his to make.

On May 16, the *Times* ran with its barnburner story about Comey's
Trump/Flynn memo.[29] This ratcheted up to new heights the calls for a
special counsel, with Democrats upbraiding the president for obstructing the FBI—both by firing Comey, who had been running the Russia
probe, and by meddling in the case of Flynn, a potential witness in the
Russia probe. One can certainly disagree with Trump's moves, and
find them foolish. Some even say indefensible. Others would argue
that Comey deserved to be removed (or, at least, that his removal was
justified), and that Flynn did not deserve to be investigated. Whatever
you think, though, these actions could not constitute obstruction—as
a matter of law, FBI investigations are not "proceedings" that can
be obstructed. Counterintelligence investigations are done for the
president, not to prosecute in judicial proceedings, so *justice* is not
obstructed; and a president's discretionary exercise of his lawful constitutional authority (such as by firing subordinates or weighing in on

the merits of continuing investigations) cannot constitute prosecutable obstruction—though, if Congress believes there have been egregious abuses of power, it can always impeach the president.[30]

Nevertheless, on May 16, in the wake of Comey's firing and on the same day as the big *Times* report about Comey's Trump/Flynn memo, Rosenstein raised with McCabe the possibility of removing Trump via the 25th Amendment. Less than twenty-four hours later, on May 17, Rosenstein suddenly announced the appointment of a special counsel.

This was Rosenstein's chance to get back into the Democrats' good graces. Indeed, the *Times* reports that the deputy AG came close to appointing his old friend and former boss, James Cole, President Obama's deputy attorney general for four years (who, the *Times* adds, was then in private practice representing such Democratic operators as Sidney Blumenthal). In the event, Rosenstein did the next best thing to restore his good standing in Washington by picking Robert Mueller, an appointment that was certain to (and did) receive ringing endorsements from Comey, Democrats, and the Beltway's bipartisan media-pundit class.[31]

Rosenstein gave the president no notice regarding the Mueller appointment. The intrepid deputy AG phoned Sessions, who was at the White House, so that he could deliver the news to Trump. The president was devastated. Sessions and his chief of staff, Jody Hunt, were embarrassed and horrified—Rosenstein had given them no heads-up, either. Slumping into his chair, as Sessions, Hunt, and White House Counsel McGahn looked on, Trump wailed, "Oh my God. This is terrible, this is the end of my presidency. I'm fucked." He berated the attorney general, "How could you let this happen, Jeff?" The president asked for Sessions's resignation but ended up not accepting it—the beleaguered attorney general finally left the Justice Department after the 2018 midterm elections.[32]

When he and Sessions returned to Main Justice, Hunt was livid. He stormed into Rosenstein's office, finding the deputy AG hunkered down behind his desk. Rosenstein asked whether the president was going to fire him. Hunt told Rosenstein that what he had done was "despicable and unprofessional."[33]

Rosenstein's first stop after installing Mueller as special counsel was Capitol Hill. There, he put on sackcloth and ashes for Senate

Democrats, promising he would impose no investigative restraints on Mueller. As *The Washington Post* later reported, the deputy AG

> emphasize[d] to the senators the independent authority that the new special counsel...has in the Russian investigation. "If one thing is clear from the meeting we just had, it is that Mr. Mueller has broad and wide-ranging authority to follow the facts wherever they go," said Senate Minority Leader Charles E. Schumer (D-N.Y.). "That gives me confidence and should give the American people some confidence."[34]

The *Post* further related that Rosenstein stressed "Mueller's wide scope" as his rationale for referring senators to Mueller rather than answering their questions about the investigation. The message: The deputy AG planned to be hands off; the special counsel would be given free rein.

The appointment of Mueller as special counsel effectively wrested control of Crossfire Hurricane from the FBI. That appeared inappropriate: the FBI investigation was counterintelligence, and Mueller was a prosecutor not an intelligence analyst. But the investigation really was criminal now. After Comey's firing, McCabe—now the Bureau's acting director—formally opened a criminal investigation of President Trump for obstruction. That it was a specious theory is, for now, beside the point. What matters is that the focus had shifted dramatically, to obstruction: a potentially criminal offense, and an abuse of power for which presidents have faced impeachment—and over which Richard Nixon would have been removed had he not resigned in 1974.

The collusion narrative had served its purpose. To be sure, Plan A had failed: The whitewashing of a criminal case against Hillary Clinton, the airbrushing of her serious misconduct, had not been able to compensate for her weaknesses as a presidential candidate. But the collusion narrative, seeded by the Obama administration, tilled by intelligence leaks, and tended by constant media care accomplished its objectives. A special counsel—effectively, an independent prosecutor—was imposed, despite the absence of a criminal predicate, to monitor the Trump presidency. This special counsel produced a report which, though unable to establish the Trump–Russia conspiracy that was its rationale, urged an impeachment road map on the Democratic-controlled House of Representatives. Though that road map will never trigger the president's removal from office, it will spawn congressional hearings on the president's asserted unfitness for office, teeing up the Democrats' 2020 campaign.

That is the Ball of Collusion: counterintelligence as a pretext for a criminal investigation in search of a crime; a criminal investigation as a pretext for impeachment without an impeachable offense; an impeachment inquiry as a pretext for rendering the Donald Trump un-reelectable; and all of it designed as a straitjacket around his presidency. Will it succeed? That depends on whether President Trump exposes and defies the narrative, or plays the role it has scripted for him.

Notes

INTRODUCTION

1. "Statement by FBI Director James B. Comey on the Investigation of Secretary Hillary Clinton's Use of a Personal Emails System" (Remarks prepared for delivery at press briefing, Jul. 5, 2016) (hereafter, "Comey July 5 press conference").

2. Andrew C. McCarthy, "'We Need to Clean This Up': More Evidence Obama Lied About Hillary's Private E-mails" (*National Review*, Oct. 25, 2016); McCarthy, "Podesta Leaks: The Clinton-Obama E-mails" (*National Review*, Oct. 15, 2016); McCarthy, "Obama's Growing Conflict of Interest in the Clinton E-mail Scandal" (*National Review*, Feb. 3, 2016).

3. Julian Hattem, "Obama's 'classified' comments strike nerve" (*The Hill*, Apr. 11, 2016).

4. The Espionage Act, codified at Title 18, United States Code, Section 793 ("Gathering, transmitting or losing defense information"), subsections (e) through (f), further discussed, *infra*. See also Title 18, United States Code, Section 1924 ("Unauthorized removal and retention of classified documents or material").

5. Kenneth Starr, *Contempt: A Memoir of the Clinton Investigation*, pp. 201-6 (Sentinel, 2018).

6. Matt Apuzzo, Michael S. Schmidt, Adam Goldman, and Eric Lichtblau, "Comey Tried to Shield the F.B.I. From Politics. Then He Shaped and Election." (*The New York Times*, Apr. 22, 2017).

7. Lisa Page Testimony before the House Judiciary and Oversight Committees, Jul. 13, 2018, pp. 94-95; Jerry Dunleavy, "Lisa Page said FBI discussed charging Hillary Clinton with 'gross negligence' in 2016, and DOJ told them no" (*Washington Examiner*, Mar. 12, 2019).

8. Matt Zapatosky, "Officials: Scant evidence that Clinton had malicious intent in handling of emails" (*The Washington Post*, May 5, 2016); "Clinton aide Cheryl Mills leaves FBI interview briefly after being asked about emails" (*The Washington Post*, May 10, 2016); see also Andrew C. McCarthy, "Clinton E-Mails: Is the Fix In?" (*National Review*, May 14, 2016).

9. Title 18, United States Code, Section 641 ("Whoever embezzles, steals, purloins, or knowingly converts to his use, or the use of another, or without authority, sells, conveys, or disposes of any record, voucher, money, or thing of value of the United States or of any department or agency thereof, or any property made or being made under contract for the United States or any department or agency thereof; or [w]hoever receives, conceals, or retains the same with intent to convert it to his use or gain, knowing it to have been embezzled, stolen, purloined or converted—[s]hall be fined under this title or imprisoned not more than ten years, or both").

10. Office of the Inspector General, U.S. Department of Justice, "A Review of Various Actions by the Federal Bureau of Investigation and Department of Justice in Advance of the 2016 Election," Executive Summary, p. iv (Jun. 2018).

11. Clinton's popular vote plurality could be credited solely to California, which she won by a staggering 4.3 million votes. Since 2010, California has employed a nominally nonpartisan "Jungle Primary" system. See, e.g., Adam Nagourney, "Here's How California's 'Jungle Primary' System Works" (*The New York Times*, May 24, 2018). In effect, this means the Golden State is not only deeply blue; it discourages Republicans from voting on Election Day. In the primaries for state and congressional races, party labels are not included on the ballot; the two top primary vote-getters, regardless of party, are awarded spots on the November ballot. In California, that generally means the two top Democrats. In 2016, for example, there was no Republican finalist in the most important statewide race, for a United States Senate seat. (In the contest between Democrats, Kamala Harris defeated Loretta Sanchez.) With Republicans thus marginalized and with Clinton a lock to win the state, Republican voter turnout was predictably weak. If California were put aside and the other 49 states were aggregated, Trump would have had more popular votes than Clinton, though still not a majority. Nevertheless, Clinton's popular-vote edge over Trump exceeded that of five elected presidents: Richard M. Nixon (1968), John F. Kennedy (1960), Grover Cleveland (1884), James A. Garfield (1880), and Polk (1844—an election in which the total number of Americans who voted was less than 3 million).

12. John McCormack, "The Election Came Down to 77,744 Votes in Pennsylvania, Wisconsin, and Michigan" (*The Weekly Standard*, Nov. 10, 2016) (later updated to reflect final results); Andrew Mercer, Claudia Deane, and Kyley McGeeney, "Why 2016 election polls missed their mark" (Pew Research Center, Nov. 9, 2016). As Mrs. Clinton's husband could tell her, it is not abnormal for a winning candidate to fail to earn a popular majority—he won twice without cracking 50 percent. Trump is the fifth president to win an electoral majority despite losing the popular vote, joining George W. Bush (2000), Benjamin Harrison (1888), Rutherford B. Hayes (1876), and John Quincy Adams (1824).

13. George F. Will, "The Electoral College is an excellent system" (*The Washington Post*, Dec. 16, 2016).

14. Andrew C. McCarthy, *Spring Fever: The Illusion of Islamic Democracy* (Encounter Books, 2012).

15. Michael Isikoff, "U.S. intel officials probe ties between Trump adviser and Kremlin" (Yahoo News, Sept. 23, 2016); Glenn Simpson Testimony before Senate Intelligence Committee, pp. 197-210 (Aug. 22, 2017); Senator Harry Reid letter to FBI Director James B. Comey (Aug. 27, 2016); Michael J. Morell, "I Ran the C.I.A. Now I'm Endorsing Hillary Clinton" (*The New York Times*, Aug. 5, 2016); Lee Smith, "How CIA Director John Brennan Targeted James Comey" (*Tablet Magazine*, Feb. 9, 2018); Andrew C. McCarthy, "Politicizing Steele's Raw, Unverified 'Intelligence'" (*National Review*, Jan. 9, 2018).

16. Sophie Tatum, "Trump defends Putin: 'You think our country's so innocent?'" (CNN, Feb. 6, 2017).

17. Andrew Kaczynski, "Trump in 2008: Hillary Clinton will go down at a minimum as a great senator" (CNN, Oct. 19, 2016); Sean McMinn, "44 Sitting Members of Congress Have Accepted Donations from Trump—Group includes prominent lawmakers from both parties" (*Roll Call*, Jan. 18, 2017); Nick Gass, "Trump has spent years courting Hillary and other Dems" (*Politico*, Jun. 16, 2015); Dan Eggen and T. W. Farnam, "Trump's donation history shows Democratic favoritism" (*The Washington Post*, Apr. 26, 2011).

18. Andrew C. McCarthy, "Bush Derangement Syndrome: Russia as a Strategic Partner" (*National Review*, Aug. 15, 2008); McCarthy, "Putin's Intentions Aren't What Matter" (*National Review*, Mar. 29, 2014); Mary Beth Nikitin, "U.S.-Russian Civilian Nuclear Cooperation Agreement: Issues for Congress" (Congressional Research Service, Jan. 11, 2011).

19. William Safire, "Ukraine Marches Out" ("misreading the forces of history in his 'chicken Kiev' speech not only made one American President appear to be anti-liberty, but jeopardized our relations with an emerging European power") (*The New York Times*, Nov. 18, 1991); David Nakamura and Debbi Wilgoren, "Caught on an open mike, Obama tells Medvedev he needs 'space' on missile defense" (*The Washington Post*, Mar. 26, 2012); Glenn Kessler, "Flashback: Obama's debate zinger on Romney's '1980s' foreign policy (with video)" (*The Washington Post*, Mar. 20, 2014).

20. Peter Schweizer, "The Clinton Foundation, State and Kremlin Connections—Why did Hillary's State Department urge U.S. investors to fund Russian research for military uses?" (*The Wall Street Journal*, Jul. 31, 2016).

21. About a fifth of U.S. electrical power is generated by nuclear energy, part of which is uranium-generated. As *The New York Times* has reported, the na-

tion produces only a fifth of the uranium needed for this purpose, and most plants have just 18 to 36 months of reserves. The U.S. is thus dependent on foreign uranium. Jo Becker and Mike McIntire, "Cash Flowed to Clinton Foundation Amid Russian Uranium Deal" (*The New York Times*, Apr. 23, 2015), citing Marin Katusa, *The Colder War: How the Global Energy Trade Slipped from America's Grasp* (Wiley Publishing, 2014).

22. Peter Schweizer, *Clinton Cash: The Untold Story of How and Why Foreign Governments and Businesses Help Make Bill and Hillary Rich* (Harper, 2015); see also *infra*.

CHAPTER 1

1. Nicholas Eberstadt, "A statistical glimpse at Russia's multiple demographic and human resource problems" (American Enterprise Institute, Apr. 7, 2018); Eberstadt, "The Dying Bear—Russia's Demographic Disaster" (*Foreign Affairs*, Nov./Dec. 2011 ed.), and "Drunken Nation: Russia's Depopulation Bomb" (*World Affairs*, Spring 2009 ed.); see also, e.g., Mark Lawrence Schrad, "Western Sanctions Are Shrinking Russia's Population" (*Foreign Policy*, Oct. 19, 2017). Russia's gross domestic product in 2017 was $1.58 trillion, well under one-tenth the size of the U.S. economy (Trading Economics, "Russia GDP") (accessed Mar. 10, 2019).

2. United Nations General Assembly Resolution 2131 (Dec. 31, 1965).

3. Sean Watts, "International Law and Proposed Responses to the D.N.C. Hack" (Just Security, Oct. 14, 2016); see also Jens David Ohlin, "Did Russian Cyber Interference in the 2016 Election Violate International Law?" (*Texas Law Review*, 2018).

4. See *United States v. Internet Research Agency LLC*, 18 Cr. 0032 (D.C., 2018), alleging conspiracy to defraud the United States under Section 371 of the federal penal code (Title 18, United States Code).

5. Scott Shane, "Russia Isn't the Only One Meddling in Elections. We Do It, Too." (*The New York Times*, Feb. 17, 2018).

6. Steven F. Hayward, *The Real Jimmy Carter: How Our Worst Ex-President Undermines American Foreign Policy, Coddles Dictators, and Created the Party of Clinton and Kerry* (Regnery Publishing, 2004).

7. Peter Robinson, "Ted Kennedy's Soviet Gambit" (*Forbes*, Aug. 28, 2009).

8. Scott Shane, "Russia Isn't the Only One Meddling in Elections. We Do It, Too," *supra*.

9. Seth Lipsky, "The hypocrisy of American election investigations into Israel" (*New York Post*, May 23, 2018); Stephen Dinan, "Obama admin. sent taxpayer money to campaign to oust Netanyahu" (*The Washington Times*,

Jul. 12, 2016); see also Andrew C. McCarthy, *The Grand Jihad* (Encounter Books, 2010), pp. 213-20 (recounting then-Senator Barack Obama's meddling in Kenya's explosive 2006 elections).

10. David M. Herszenhorn and Ellen Barry, "Putin Contends Clinton Incited Unrest Over Vote" (*The New York Times*, Dec. 8, 2011).

11. Nolan D. McCaskill, "Trump tells Wisconsin: Victory was a surprise" (*Politico*, Dec. 13, 2016).

12. Andrew C. McCarthy, "Putin's Intentions Aren't What Matter" (*National Review*, Mar. 29, 2014).

13. "After the Summit; Excerpts From Bush's Ukraine Speech: Working 'for the Good of Both of Us'" (*The New York Times*, Aug. 2, 1991), William Safire, "Ukraine Marches Out" (*The New York Times*, Nov. 18, 1991); James Jay Carafano, "How to be a freedom fighter" (*Washington Examiner*, Apr. 3, 2011).

14. Robert McConnell, "Keep America's Word Again—and Protect Ukraine" (*The Wall Street Journal*, Jan. 9, 2017); Andrew C. McCarthy, "Obama Won't Arm Ukraine Because He Led the Disarming of Ukraine" (*National Review*, Jul. 23, 2014); Sen. Richard Lugar Press Release, "Lugar and Obama Urge Destruction of Conventional Weapons Stockpiles" (Aug. 30, 2005).

15. Francis Fukuyama, *The End of History and the Last Man* (Free Press, Reissue Edition, 2006); William Anthony Hay, "Squandering the Post-Cold War Peace Dividend" (Law & Liberty, Sept. 1, 2016).

16. Steven Pifer, "Ukraine, nuclear weapons, and the trilateral statement 25 years later" (Stanford University Freeman Spogli Institute for International Studies, Jan. 4, 2019); United States Department of State, Office of the Historian, "Bill Clinton, Boris Yeltsin, and U.S.-Russian Relations" (Milestone Books, 1993-2000); International Monetary Fund, World Economic Outlook, Global Economic Prospects and Policies, Advanced Economies (Oct. 1997).

17. "Bush Trusts Putin—Bush looked into Putin's eyes and got a sense of his soul, and he trusts him" (C-SPAN, Jun. 16, 2001); Andrew C. McCarthy, "Bush Derangement Syndrome: Russia as a Strategic Partner" (Aug. 15, 2008); Mary Beth Nikitin, "U.S.-Russian Civilian Nuclear Cooperation Agreement: Issues for Congress" (Congressional Research Service, Jan. 11, 2011).

18. McCarthy, "Obama Won't Arm Ukraine Because He Led the Disarming of Ukraine," *supra.*

19. Luke Coffey, "10 Years After Putin's Invasion, Russia Still Occupies Parts of Georgia" (The Daily Signal, Mar. 1, 2018); Nikitin, "U.S.-Russian Civilian Nuclear Cooperation Agreement: Issues for Congress," *supra.*

20. Claudia Rosett, "Ten Years into Obama's Russia 'Reset'" (PJ Media, Mar. 6, 2019).

21. Peter Baker, "White House Scraps Bush's Approach to Missile Shield" (*The New York Times*, Sept. 17, 2009); Michaela Dodge, "President Obama's Missile Defense Policy: A Misguided Legacy" (Heritage Foundation, Sept. 15, 2016); Nikitin, "U.S.-Russian Civilian Nuclear Cooperation Agreement: Issues for Congress," *supra*.

22. Hillary Clinton, "Trade with Russia Is a Win-Win—By making Moscow a normal trading partner, Congress would create American jobs and advance human rights" (*The Wall Street Journal*, Jun. 19, 2012).

23. U.S. European Command, "Russia's Skolkovo Innovation Center" (EUCOM Strategic Foresight pamphlet, Jul. 29, 2013), p. 6 (emphasis in original); John Solomon, "The case for Russia collusion...against the Democrats" (*The Hill*, Feb. 10, 2019).

24. Peter Schweizer, "The Clinton Foundation, State and Kremlin Connections" (*The Wall Street Journal*, Jul. 31, 2016).

25. Solomon, "The case for Russia collusion...against the Democrats," *supra*; Lucia Ziobro, "FBI Boston office warns businesses of venture capital scams" (*Boston Business Journal*, Apr. 4, 2014); Michael B. Farrell, "FBI warns Mass. Tech companies on Russian investors" (*The Boston Globe*, Apr. 8, 2014) (republished by telegram.com).

26. U.S. Department of State, 2012 Country Reports on Human Rights Practies, Russia Report (Apr. 19, 2013).

27. Schweizer, "The Clinton Foundation, State and Kremlin Connections," *supra*.

28. Schweizer, *Clinton Cash, supra*; Jo Becker and Mike McIntire, "Cash Flowed to Clinton Foundation Amid Russian Uranium Deal" (*The New York Times*, Apr. 23, 2015).

29. U.S. Energy Information Administration, "What is the status of the U.S. nuclear industry"; and "Where Our Uranium Comes From" (accessed Mar. 11, 2019).

30. U.S. Department of State, "Kazakhstan 2017 Human Rights Report"; Andrew Osborn, "Kazakhstan to Britain: Don't lecture us on human rights" (Reuters, Jul. 1, 2013); Peter Baker, "As Kazakh scandal unfolds, Soviet-style reprisals begin" (*The Washington Post*, Jun. 11, 2002) (republished by *Chicago Tribune*).

31. Andrew C. McCarthy, "Uranium One Focus: Corruption, Not National Security" (*National Review*, Nov. 15, 2017).

32. Schweizer, *Clinton Cash, supra*.

33. Title 18, U.S. Code, Section 1956.

34. Title 18, U.S. Code, Section 371.

35. *United States v. Vadim Mikerin*, No. 14 Cr. 529 (District of Maryland,

2014), Plea Agreement (Aug. 14, 2015); John Solomon and Alison Spann, "FBI uncovered Russian bribery plot before Obama administration approved controversial nuclear deal with Moscow" (*The Hill*, Oct. 17, 2017).

36. That may not be the end of the story. Campbell, the informant, has claimed that he learned, through conversations with Mikerin and other conspirators, that Russian nuclear officials tried to ingratiate themselves with the Clintons. He further alleges that the FBI induced him to sign a nondisclosure agreement, and that the Obama Justice Department threatened to enforce it against him—including to prevent him from disclosing information to Congress and from filing a civil lawsuit to recover losses he says he sustained because of the criminal scheme. President Trump's original attorney general, Jeff Sessions, waived any nondisclosure sanctions in order to permit Campbell to speak with congressional investigators. Republicans claim he provided information about a possible Russian scheme to channel funds to a lobbying firm that would contribute to the Clinton Global Initiative (a Clinton Foundation project). Democrats launched a stinging attack against Campbell's credibility, highlighting medical problems and other issues that caused him significant memory lapses. The matter is reportedly under investigation by Utah U.S. Attorney John Huber, appointed by Sessions in 2017 to probe matters related to the 2016 election. *The Hill*'s John Solomon, who has reported extensively on Uranium One, noted in October 2018 that the FBI has thus far refused to disclose 37 pages of relevant documents, which are the subject of Freedom of Information Act litigation. Solomon, "FBI's 37 secret pages of memos about Russia, Clintons and Uranium One" (*The Hill*, Oct. 1, 2018); see also Solomon and Alison Spann, "Russian uranium informant says FBI sought new information from him about the Clintons" (*The Hill*, Mar. 22, 2018); Dan Friedman, "Here's Why Republicans Stopped Talking about a Uranium One 'Whistleblower'" (*Mother Jones*, Mar. 8, 2018).

37. Karen Tumulty and Philip Rucker, "At third debate, Trump won't commit to accepting election results if he loses" (*The Washington Post*, Oct. 19, 2016).

38. Eric Lipton, David E. Sanger, and Scott Shane, "The Perfect Weapon: How Russian Cyberpower Invaded the U.S." (*The New York Times*, Dec. 13, 2016); Greg Miller, Ellen Nakashima, and Adam Entous, "Obama's secret struggle to punish Russia for Putin's election assault" (*The Washington Post*, Jun. 23, 2017); Philip Bump, "What Obama did, didn't do and couldn't do in response to Russian interference" (*The Washington Post*, Feb. 21, 2018); Emily Birnbaum, "Trump: Obama didn't warn about Russia before election because 'it is all a big hoax'" (*The Hill*, Jul. 22, 2018).

39. Chiara Palazzo, "Barack Obama tells The Daily Show's Trevor Noah that Russian hacking was no 'big surprise'" (*The Telegraph*, Dec. 13, 2016).

40. Debra Heine, "RussiaGate: Hillary Clinton and John Podesta's Troubling Ties to Russia" (PJ Media, Mar. 29, 2017).

CHAPTER 2

1. Justin Baragona, "Fox News' Chris Wallace Sets Record Straight: Russia Investigation Did Not Start With Trump Dossier" (*The Daily Beast*, Mar. 29, 2019).

2. Intelligence leaks have suggested that there was FISA surveillance of Paul Manafort and his assistant, Richard Gates, but these appear to have been dispelled during Manafort's prosecution. It has been reported, though not confirmed, that Manafort's Russian associate, Konstantin Kilimnik, was a subject of FISA surveillance. Michael Flynn appears to have been captured by FISA surveillance, but the target of that effort was likely Russian ambassador Sergey Kislyak, with Flynn monitored incidentally when the two communicated. As further detailed subsequently, it has also been reported that there was an effort to get FISA coverage on a Trump Tower server once suspected of being a back channel to Russia through two Kremlin-connected financial institutions, including Alfa Bank.

3. Max Boot, "Everybody spies on allies—get over it" (*New York Post*, Oct. 23, 2013) (The "five eyes" alliance is an exception to the usual rule in that they "probably don't spy on each other's leaders—but they do spy on each other's citizens. In fact this intelligence sharing allows them to do an end-run around prohibitions on domestic surveillance: The Brits can spy on our citizens, we can spy on theirs and then we can share the results."; Scarlet Kim, Diana Lee, and Paulina Perlin, "Newly Disclosed Documents on the Five Eyes Alliance and What They Tell Us about Intelligence-Sharing Agreements" (Lawfare, Apr. 23, 2018); Margaret Warner, "An exclusive club: The 5 countries that don't spy on each other" (PBS, Oct. 25, 2013).

4. John O. Brennan (@JohnBrennan) Jul. 16, 2018, Tweet ("Donald Trump's press conference performance in Helsinki rises to & exceeds the threshold of 'high crimes & misdemeanors.' It was nothing sort of treasonous. Not only were Trump's comments imbecilic, he is wholly in the pocket of Putin. Republican Patriots: Where are you???"); Tim Hains, "Brennan: 'I Stand Very Much By' Accusing President Trump of Treason; 'He's Bringing This Country Down," (Real Clear Politics, Aug. 19, 2018).

5. House Permanent Select Committee on Intelligence, Minority Memo of January 29, 2018 (Schiff Memo), p. 3; Andrew C. McCarthy, "The Schiff Memo Harms Democrats More Than It Helps Them" (*National Review*, Feb. 25, 2018).

6. See, e.g., Schiff Memo, *supra*, p. 3; Scott Shane, Mark Mazzetti, and Adam Goldman (with reporting contributions from Nicholas Confessore, Andrew

E. Kramer, Michael S. Schmidt, and research assistance by Kitty Bennett), "Trump Advisor's Visit to Moscow Got the F.B.I.'s Attention" (*The New York Times*, Apr. 19, 2017).

7. *Ibid.*

8. Sharon LaFraniere, Mark Mazzetti, and Matt Apuzzo (with reporting contributions from Adam Goldman, Eileen Sullivan, and Matthew Rosenberg), "How the Russia Inquiry Began: A Campaign Aide, Drinks and Talk of Political Dirt" (*The New York Times*, Dec. 30, 2017).

9. Adam Entous, Devlin Barrett, and Rosalind Helderman, "Clinton campaign, DNC paid for research that led to Russia dossier" (*The Washington Post*, Oct. 24, 2017); Andrew C. McCarthy, "When Scandals Collide" (*National Review*, Oct. 25, 2017).

10. FBI Director James B. Comey, testimony before Senate Intelligence Committee (Jun. 8, 2017) (reproduced by *The Washington Post*) (questioning by Senator Susan Collins (R., Maine)).

11. *Gubarev et al. v. Orbis Business Intelligence Ltd. and Christopher Steele*, High Court of Justice, Queens Bench Division, Claim No. HQ17D00413, Defendants' Response to Claimants' Request for Further Information (May 18, 2017); Andrew C. McCarthy, "Politicizing Steele's Raw, Unverified 'Intelligence'" (*National Review*, Jan. 9, 2018).

12. Grassley and Graham Letter to Deputy Attorney General Rod Rosenstein and FBI Director Christopher Wray (Jan. 4, 2018); Andrew C. McCarthy, "Grassley-Graham Memo Affirms Nunes Memo—Media Yawns" (*National Review*, Feb. 10, 2018).

13. Tim Haines, "Gowdy: Did Obama Justice Department Rely on Steele Dossier to Get FISA Warrant?" (Real Clear Politics, Oct. 29, 2017); Evan Perez, Shimon Prokupecz, and Manu Raju, "FBI used dossier allegations to bolster Trump–Russia investigation" (CNN, Apr. 18, 2017).

14. Louis Nelson and Brent D. Griffiths, "Carter Page: I've never communicated with Trump" (*Politico*, Feb. 5, 2018).

15. *United States v. Evgeny Buryakov, Igor Sporyshev, and Victor Podobnyy*, Sealed Complaint Affidavit of FBI Agent Gregory Monaghan (Jan. 23, 2015), pp. 12-13 (referring to Carter Page as "Male-1"); Byron York, "Assessing the new Democratic intel memo" (*Washington Examiner*, Feb. 24, 2018); Andrew C. McCarthy, "A Foreign Power's Recruitment Effort Is Not a Basis for a FISA Court Warrant" (*National Review*, Feb. 26, 2018). Because of redactions to the Page surveillance warrant applications, we do not know exactly what the Justice Department and the FBI told the court about Page's involvement in the Russian spy prosecution. In the Schiff memo, *supra*, House Democrats highlight the fact that Page was the subject of a recruitment effort in arguing that there were reasons for grave concern about

Page's interactions with Russia. The memo mentions the *Buryakov* spy case and cites to the arrest complaint, but redactions render it impossible to say whether these mentions (a) are merely meant to underscore that Page was a recruitment target, or (b) acknowledge Page's cooperation with the Justice Department's prosecution. Schiff Memo, pp. 3-4 & n.10.

16. For example, we learned in mid-2017 that Aras Agalarov, a Russian oligarch close to Putin, had coordinated the dispatch of Natalia Veselnitskaya, a Kremlin-connected lawyer, to pass to the Trump campaign what Don Trump Jr. was told would be information devastating to Hillary Clinton. The information was apparently nonsense, but the campaign took the June 2016 meeting at Trump Tower in New York City because of Donald Trump's personal relationship and prior business history with Agalarov. See Andrew C. McCarthy, "The Curious Case of Natalia Veselnitskaya" (*National Review*, Jul. 19, 2017).

CHAPTER 3

1. Jeff Horowitz and Chad Day, "AP Exclusive: Before Trump job, Manafort worked to aid Putin" (Associated Press, Mar. 22, 2017).

2. Oksana Grytsenko, "WikiLeaks: Regions Party partly composed of 'criminals'" (*Kyiv Post*, Jan. 24, 2012).

3. Glenn R. Simpson and Mary Jacoby, "How Lobbyists Help Ex-Soviets Woo Washington" (*The Wall Street Journal*, Apr. 17, 2007) (updated); Christina Sterbenz, "The Worst Gangster Most People Have Never Heard Of" (*Business Insider*, Dec. 1, 2014); on Sessions, see Michael Isikoff and Ruth Marcus, "Clinton Fires Sessions as FBI Director" (*The Washington Post*, Jul. 20, 1993).

4. Foreign Agents Registration Act (FARA), Title 22, U.S. Code, Sections 611 et seq. See, generally, Congressional Research Service, "Foreign Agents Registration Act: An Overview" (Feb. 15, 2019) (updated).

5. Office of the Inspector General, U.S. Department of Justice, "Audit of the National Security Division's Enforcement and Administration of the Foreign Agents Registration Act" (Sept. 2016); Ken Silverstein, "I've Covered Foreign Lobbying for 20 Years and I'm Amazed Manafort Got Busted— That's because foreign lobbying laws are so toothless that you can count on one hand the number of people prosecuted for what Manafort is accused of" (*Politico*, Oct. 30, 2017). (Of the seven cases, one was convicted at trial, two pled guilty, two were convicted of non-FARA charges, and two saw their cases dismissed.)

6. Byron York, "In Trump–Russia probe, was it all about the Logan Act?" (*Washington Examiner*, Dec. 3, 2018); Stephen Mihm, "The Logan Act:

Never Used, Often Abused" (Bloomberg, Dec. 8, 2017); Dan McLaughlin, "Repeal the Logan Act" (*National Review*, May 5, 2018).

7. "Donbas" (sometimes "Donbass") is a large mining and industrial region. The name is derived from the region's serving as the basin of the Donets River, where the vast coal fields of eastern Ukraine spill into southwestern Russia.

8. Andrew C. McCarthy, "If Working with Moscow is 'Collusion,' It's a Bipartisan Offense—D.C. has been delusional about the Kremlin since the 1990s" (*National Review*, Feb. 23, 2019); see also, e.g., McCarthy, "The Obama Administration's Hypocritical Pretext for Spying on the Trump Campaign— Where was its concern about Russia during its eight years in power?" (*National Review*, May 29, 2018); McCarthy, "Putin's Intentions Aren't What Matter" (*National Review*, Mar. 19, 2014); McCarthy, "Missile Malpractice" (*National Review*, Dec. 4, 2010); McCarthy, "Bush Derangement Syndrome: Russia as a Strategic Partner" (*National Review*, Aug. 15, 2008).

9. Graham Stack, "Everything you know about Paul Manafort is wrong" (*Kyiv Post*, Sept. 17, 2018); Chuck Ross, "Former Fusion GPS Employee Shreds Firm's Work on Paul Manafort" (The Daily Caller, Sept. 18, 2018).

10. Andrew C. McCarthy, "Collusion: The Criminalization of Policy Disputes" (*National Review*, Feb. 16, 2019).

11. McCarthy, "If Working with Moscow is 'Collusion,' It's a Bipartisan Offense—D.C. has been delusional about the Kremlin since the 1990s," *supra*.

12. Frankin Foer, "Paul Manafort, American Hustler" (*The Atlantic*, Mar. 2018 ed.).

13. James Kirchick, "Devils' Advocates" (*The New Republic*, Aug. 13, 2008); Mary Jacoby and Glenn R. Simpson, "McCain Consultant Is Tied To Work for Ukraine Party" (*The Wall Street Journal*, May 14, 2008); Foer, "Paul Manafort, American Hustler," *supra*.

14. Kenneth P. Vogel and Matthew Rosenberg, "Agents Tried to Flip Russian Oligarchs. The Fallout Spread to Trump." (*The New York Times*, Sept. 1, 2018); John Solomon, "Russian oligarch, Justice Department and a clear case of collusion" (*The Hill*, Aug. 28, 2018); see also Solomon, "Mueller may have a conflict—leads directly to a Russian oligarch" (*The Hill*, May 14, 2018); Lee Smith, "Was Christopher Steele Paid by Russian Oligarch Deripaska?" (RealClearPolitics, Feb. 13, 2018); Michael Isikoff, "Trump's campaign chief is questioned about ties to Russian billionaire" (Yahoo News, Apr. 26, 2016); Simpson and Jacoby, "How Lobbyists Help Ex-Soviets Woo Washington," *supra*.

15. Simpson and Jacoby, "How Lobbyists Help Ex-Soviets Woo Washington," *supra*; J. E. Dyer, "A really big clue: The close Clinton connection of Fusion GPS founder Glenn Simpson" (Liberty Unyielding, Dec. 22, 2017); Lee Smith, "Did President Obama Read the 'Steele Dossier' in the White House Last August?" (*Tablet Magazine*, Dec. 20, 2017).

16. Jacoby and Simpson, "McCain Consultant Is Tied To Work for Ukraine Party," *supra*.

17. Oksana Grytsenko, "WikiLeaks: Regions Party partly composed of 'criminals'" (*Kyiv Post*, Jan. 24, 2012).

18. Vlad Lavrov, "Libel Warriors" (*Kyiv Post*, Feb. 11, 2011); Mark Rachkevych, "WikiLeaks: Nation's businessmen tell tales on each other in chats with US ambassadors" (*Kyiv Post*, Sept. 15, 2011).

19. CIA World Fact Book, Ukraine section (accessed Jan. 2019).

20. Taras Kuzio, "Oligarchs Wield Power in Ukrainian Politics" (Jamestown Foundation, Jul. 1, 2008).

21. Oksana Grytsenko, "WikiLeaks: Regions Party partly composed of 'criminals,'" *supra*.

22. Federal Bureau of Investigation, "Top Ten Fugitives—Global Con Artist and Ruthless Criminal Semion Mogilevich" (Oct. 2009).

23. *United States v. Semion Mogilevich*, Criminal No. 02-157 (Eastern District of Pennsylvania, 2002).

24. Christina Sterbenz, "The Worst Gangster Most People Have Never Heard Of" (*Business Insider*, Dec. 1, 2014); Craig Unger, "Understanding Trump v. Bruce Ohr: Think Russia's top crime boss, Semion Mogilevich" (Just Security, Aug. 30, 2018).

25. WikiLeaks, State Department cable "Ukraine: Firtash Makes His Case to the USG" (Dec. 10, 2008); Tom Winter, "DOJ: Ex-Manafort Associate Firtash Is Top-Tier Comrade of Russian Mobsters" (NBC News, Jul. 26, 2017).

26. Seth Hettena, "Why a Powerful Russian Oligarch Was Furious with Paul Manafort" (*Kyiv Post*, May 7, 2018); Jacoby and Simpson, "McCain Consultant Is Tied To Work for Ukraine Party," *supra* (*The Wall Street Journal*, Apr. 17, 2007).

27. Walt Bogdanich and Michael Forsythe, "'Exhibit A': How McKinsey Got Entangled in a Bribery Case—The consultancy's report became key evidence in a battle over the extradition of a powerful Ukrainian oligarch charged in a scheme to help Boeing" (*The New York Times*, Dec. 30, 2018).

28. Garrett M. Graff, "Robert Mueller Chooses His Investigatory Dream Team" (*Wired*, Jun. 14, 2017) (noting Lisa Page experience in international organized crime and investigation of Ukrainian oligarch Firtash, Manafort's former business partner); Federal Bureau of Investigation, National Press Office, "Andrew G. McCabe Named Executive Assistant Director of National Security Branch" (Oct. 23, 2013) (noting that McCabe began his FBI career in the New York field office and was supervisor of the Eurasian Organized Crime Task Force); U.S. Department of Justice, Office of Public Affairs, "Six

Defendants Indicted in Alleged Conspiracy to Bribe Government Officials in India to Mine Titanium Materials" (Apr. 2, 2014) (noting indictment of Firtash and participation in the investigation by Justice Department's Fraud Section); Jeff Carlson, "Little-Known FBI Unit Played Major Role in Disseminating Steele Dossier" (*The Epoch Times*, Sept. 29, 2018).

29. Kim Sengupta, "Viktor Yushchenko: 'Every politician in Ukraine who turns to the West is in danger'" (*UK Independent*, Oct. 14, 2015).

30. Kenneth P. Vogel, "Manafort's man in Kiev" (*Politico*, Aug. 18, 2016); Clifford J. Levy, "Toppled in Ukraine but Nearing a Comeback" (*The New York Times*, Jan. 14, 2010).

31. Levy, "Toppled in Ukraine but Nearing a Comeback," *supra*.

32. Jessica Donati, "Ukraine's Yulia Tymoshenko Courts Washington After Manafort Revelations" (*The Wall Street Journal*, Dec. 8, 2018); Morgan Henson, "Yulia Tymoshenko & Batkivshchyna (Fatherland) Party" (Geohistory Today, Jan. 9, 2009); Warsaw Institute, "Does Yulia Tymoshenko collaborate with the Kremlin?" (Ukraine Monitor, Jul. 17, 2018).

33. Stephanie Petrella, "Yulia Tymoshenko: Ukraine's Candidate of Uncertainty" (Foreign Policy Research Institute, Eurasia Program, Jan. 28, 2019); Andrzej Szeptycki, "The Putin-Tymoshenko Gas Agreement and Political Developments in Ukraine" (Polish Institute of International Affairs, Jan. 23, 2009).

34. Tom Lasseter, "A Ukraine mystery: Who did Russian gas sales benefit?" (McClatchy, Feb. 11, 2009); Warsaw Institute, "Does Yulia Tymoshenko collaborate with the Kremlin?" *supra*.

35. Donati, "Ukraine's Yulia Tymoshenko Courts Washington After Manafort Revelations," *supra*; Lally Weymouth, "Yulia Tymoshenko and the fight for Ukraine: 'We cannot accept peace on Putin's terms'" (*The Washington Post*, Sept. 19, 2018); Andrew Roth, "Russia announces sanctions against senior Ukraine figures" (*The Guardian*, Nov. 1, 2018); Yevgeny Kiselyov, "Putin's Shrewd Endorsement of Tymoshenko" (*The Moscow Times*, Mar. 10, 2014); Warsaw Institute, "Does Yulia Tymoshenko collaborate with the Kremlin?" *supra*.

36. Taras Kuzio, "Yulia Tymoshenko's policies sit uneasily with her image as a pro-European politician" (London School of Economics and Political Science, May 4, 2018); see also Petrella, "Yulia Tymoshenko: Ukraine's Candidate of Uncertainty," *supra*.

37. Michael Isikoff, "Firm With Obama Ties Cashes in Overseas" (*Newsweek*, Oct. 19, 2009); Ben Smith and Kenneth P. Vogel, "Obama consultants land abroad" (*Politico*, Nov. 18, 2009); Robert Schlesinger, "Ukraine's American Imports—American political consultants and lobbyists have been working on all sides of the tempestuous Ukrainian situation" (*U.S. News & World Report*, Feb. 21, 2014); Matthew Mosk, "Top McCain Adviser Has Found

Success Mixing Money, Politics" (*The Washington Post*, Jun. 26, 2008); Seth Hettena, "Why a Powerful Russian Oligarch Was Furious With Paul Manafort" (*Kyiv Post*, May 7, 2018).

38. Mueller Report, Vol. I, pp. 132-34.

39. Kenneth P. Vogel and Andrew E. Kramer, "Russian Spy of Hustling Political Operative? The Enigmatic Figure at the Heart of Mueller's Inquiry" (*The New York Times*, Feb. 23, 2019); "Russian charged with Trump's ex-campaign chief was key figure in pro-Russia strategy" (Associated Press, Jul. 3, 2018).

40. "Russian charged with Trump's ex-campaign chief was key figure in pro-Russia strategy," *supra*.

41. Michael Isikoff, "Trump's campaign chief is questioned about ties to Russian billionaire" (Yahoo News, Apr. 26, 2016); Hettena, "Why a Powerful Russian Oligarch Was Furious With Paul Manafort," *supra*.

42. "Profile: Viktor Yanukovych" (BBC News, Mar. 2, 2010).

43. Ellen Barry, "Former Ukraine Premier Is Jailed for 7 Years" (*The New York Times*, Oct. 11, 2011); "Ukraine ex-PM Yulia Tymoshenko jailed over gas deal" (BBC News, Oct. 11, 2011).

44. Lachlan Markay, "Robert Mueller Targeted Two Lobbying Firms. Thriving in Trump's D.C." (The Daily Beast, Jul. 30, 2018); Hettena, "Why a Powerful Russian Oligarch Was Furious With Paul Manafort," *supra*.

45. *United States v. Gregory B. Craig* (District of Columbia, 2019), Indictment (Apr. 11, 2019); *United States v. Alex van der Zwaan*, No. 18 Crim. 31 (ABJ) (District of Columbia, 2018), Statement of the Offense (Feb. 20, 2018); Kenneth P. Vogel and Katie Benner, "Gregory Craig, Ex-Obama Aide, Is Indicted on Charges of Lying to Justice Dept" (*The New York Times*, Apr. 11, 2019); Hettena, "Why a Powerful Russian Oligarch Was Furious With Paul Manafort," *supra*.

46. "Where is Viktor Yanukovych?" (*Kyiv Post*, Feb. 23, 2014).

47. Chuck Ross, "Manafort Meeting with Alleged Russian Operative Is at 'the Heart' of Mueller Probe, Prosecutors Say" (The Daily Caller, Feb. 7, 2019); Tom Hamburger, Rosalind S. Helderman, Carol D. Leonnig, and Adam Entous, "Manafort offered to give Russian billionaire 'private briefings' on 2016 campaign" (*The Washington Post*, Sept. 20, 2017).

48. Sharon LaFraniere, Kenneth P. Vogel, and Maggie Haberman, "Manafort Accused of Sharing Trump Polling Data With Russian Associate" (*The New York Times*, Jan. 8, 2019) (the *Times* corrected the original version of its story, which incorrectly said the polling data was to be shared with Deripaska); Tom Winter, "Manafort kept working in Ukraine after Mueller indictment, transcript shows" (NBC News, Feb. 7, 2019); Jonathan Turley, "Could Robert Mueller actually be investigating Ukrainian collusion?" (*The Hill*, Feb. 21, 2019).

49. *United States v. Paul J. Manafort, Jr., and Konstantin Kilimnik*, No. 17 Cr. 201 (ABJ) (District of Columbia, 2017), Superseding Indictment (Jun. 8, 2018); *United States v. Paul J. Manafort, Jr., and Richard W. Gates III*, No. 17 Cr. 201 (Eastern District of Virginia, 2018), Indictment (Feb. 22, 2018); *United States v. Richard W. Gates III*, No. 17 Cr. 201 (ABJ), (District of Columbia, 2018) Superseding Criminal Information (Feb. 2, 2018);Andrew C. McCarthy, "Manafort's Light Sentence in Washington Owes to How Mueller Charged Him" (*National Review*, Mar. 13, 2019); McCarthy, "Mueller's Investigation Flouts Justice Department Standards—Gates was charged with $100 million in financial crimes—and pled guilty to two minor offenses, one of them highly questionable" (*National Review*, Mar. ͳͲ, ͳͰͱͷ); McCarthy, "More Thoughts on the Mueller Indictment" (*National Review*, Nov. 1, 2017).

50. *United States v. W. Samuel Patten*, No. 18 Cr. 260 (ABJ) (District of Columbia, 2018), Criminal Information (Aug. 31, 2018); Jon Swaine, "Manafort associate paid Trump inauguration $50,000 in Ukrainian cash" (*The Guardian*, Aug. 31, 2018); Mike Eckel, "Washington Operative Who Lobbied for Ukrainian Party Charged" (Radio Free Europe/Radio Liberty, Aug. 31, 2018).

CHAPTER 4

1.   Shane Harris and Elias Groll, "Nothing Could Be Further From the Truth—As Washington awaits the release of the highly classified probe into the CIA's torture program, John Brennan's integrity is being questioned just when the agency needs it most" (*Foreign Policy*, Aug. 1, 2014); Gregory D. Johnsen, "The Untouchable John Brennan" (BuzzFeed, Apr. 23, 2015) ("'As far as the allegations of, you know, CIA hacking into Senate computers,' CIA Director John Brennan told Andrea Mitchell of NBC News, shaking his head and rolling his eyes to demonstrate the ridiculousness of the charges, 'nothing could be further from the truth. I mean, we wouldn't do that.'"); Matt Apuzzo and Mark Mazzetti, "Investigators Said to Seek No Penalty for C.I.A.'s Computer Search" (*The New York Times*, Dec. 19, 2014); Greg Miller, "CIA director John Brennan apologizes for search of Senate committee's computers" (*The Washington Post*, Jul. 31, 2014); Andrew C. McCarthy, "Clinton's Republican Guard" (PJ Media, May 7, 2013); Jonah Goldberg, "Truth and Consequences for Benghazi" (*National Review*, Sept. 20, 2013).

2.   U.S. Department of State, Office of the Historian, "How many U.S. Ambassadors have been killed by militants?".

3.   Andrew C. McCarthy, "New Benghazi Indictment Still Doesn't Mention Al-Qaeda" (*National Review*, Oct. 15, 2014); see also Declassified Defense Intelligence Agency Email (Sept. 16, 2012) ("The attack was planned ten or

more days prior on approximately 01 September 2012. The intention was to attack the consulate and kill as many Americans as possible to seek revenge for U.S. killing of Aboyahiye ((ALALIBY)) in Pakistan and in memorial of the 11 September 2001 attacks on the World Trade Center buildings.").

4.   United Nations Security Council Resolution 1973 (Mar. 17, 2011); Caroline D. Krass, Principal Deputy Assistant Attorney General, Memorandum Opinion for the Attorney General, "Authority to Use Military Force in Libya" (Apr. 1, 2011); Micah Zenko, "The Big Lie About the Libyan War—The Obama administration said it was just trying to protect civilians. Its actions reveal it was looking for regime change." (*Foreign Policy*, Mar. 22, 2016); "Global Post: Qaddafi apparently sodomized after capture" (Oct. 24, 2011); Anthony Fisher, "Libyans Would Have Preferred Hillary Clinton Kept Her 'Smart Power' Away From Their Country" (Reason, Oct. 18, 2016); Andrew C. McCarthy, *Faithless Execution* (Encounter Books, 2014), pp. 113-14 & nn.; McCarthy, "Our Libyan Adventure" (*National Review*, Oct. 27, 2011).

Secretary Clinton stated:

> Some have sought to justify this vicious behavior as a response to inflammatory material posted on the Internet. The United States deplores any intentional effort to denigrate the religious beliefs of others. Our commitment to religious tolerance goes back to the very beginning of our nation.

5.   See, e.g., McCarthy, *Faithless Execution, supra*, pp. 116-18; see also McCarthy, "The 10 P.M. Phone Call—Clinton and Obama discussed Benghazi. What did they say?" (*National Review*, May 18, 2013).

6.   Stephen F. Hayes, "The Benghazi Lie in Black and White" (*The Weekly Standard*, Jun. 28, 2016); Andrew C. McCarthy, "Hillary's Breathtaking Mendacity" (*National Review*, Oct. 24, 2015).

7.   Stephen F. Hayes, "The Spin Never Stops" (*Weekly Standard*, May 25, 2015) (assessing Morell's *The Great War of Our Time: The CIA's Fight Against Terrorism—From al Qa'ida to ISIS* (Twelve Books, 2015)); McCarthy, *Faithless Execution, supra*.

8.   Stephen F. Hayes, "The Benghazi Cover-up (cont.)—How the CIA's No. 2 misled Congress" (*The Weekly Standard*, Mar. 3, 2014).

9.   The White House, Office of the Press Secretary, "Remarks by the President at a Campaign Event—Las Vegas, NV" (Sept. 12, 2012).

10.   Thomas Joscelyn, "Al Qaeda Responsible for 4 Attack on U.S. Embassies in September" (*The Weekly Standard*, Oct. 3, 2012); Joscelyn, "Al Qaeda's expansion into Egypt" (*Long War Journal*, Feb. 11, 2014); Andrew C. McCarthy, *Faithless Execution, supra*, pp. 118-19 &nn.; McCarthy, "Obama's 'Blame It on the Video' Was a Fraud for Cairo as Well as Benghazi—More Proof" (*National Review*, Feb. 20, 2014).

11. Hayes, "The Benghazi Cover-up (cont.)—How the CIA's No. 2 misled Congress," *supra*.

12. Deroy Murdock, "How Hillary Lied to Parents of Benghazi Dead" (*National Review*, Aug. 4, 2016); McCarthy, "Hillary's Breathtaking Mendacity," *supra*; The White House, Office of the Press Secretary, "Remarks by the President to the UN General Assembly" (Sept. 25, 2012).

13. Rich Lowry, "The Benghazi patsy" (*Politico*, May 9, 2013); Editorial, "Obama's Benghazi Scapegoat Gets Year In Prison" (*Investor's Business Daily*, Nov. 9, 2012); Andrew C. McCarthy, "Amnesty, but Not for D'Souza" (*National Review*, Feb. 1, 2014); McCarthy, "Hillary's Breathtaking Mendacity" (*National Review*, Oct. 11, 2015)

14. Stephen F. Hayes, "John Brennan: Political Hack" (*The Weekly Standard*, Aug. 17, 2018).

15. Natalie Johnson, "CIA Director Once Voted for Communist Presidential Candidate" (The Washington Free Beacon, Sept. 21, 2016); National Commission on Terrorist Attacks Upon the United States, The 9/11 Commission Report (Jul. 22, 2004), pp. 110-14 (recounting abandoned CIA plan to capture bin Laden); Johnsen, "The Untouchable John Brennan," *supra*.

16. John Diamond, "CIA director's allies outrank his enemies" (*USA Today*, Oct. 9, 2002); "CIA criticizes ex-chief over 9/11" (BBC News, Aug. 22, 2007); Michelle Nichols, "Ex-CIA chief says 'slam dunk' Iraq quote misused" (Reuters, Apr. 26, 2007).

17. *Ibid.* See also Douglas Jehl, John Kifner, and Eric Schmitt, "Fatal Lapses: How U.S. Missteps and Delay Opened Door to Saudi Blast" (*The New York Times*, Jul. 7, 1996) ("The Central Intelligence Agency and other Government experts consulted by the Air Force significantly misjudged the bomb-making capabilities of militants in Saudi Arabia, concluding that they could not build a bomb larger than the 200-pound device that killed five Americans and two Indians in Riyadh last November. American officials acknowledge that they had virtually no basis for that assumption because they know almost nothing about Saudi militants. In fact, the bomb that detonated outside the military housing complex in Dhahran, Saudi Arabia, on June 25, leaving a crater 85 feet wide, was packed with as much as 5,000 pounds of high explosive, American officials now estimate."); Jennifer Kerns, "John Brennan's intelligence failures have hurt our security and our democracy" (*Washington Examiner*, Nov. 2, 2017).

18. Johnsen, "The Untouchable John Brennan," *supra*.

19. *Ibid.*; see also Jane Mayer, "The Secret History" (*The New Yorker*, Jun. 14, 2009); Mark Hosenball, "CIA nominee had detailed knowledge of 'enhanced interrogation techniques'" (Reuters, Jan. 30, 2013); "Interrogating Brennan" (*Los Angeles Times*, Jan. 9, 2013).

20. Department of Homeland Security, "Rightwing Extremism: Current Economic and Political Climate Fueling Resurgence in Radicalization and Recruitment" (Apr. 7, 2009). For a comprehensive exposition of CVE, see Stephen Coughlin, *Catastrophic Failure: Blindfolding America in the Face of Jihad* (Create Space Independent Publishing Platform, 2015); see also, e.g., Michelle Malkin, "You might be a radicalized rightwing extremist if..." (MichelleMalkin.com, Apr. 15, 2009); Peter Roff, "The New McCarthyism: DHS Reports on Right-Wing Extremism" (*U.S. News & World Report*, Apr. 15, 2009).

21. The White House, "Empowering Local Partners to Prevent Violent Extremism in the United States" (Aug. 2011); Victor Davis Hanson, "More from the Man-Caused Disaster and Overseas Contingency Operations Front" (*National Review*, Apr. 12, 2010); Andrew C. McCarthy, "Does Trump Grasp the Reality of 'Radical Islam'?" (*National Review*, Dec. 31, 2016); McCarthy, "Fifteen Years After 9/11, Blindness to the Islamist Threat Is Official Policy" (*National Review*, Sept. 11, 2016); McCarthy, "Defenseless in the Face of Our Enemies" (*National Review*, Jun. 25, 2016); McCarthy, "An Islam of Their Very Own...Cont'd" (*National Review*, Dec. 4, 2015); McCarthy, "Find the 'Countering Violent Extremism Summit' at the Intersection of Islamists and Leftists" (*National Review*, Feb. 19, 2015); McCarthy, "In Search of the 'Moderate Islamists'—The Muslim Brotherhood is the best Obama can do" (*National Review*, Sept. 15, 2014); McCarthy, "It's Not a Misnomer—The Islamic State has everything to do with Islam" (*National Review*, Sept. 12, 2014); McCarthy, "How the NYPD Gets Jihad Right" (*National Review*, Sept. 3, 2011); McCarthy, "The 'Secular' Muslim Brotherhood" (*National Review*, Feb. 12, 2011).

22. Daniel Halper, "Brennan to Be Named CIA Director" (*The Weekly Standard*, Jan. 6, 2013); Andrew C. McCarthy, "Obama's 'Moderate' Hezbo Guy: 'The city I have come to love most is al-Quds'" (*National Review*, May 20, 2013).

23. John O. Brennan, "The Conundrum of Iran: Strengthening Moderates without Acquiescing to Belligerence" (Annals of the American Academy of Political and Social Science, Jul. 2008); Michael Rubin, "Brennan's Quest for a Moderate Hezbollah" (*Commentary*, Jan. 7, 2013); Andrew C. McCarthy, "Next Up: Cultivating the Moderate Hezbos" (*National Review*, May 19, 2010); cf. Steven Emerson and John Rossomando, "Obama CIA Nominee John Brennan Wrong for the Job" (Investigative Project on Terrorism, Feb. 5, 2013); Marc C. Johnson, "Hezbollah Remains a Very Real Threat to the U.S.—Despite what John Kerry may think, the world's most sophisticated terrorist organization continues to plot attacks against the United States at home and abroad" (*National Review*, Jun. 13, 2017); Thomas Joscelyn, "Death by Car Bomb in Damascus" (retrospective on the career of Hezhollah leader Imad Mughiyah after his killing in Syria) (*The Weekly Standard*, Feb. 25, 2008); McCarthy, "Negotiate with Iran? How many Americans do they need to kill before we get the point?" (*National Review*, Dec. 8, 2006).

24. John Brennan Speaks on National Security at NYU (Sept. 16, 2012) (You-Tube video); Thomas Joscelyn, "John Brennan On Gitmo Recidivism" (*The Weekly Standard*, Feb. 14, 2010); Michelle Malkin, "National security nightmare: John Brennan and the notorious flying imam" (MichelleMalkin.com, Feb. 17, 2010); Emerson and Rossomando, "Obama CIA Nominee John Brennan Wrong for the Job," *supra*.

25. Andrew C. McCarthy, "An Islam of Their Very Own—Obama's counterterrorism chief trivializes jihad" (*National Review*, Jun. 1, 2010); Bernard Lewis, *The Middle East: A Brief History of the Last 2,000 Years* (Scribner, 1997) ("The overwhelming majority of early authorities…citing relevant passages in the Qur'an and in the tradition, discuss jihad in military terms."); Thomas Patrick Hughes, A Dictionary of Islam—A Cyclopaedia of the Doctrines, Rites, Ceremonies, and Customs, Together with the Technical and Theological Terms, of the Muhammadan Religion (W.H. Allen & Co., London, 1895) (republished by Kazi Publications Inc., 2007); Andrew G. Bostom, "Geert Wilders, Western Sages, and Totalitarian Islam" (PJ Media, Oct. 18, 2010); McCarthy, "Who Says Islam Is Totalitarian?" (*National Review*, Oct. 19, 2010).

26. Letter of John O. Brennan, Assistant to the President for Homeland Security and Counterterrorism, to Ms. Farhana Khera, President and Executive Director, Muslim Advocates (Nov. 3, 2011); Letter of 57 "Muslim, Arab, and South Asian organizations" to John Brennan, Assistant to the President for Homeland Security and Counterterrorism and Deputy National Security Advisor (Oct. 19, 2011); Kerry Picket, "Muslim advocacy groups influence heavily on U.S. national security protocol and lexicon" (*The Washington Times*, Sept. 24, 2012); Rowan Scarborough, "Obama's scrub of Muslim terms under question; common link in attacks" (*The Washington Times*, Apr. 25, 2013); Robert Spencer, "Law Enforcement 'Never Guessed Gay Club Would Be Targeted by Jihad" (PJ Media, Jun. 13, 2016).

27. I wrote about the CVE document in "Defenseless in the Face of Our Enemies" (*supra*) a column that followed the Jun. 12, 2016, mass-murder attack by jihadist Omar Mateen at the Pulse, a gay nightclub in Orlando, Florida. Subsequently, it was withdrawn from the DHS website and is no longer available to the public.

28. United Nations General Assembly, Human Rights Council, Resolution 16/18, "Combatting intolerance, negative stereotyping and stigmatization of, and discrimination, incitement to violence and violence against, persons based on religion or belief" (Apr. 12, 2011); Andrew C. McCarthy, "Blasphemy and Islam—Our fundamental rights are under attack" (*National Review*, Dec. 15, 2012).

29. Charles C. W. Cooke, "John Kerry Is a Disgrace" (*National Review*, Nov. 17, 2015); Andrew C. McCarthy, "John Kerry's Reprehensible Charlie Hebdo Comments Perfectly Reflect Obama Administration Policy" (*National Review*, Nov. 23, 2015).

30. Kori Schake, "The Obama administration's troubling history of politicizing intelligence" (*Foreign Policy*, Apr. 25, 2013).

31. Thomas Joscelyn and Bill Roggio, "Analysis: CIA releases massive trove of Osama bin Laden's files" (*Long War Journal*, Nov. 1, 2017); Hayes, "John Brennan Political Hack," *supra*; Hayes, "Spinning the bin Laden Documents" (*The Weekly Standard*, Nov. 10, 2017); Joscelyn, "Documenting al Qaeda's Durability" (*The Weekly Standard*, Nov. 3, 2017); Joscelyn, "Al Qaeda Is Very Much Alive" (*The Weekly Standard*, Sept. 11, 2018); Hayes and Joscelyn, "Top Intel Official: Al Qaeda Worked on WMD in Iran" (*The Weekly Standard*, Jul. 12, 2016); Michael T. Flynn and Michael Ledeen, *The Field of Fight: How We Can Win the Global War Against Radical Islam and Its Allies* (St. Martin's Press, 2016).

32. Thomas Joscelyn, "The Al-Qaeda-Iran Connection" (*The Weekly Standard*, Aug. 7, 2018); Andrew C. McCarthy, "Negotiate with Iran? How many Americans do they need to kill before we get the point?," *supra*.

33. Hayes, "John Brennan: Political Hack," *supra*.

34. Lee Smith, "Obama's Foreign Policy Guru Boasts of How the Administration Lied to Sell the Iran Deal" (*The Weekly Standard*, May 5, 2016).

35. Andrew C. McCarthy, "Mr. President, Decertify the Iran Deal and Then Walk Away" (*National Review*, Oct. 5, 2017); McCarthy, "Distorting the Iran-Deal Bill" (*National Review*, Nov. 19, 2016); McCarthy, "Obama's Iran Deal Is a Fraud on the American People" (*National Review*, Sept. 3, 2016); Fred Fleitz, "In Yet Another Secret Side Deal, Iran's Nuclear Violations Won't Be Publicly Disclosed" (*National Review*, Mar. 9, 2016); Claudia Rosett, "Riddle of $1.3 Billion for Iran Might Relate to 13 Outlays of Exactly $99,999,999.99" (*The New York Sun*, Aug. 22, 2016); Fleitz, "More U.S. Ransom Payments to Iran Revealed" (*National Review*, Sept. 7, 2016); McCarthy, "Why Is Obama Stonewalling on Details of the $1.7 Billion in Iransom Payoffs?" (*National Review*, Aug. 27, 2016); McCarthy, "Besides Being Illegal, Obama's $400M Cash Payment to Iran Was a Ransom" (Aug. 18, 2016); McCarthy, "President Obama Violated the Law with His Ransom Payment to Iran" (*National Review*, Aug. 6, 2017); Gregory Korte, "Despite plane full of cash to Iran, White House denies ransom deal" (*USA Today*, Aug. 3, 2016).

36. David Samuels, "The Aspiring Novelist Who Became Obama's Foreign-Policy Guru—How Ben Rhodes rewrote the rules of diplomacy for the digital age" (*The New York Times*, May 5, 2016).

37. Andrew C. McCarthy, "The Khamenei Fatwa Hoax Is Absurd on Its Face" (*National Review*, Apr. 16, 2015).

38. Samuels, "The Aspiring Novelist Who Became Obama's Foreign-Policy Guru," *supra*.

39. Saul D. Alinsky, *Rules for Radicals* (1971) (Vintage Books ed., 1989).

40. Shane Harris and Nancy A. Yousef, "50 Spies Say ISIS Intelligence Was Cooked" (The Daily Beast, Sept. 9, 2015); Andrew C. McCarthy, "Unsolicited Advice for the Trump Transition Team on National Security Intelligence" (PJ Media, Nov. 10, 2016).

41. Lee Smith, "Did the Obama Administration's Abuse of Foreign-Intelligence Collection Start Before Trump—One clue: The Russia story is a replay of how the former White House smeared pro-Israel activists in the lead-up to the Iran Deal" (*Tablet Magazine*, Apr. 5, 2017).

42. Adam Entous and Danny Yadron, "U.S. Spy Net on Israel Snares Congress: NSA's targeting of Israeli leaders swept up the content of private conversations with U.S. lawmakers" (*The Wall Street Journal*, Dec. 29, 2015).

43. Former Democratic Congressman Dennis Kucinich also suspects that he was subjected to electronic surveillance. In 2011, he was an ardent opponent of President Obama's unauthorized military intervention in Libya. While trying to broker negotiations between the administration and Qaddafi, Rep. Kucinich took a call in his Washington office from the dictator's son, Saif al-Islam Qaddafi. That the call was recorded is not surprising; the intelligence community should have been monitoring phone calls by members of Qaddafi's regime, and it is entirely possible, even likely, that the Libyans themselves were recording. What was not to be expected, however, was that the call was leaked to *The Washington Times*. As Kucinich has rightly acknowledged, it is not at all clear that the Obama administration was at fault for the leak—there are good reasons to doubt it. Nevertheless, the Obama administration's record of abusing its counterintelligence authorities certainly makes it reasonable for Kucinich to press for answers. See Andrew C. McCarthy, "Obama Political Spying Scandal: Trump Associates Were Not the First Targets" (*National Review*, Apr. 18, 2017).

44. Sharyl Attkisson, "Obama-era Surveillance Timeline" (SharylAttkisson. com, Dec. 5, 2017).

45. Bradley A. Smith, "Remember the IRS targeting scandal? No one ever got punished for it" (*Washington Examiner*, Jan. 18, 2018); Zachary A. Goldfarb and Karen Tumulty, "IRS admits targeting conservatives for tax scrutiny in 2012 election" (*The Washington Post*, May 10, 2013).

46. U.S. Department of Justice, Office of the Inspector General, "Report of Investigation Concerning the Improper Disclosure of U.S. Department of Justice Information to a Member of the Media" (May 2013); Andrew C. McCarthy, "A 'Fast & Furious' I Told You So" (*National Review*, Jun. 5, 2012); John Bresnahan, "Holder held in contempt" (*Politico*, Jun. 28, 2012); "Fast and Furious: A Timeline" (*National Review*, Jun. 28, 2012).

47. Andrew C. McCarthy, "Amnesty, but Not for D'Souza" (*National Review*,

Feb. 1, 2014); "Obama 2008 campaign fine conciliation agreement" (*Politico*, Jan. 4, 2013).

48.　See, e.g., Heather Mac Donald, *The War on Cops—How the Attack on Law and Order Makes Everyone Less Safe* (Encounter Books, 2016); Adams, *Injustice: Exposing the Racial Agenda of the Obama Justice Department* (Regnery Publishing, 2011); Gardiner Harris, "Obama, Pushing Criminal Justice Reform, Defends 'Black Lives Matter'" (*The New York Times*, Oct. 22, 2015); Mac Donald, "The Myths of Black Lives Matter—The movement has won over Hillary Clinton and Bernie Sanders. But what if its claims are fiction" (*The Wall Street Journal*, Feb. 11, 2016); Victor Davis Hanson, "'Black Lives Matter'—a Year from Now" (PJ Media, Sept. 5, 2015); Andrew C. McCarthy, "Progressive Mythography" (*National Review*, Nov. 29, 2014); Adams, "Breaking: Inspector General Report on Racialist Dysfunction Inside DOJ" (PJ Media, Mar. 12, 2013) (discussing U.S. Dept. of Justice, Office of the Inspector General, "A Review of Operations of the Voting Rights Section of the Civil Rights Division") (Mar. 2013); Hans von Spakovsky, "The Justice Department Condones Perjury...Again" (PJ Media, Dec. 21, 2011); Adams and von Spakovsky, "Every Single One: PJ Media's Investigation of Justice Department Hiring Practices" (collecting links to 12-part series); McCarthy, "What's Really Going on with Holder's Civil-Rights Crusade against Police Departments" (*National Review*, Dec. 6, 2014); McCarthy, "The Obama Administration Race-Baiting Campaign" (*National Review*, Jul. 20, 2013); McCarthy, "Holder Meets Sharpton" (*National Review*, Apr. 14, 2012); Michelle Malkin, "Team Obama's Brother Sharpton Moment" (MichelleMalkin.com, Jun. 27, 2012); McCarthy, "Holder Revives Bogus Civil-Rights Investigation against Zimmerman" (*National Review*, Jul. 15, 2013); McCarthy, "The Case Against the New Black Panthers" (*National Review*, Jul. 20, 2010).

49.　*United States v. Kenneth Bowen, et al.*, No. 13-31078 (5th Cir. 2015); Andrew C. McCarthy, "The Justice Department's 'Grotesque' Misconduct Against New Orleans Cops" (*National Review*, Aug. 22, 2015); J. Christian Adams, "Justice Dept. Lawyer Karla Dobinski's Misconduct Sends Cops to Prison" (PJ Media, Sept. 18, 2013).

CHAPTER 5

1.　James Clapper Testimony before the Senate Intelligence Committee (Mar. 12, 2013), questioning by Senator Ron Wyden (D., Ore.).

2.　Edward Lucas, *The Snowden Operation: Inside the West's Greatest Intelligence Disaster* (Amazon Digital Services, 2014); Fred Fleitz, "Snowden Is a Traitor and a Fraud, Period" (*National Review*, Sept. 16, 2016); Andrew C. McCarthy, "Not all Truth Telling Is Virtuous" (*National Review*, Jun. 23, 2013); McCarthy, "Rewriting FISA History" (*National Review*, Jun. 22, 2013).

3.   Madeline Osburn, "4 Different Lies James Clapper Told About Lying To Congress" (*The Federalist*, Mar. 6, 2019); Steven Nelson, "James Clapper avoids charges for 'clearly erroneous' surveillance testimony" (*Washington Examiner*, Mar. 10, 2018).

4.   U.S. Foreign Intelligence Surveillance Court, Case Caption Redacted, Memorandum and Order (Apr. 26, 2017) (hereafter, "FISC 2017 Mem. and Order"), p. 19.

5.   Title 50, U.S. Code, §§ 1801 *et seq.*

6.   U.S. Foreign Intelligence Surveillance Court Rules of Procedure (Nov. 1, 2010), Rule 13 (Correction of Misstatement or Omission; Disclosure of Non-Compliance).

7.   See Jeff Carlson, "The Uncovering—Mike Rogers' Investigation, Section 702 FISA Abuse & the FBI" (*The Epoch Times*, Apr. 5, 2018); Carlson, "The Uncovering—Section 702 "About" Queries, Independent Contractors & a New Narrative" (*The Epoch Times*, Jan. 15, 2018); Carlson, "FISA Surveillance—Title I & III and Section 702" (*The Epoch Times*, Apr. 1, 2018). See also John Solomon and Sara Carter, "Obama intel agency secretly conducted illegal searches on Americans for years" (Circa, May 23, 2017); Andrew C. McCarthy, "Explosive Revelation of Obama Administration Illegal Surveillance of Americans" (*National Review*, May 25, 2017).

8.   Executive Order 12333 (Dec. 4, 1981) (as amended).

9.   See, e.g., Andrew C. McCarthy, "Mr. President, the Problem Is FISA, Not the Lack of Hearings on FISA Warrants" (*National Review*, Sept. 4, 2018).

10. *Chicago & Southern Air Lines v. Waterman S.S. Corp.*, 333 U.S. 103, 111-12 (1948).

11. *United States v. United States District Court*, 407 U.S. 297 (1972) (the *Keith* case), ("the scope of our decision…involves only the domestic aspects of national security. We have not addressed, and express no opinion as to, the issues which may be involved with respect to activities of foreign powers or their agents"). The criminal wiretap statute is known as "Title III" because that is where it is found in the Omnibus Crime Control and Safe Street Act of 1968; in a provision since amended (Section 2511(3) of Title 18, U.S. Code) it stated that nothing in Title III "shall limit the constitutional power of the President to take such measures as he deems necessary to protect the Nation against actual or potential attack or other hostile acts of a foreign power, to obtain foreign intelligence information deemed essential to the security of the United States, or to protect national security information against foreign intelligence activities." See Andrew C. McCarthy, David B. Rivkin, Jr., and Lee A. Casey, "NSA's Warrantless Surveillance Program: Legal, Constitutional, and Necessary" (reprinted in *Federalist Society, Terrorist Surveillance and the Constitution* (2006), pp. 23 & ff), pp. 37-39).

12. It is necessary to qualify this proposition as "ostensible," because the question whether FISA effectively reduces the president's constitutional authority, something Congress cannot, in principle, accomplish by statute, is unresolved. President Carter's attorney general, Griffin Bell, strongly supported FISA, but took the position that it could not invalidate the chief executive's power to collect foreign intelligence in the absence of judicial permission. The Clinton administration took the same position in the early 1990s, when FISA was extended to physical searches (in addition to electronic surveillance). And in litigation stemming from President Bush's post-9/11 warrantless surveillance program, the Foreign Intelligence Court of Review (which hears rare government appeals of FISC decisions), observed, "The *Truong* court, as did all the other courts to have decided the issue, held that the President did have inherent authority to conduct warrantless searches to obtain foreign intelligence information. … We take for granted that the President does have that authority and, assuming that is so, FISA could not encroach on the President's constitutional power." See *In re Sealed Case*, U.S. Foreign Intelligence Surveillance Court of Review, No. 02-001 (Nov. 18, 2002), citing *United States v. Truong Dinh Hung*, 629 F. 2d 908 (4th Cir. 1980); see also Statement of Attorney General Griffin B. Bell to the Senate Judiciary Committee on the Foreign Intelligence Surveillance Act (Jun. 13, 1977); Testimony of Attorney General Griffin Bell before the Senate Judiciary Committee (Sept. 2, 1977), pp. 26-28 (answering questions of, and submitting a letter to, Senator Robert Morgan (D., N.C.), opining that the president retains inherent constitutional authority to engage in electronic surveillance); Byron York, "Clinton Claimed Authority to Order No-Warrant Searches" (*National Review*, Dec. 20, 2005).

13. See *In re Sealed Case, supra*; Andrew C. McCarthy, Written Testimony before the Senate Judiciary (May 10, 2005); McCarthy, "FISA's Fate Should Be the Funeral Pyre" (*National Review*, Aug. 7, 2007).

14. See, e.g., Andrew C. McCarthy, "The globalist legal agenda" (*The New Criterion*, Feb. 2016) (reviewing Justice Stephen Breyer's *The Court and the World: American Law and the New Global Realities* (Knopf, 2015)).

15. Andrew C. McCarthy, "FISA Fiasco—A 'rubber stamp' would be an improvement" (*National Review*, Jun. 26, 2013); David Kris, "How the FISA Court Really Works" (Lawfare, Sept. 2, 2018).

16. Brooke Singman, "Comey scoffs at Barr testimony, claims 'surveillance' is not 'spying'" (Fox News, Apr. 12, 2019).

17. FISA Section 702 is codified at Title 50, U.S. Code, Section 1881a.

18. See, e.g., Privacy and Civil Liberties Oversight Board, "Report on the Surveillance Program Operated Pursuant to Section 702 of the Foreign Intelligence Surveillance Act" (hereafter, "Section 702 Report" (Jul. 2, 2014), pp. 9-10).

19. Statement for the Record of J. Michael McConnell, Director of National

Intelligence, House Permanent Select Committee on Intelligence (Sept. 20, 2007), pp. 3-9; see also U.S. Department of Justice, Office of the Inspector General, "A Review of the Federal Bureau of Investigation's Activities Under Section 702 of the Foreign Intelligence Surveillance Act Amendments Act of 2008" (Sept. 2012), pp. ix-x (hereafter, "DOJ-IG Section 702 Report"); Charlie Savage, "F.B.I. Is Broadening Its Surveillance Role, Report Shows" (*The New York Times*, Jan. 11, 2015).

20. We do not have a cognizable expectation of privacy in our conversations with third parties. The law, however, has long required court authorization before the government may tap a phone (or, similarly, surreptitiously monitor traffic on a person's email account). At the end of every court-authorized electronic surveillance (e.g., wiretap) in criminal cases, furthermore, the Justice Department is supposed to provide notice to people whose communications have been intercepted—a mandate known as the "inventory notice" (which is often overlooked). See Title 18, U.S. Code, Section 2518(8)(d); see also U.S. Department of Justice, Criminal Division's Office of Enforcement Operations (Electronic Surveillance Unit), "Electronic Surveillance Manual—Procedures and Case Law[, and] Forms" (Revised Jun. 2005), pp. 31-32. For discussion of the applicable Fourth Amendment and privacy law principles, see, e.g., Andrew C. McCarthy, "If the Government Cannot Be Trusted, Can It Protect the Nation?" (*National Review*, Apr. 15, 2017); McCarthy, "Rand Paul's Metadata Concerns Are Misplaced" (*National Review*, May 28, 2015); McCarthy, "Why National-Security Republicans Lost the Patriot Act Debate" (*National Review*, May 23, 2015); McCarthy, "The WHY Question—Why the National-Security Right Is Gradually Losing the NSA Debate" (PJ Media, Jul. 30, 2013); McCarthy, Rivkin, and Casey, "NSA's Warrantless Surveillance Program: Legal, Constitutional, and Necessary," *supra*.

21. DOJ-IG Section 702 Report, *supra*, pp. x, 2, 17; Office of the Director of National Intelligence, "Section 702 Overview" (undated); Paul Rosenzweig, "Anti-Terror Law's Safeguards Against Incidental Collection of Domestic Data Are Sufficient" (The Daily Signal, Nov. 28, 2017); Mario Loyola and Richard Epstein, "Libertarians of La Mancha" (*The Weekly Standard*, Jul. 8, 2013) (observing that Congress's 2008 reform of FISA "prohibited 'reverse targeting,' the indirect targeting of U.S. persons' communications via targeting the communications of known terrorists abroad."); cf. Robyn Greene, "A History of FISA Section 702 Compliance Violations" (*New America*, Open Technology Institute, Sept. 28, 2017) (cataloguing hundreds of compliance violations, which are attributed not to willfulness but to the scope and complexity of Section 702 surveillance).

22. George W. Croner, "2017 FISA Reporting Season Has Ended: What Do the Numbers Mean?" (Foreign Policy Research Institute, May 15, 2018). The Office of the Director of National Intelligence provides a sample (redacted) certification on its website. See ODNI, "IC on the Record—Statement by the

Office of the Director of National Intelligence and the Department of Justice on the Declassification of Documents Related to Section 702 of the Foreign Intelligence Surveillance Act," and sample Section 702 certification. See also Charlie Savage and Scott Shane, "Secret Court Rebuked N.S.A. on Surveillance" (*The New York Times*, Aug. 21, 2013) (noting recent FISC estimate that 250 million communications were intercepted each year) (citing U.S. Foreign Intelligence Surveillance Court, Redacted Caption, Memorandum Opinion (Oct. 3, 2011) (hereafter, "FISC 2011 Memorandum Opinion").

23. See, e.g., Ellen Nakashima, "NSA gathered thousands of Americans' e-mails before court ordered it to revise its tactics" (*The Washington Post*, Aug. 21, 2013) (quoting FISC Judge John D. Bates): Because of the "sheer volume" of transactions acquired by the NSA, "any meaningful review of the entire body of the transactions" was not feasible. . . . "As a result, the court cannot know for certain the exact number" of wholly domestic communications but was reliant on the NSA's samples of data.) (FISC 2011 Memorandum Opinion); Carol D. Leonnig, "Court: Ability to police U.S. spying program limited" (*The Washington Post*, Aug. 15, 2013), quoting Judge Reggie B. Walton, then chief judge of the FISC: "The FISC is forced to rely upon the accuracy of the information that is provided to the Court. ... The FISC does not have the capacity to investigate issues of noncompliance, and in that respect the FISC is in the same position as any other court when it comes to enforcing compliance with its orders." With due respect to Judge Walton, the FISC is decidedly *not* in the same position as any other court because FISA proceedings are not normal judicial proceedings in which an adversary litigant can be relied on to ferret out government noncompliance; in FISA, the court is a participant in an executive function.

24. National Security Agency website, "NSA/CSS" (explaining the Central Security Service); see also, e.g., Mark Pomerleau, "The renewed debate over the NSA-CYBERCOM split" (The Fifth Domain Cyber, Mar. 15, 2019).

25. The term derives from longstanding procedures in criminal wiretaps, in which monitoring agents "minimize" the eavesdropping (i.e., they stop listening and turn off the recording device) once a "pattern of innocence" is detected—usually, people who use the targeted phone regularly but are clearly not involved in the criminal scheme (e.g., the suspect's children).

26. Andrew C. McCarthy, "On Susan Rice, the Issue Is Abuse of Power, Not Criminality" (*National Review*, Apr. 5, 2017).

27. Nakashima, "NSA gathered thousands of Americans' e-mails before court ordered it to revise its tactics," *supra*; citing FISC 2011 Memorandum Opinion, *supra*.

28. See, e.g., Privacy and Civil Liberties Oversight Board, "Section 702 Report," pp. 5-8; Stephen Braun, Anne Flaherty, Jack Gillum, and Matt Apuzzo, "PRISM Is Just Part Of A Much Larger, Scarier Government Surveillance Program" (As-

sociated Press, Jun. 15, 2013); Paul Rosensweig, "The NSA's phone collection order—it may be legal, but is it wise?" (Fox News, Jun. 6, 2013).

29. On his website, Charlie Savage, a superb *New York Times* reporter and author of *Power Wars: The Relentless Rise of Presidential Authority and Secrecy* (Back Bay Books, 2015, rev'd 2017), explains that a commonly cited statistic, putting upstream collection at 9 percent of the total, is wrong. The figure is drawn from a declassified 2011 FISC opinion, and is based on mistaken assumptions of what counts as a *communication*—not a straightforward computation because many contacts that are vacuumed up are "multi-communications transactions" (MCTs) not discrete or single communications. Since there is no formula for how many communications are in an MCT, it cannot be said with certainty what the MCT multiplier should be. See Savage, "Don't cite the Prism v. Upstream collection numbers from Judge Bates' 2011 FISC opinion anymore" (CharlieSavage. com, Sept. 13, 2017).

30. For a good explanation of this process, see Charlie Savage, "Federal Court Revives Wikimedia's Challenge to N.S.A. Surveillance" (*The New York Times*, May 23, 2017). As I have elsewhere noted, there are profound Fourth Amendment issues, too. Even if the NSA does exactly what it is supposed to do (i.e., sift and discard), this means American communications are being seized and subjected to an inspection—however cursory—in the absence of any warrant, probable cause, or foreign-intelligence relevance. The traditional Fourth Amendment paradigm is that the government must show probable cause *before* searching or seizing; modern technology is challenging this paradigm on many fronts, with government seeking to seize without a particularized showing of cause, with the understanding that it will not search what it now possesses until such a showing has been made. McCarthy, "Explosive Revelation of Obama Administration Illegal Surveillance of Americans," *supra.*

31. 50 U.S. Code, Section 1881a(m)(4); see also FISC 2017 Mem. and Order, pp. 16-17; DOJ-IG Section 702 Report, *supra*, p. 7 & n.5; Charlie Savage, "N.S.A. Said to Search Content of Messages to and From U.S" (*The New York Times*, Aug. 8, 2013).

32. See Charlie Savage, "N.S.A. Gets More Latitude to Share Intercepted Communications" (*The New York Times*, Jan. 12, 2017). Critics refer to the FBI's law-enforcement access as the "backdoor search loophole." That's because agents are not required to seek a warrant to sift through information in the database—even though that information has been obtained without a warrant; and even though, in a normal criminal-law wiretap, agents would have to get a warrant based on probable cause that a crime has been committed before seizing and examining communications. In certain instances, FISA requires the FBI to apply for court permission to access captured communications if the Bureau is conducting a criminal in-

vestigation that does not relate to national security. 50 U.S. Code, Section 1881a(f)(2).

33. FISC 2011 Memorandum Opinion, *supra*; Nakashima, "NSA gathered thousands of Americans' e-mails before court ordered it to revise its tactics," *supra*.

34. Other minimization changes included the segregation of domestic communications, special handling and marking of such communications if they could not be segregated, and a reduction to two years (from five) of the period of retaining upstream-collected communications. See FISC 2017 Mem. and Order, pp. 17-19; Edward C. Liu, "Surveillance of Foreigners Outside the United States Under Section 702 of the Foreign Intelligence Surveillance Act" (Congressional Research Service, Apr. 13, 2016), pp. 4-5.

35. David E. Sanger and Thom Shanker, "N.S.A. Choice Is Navy Expert on Cyberwar" (*The New York Times*, Jan. 30, 2014).

36. DOJ-IG Section 702 Report, *supra*.

37. Statement of Michael E. Horowitz, Inspector General, U.S. Dept. of Justice, before the House Judiciary Committee, "Access to Justice?: Does DOJ's Office of the Inspector General Have Access to Information Needed to Conduct Proper Oversight?" (Sept. 9, 2014).

38. U.S. Dept. of Justice, Office of Legal Counsel, Memorandum for Deputy Attorney General Sally Quillian Yates, "The Department of Justice Inspector General's Access to Information Obtained by the Federal Wiretap Act, Rule 6(e) of the Federal Rules of Criminal Procedure, and Section 626 of the Fair Credit Reporting Act" (Jul. 15, 2015), pp. 32-37.

39. National Security Agency/Central Security Service, Office of the Inspector General, "Report on the Special Study of NSA Controls to Comply with the FISA Amendments Act §§ 704 and 705(b) Targeting and Minimization Procedures" (Jan. 7, 2016), pp. 2, 4-7 & Table 3; see also Carlson, "The Uncovering—Mike Rogers' investigation, Section 702 FISA Abuse & the FBI," *supra*.

40. FISC 2017 Mem. and Order, *supra*, pp. 83-86; Carlson, "The Uncovering—Mike Rogers' investigation, Section 702 FISA Abuse & the FBI," *supra*.

41. Senate Intelligence Committee Hearing, Jun. 7, 2017, Testimony of Admiral Michael Rogers (questions by Senator James Lankford (R., Okla.)); Carlson, "The Uncovering—Mike Rogers' investigation, Section 702 FISA Abuse & the FBI," *supra*.

42. FISC 2017 Mem. and Order, *supra*, pp. 81-82: Savage, "N.S.A. Said to Search Content of Messages to and From U.S," *supra*.

43. There has been some speculation that Fusion GPS, generator of the Clinton campaign–sponsored Steele dossier, was among the contractors. That seems highly unlikely. As further detailed, *infra*, Steele did not start writing his

reports until June, and the FBI does not seem to have known about them at any level until early July—months after the April 2016 discovery that contractors had received raw FISA data. Moreover, the main problem with the dossier is that it is unverified and apparently inaccurate. That is not suggestive of a process in which it was carefully checked against factual information, let alone classified FISA information. Although Glenn Simpson testified that the FBI gave Steele some information about having a source inside the Trump campaign (a claim that has not been confirmed), there has been no publicly reported testimony indicating that the FBI gave FISA information to Fusion GPS.

44. Government's Ex Parte Submission of Reauthorization Certifications and Related Procedures, Ex Parte Submission of Amended Certifications, and Request for an Order Approving Such Certifications and Amended Certifications (Sept. 26, 2016); FISC 2017 Mem. and Order, *supra*, pp. 2-3 (noting supporting affidavits from directors of the NSA, the FBI, the CIA, and the National Counterterrorism Center, in addition to two sets of targeting procedure guidance, and four sets of minimization procedures—one for each of the four relevant agencies); see also Title 50, U.S. Code, Section 1881a(j)(1)(B) and 1881a(h)(2)(D)(i) (requiring FISC to complete review and issue order within 30 days of submission of certifications).

45. Carlson, "The Uncovering—Mike Rogers' investigation, Section 702 FISA Abuse & the FBI," *supra*; Ellen Nakashima, "Head of Justice Department's National Security Division to step down" (*The Washington Post*, Sept. 27, 2016); U.S. Department of Justice, U.S. Attorney's Office, Southern District of New York, Press Release, "Evgeny Buryakov Pleads Guilty In Manhattan Federal Court In Connection With Conspiracy To Work For Russian Intelligence" (Mar. 11, 2016).

46. FISC 2017 Mem. and Order, *supra*, p. 19; Eric Geller, "DOJ official leading Trump–Russia probe to step down" (*Politico*, Apr. 20, 2017); Morrison & Foerster Press Release, "Top Justice Department Official John P. Carlin Joins Morrison & Foerster; Will Lead Firm's Global Risk & Crisis Management Practice" (Jan. 10, 2017).

47. Senate Intelligence Committee Hearing, Jun. 7, 2017, Testimony of Admiral Michael Rogers, *supra*; Charlie Savage, "N.S.A. Halts Collection of Americans' Emails About Foreign Targets" (*The New York Times*, Apr. 28, 2017); Carlson, "The Uncovering—Mike Rogers' investigation, Section 702 FISA Abuse & the FBI," *supra*.

48. FISC 2017 Mem. and Order, *supra*, p. 19.

49. *Ibid.*, pp. 19-20.

50. David E. Sanger, Julie Hirschfeld David, and Eric Schmitt, "Obama Is Considering Removing N.S.A. Leader" (*The New York Times*, Nov. 19, 2016);

S. A. Miller, "Donald Trump moves transition meetings to private golf club in New Jersey" (*The Washington Times*, Nov. 17, 2016).

51.   Donald J. Trump (@realDonaldTrump), Mar. 4, 2017, Tweet.

52.   House Intelligence Committee Hearing, Mar. 20, 2017, Testimony of Admiral Michael Rogers (questioning by then–Ranking Member Adam Schiff (D., Calif.)) ("No sir, and again, my view is the same as Director Comey, I've seen nothing on the NSA side that we engaged in any such activity, nor that anyone ever asked us to engage in such activity"); Matthew Rosenberg, Enmarie Huetteman, and Michael S. Schmidt, "Comey Confirms F.B.I. Inquiry on Russia; Sees No Evidence of Wiretapping" (*The New York Times*, Mar. 20, 2017).

53.   Ellen Nakashima, "Pentagon and intelligence community chiefs have urged Obama to remove the head of NSA" (*The Washington Post*, Nov. 19, 2016); Sanger et al., "Obama Is Considering Removing N.S.A. Leader," *supra*; W. J. Hennigan, "Top Obama military official under fire as he meets Trump" (*Los Angeles Times*, Nov. 19, 2016); Shane Harris and Nancy A. Youssef, "Why Did Team Obama Try to Take Down Its NSA Chief?" (The Daily Beast, Nov. 25, 2016).

54.   Olivia Gazis, "Ex-NSA chief says he never discussed collusion with Trump" (CBS News, Sept. 12, 2018). Whether Cyber Command will be split off from the NSA, which the Defense Department has favored, remains in doubt due to some congressional skepticism. See, e.g., Pomerleau, "The renewed debate over the NSA-CYBERCOM split," *supra*.

55.   Jeff Carlson, "A Quiet Hero—NSA Director Mike Rogers Retires" (*The Epoch Times*, May 5, 2018).

CHAPTER 6

1.   NBC News, Meet the Press (Feb. 14, 2018).

2.   Gregory D. Johnsen, "The Untouchable John Brennan" (BuzzFeed, Apr. 23, 2015), *supra*.

3.   Nico Hines and Jamie Ross, "Trump's Source on Fake Story That Britain Spied on Campaign: There's a Conspiracy to Frame Me as 'Conspiracy Nut'" (The Daily Beast, Apr. 24, 2019); Amy B. Wang, "Suspended Fox News expert returns—and doubles down on baseless wiretapping claims" (*The Washington Post*, Mar. 29, 2017).

4.   House Intelligence Committee Hearing, Mar. 20, 2017, FBI Director James B. Comey (questioning by then-Ranking Member Adam Schiff (D., Calif.)).

As noted above, in NSA Director Michael Rogers's testimony, he seconded Comey. (See Ch. 5, n.52, *supra*.) Director Comey's testimony that the Justice Department had asked him to share this information with the committee is interesting. Comey, of course, had been widely rebuked for usurping the role of the Obama Justice Department in proclaiming that no charges should be brought against Hillary Clinton. At the time of the March 20 testimony, there were no Trump appointees in the Justice Department chain of command: Attorney General Sessions had recused himself from Trump–Russia matters; the Acting Attorney General, Dana Boente, was the Obama-appointed U.S. attorney for the Eastern District of Pennsylvania whom Trump had abruptly promoted upon firing Obama holdover Sally Yates for insubordinately defying him on an executive order restricting travel by aliens from several countries with terrorism problems. Trump did not know Boente; one suspects he chose him because Obama had issued an executive order right before leaving office that cut Boente out of the Justice Department order of succession (in the apparent hope that, if the Russia investigation forced Trump DOJ officials to recuse themselves, the probe might end up in the hands of Channing Phillips, a protégé of former Obama Attorney General Eric Holder whom Obama had unsuccessfully tried to get confirmed as U.S. attorney in Washington, D.C.). In any event, the Justice Department that "asked" Comey to share its rejection of Trump's tweets about Obama surveillance of Trump was still being run by Obama appointees. See President Barack Obama Executive Order 13762, "Providing an Order of Succession Within the Department of Justice" (Jan. 13, 2017).

5. Kailani Koenig, "Former DNI James Clapper: 'I Can Deny' Wiretap of Trump Tower" (NBC News, Mar. 5, 2017); see also Andrew C. McCarthy, "Parsing Clapper—What he said was probably true, but what he didn't say was more revealing" (*National Review*, Mar. 8, 2017).

6. Fiona Hamilton, "GCHQ ridicules White House over claims it spied on Trump" (*The Times*, Mar. 17, 2017).

7. David E. Sanger and Maggie Haberman, "Transcript: Donald Trump on NATO, Turkey's Coup Attempt and the World" (*The New York Times*, Jul. 21, 2016).

8. See, e.g., Bojan Pancevski, "How a Russian Gas Pipeline Is Driving a Wedge Between the U.S. and Its Allies—The Nord Stream 2 gas-transport project is a bone of contention with Washington, which fears it will make Germany too reliant on Moscow" (*The Wall Street Journal*, Mar. 10, 2019); "Tough to stop Nord Stream 2 now it's being built—EU's Oettinger" (Reuters, Dec. 28, 2018).

9. Wolf Blitzer, "Donald Trump Interview" (CNN, Mar. 21, 2016).

10. John O. Brennan (@JohnBrennan) Jul. 16, 2018, Tweet; see also Brennan Apr. 23, 2019, Tweet; Nancy LeTourneau, "John Brennan Says That Trump Is in Putin's Pocket" (*Washington Monthly*, Mar. 6, 2019); Stephen F. Cohen, "What the Brennan Affair Really Means" (*The Nation*, Aug. 22, 2018);

McCarthy, "Revoking Brennan's Security Clearance: The Right Thing, Even if for the Wrong Reason," *supra*.

11. James Clapper, testimony before the Senate Intelligence Committee (questioning by Sen. Dianne Feinstein (D., Calif.)), May 9, 2017. Luke Harding, "British spies were first to spot Trump team's links with Russia" (*The Guardian*, Apr. 13, 2017).

12. Lee Smith, "Did President Obama Read the 'Steele Dossier' in the White House Last August?" (*Tablet Magazine*, Dec. 20, 2017); Devin Nunes interview by Jake Tapper (CNN, Apr. 12, 2016).

13. The U.S. embassy in Ashgabat passed the information along in a cable to the State Department in Washington. Kevin G. Hall, "Why did FBI suspect Trump campaign adviser was a foreign agent?" (McClatchy, Apr. 14, 2017).

14. Hall, "Why did FBI suspect Trump campaign adviser was a foreign agent?," *supra*; Julia Ioffe, "Who Is Carter Page?: The mystery of Trump's man in Moscow" (*Politico*, Sept. 23, 2016); Jason Zengerle, "What (if Anything) Does Carter Page Know?" (*The New York Times*, Dec. 18, 2017); Scott Shane, Mark Mazzetti, and Adam Goldman, "Trump Adviser's Visit to Moscow Got the F.B.I.'s Attention" (*The New York Times*, Apr. 19, 2017); Goldman, "Russian Spies Tried to Recruit Carter Page Before He Advised Trump" (*The New York Times*, Apr. 4, 2017).

15. See, e.g., Robert Zubrin, "Trump: The Kremlin's Candidate—Donald Trump's energy adviser is all in for Putin" (*National Review*, Apr. 4, 2016); Stephanie Kirchgaessner, Spencer Ackerman, Julian Borger, and Luke Harding, "Former Trump adviser Carter Page held 'strong pro-Kremlin views', says ex-boss" (*The Guardian*, Apr. 14, 2017); Hall, "Why did FBI suspect Trump campaign adviser was a foreign agent?" *supra*; Shane et al., "Trump Adviser's Visit to Moscow Got the F.B.I.'s Attention," *supra*.

16. Dan Freedman, "N.Y. GOP's Cox introduced Carter Page to Trump campaign" (*Times Union*, Feb. 5, 2018).

17. See, e.g., David Lightman and William Douglas, "Trump slams George W. Bush in freewheeling GOP debate" (McClatchy, Feb. 13, 2016); MJ Lee, "How Donald Trump blasted George W. Bush in S.C.—and still won" (CNN, Feb. 21, 2016); John Solomon and Buck Sexton, "Trump slams Bush for 'worst single mistake' in U.S. history" (*The Hill*, Sept. 18, 2018); "Letter from G.O.P. National Security Officials Opposing Donald Trump" (*The New York Times*, Aug. 8, 2016).

18. Michael Crowley, "Trump's foreign policy team baffles GOP experts" (*Politico*, Mar. 21, 2016).

19. Title 18, U.S. Code, Section 2384.

20. See, e.g., Title 50, U.S. Code, Section 1861(2)(B): "An investigation con-
    ducted under this section shall...not be conducted of a United States person
    solely upon the basis of activities protected by the first amendment to the
    Constitution of the United States."

21. Title 50, U.S. Code, Section 1801(b)(2).

22. Mueller Report, Vol. I, pp. 96-97.

23. *United States v. Evgeny Buryakov, Igor Sporyshev, and Victor Podobnyy*,
    Arrest Complaint (Southern District of New York, Jan. 23, 2015) pp. 12-
    13 (Page is "Male-1," whom the Russian spy Victor Podobnyy refers to
    as "an idiot," and one of whose 2013 interviews by the FBI is described
    in paragraph 34), Andrew C. McCarthy, "A Foreign Power's Recruitment
    Effort Is Not a Basis for a FISA Court Warrant" (*National Review*, Jan.
    26, 2013); McCarthy, "The Schiff Memo Harms Democrats More Than It
    Helps Them" (*National Review*, Feb. 25, 2013).

24. *United States v. Buryakov, et al.*, Complaint, *supra*, p. 13, para. 34.

25. Schiff Memo, *supra*, p. 4 (the relevant footnote (no. 10) is redacted except
    for a cite to the *Buryakov* complaint).

26. Mike Levine, "Trump 'dossier' stuck in New York, didn't trigger Russia
    investigation, sources say" (ABC News, Sept. 18, 2018) ("sources told ABC
    News [Page's] file, like many counterintelligence files, was never closed").

27. Mueller Report, Vol. I, pp. 95-101.

28. Title 50, U.S. Code, Section 1701, et seq. See also Andrew C. McCarthy,
    "Legislative Emergencies and the Long-Lost Legislative Veto" (*National Re-
    view*, Jan. 12, 2019).

29. "Text: Obama's Speech at the New Economic School" (*The New York
    Times*, Jul. 7, 2009).

30. Mueller Report, Vol. I, pp. 95-101.

31. *Ibid.*

32. Under state and party rules, the results of primary elections tend to be advi-
    sory; they do not bind the delegate to vote for the popular-vote winner. See
    also Alexander Burns and Maggie Haberman, "Donald Trump Hires Paul
    Manafort to Lead Delegate Effort" (*The New York Times*, Mar. 28, 2016).

33. Glenn Thrush, "To Charm Trump, Paul Manafort Sold Himself as an Af-
    fordable Outsider" (*The New York Times*, Apr. 8, 2017).

34. Evan Perez, Shimon Prokupecz, and Pamela Brown, "US government wire-
    tapped former Trump campaign chairman" (CNN, Sept. 17, 2017).

35. Josh Gerstein, "New scrutiny of potential Manafort link with Russia"
    (*Politico*, May 1, 2018). Federal discovery rules require the prosecutor to

disclose to the defendant prior to trial "any relevant written or recorded statement by the defendant" if it is within the government's possession. Rule 16(a)(1)(B), Fed. R. Crim. P.

36. See Josh Gerstein, "How Paul Manafort could put the FBI on trial" (*Politico*, Apr. 8, 2018). FBI Agent Peter "Strzok also appears to have been involved in preparing Foreign Intelligence Surveillance Act applications related to the Russia probe. Whether any of those relate directly to Manafort is unclear, although the FBI placed one of Manafort's associates, Russian-Ukrainian national Konstantin Kilimnik, under court-ordered surveillance."

37. Peter Schweizer, *Secret Empires: How the American Political Class Hides Corruption and Enriches Family and Friends* (Harper, 2018), chapters 2 and 3; Chuck Ross, "Nellie Ohr: Ukrainian Lawmaker Was Fusion GPS Source" (The Daily Caller, Feb. 6, 2019); Jeff Carlson, "Joe Biden, Obama Officials Stood to Gain from Ukrainian Influence—New evidence suggests Ukraine played a key role in creating Trump–Russia collusion narrative at behest of Obama officials" (*The Epoch Times*, Apr. 26, 2019); John Solomon, "How the Obama White House engaged Ukraine to give Russia collusion narrative an early boost" (*The Hill*, Apr. 25, 2019).

38. Schweizer, *Secret Empires, supra.*

39. See McCarthy, "Is 'Collusion with Russia' Over?", *supra*; McCarthy, "A Bipartisan Dossier of Collusion" (*National Review*, Oct. 28, 2017). In April 2019, Craig was indicted for lying to the government about his work for Ukraine. *United States v. Gregory B. Craig* (U.S. District Court, District of Columbia) (Indictment, Apr. 11, 2019). Like Craig, Tony Podesta (among other lobbyists said to have done work for foreign countries) was referred by Trump–Russia Special Counsel Robert Mueller for investigation by other Justice Department components. See, e.g., Associated Press, "Feds ramp up probe into Podesta lobbying firm with ties to Manafort" (*New York Post*, Dec. 5, 2018).

40. Marc Caputo, "Sources: Roger Stone quit, wasn't fired by Trump in campaign shakeup" (*Politico*, Aug. 8, 2015).

41. Kenneth Vogel, David Stern, and Josh Meyer, "Manafort faced blackmail attempt, hacks suggest" (*Politico*, Feb. 3, 2017); see also Matthew Kupfer, "UPDATE: Publication of Manafort Payments violated law, interfered in US election, Kyiv court rules" (*Kyiv Post*, Dec. 12, 2018).

42. Perez et al., "US government wiretapped former Trump campaign chairman," *supra.*

43. Kimberley Strassel, "Was Trump's Campaign 'Set Up'? At some point, the Russia investigation became political. How early was it?" (*The Wall Street Journal*, May 17, 2018).

44. Schiff Memo (HPSCI Minority Memo, Jan. 29, 2018) p. 3 & n.10 (though this footnote remains redacted).

CHAPTER 7

1. Mueller Report, Vol. 1, pp. 80-95, 192-93.

2. *United States v. Papadopoulos*, No. 17 Cr. 182 (RDM), Statement of the Offense (Oct. 5, 2017).

3. Jeff Carlson, "Ties that Bind—Stefan Halper, Joseph Mifsud & Alexander Downer (& Papadopoulos)" (*The Epoch Times*, May 10, 2018); see also Griff Witte and Karla Adam, "Is there more than meets the eye with the professor at the center of the Trump–Russia probe—or less?" (*The Washington Post*, Nov. 4, 2017).

4. It is unclear whether the Model UN participation claim is an exaggeration. Brian Whitaker, "What George Papadopoulos did before joining the Trump campaign: a chronology" (Medium.com, Aug. 24, 2018); Jason Meisner and Patrick M. O'Connell, "Week after bombshell, George Papadopoulos largely remains a mystery man" (*Chicago Tribune*, Nov. 7, 2017).

5. Lee Smith, "The Maltese Phantom of Russiagate" (RealClearInvestigations, May 30, 2018).

6. Smith, "The Maltese Phantom of Russiagate," *supra*; Stephan C. Roh and Thierry Pastor, *The Faking of Russia-gate: The Papadopoulos Case, an Investigative Analysis* (ILS Publishing Ltd., 2018).

7. Mueller Report, Vol. II, p. 83.

8. Mrs. Polonskaya was originally introduced to Papadopoulos by as "Olga Vinogradova," which is reportedly her maiden name. Her brother told *The New York Times* she had no connection to Putin or the Russian government ("She's not interested in politics. She can barely tell the difference between Lenin and Stalin.") The brother, it should be noted, further denied that she portrayed herself as Putin's niece, though that is alleged in the special prosecutor's statement of the offense—a claim that Papadopoulos did not dispute but which was irrelevant to the lie he admitted telling FBI agents. Sharon LaFraniere, David D. Kirkpatrick, Andrew Higgins, and Michael Schwirtz, "A London Meeting of an Unlikely Group: How a Trump Adviser Came to Learn of Clinton 'Dirt'" (*The New York Times*, Nov. 10, 2017); see also Mueller Report, Vol. I, pp. 84, 87-89, 193.

9. Mueller Report, Vol. I, pp. 89-90.

10. Mueller Report, Vol. I, p. 193.

11. See, e.g., Andrew C. McCarthy, "The Travel Ban Is about Vetting—Which Means It's about Islam" (*National Review*, Mar. 18, 2017).

12. Andrew C. McCarthy, *The Grand Jihad* (Encounter Books, 2010); McCarthy, "The Jihad in London" (*National Review*, Mar. 25, 2017); John O'Sullivan, "Britain Needs to Have an Uncomfortable Conversation about Islamic Terrorism" (*National Review*, Jun. 7, 2017).

13. Associate Press, "Say sorry to Trump or risk special relationship, Cameron told" (*The Times*, May 4, 2016); "David Cameron stands by attack on Donald Trump over Muslim 'ban'" (BBC News, May 16, 2016). Papadopoulos was eventually dumped from the Trump campaign after making foolish comments to a Russian news agency about how sanctions were incentivizing Russia into closer relations with China. Mueller Report, Vol. I, p. 93 & n.492.

14. John Solomon and Alison Spann, "Australian diplomat whose tip prompted FBI's Russia-probe has tie to Clintons" (*The Hill*, Mar. 5, 2018); Brennan Weiss, "Some Republicans are latching onto a dubious new theory about the Australian diploma who was pivotal to launching the Trump–Russia probe" (*Business Insider*, Mar. 5, 2018); Australian Associated Press, "Ex-Trump adviser takes aim at Alexander Downer after Mueller Report" (*The Guardian*, Mar. 25, 2019).

15. Stephen Robinson, "MI6, a death in China and the very secretive Mayfair company full of spooks: Labelled a 'convenient rest home' for spies, Hakluyt had always managed to stay in the shadows—until a top intelligence operator lost his life in murky circumstances" (*Evening Standard*, Mar. 30, 2012).

16. A well-informed researcher who tweets under the name Undercover Huber (@JohnWHuber—an homage (or perhaps a prod) to the Utah U.S. attorney appointed by then–Attorney General Jeff Sessions to examine actions by the FBI and Justice Department relevant to the 2016 campaign), notes that Hakluyt is an homage to Richard Hakluyt, a 16th-century British explorer who promoted the colonization of North America and published maps under of what he called "Novus Orbis." When former British spy Christopher Steele, an acquaintance of several Hakluyt figures, left British intelligence to start his own private-eye firm, he named it "Orbis.". Undercover Huber's thread relates the Halper–Downer panel at Cambridge. Undercover Huber (@JohnWHuber), "Is a mysterious British private spy firm linked to a series of 'collusion' stings on the @realDonaldTrump team? Is HAKLUYT the 'British Fusion GPS'?" (TreadReader app., May 8, 2018); "Pembroke College William Pitt seminar—Geopolitics: crisis and change" (Oct. 15, 2010). See also Jeff Carlson, "Dearlove Connections—UK Intel Firm Hakluyt, Alexander Downer, Stefan Halper & Papadopoulos" (*Epoch Times*, May 9, 2018); @The_War_Economy Jan. 17, 2018, Tweet (Facebook entry with photos of former CIA Director John Brennan appearing at the Hakluyt Leadership Seminar); Tim Shipman, "Louis Susman: Obama's choice as London envoy—Barack Obama might very well owe his national political career to Louis Susman" (*The Telegraph*, Feb. 21, 2009); Stefan Halper and Jonathan Clarke, *America*

Alone: The Neo-Conservatives and the Global Order (Cambridge University Press, 2005); Halper and Clarke, *The Silence of the Rational Center—Why American Foreign Policy Is Failing* (Basic Books, 2007); World Affairs Council, Premium Member and Trustee Event announcement, "Jonathan Clarke, a Scholar at the Cato Institute and co-author of America Alone: The Neo-Conservatives and the Global Order" (Oct. 2004).

17. Smith, "The Maltese Phantom of Russiagate," *supra*; see also Elizabeth Lea Vos, "All Russiagate Roads Lead to London as Evidence Emerges of Joseph Misfud's Links to UK Intelligence" (ZeroHedge, Apr. 4, 2018) (including photo of Mifsud and Smith together at a training program on international security organized by Link Campus University and the London Academy of Diplomacy).

18. Chuck Ross, "Alexander Downer Describes Barroom Meeting with Trump Adviser George Papadopoulos" (The Daily Caller, May 27, 2018) (discussing Downer interview with *The Australian* on Apr. 28, 2018).

19. Rudy Takala, "Leaked papers appear to reveal Dem 'pay for play' scheme" (*Washington Examiner*, Sept. 14, 2016); Michael Sainato, "Corruption doesn't start or end with Hillary" (*Observer*, Sept. 14, 2016); Ryan Lizza, "Let's Be Friends—Two presidents find a mutual advantage" (*The New Yorker*, Sept. 3, 2012).

20. Greg Miller, *The Apprentice: Trump, Russia and the Subversion of American Democracy* (Custom House, 2018).

21. Statement of the Offense, *supra*, pp. 7-8.

22. Mueller Report, Vol. I, p. 89 n.465.

23. Mueller Report, Vol. I, p. 89 n.464.

24. Chuck Ross, "Papadopoulos Addresses Key Question Looming Over Collusion Conspiracy Theory" (The Daily Caller, Sept. 14, 2018).

25. Andrew C. McCarthy, "The Steele Dossier's 'Corroborated' Claims Were Old News" (*National Review*, Mar. 4, 2019).

CHAPTER 8

1. Tom Kertscher, "Donald Trump wants to pull the U.S. out of NATO, Hillary Clinton says" (PolitiFact, Apr. 1, 2016).

2. Russia is the EU's fourth largest trading partner, while the EU is Russia's largest. Russia report: Trade picture (European Commission, data as of Apr. 17, 2019); see, e.g., Andrew E. Kramer, "French Leader Urges End to Sanctions Against Russia Over Ukraine" (*The New York Times*, Jan. 5, 2015); Jeanne Whalen, "Europe urges Congress to support lifting U.S. sanctions on Russian

firm controlled by Vladimir Putin ally" (*The Washington Post*, Jan. 11, 2019) the EU complains that sanctions on aluminum oligarch Deripaska harm factories in Austria, France, Germany, Ireland, Italy, Sweden, and the U.K.).

3. Gingrich obviously was not saying that Estonia (which is about 85 miles from St. Petersburg) was part of Russia. His point was that the country has a robust Russian minority population, and thus that Russia would not have to invade but—as it has done in Georgia and Ukraine—mainly rely on insurrection by ethnic Russian Estonians. His question was whether Americans would feel obliged to chance war with nuclear-armed Russia if the latter orchestrated an uprising in a country with a significant Russian population, situated on Russia's doorstep. See Andrew Stuttaford, "Estonia, Newt Gingrich and Strategery" (*National Review*, Jul. 23, 2016). See also, Miriam Elder, "Estonia's President Wants Some of His Fellow Leaders to End 'Naïveté' Toward Russia" (BuzzFeed, Sept. 20, 2016); Kristin Salaky, "Estonian Prez Appears to Push Back on Trump's NATO Comments" (Talking Points Memo, Jul. 21, 2016) (collecting Ilves tweets); George Neumayr, "John Brennan and Baltic Spies Teamed Up to Defeat Trump" (The American Spectator, Mar. 28, 2017).

4. Stanford University, Freeman Spogli Institute for International Studies, pages on Michael A. McFaul and Toomas Hendrik Ilves; Neumayr, "John Brennan and Baltic Spies Teamed Up to Defeat Trump," *supra*.

5. Paul Wood, "Trump 'compromising' claims: How and why did we get here" (BBC News, Jan. 12, 2017); Luke Harding, "British spies were first to spot Trump team's links with Russia—Exclusive: GCHQ is said to have alerted US agencies after becoming aware of contacts in 2015" (*The Guardian*, Apr. 13, 2017); see also Peter Stone and Greg Gordon, "FBI, 5 other agencies probe possible covert Kremlin aid to Trump" (McClatchy, Jan. 18, 2017) (six U.S. government agencies investigating "whether money from the Kremlin covertly aided President-elect Donald Trump").

6. John O. Brennan, House Intelligence Committee Testimony (hearing on "Russian Active Measures during the 2016 Election Campaign), May 23, 2017, p. 17.

7. Michael S. Schmidt, Matthew Rosenberg, Adam Goldman, and Matt Apuzzo, "Intercepted Russian Communications Part of Inquiry Into Trump Associates" (*The New York Times*, Jan. 19, 2017) ("The F.B.I. is leading the investigations, aided by the National Security Agency, the C.I.A. and the Treasury Department's financial crimes unit. ... One official said intelligence reports based on some of the wiretapped communications had been provided to the White House."); see also Stone and Gordon, "FBI, 5 other agencies probe possible covert Kremlin aid to Trump," *supra*.

8. Edward William Priestap, Testimony before the House Judiciary Committee, Jun. 5, 2018, pp. 76-80; Eric Felten, "FBI Man's Testimony Points to Wrongdoing Well Beyond Spying" (RealClearInvestigations, Apr. 12, 2019).

9.   John O. Brennan, Meet the Press interview by Chuck Todd (NBC News, Feb. 4, 2018); Jeff Carlson, "John Brennan's Role in the FBI's Trump–Russia Investigation" (*The Epoch Times*, Apr. 9, 2018).

10.   "FBI Records Show Dossier Author Deemed 'Not Suitable For Use' as Source, Show Several FBI Payments in 2016" (Judicial Watch, Aug. 3, 2018) (collecting documents released in FOIA litigation, *Judicial Watch v. U.S. Dept. of Justice*, No. 17 cv 916).

11.   Carlson, "John Brennan's Role in the FBI's Trump–Russia Investigation," *supra*. Gordon Rayner, "GCHQ boss Robert Hannigan quits for 'personal reasons' after just two years" (*The Telegraph*, Jan. 23, 2017).

12.   The Justice Department and the FBI stiff-armed congressional investigators through the Trump administration's first two years. Though the president groused about this, he seems to have been reluctant to issue a firm order that they cooperate, at least in part out of fear that doing so would be portrayed as obstruction of the Mueller probe. After the Mueller report was issued, we learned that newly appointed Attorney General Bill Barr has assigned a Justice Department prosecutor, John Durham (the U.S. attorney for Connecticut), to probe the investigative decisions made in connection with the 2016 campaign. The president also delegated the attorney general to exercise declassification authority to ensure that all relevant information is made available to Durham's investigation. See Andrew C. McCarthy, "Bill Barr's Declassification Kerfuffle" (*National Review*, May 28, 2019).

13.   Senators Charles E. Grassley and Lindsey O. Graham letter to Deputy Attorney General Rod J. Rosenstein and FBI Acting Director Andrew McCabe (Jun. 27, 2017), citing Julian Borger, "John McCain Passes Dossier Alleging Secret Trump–Russia Contacts to FBI" (*The Guardian*, Jan. 11, 2017), and Wood, "Trump 'compromising' claims: How and why did we get here?" *supra*.

14.   Louise Mensch, "EXCLUSIVE: FBI 'Granted FISA Warrant' Covering Trump Camp's Ties to Russia" (*Heat Street*, Nov. 8, 2016); Erick Lichtblau and Steven Lee Myers, "Investigating Donald Trump, F.B.I. Sees No Clear Link to Russia" (*The New York Times*, Oct. 31, 2016).

15.   Webster Stone, "Moscow's Still Holding" (*New York Times*, Sept. 18, 1988) (detailing that the so-called hotline between Washington and Moscow was not actually a telephone; begun in 1963, it was a 24-hour electronic link between the Pentagon and Communist Party headquarters).

16.   Franklin Foer, "Was a Trump Server Communicating with Russia?" (*Slate*, Oct. 31, 2016).

17.   Rowan Scarborough, "Simpson pushed Justice Department to investigate debunked Trump-Alfa bank theory" (*The Washington Times*, Sept. 9, 2018).

18.   Wood, "Trump 'compromising' claims: How and why did we get here?", *supra*; Stone and Gordon, "FBI, 5 other agencies probe possible covert

Kremlin aid to Trump," *supra*; cf. Title 50, U.S. Code, Sections 1861 (access to certain business records for foreign-intelligence and international terrorism investigations) and 3162 (requests by authorized investigative agencies for financial records necessary to the conduct of counterintelligence and other investigations).

19. Everett Rosenfeld, "Hillary Clinton will campaign in Arizona—a normally red state" (CNBC, Oct. 28, 2016).

20. Office of the Inspector General, U.S. Dept. of Justice, "A Review of Various Actions by the Federal Bureau of Investigation and Department of Justice in Advance of the 2016 Election" (Jun. 2018), pp. 333-90; Devlin Barrett, "FBI in Internal Feud Over Hillary Clinton Probe" (*The Wall Street Journal*, Oct. 30, 2016).

21. Liz Spayd, "The Public Editor: Trump, Russia, and the News Story That Wasn't" (*The New York Times*, Jan. 20, 2017).

22. See, e.g., Sam Roberts, "A Spy Confesses, and Still Some Weep for the Rosenbergs" (*New York Times*, Sept. 20, 2008).

23. Franklin Foer, "Suspended Animation in the Age of Trump—Before Donald Trump was elected, I reported on strange activity liking a Trump-campaign computer server to Moscow. A new report shows how much has changed since 2016—and how many questions still remain" (*The Atlantic*, Oct. 8, 2018); Dexter Filkins, "Was There a Connection Between a Russian Bank and the Trump Campaign?" (*The New Yorker*, Oct. 15, 2018).

24. Glenn Simpson Testimony before Senate Intelligence Committee, pp. 304-5 (Aug. 22, 2017).

25. Scarborough, "Simpson pushed Justice Department to investigate debunked Trump-Alfa bank theory," *supra*.

CHAPTER 9

1. Nick Hopkins and Luke Harding, "Donald Trump dossier: intelligence sources vouch for author's credibility—Ex-MI6 officer Christopher Steele, named as writer of Donald Trump memo, is 'highly regarded professional'" (*The Guardian*, Jan. 12, 2017); Gordon Rayner, "Who is Christopher Steele, author of the explosive Trump–Russia dossier?" (Reuters, Jan. 13, 2017) (noting that Steele was case officer for murdered Russian defector Alexander Litvenenko); Lee Smith, "Did Glenn Simpson Lie to Congress? And could Christopher Steele, the British spy who spent his life as a Cold Warrior, have become an unwitting Kremlin pawn?" (*Tablet Magazine*, Jan. 12, 2018); Esther Addley and Luke Harding, "Litvinenko probably murdered on personal orders of Putin" (*The Guardian*, Jan. 21, 2016).

2. Andrew C. McCarthy, "Anatomy of a Farce" (*National Review*, Jan. 13, 2018); McCarthy, "The Curious Case of Natalia Veselnitskaya" (*National Review*, Jul. 19, 2017); McCarthy, "Is Collusion with Russia Over?" (*National Review*, Feb. 24, 2018); John Solomon, "Russian Oligarch, Justice Department and a clear case of collusion" (*The Hill*, Aug. 28, 2018).

3. Eric Felten, "Was Christopher Steele disseminating Russian disinformation to the State Department?" (*The Weekly Standard*, Sept. 14, 2018).

4. Jerry Dunleavy, "Christopher Steele admitted using posts by 'random individuals' on CNN website to back up Trump Dossier" (*Washington Examiner*, Mar. 15, 2019).

5. Asha Schow, "Christopher Steele's Former MI6 Boss Slams Dossier as 'Overrated'" (Daily Wire, Mar. 18, 2019).

6. McCarthy, "Anatomy of a Farce," *supra*.

7. Lee Smith, "Did President Obama Read the 'Steele Dossier' in the White House Last August?" (*Tablet Magazine*, Dec. 20, 2017).

8. John Solomon, "FBI's Steele story falls apart: False intel and media contacts were flagged before FISA" (*The Hill*, May 9, 2019).

9. Andrew C. McCarthy, "Politicizing Steele's Raw, Unverified 'Intelligence'" (*National Review*, Jan. 9, 2018).

10. Des Bieler, "The British spy behind the Trump dossier helped the FBI bust FIFA" (*The Washington Post*, Jan. 13, 2017).

11. Glenn Simpson Testimony before Senate Intelligence Committee, pp. 58-63 (Aug. 22, 2017); Glenn Simpson Testimony before House Permanent Select Committee on Intelligence, pp. 7-12 (Nov. 14, 2017); Kenneth P. Vogel and Maggie Haberman, "Conservative Website First Funded Anti-Trump Research by Firm That Later Produced Dossier" (*The New York Times*, Oct. 27, 2017).

12. Matthew J. Gehringer, General Counsel, Perkins Coie LLP, Letter "Re: Fusion GPS" to William W. Taylor III, Zuckerman Spaeder LLP, Counsel for Fusion GPS (Oct. 24, 2017); Jack Gillum and Shawn Boburg, "'Journalism for rent': Inside the secretive firm behind the Trump dossier" (*The Washington Post*, Dec. 11, 2017); Adam Entous, Devlin Barrett, and Rosalind S. Helderman, "Clinton campaign, DNC paid for research that led to Russia dossier" (*The Washington Post*, Oct. 24, 2017); Kenneth P. Vogel, "Clinton Campaign and Democratic Party Helped Pay for Russia Trump Dossier" (*The New York Times*, Oct. 24, 2017); Andrew C. McCarthy, "When Scandals Collide" (*National Review*, Oct. 25, 2017).

13. In the 2016 campaign, Perkins Coie was also paid $798,047 by President Obama's political organization, Obama for America. See Sean Casey, "Obama's Campaign Paid $972,000 to Law Firm That Secretly Paid Fusion GPS in 2016" (*The Federalist*, Oct. 29, 2017).

14. John Breslin, "Allegations That Clinton Campaign Funded Trump–Russia Research Still Pending At Now-Closed FEC" (*Forbes*, Jan. 15, 2019) (In FEC filings, Hillary for America reported paying Perkins Coie $5,631,421 for "Legal Services"; the DNC reported paying the firm $6,466,722 for "Legal and Compliance Consulting"; there was no mention of Fusion GPS); Mark Hosenball, "Ex-British spy paid $168,000 for Trump dossier, U.S. firm discloses" (Reuters, Nov. 1, 2017); see also John Solomon, "State Department's red flag on Steele went to a senior FBI man well before FISA warrant" (*The Hill*, May 14, 2019); "Judicial Watch Sues FBI for Records of Communications and payments to Anti-Trump Dossier Author Steele" (Judicial Watch, Apr. 16, 2009) (records show at least 11 FBI payments to Steele in 2016); Tom Winter, "FBI releases documents showing payments to Trump dossier author Steele" (NBC News, Aug. 3, 2018).

15. See Open Source Center website (accessed Nov. 22, 2018); see also Steven Aftergood, "Charter of Open Source Org Is Classified, CIA Says" (Federation of American Scientists, Dec. 12, 2011).

16. Nellie Ohr, House Judiciary and Oversight Committees Testimony (Oct. 19, 2018) p. 105; see also Diana West, "Nellie Ohr: Woman in the Middle" (The American Spectator, Feb. 22, 2018).

17. Ohr was not "the fourth highest-ranking official in the Justice Department," as media reporting commonly misstates; but his job was important—among the Department's top career (i.e., nonpolitical) slots. He was demoted from it in 2017. Jake Gibson, "Top DOJ official demoted amid probe of contacts with Trump dossier firm" (Fox News, Dec. 7, 2017). I've known Bruce Ohr for years, cordially though not well. In an amusing moment in Mr. Ohr's otherwise tense congressional testimony, he explained that after an important meeting with Christopher Steele, his "first move was to reach out to Andrew McCarthy." With the help of his questioner, he corrected himself and said he'd meant Andrew *McCabe*, adding, "Andrew McCarthy will be angry." Bruce Ohr, House Judiciary and Oversight Committees Testimony (Aug. 28, 2018), p. 79.

18. Des Beiler, "The British spy behind the Trump dossier helped the FBI bust FIFA" (*The Washington Post*, Jan. 13, 2017).

19. Toby Harnden, "Trump allies cry foul after former MI6 agent's [sic] Christopher Steele dossier linked to Obama official" (*The Times*, Dec. 10, 2017); Bruce Ohr Testimony before the House Judiciary and Oversight Committees (Aug. 28, 2018), pp. 13-14, 177, 185-86.

20. John T. Picarelli, "Expert Working Group Report on International Organized Crime" (National Institute of Justice, Jun. 2010) (see p. 30, listing Bruce Ohr as chief of the Justice Department's Organized Crime and Racketeering Section, Nellie Ohr as a researcher for Open Source Works (i.e., the CIA), and Glenn Simpson as a senior fellow at the International Assessment and Strategy Center in Arlington, Virginia).

21. Nellie Ohr Testimony before the House Judiciary and Oversight Committees, (Oct. 19, 2018), pp. 10-12; Bruce Ohr, House Testimony, *supra*, p. 186; McCarthy, "Anatomy of a Farce," *supra*. Bruce Ohr, Executive Branch Personnel Public Financial Disclosure Report (OGE Form 278e, 2017) (listing Dr. Ohr as an independent contractor, with no reference to Fusion or a compensation amount).

22. John Solomon, "How a senior DOJ official helped Dem researchers on Trump–Russia case" (*The Hill*, Aug. 7, 2018).

23. Simpson House testimony, *supra*, pp. 78-79.

24. Bruce Ohr testimony, *supra*, p. 80 (noting he supervised trial attorney Lisa Page for five years); see also Chapter 3, n. 18

25. The Steele dossier is available here: https://www.documentcloud.org/documents/3259984-Trump-Intelligence-Allegations.html. It appears somewhat shopworn with yellow highlighting, the form in which it was published by BuzzFeed on January 10, 2017. As further described, *infra*, BuzzFeed's reporter, Ken Bensinger, is said to have photographed its pages without authorization when they were made available to him by David Kramer, an aide to the now-deceased Senator John McCain (R., Ariz.), who received a copy of the dossier from Simpson after meeting in London with Steele, and who met with Bensinger pursuant to a request by Steele. *Gubarev v. BuzzFeed*, No. 17 Civ. 60426-UU (Southern District of Florida), Deposition of David Kramer (Dec. 13, 2017) pp. 58-67; see also Chuck Ross, "John McCain Associate Had Contact with a Dozen Reporters Regarding Steele Dossier" (*The Daily Caller*, Mar. 14, 2019). The penultimate dossier report is dated October 19. The final report, written nearly two months later (i.e., over a month after Trump won the 2016 election), doubles down on Steele's earlier reporting that Trump's then-lawyer, Michael Cohen, met with Russian government operatives in Prague—a claim that was never corroborated, was heatedly denied by Cohen and Trump, and was ultimately rejected by Special Counsel Mueller.

26. Glenn Simpson Senate Testimony, *supra*, p. 83, 103-4; Diana West, "Nellie Ohr: Woman in the Middle," *supra*.

27. Trump encouraged the FBI to investigate the incident, insisting it did not happen and concerned that it would upset his wife. His recollection, in reliance on staffers, that he had not stayed overnight in Russia, is almost certainly wrong: He appears to have arrived in Moscow on Friday, November 8, 2013, and left Sunday, November 10, following the pageant. A witness, Trump bodyguard Keith Schiller, told a congressional committee that he had escorted Trump to a hotel room, where he retired, alone. Schiller recalled that, in what he regarded as a joke, a Russian (not identified in press reports of Schiller's testimony) had offered to send five women to Trump's room; Schiller and Trump laughed about the offer as they walked to the latter's room. Mark Murray, "Did Trump stay overnight in Russia in 2013? Evi-

dence points to yes" (NBC News, Apr. 20, 2018). The Mueller report found no evidence that Trump was compromised by the Kremlin.

28. James B. Comey, Senate Intelligence Committee Testimony (Jun. 8, 2017) ("I was briefing [then-President-elect Trump] about salacious and unverified material"); Andrew Prokop, "The 'pee tape' claim, explained" (Vox, Apr. 23, 2018); see also James R. Clapper, "DNI Clapper Statement on Conversation with President-elect Trump" (Office of the Director of National Intelligence, Jan. 11, 2017) (the day after BuzzFeed published the dossier, Clapper explained that U.S. intelligence agencies had "not made any judgment that the information in this document is reliable").

29. "According to Source D, where s/he had been present [sic], TRUMP's (perverted) conduct in Moscow included hiring the presidential suite of the Ritz Carlton Hotel, where he knew President and Mrs. Obama (whom he hated) had stayed on one of their official trips to Russia, and defiling the bed where they had slept by employing a number of prostitutes to perform a 'golden showers' (urination) show in front of him. The hotel was known to be under FSB control with microphones and concealed cameras in all the main rooms to record anything they wanted to."

30. Brian Ross and Matthew Mosk, "US-Russian Businessman Said to Be Source of Key Trump Dossier Claims" (ABC News, Jan. 30, 2017) ("a version provided to the FBI included Millian's name as a source, according to someone who has seen the version given to the FBI").

31. *Ibid*; Mark Maremont, "Key Claims in Trump Dossier Said to Come From Head of Russian-American Business Group" (*The Wall Street Journal*, Jan. 24, 2017); see also Chuck Ross, "Papadopoulos Details His Interactions with 'Spygate' Figure and Steele Dossier Source" (The Daily Caller, Sept. 8, 2018).

32. D claims to have been in Moscow (if not in the hotel) with Trump, while E is said to have "been aware" of the incident but is not alleged to have been in the vicinity. Millian has claimed (at times) to have been in Moscow with Trump at the time, so he must be D—meaning someone else must be E.

33. The most common speculation centers around Felix Sater, a longtime FBI and CIA informant. We will discuss Sater in due course, but there has been no confirmation that he is among Steele's sources. Interestingly, Sater was originally inked as a government cooperator in the late 1990s by Andrew Weissmann, then a prosecutor working for then–U.S. Attorney Loretta Lynch in the Eastern District of New York. Weissmann, of course, was Special Counsel Mueller's top lieutenant and an author of the Mueller report, in which Sater is benignly described as "a New York based real estate advisor" who dealt with Trump Organization lawyer Michael Cohen (Sater's friend and high school classmate) on the Trump Tower Moscow project. There is no mention in the report of Sater's colorful career as a covert government informant in organized-crime and terrorism investigations—on which he embarked to get

out from under his complicity in a $40 million fraud conspiracy. I guess it wasn't deemed important—or at least as important as, say, lying about the date of a meeting (for which Mueller prosecuted George Papadopoulos). See, e.g., Anthony Cormier and Jason Leopold, "The Asset: How a Player in the Trump–Russia Scandal Led a Double Life as an American Spy" (BuzzFeed, Mar. 12, 2018); Jason Haltiwanger, "Meet Felix Sater, the Russian-born, bar-fighting felon with ties to the mob at the center of Mueller's Russia investigation" (*Business Insider*, May 17, 2018); Rosalind S. Helderman and Tom Hamburger, "'We will be in Moscow': The story of Trump's 30-year quest to expand his brand to Russia" (*The Washington Post*, Nov. 29, 2018).

34. Simpson is well known to leak information to the media, which he sees as part of Fusion GPS's services for clients. Simpson Senate Testimony, *supra*, p. 210; Simpson House testimony, pp. 103-4. He reportedly outed Millian to ABC's Brian Ross. See Isikoff and Corn, *Russian Roulette, supra*. Moreover, on the day of Donald Trump's inauguration, just four days before the *Journal* reported that Millian was a major dossier source, Simpson told Justice Department official Bruce Ohr that there was about to be media reporting about a major dossier source. In addition, Simpson had previously told Ohr that Millian was a potential "intermediary" between Trump and the Putin regime. Bruce Ohr House Testimony, *supra*, pp. 13-19, 22; see also Chuck Ross, "Bruce Ohr Told of Safety Concerns for Steele Dossier Source" (The Daily Caller, Feb. 21, 2019); Ross, "In Newly Released Interview, Alleged Dossier Source Made Cryptic Remarks About Trump" (Daily Caller, Sept. 7, 2018).

35. U.S. Dept. of State, Case No. F-2018-04736, Doc. No. C06679743, Deputy Assistant Secretary of State Kathleen Kavalec, "Notes from Meeting with Chris Steele and Tatyana Duran of Orbis Security, October 11, 2016" (Disclosed May 6, 2019); John Solomon, "FBI's Steele story falls apart: False intel and media contacts were flagged before FISA" (*The Hill*, May 9, 2013).

36. Relying on reporting by the *Financial Times*, ABC News recounted that Millian's organization collaborated on a 2011 trip to Moscow for 50 American businessmen. The FBI later asked some of the Americans whether Russian intelligence tried to recruit them, implying that at least some of the people behind the junket were spies. An intelligence expert told ABC News that the Russian-American Chamber of Commerce reminded him of a classic Soviet front organization. Ross and Mosk, "US-Russian Businessman Said to Be Source of Key Trump Dossier Claims," *supra*.

37. Isikoff and Corn, *Russian Roulette, supra*; Chuck Ross, Bruce Ohr Told of Safety Concerns for Steele Dossier Source," *supra*.

38. Ross and Mosk, "US-Russian Businessman Said to Be Source of Key Trump Dossier Claims," *supra*; Maremont, "Key Claims in Trump Dossier Said to Come From Head of Russian-American Business Group," *supra*. Millian told ABC News he was in Moscow at the time but did not see Trump. He

told The Daily Caller that "he was not in Moscow with Trump"—confirming that he knew nothing about any episode with prostitutes but leaving ambiguous whether he was in the city at the time. Chuck Ross, "Bruce Ohr Told of Safety Concerns for Steele Dossier Source," *supra*.

39. Chuck Ross, "Steele Identified Russian Dossier Sources, Notes Reveal" (The Daily Caller, May 16, 2019); Peter Pomerantsev, "Putin's Rasputin" (*London Review of Books*, Oct. 20, 2011); Matt Thomas, "Vladislav Surkov: Who is Vladimir Putin's 'grey cardinal'? Putin's chief political technologist, postmodern novelist, PR man—Surkov has been all of these and more" (*International Business Times*, Oct. 29, 2016).

40. "Russia Is Selling a Big Chunk of This State-Controlled Oil Giant" (Reuters, Dec. 8, 2016).

41. See Mueller Report, Vol. II, pp. 23, 27 & n.12, 28. [Kindle locations Vol. I at 7092, 7176, 7188, Vol. II at 10632—search term "unverified."]

42. Eric Lipton, David E. Sanger, and Scott Shane, "The Perfect Weapon: How Russian Cyberpower Invaded the U.S." (*The New York Times*, Dec. 13, 2016).

43. Mark Tran, "WikiLeaks to publish more Hillary Clinton emails—Julian Assange" (*The Guardian*, Jun. 12, 2016).

44. Simpson House Intelligence Committee Testimony, *supra*, p. 234.

45. Alan Yuhas, "Hillary Clinton campaign blames leaked DNC emails about Sanders on Russia" (*The Guardian*, Jul. 24, 2016).

46. *Gubarev v. Orbis Business Intelligence Ltd. and Christopher Steele*, High Court of Justice, Queen's Bench Div., No. HQ17D00413, Defendants Orbis and Steele Response to Interrogatories (May 18, 2017); Rowan Scarborough, "Faced with libel lawsuit, dossier drafter Christopher Steele hedges on liking Trump to Russia" (*The Washington Times*, Dec. 20, 2017); Andrew C. McCarthy, "Politicizing Steele's Raw, Unverified 'Intelligence'" (*National Review*, Jan. 9, 2018).

CHAPTER 10

1. Peter S. Goodman, "The Post World War II Order Is Under Assault From the Powers That Built It" (*The New York Times*, Mar. 26, 2018) (Post–World War II order forged by victorious Western powers that "forged institutions— NATO, the European Union, and the World Trade Organization—that aimed to keep the peace through collective military might and shared prosperity. They promoted democratic ideals and international trade while investing in the notion that coalitions were the antidote to destructive nationalism.").

2. Peter Schweizer, *Clinton Cash*, *supra*; Marc A. Theissen, "Yes, the Clintons should be investigated" (*The Washington Post*, Nov. 19, 2017); John

Solomon, "The case for Russian collusion...against the Democrats" (*The Hill*, Feb. 10, 2019); Schweizer, "Uncovering the Russia ties of Hillary's campaign chief" (*New York Post*, Jul. 5, 2017).

3. Office of the Director of National Intelligence, "Background to 'Assessing Russian Activities and Intentions in Recent US Elections': The Analytic Process and Cyber Incident Attribution" (Jan. 6, 2017), p. 13, Annex B (explaining "Estimative Language").

4. John Solomon, "Comey: DNC denied FBI's requests for access to hacked servers" (*The Hill*, Jan. 10, 2017).

5. Eric Lipton, David E. Sanger, and Scott Shane, "The Perfect Weapon: How Russian Cyberpower Invaded the U.S." (*The New York Times*, Dec. 13, 2016).

6. The International Institute for Strategic Studies, an influential British think-tank, concluded that CrowdStrike erroneously used IISS data as proof of the intrusion, and the Ukrainian defense ministry denied that the claimed hacking and combat losses had not happened. CrowdStrike, nevertheless, maintained that its analysis was sound. Oleksiy Kuzmenko and Pete Cobus, "Think Tank: Cyber Firm at Center of Russian Hacking Charges Misread Data" (Voice of America, Mar. 21, 2017).

7. Patrick Lawrence, "A New Report Raises Big Questions About Last Year's DNC Hack" (*The Nation*, Aug. 9, 2017).

8. Various Contributors, "A Leak or a Hack? A Forum on the VIPS Memo" (*The Nation*, Sept. 1, 2017).

9. Sam Biddle, "Here's the Public Evidence Russia Hacked the DNC—It's Not Enough" (*The Intercept*, Dec. 14, 2016); see also Jeffrey Carr, "FBI/DHS Joint Analysis Report: A Fatally Flawed Effort" (Medium.com, Dec. 30, 2016) ("Once malware is deployed, it is no longer under the control of the hacker who deployed it or the developer who created it. It can be reverse-engineered, copied, modified, shared and redeployed again and again by anyone. In other words—malware deployed is malware enjoyed!").

10. U.S. Dept. of Justice, "Deputy Attorney General Rod J. Rosenstein Delivers Remarks Announcing the Indictment of Twelve Russian Intelligence Officers for Conspiring to Interfere in the 2016 Presidential Election Through Computer Hacking and Related Offenses" (Office of Public Affairs, Jul. 13, 2018).

11. *United States v. Julian Paul Assange*, No. 18 Crim. 111 (E.D.Va. 2018), Indictment (Mar. 6, 2018).

12. Title 18, U.S. Code, Section 371.

13. President Obama commuted Manning's 35-year sentence to 7 years, rationalizing that it was warranted due to the distress a transgender woman (who had attempted suicide) faced from the prospect of decades of imprisonment in a men's military prison. Manning was released in May 2017.

Charlie Savage, "Chelsea Manning to Be Released Early as Obama Commutes Sentence" (*The New York Times*, Jan. 17, 2017) See also Andrew C. McCarthy, "Why Isn't Assange Charged with 'Collusion with Russia'?" (*National Review*, Apr. 13, 2019).

14. The 2010 Assange–Manning cyber-theft conspiracy charge is outside the standard 5-year statute of limitations for federal crimes: The limitations period was already exhausted when the original indictment was filed in 2018. The superseding indictment, filed on May 23, 2019 (as this book was being finalized), is even more blatantly time-barred. The new indictment will only survive a motion to dismiss if prosecutors convince courts in both Britain (which will rule on extradition) and the U.S. (where the case would be prosecuted) that each of the charges is actually a "federal crime of terrorism," triggering a 3-year statute-of-limitations extension. I am skeptical that the Justice Department's cyber-theft charge qualifies. The extension statute, Section 2332b(g)(5)(B) of the penal code (Title 18), makes the extra 3 years applicable to cyber-theft offenses under Section 1030 of the penal code, but not to Espionage Act offenses under Section 793. Prosecutors haven't charged a substantive cyber-theft violation under Section 1030; they have charged a *conspiracy* (under Section 371) to commit the Section 1030 offense. That is not the same thing. Typically, if Congress intends that its mention of a crime should be understood to include a conspiracy to commit that crime, it says so. It did not say so in the extension statute. See *United States v. Julian Paul Assange*, No. 18 Crim. 111 (CMH) (Eastern District of Virginia, 2019), Superseding Indictment (May 23, 2019) (and note that, like the original indictment, the superseding indictment contains no charges related to the cyberespionage operations directed at the 2016 campaign).

15. On May 23, 2019, the Justice Department superseded the indictment against Assange. It now charges 18 felony counts arising out of the scheme with Manning to steal and expose classified information. Again, the government brought no charges related to the cyberespionage operations directed at the 2016 presidential campaign. *United States v. Julian Paul Assange*, No. 18 Crim. 111 (CMH) (Eastern District of Virginia, 2019), Superseding Indictment (May 23, 2019).

CHAPTER 11

1. Comey Senate Testimony (Jun. 8, 2017), *supra*.

2. James B. Comey, "How Trump Co-opts Leaders Like Bill Barr—Accomplished people lacking inner strength can't resist the compromises necessary to survive this president" (*The New York Times*, May 1, 2019); Nancy Cook, "Comey calls Trump 'morally unfit to be president'" (*Politico*, Apr. 15, 2018).

3. Andrew C. McCarthy, "Trump's Berating of Comey for the Consumption of Our Enemies" (*National Review*, May 20, 2017).

4. Andrew C. McCarthy, "Comey Confirms: In Clinton Emails Caper, the Fix Was In" (*National Review*, Apr. 28, 2018).

5. Inspector General Report, *supra*, pp. 130-31.

6. Steele and his company (Orbis) worked for Deripaska in an arrangement similar to the one under which Simpson and Fusion worked for the son of Putin ally Pyotr Katsyv. They were retained by law firms that represented the oligarchs to perform research in support of litigation. John Solomon, "Russian oligarch, Justice Department and a clear case of collusion" (*The Hill*, Aug. 28, 2018); *see also* Lee Smith, "Was Christopher Steele Paid by Russian Oligarch and Putin Ally Oleg Deripaska?" (*Tablet Magazine*, Feb. 12, 2108) (embedding letter of Feb. 9, 2018, from Senate Judiciary Chairman Charles Grassley (R., Iowa) to Paul E. Hauser, a lawyer for Deripaska believed to have retained Steele, inquiring about Steele's work for Deripaska); Byron York, "Emails show 2016 links among Steele, Ohr, Simpson—with Russian oligarch in background" (*Washington Examiner*, Aug. 8, 2018) (relating that the lawyer declined to answer Senator Grassley's question).

7. York, "Emails show 2016 links among Steele, Ohr, Simpson—with Russian oligarch in background," *supra*.

8. Kenneth P. Vogel and Matthew Rosenberg, "Agents Tried to Flip Russian Oligarchs. The Fallout Spread to Trump." (*The New York Times*, Sept. 1, 2018); Andrew E. Kramer, "Praise for Mueller Report, From an Unlikely Source: Oleg Deripaska" (*The New York Times*, Apr. 3, 2019).

9. Schiff Memo, *supra*, pp. 3-4; Mike Levine, "Trump 'dossier' stuck in New York, didn't trigger Russia investigation, sources say," *supra* ("two months after Page started advising Trump's campaign, the FBI paid him a visit in New York, asking about contacts with Russian intelligence, according to a [not further described] government document").

10. Paul Sperry, "Flashback: The Real Carter Page vs. the One People Suspect" (RealClearInvestigations, Jun. 7, 2018).

11. Benjamin Weiser, "Bank Employee Pleads Guilty to Conspiring to Work as Secret Russian Agent" (*The New York Times*, Mar. 11, 2016).

12. *United States v. Viktor Borisovich Netyksho*, No. 18 Crim. 215 (ABJ) (S.D.N.Y. 2019), Indictment (Jul. 13, 2018), p. 12.

13. Eric Lipton, David E. Sanger, and Scott Shane, "The Perfect Weapon: How Russian Cyberpower Invaded the U.S." (*The New York Times*, Dec. 13, 2016); *United States v. Netyksho*, Indictment, *supra*, pp. 6-12.

14. Issie Lapowsky, "Wait, Clinton Didn't Have a Computer in Her Office?" (*Wired*, Oct. 22, 2015).

15. Lipton et al., "The Perfect Weapon: How Russian Cyberpower Invaded the U.S.," *supra*; Ellen Nakashima, "Russian government hackers penetrated DNC, stole opposition research on Trump" (*The Washington Post*, Jun. 14, 2016).

16. Jeff Carlson, "Baker Testimony Reveals Perkins Coie Lawyer Provided FBI With Information on Alfa Bank Allegations" (*The Epoch Times*, Jan. 21, 2019).

17. John Solomon, "Comey: DNC denied FBI's requests for access to hacked servers" (*The Hill*, Jan. 10, 2017). CrowdStrike is "Company 1" in Special Counsel Mueller's indictment of the Russian intelligence officers. *United States v. Netyksho*, Indictment, *supra*, pp. 12, 14, 15.

18. Adam Pasick and Tim Fernholz, "The stealthy, Eric Schmidt-backed startup that's working to put Hillary Clinton in the White House" (*Quartz*, Oct. 9, 2015); Ron Miller, "Security Company CrowdStrike Scores $100M Led By Google Capital" (*TechCrunch*, Jul. 13, 2015); Justin Caruso, "Crowdstrike: Five Things Everyone Is Ignoring About the Russia-DNC Story" (The Daily Caller, Jun. 24, 2017); Jack Nicas, "Alphabet's Eric Schmidt Gave Advice to Clinton Campaign, Leaked Emails Show—The executive backed a startup that helped develop some of the technology behind Mrs. Clinton's website" (*The Wall Street Journal*, Nov. 2, 2016).

19. In the drafting process, Comey's remarks were edited: The assertion that it was "reasonably likely" that a foreign government had accessed Clinton's emails was watered down to a statement that it was "possible" but that the FBI had no concrete evidence that it had happened. "Did the FBI Cover Up Evidence that China Hacked Clinton's State Dept. Emails?" (*Investor's Business Daily*, Aug. 28, 2018). President Trump has publicly claimed that hackers working for China stole Mrs. Clinton's emails, an allegation that the FBI has shot down. ("The FBI has not found any evidence the servers were compromised.") John Wagner, "FBI pushes back on unfounded Trump claim that China hacked Hillary Clinton's email" (*The Washington Post*, Aug. 29, 2018) (embedding Donald J. Trump (@realDonaldTrump) Aug. 28 and 29, 2018, Tweets); but see Richard Pollock, "Sources: China Hacked Hillary Clinton's Private Email Server" (The Daily Caller, Aug. 27, 2018) (two unidentified government sources claim the Intelligence Community Inspector General believed Clinton's emails had been penetrated by a Chinese-controlled company in Washington and alerted the FBI's Agent Peter Strzok—again, note that the FBI denied having such evidence). See also David E. Sanger, "Hillary Clinton's Email Was Probably Hacked, Experts Say" (*The New York Times*, Jul. 6, 2016); Elias Groll and David Francis, "FBI: An Accont on Clinton's Private Email Server Was Hacked—An unidentified hacker compromised the email of a Bill Clinton staffer" (*Foreign Policy*, Sept. 2, 2016).

20. *United States v. Netyksho*, Indictment, *supra*, pp. 13-18.

21. Special Counsel Mueller indicted Stone for obstructing the congressional investigations of Russia's interference in the election. *United States v. Roger Jason Stone, Jr.*, No. 19 Crim. 18 (ABJ) (D.C. 2019), Indictment (Jan. 24, 2019); see also Andrew C. McCarthy, "Fever Dream: Mueller's Collusion-Free Collusion Indictment of Roger Stone" (*National Review*, Feb. 2, 2019). As we shall discuss, *infra*, Assange was indicted by the Justice Department...but not for conduct arising out of the 2016 campaign.

22. Isikoff and Corn, *Russian Roulette, supra*.

23. *Ibid.* See also Jonathan M. Winer, "Devin Nunes is investigating me. Here's the truth." (*The Washington Post*, Feb. 8, 2018); Rowan Scarborough, "Obama aide started Christopher Steele-FBI alliance" (*The Washington Times*, Mar. 13, 2018); Chuck Ross, "Here's How the Steele Dossier Spread through the Media and Government" (The Daily Caller, Mar. 18, 2019).

24. Eric Felten, "Was Christopher Steele disseminating Russian disinformation to the State Department?" (*The Weekly Standard*, Sept. 14, 2018).

25. Isikoff and Corn, *Russian Roulette, supra*.

26. Bruce Ohr House Testimony, *supra*; Carter Page FISA warrant application (second) (Jan. 2017), p. 17 & n.8 (p. 100 of disclosure package).

27. See, e.g., Schiff Memo, *supra*, p. 3 (allegedly supporting endnote 6 (p. 8) is redacted); Lisa Page Testimony, House Judiciary Committee (Jul. 13, 2018), pp. 126-27; see also Jeff Carlson, "Exclusive: Transcripts of Lisa Page's Closed-Door Testimonies Provide New Revelations in Spygate Scandal" (*The Epoch Times*, Jan. 11, 2019) (in House testimony, Lisa Page replied "That is correct, sir," to question stating that she did not have knowledge of Steele's unverified memos "prior to the middle part of September"); Mike Levine, "Trump 'dossier' stuck in New York, didn't trigger investigation, sources say" (ABC News, Sept. 18, 2018); Chuck Ross, "Ex-FBI Lawyer Claims He Was 'Concerned' with Steele Dossier, But Still Used It to Get Carter Page Spy Warrant" (The Daily Caller, May 18, 2018); Margot Cleveland, "Strzok Testimony Suggests Steele Dossier Did Help Launch FBI's Trump Investigation" (*The Federalist*, Mar. 15, 2019).

28. Bruce Ohr House Testimony, *supra*, pp. 10-48, 70-83, 168-84; John Solomon, "FISA shocker: DOJ official warned Steele dossier was connected to Clinton, might be biased" (*The Hill*, Jan. 16, 2019); Kim Strassel, "What Bruce Ohr Told Congress" (*The Wall Street Journal*, Aug. 30, 2018); York, "Emails show 2016 links among Steele, Ohr, Simpson—with Russian oligarch in background," *supra*.

29. Victoria Nuland, Testimony before the Senate Intelligence Committee (Jun. 20, 2018); Chuck Ross, "Revealed: Christopher Steele Visited State Department Shortly Before 2016 Election" (Jun. 20, 2018).

30. Emily Tillett, "Victoria Nuland says Obama State Dept. informed FBI of

reporting from Steele dossier" (CBS News *Face the Nation*, Feb. 4, 2018); Ross, "Revealed: Christopher Steele Visited State Department Shortly Before 2016 Election," *supra.*

31. Marisa Schultz, "CNN drops Brazile for feeding debate questions to Clinton" (*New York Post*, Oct. 31, 2016).

32. Chuck Ross, "Exclusive: Cambridge Prof with CIA, MI6 Ties Met with Trump Adviser During Campaign, Beyond" (The Daily Caller, May 17, 2018); Jerry Dunleavy, "Stefan Halper: The Cambridge don the FBI sent to spy on Trump" (*Washington Examiner*, Apr. 10, 2019).

33. It was not until a private briefing in August that CIA Director Brennan informed Senate Majority Leader Harry Reid that Russia was responsible for hacking the DNC...and suggested that Trump could be complicit. Isikoff and Corn, *Russian Roulette*, *supra*; Scarborough, "Obama aide started Christopher Steele-FBI alliance," *supra.*

CHAPTER 12

1. Josh Marshal, "Trump & Putin. Yes, It's Really a Thing" (Talking Points Memo, Jul. 23, 2016); Strzok-Page Texts, Justice Department Production to Senate Judiciary Committee (2018), pp. 0000199 & ff.

2. In point of fact, as Byron York has related, the party platform was tough on the Kremlin, promising to "meet the return of Russian belligerence with the same resolve that le to the collapse of the Soviet Union," and to refuse to "accept territorial change in Eastern Europe imposed by force, in Ukraine or elsewhere." One delegate proposed an amendment, urging the provision of "lethal defense weapons." One Trump campaign national-security adviser, J. D. Gordon, found this objectionable as not in keeping with the candidate's preference to improve relations with Russia and induce Europeans to take more responsibility for European conflicts. Trump never weighed in on the platform. Gordon suggested tweaking "lethal defense weapons" to "appropriate assistance." He claims not to have gotten firm guidance on this point from his campaign superiors; the campaign's policy director, John Mashburn, says he countered that the candidate had not taken a position so the campaign should not interfere. Meanwhile, the alternative language was adopted, with Mashburn concluding Gordon had disregarded his directive that the campaign take a hands-off approach to the platform. Mueller Report, Vol. I, pp. 124-27; York, "What really happened with the GOP platform and Russia" (*Washington Examiner*, Nov. 26, 2017).

3. Matt Apuzzo, Adam Goldman, and Nicholas Fandos, "Code Name Crossfire Hurricane: The Secret Origins of the Trump Investigation" (*The New York Times*, May 16, 2018); Andrew C. McCarthy, "The Strzok-Page

Texts and the Origins of the Trump–Russia Investigation" (*National Review*, May 14, 2018).

4.   Michael Burke, "Brennan on Mueller summary: 'I suspected there was more than there actually was'" (*The Hill*, Mar. 25, 2019).

5.   Andrew C. McCarthy, "The Steele Dossier and the 'Verified Application' That Wasn't" (*National Review*, May 18, 2018); Gregg Re and Catherine Herridge, "Dispute erupts over whether Brennan, Comey pushed Steele dossier, as DOJ probe into misconduct begins" (Fox News, May 15, 2019).

6.   Greg Miller, Ellen Nakashima, and Adam Entous, "Obama's secret struggle to punish Russia for Putin's election assault" (*The Washington Post*, Jun. 23, 2017).

7.   These are the Senate majority and minority leaders, the Speaker of the House and the House minority leader, and the chairperson and ranking member of both the Senate Select Committee on Intelligence and the House Permanent Select Committee on Intelligence. In summer 2016, these were, respectively, Senators Mitch McConnell and Harry Reid, Speaker Paul Ryan and Minority Leader Nancy Pelosi, Senators Richard Burr and Dianne Feinstein, and Representatives Devin Nunes and Adam Schiff.

      See, e.g., Title 50, U.S. Code, Section 3093(c)(2).

8.   Chris Cillizza, "Harry Reid lied about Mitt Romney's taxes. He's still not sorry." (*The Washington Post*, Sept. 15, 2016).

9.   Brennan Testimony, House Intelligence Committee (May 23, 2017); Jeff Carlson, "John Brennan Heads for the Exits" (*The Epoch Times*, May 25, 2017).

10.   Letter of Senator Harry Reid (D., Nev.), Minority Leader, to FBI Director James Comey (Aug. 27, 2018).

11.   See Lee Smith, "How CIA Director John Brennan Targeted James Comey—The Russia investigation put the FBI in a bind well before Trump ever landed in the White House" (*Tablet Magazine*, Feb. 9, 2018).

12.   Stefan A. Halper and Jonathan Clarke, *The Silence of the Rational Center: Why American Foreign Policy is Failing* (Basic Books, 2007); see also Halper and Clarke, *America Alone: The Neo-Conservatives and the Global Order* (Cambridge University Press, 2004). To be sure, Halper's thoughtful work would appeal to Trump supporters' distaste for the Wilsonian impulses of Bush-43 foreign policy, particularly the "pre-emptive" war in Iraq and "Big Ideas" like Islamic democracy promotion. Halper, however, is a devotee of Trump's bugaboo, "the Swamp," arguing for more reliance on the stabilizing influence of government experts, think-tankers, and academics, rather than what he regards as sloganeering and appeals to emotion and bias.

13.   Andrew Kaczynski, "Trump in 2008: Hillary Clinton will 'go down at a

minimum as a great senator'" (CNN, Oct. 19, 2016).

14. Khorri Atkinson, "Trump meets with Kissinger for the third time" (Axios, Feb. 8, 2018).

15. Byron York, "Trump campaign vet: Informant used me to get to Papadopoulos" (*Washington Examiner*, May 28, 2018).

16. Adam Goldman, Michael S. Schmidt, and Mark Mazzetti, "F.B.I. Sent Investigator Posing as Assistant to Meet With Trump Aide in 2016" (*The New York Times*, May 2, 2019).

17. *Ibid.*

18. *Ibid.*; see also Dunleavy, "Stefan Halper: The Cambridge don the FBI sent to spy on Trump," *supra* (noting that the FBI tasked Halper to meet with Page and Papadopoulos, but that "it is not known if [Halper's contact with Clovis] was done with the authorization of the FBI").

19. Goldman et al., "F.B.I. Sent Investigator Posing as Assistant to Meet With Trump Aide in 2016," *supra*.

20. Chuck Ross, "Cambridge Professor Spied on Trump Campaign Advisers" (The Daily Caller, May 19, 2018).

21. Chuck Ross, "Papadopoulos Details His Interactions with 'Spygate' Figure and Steele Source" (The Daily Caller, Sept. 8, 2018); Marshall Cohen, "Papadopoulos breaks silence, 'can't guarantee he didn't tell Trump campaign about Russian dirt'" (CNN, Sept. 8, 2018); Ross, "Exclusive: Cambridge Prof with CIA, MI6 Ties Met with Trump Adviser During Campaign, Beyond" (The Daily Caller, May 17, 2018); Daniel Chaitan, "FBI informant's assistant who met George Papadopoulos was undercover" (*Washington Examiner*, May 2, 2019); Goldman et al, "F.B.I. Sent Investigator Posing as Assistant to Meet With Trump Aide in 2016," *supra*.

22. Goldman et al, "F.B.I. Sent Investigator Posing as Assistant to Meet With Trump Aide in 2016," *supra*.

23. Papadopoulos later falsely told *The Washington Post* that the Trump campaign had arranged the interview, told him what to say, and complimented him afterward; in fact, the Russian outlet *Interfax* contacted Papadopoulos directly, and, though the campaign authorized him to do the interview, its reaction was disapproving. T. A. Frank, "The Surreal Life of George Papadopoulos" (*Washington Post Magazine*, May 20, 2019).

24. Rosalind Helderman and Tom Hamburger, "Sergey Millian, identified as an unwitting source for the Steele dossier, sought proximity to Trump's world in 2016" (*The Washington Post*, Feb. 7, 2019); Ross, "Papadopoulos Details His Interactions with 'Spygate' Figure and Steele Source," *supra*; Brooke Singman, "Ex-Trump campaign aide George Papadopoulos says FBI asked him to wear a wire: transcript" (Fox News, Mar. 29, 2019); George

Papadopoulos, *Deep State Target: How I Got Caught in the Crosshairs of the Plot to Bring Down President Trump* (Diversion Books, 2019).

25. Mueller Report, Vol. I, p. 94.

26. Josh Gerstein, "George Papadopoulos' late night with the FBI—'Law enforcement likes to get somebody's attention as much as they can in a lawful way,' one of his lawyers said of the July arrest" (*Politico*, Dec. 4, 2017); Singman, "Ex-Trump campaign aide George Papadopoulos says FBI asked him to wear a wire: transcript," *supra*.

CHAPTER 13

1. Jessica Durando, "Trump says 'I have nothing to do with Russia.' That's not exactly true" (*USA Today*, Jan. 11, 2017); Donald J. Trump (@realDonaldTrump) Jan. 11, 2019, Tweet.

2. Cohen is the infamous figure at the center of payoffs made to the pornographic actress "Stormy Daniels" (real name Stephanie Clifford) and former *Playboy* model Karen McDougal to buy their silence about trysts they claim to have had with Donald Trump about a decade before he ran for president. In addition to tax- and bank-fraud offenses, Cohen has pled guilty to election-law violations, on the legally debatable theory that the nondisclosure payments were in-kind campaign contributions required to be reported under federal law. In entering his plea in Manhattan federal court (the Southern District of New York), Cohen allocuted that Donald Trump had directed him to make the payments. Subsequently, Cohen pled guilty in the Mueller probe to lying to Congress about the temporal extent of the Trump Tower Moscow negotiations. Andrew C. McCarthy, "Cohen's Congressional Testimony Portends Danger for Trump" (*National Review*, Mar. 7, 2019); McCarthy, "Takeaways from the House Democrats' Cohen Hearing" (*National Review*, Mar. 1, 2019); McCarthy, "Trump Tower Meeting Silently Looms Over Cohen's False-Statements Plea" (*National Review*, Nov. 29, 2018); McCarthy, "On Hush Money, the President's Best Defense Is Lack of Criminal Intent" (*National Review*, Aug. 25, 2018).

3. *United States v. Michael Cohen*, No. 18 Crim. 850 (S.D.N.Y., 2018), Criminal Information (Nov. 2018); Ilya Arkhipov, "Russia's Peskov Shares 2016 Emails from Ex-Trump Lawyer Cohen" (Bloomberg, Nov. 30, 2018).

4. We met Sater briefly in Chapter 9 (endnote 33), detailing the surmise, never established as fact, that he was a source for the Steele dossier; as well as the intriguing fact that he was prosecuted and induced to become an informant by Loretta Lynch and Andrew Weissmann Obama's attorney general, and the chief of the Obama Justice Department's fraud section, respectively—and, later, Robert Mueller's deputy in the Trump–Russia probe. On the

question whether Sater was a Steele source, it should be noted that there is nothing in the Steele dossier about Trump Tower Moscow; to the contrary, the dossier states that while the Kremlin had tried to entice Trump with favorable real-estate deals, Trump did not bite. In fact, Trump had a major real-estate deal under negotiation, but there is no evidence that the Kremlin initiated it...though, in Russia, regime approval would plainly be needed for a project of that kind—which is why Cohen was talking to Peskov's office. See also Matt Apuzzo and Maggie Haberman, "Trump Associate Boasted That Moscow Business Deal 'Will Get Donald Elected'" (*The New York Times*, Aug. 28, 2017). See also Grace Segers, "Who is Felix Sater and what's his role in Michael Cohen's plea deal?" (CBS News, Nov. 29, 2018); Kerry Picket, "House Intel Witness Felix Sater Was Part of Loretta Lynch's Secret Docket" (The Daily Caller, Mar. 2, 2019); Chuck Ross, "Russian-born Businessman Linked to Trump Claims to Have Been US Spy" (The Daily Caller, Mar. 12, 2018).

5.   Medvedev is Russia's prime minister and Putin's flunkey. He kept the president's chair warm for four years beginning in 2008 so the dictator could pretend to honor Russia's constitutional term limits. In 2012, Putin went back to being president and Medvedev (who had been deputy prime minster prior to standing in as president in 2008) became being prime minister—all elected in Russia's thriving democracy, of course.

6.   Cameron Sperance, "Meet Aras Agalarov, The Russian Developer Connecting the Trumps and Putin" (*Forbes*, Jul. 12, 2017); David Ignatius, "A History of Donald Trump's business dealings in Russia" (*The Washington Post*, Nov. 2, 2017); Michael Birnbaum, "Here's what the businessman who brokered the Russia meeting with Trump Jr. said in an interview last year" (*The Washington Post*, Jul. 11, 2017).

7.   Andrew C. McCarthy, "A Second Fusion GPS Dossier Implicated Clinton Foundation Donors" (*National Review*, Nov. 10, 2017).

8.   *United States v. Prevezon Holdings LTD, et al.*, No. 13 Civ. 632 (TPG) (S.D.N.Y. 2018), Complaint (Sept. 10, 2013).

9.   Jamila Trindle, "The Magnitsky Flip-Flop—The Obama administration was against Russia sanctions before it was for them" (*Foreign Policy*, May 15, 2014).

10.   Safely back in Russia, Ms. Veselnitskaya will never be extradited to face U.S. prosecution. *United States v. Natalya Vladimirovna Veselnitskaya*, No. 18 Cr. 908 (S.D.N.Y. 2018), Indictment (Jan. 8, 2018); Benjamin Weiser and Sharon LaFraniere, "Veselnitskaya, Russian in Trump Tower Meeting, Is Charged in Case That Shows Kremlin Ties" (*The New York Times*, Jan. 8, 2019).

11.   Putin is peddling the claim that Browder, not the Kremlin, is the mastermind of the fraud. He managed to have Browder, a British national, placed on an

Interpol watch list in hopes of apprehending him. Remarkably, even as it sued Prevezon on theory that the regime was the culprit, the U.S. government revoked Browder's passport based on Putin's machinations. The revocation has since been lifted. See "Interpol Should Remove William Browder from Its Watch List" (*National Review*, Oct. 24, 2017); Jay Nordlinger, "Why Is Bill Browder Banned from America?" (*National Review*, Oct. 22, 2017); see also Bill Browder, *Red Notice—A True Story of High Finance, Murder, and One Man's Fight for Justice* (Simon & Schuster, 2015); David J. Kramer, "I'm on Putin's hit list but I'm not the real victim" (*Politico*, Jul. 22, 2018).

12. Glenn Simpson Senate Testimony, *supra*, pp. 114, 131-35.

13. Simpson Senate Testimony, *supra*, pp. 27-52, 83, 99-101, 107-36. Edward Baumgarten, a Russian translator, worked on both cases, as did Simpson himself.

14. *Forbes* ranks the Ziff family as among the nation's wealthiest. Three brothers, Daniel, Robert, and Dirk, used a vehicle called Ziff Brothers Investments for various purposes, including political donations. Russia's general prosecutor, Yuri Chaika, announced in June 2017 that his agency had presented to U.S. officials "serious evidence of violations of the law by Browder and the Ziff brothers." Russia's Browder obsession was on display in June 2018, when Putin met with President Trump in Helsinki; the Russian strongman repeated his standing allegation that Browder and his associates have evaded taxes on over a billion dollars in Russian income, then added the absurd claim that "they sent a huge amount—$400 million—as a contribution to the campaign of Hillary Clinton." Andrew C. McCarthy, "Trump Bites on Putin's 'Incredible Offer'" (*National Review*, Jul. 21, 2018); David Kocieniewski, Greg Farrell, Peter Robinson, and Bob Van Voris, "Russian Lawyer Who Met Trump Jr. Saw Clinton Scandal in Tax Inquiry" (*Forbes*, Jul. 12, 2017); "Ziff Family Profile" (*Forbes*, Jun. 29, 2016) (estimating net worth at $14.4 billion); Mueller Report, Vol. I, p. 117.

15. Jo Becker, Matt Apuzzo, and Adam Goldman, "Trump's Son Met With Russian Lawyer After Being Promised Damaging Information on Clinton" (*The New York Times*, Jul. 9, 2017).

16. Simpson Senate Testimony, *supra*, pp. 114-19, 131-35.

17. Mueller Report, Vol. I, pp. 114-15.

18. Sharon LaFraniere, David D. Kirkpatrick, and Kenneth Vogel, "Lobbyist at Trump Campaign Meeting Has a Web of Russian Connections" (*The New York Times*, Aug. 21, 2017); Mike Eckel, "Who Is Rinat Akhmetshin, the Russian-American Lobbyist Who Met With Trump's Son?" (Radio Free Europe/Radio Liberty, Jul. 14, 2017); Simpson Senate Testimony, *supra*, pp. 107-13, 121, 254, 273-74.

19. In December 2016, Simpson assured Justice Department official Bruce Ohr (according to Ohr's notes, "Much of the collection about the Trump cam-

paign ties to Russia comes from a former Russian intelligence officer (? not entirely clear) who lives in the U.S." Lee Smith reports that Akhmetshin "served in the Soviet Union's military counterintelligence service"; *The New York Times* is less assertive, reporting that Akhmetshin "worked with a military counterintelligence unit" after being drafted at age 18 to fight in the Red Army's war in Afghanistan, "but said he never joined Russian intelligence services—unlike his father, sister and godfather." As we noted in Chapter 12, Steele told the State Department that Vyacheslav Trubnikov, the former head of Russia's external intelligence service, was one of his main sources. Unlike Akhmetshin, Trubnikov is not U.S.-based, and his intelligence experience is with the KGB and the SVR, not military intelligence (GRU). Interestingly, Simpson, who was trying to protect sources when he testified before the Senate, told congressional investigators that he does not know whether Steele knows Akhmetshin. Lee Smith, "2016 Trump Tower Meeting Looks Increasingly Like a Setup by Russian and Clinton Operatives" (RealClearInvestigations, Aug. 13, 2018); John Solomon, "The handwritten notes exposing what Fusion GPS told DOJ about Trump" (*The Hill*, Aug. 9, 2018); LaFraniere, et al., "Lobbyist at Trump Campaign Meeting Has a Web of Russian Connections," *supra*; Simpson Senate Testimony, *supra*, pp. 254, 273-74.

20. Mueller Report, Vol. I., pp. 114-19.

21. *Ibid.*; see also Erik Larson and Bloomberg, "Why the Infamous Trump Tower Meeting Didn't Take Down Trump" (*Fortune*, Apr. 20, 2019).

22. *Ibid.*

23. Mueller Report, Vol. II, pp. 98-105; Jo Becker, Matt Apuzzo, and Adam Goldman, "Trump Team Met With Lawyer Linked to Kremlin During Campaign" (*The New York Times*, Jul. 8, 2017).

24. Mueller Report, Vol. II, p. 105 & n.732 (citing remarks by President Trump in a Jun. 15, 2018, press gaggle).

25. Andrew C. McCarthy, "The Curious Case of Natalia Veselnitskaya" (*National Review*, Jul. 19, 2017).

CHAPTER 14

1. Director Comey was scathing in his critique of Mrs. Clinton's misconduct, even if he announced the conclusion that it did not reach the threshold of criminality worth prosecuting. Lisa Page, who has been portrayed in right-leaning media as the second coming of Emma Goldman, is a law-and-order-oriented former organized-crime prosecutor who was proud to work in an FBI she regarded as a conservative institution and opined in her House testimony that, while her politics were irrelevant to her professional judgments, she was not a Hillary Clinton fan (though she did not find her as "loathsome" as she

described Donald Trump to be—and, like many Americans of diverse sensibilities, she was angered by candidate Trump's unwise decision to engage in a political back-and-forth with Gold Star Muslim parents (of slain U.S. Captain Humayan Kahn) who dissented from his immigration policies). Page House Testimony, pp. 84-85. Similarly, Justice Department official Bruce Ohr did not tell his direct boss, Obama-appointed Deputy Attorney General Sally Yates, about his interactions with Christopher Steele because he thought the matter should be dealt with by career investigators rather than political appointees. Ohr House Testimony, pp. 86-87.

2.   Grassley-Graham Memo, *supra*, p. 2.

3   The IG used an analytical formula by which, if there were potentially proper and improper motivations for a particular investigative action, law-enforcement officials were entitled to a presumption of proper motivation. As a practical matter, that meant there could be no conclusively biased decision unless the action involved was indisputably improper—in which case, of course, the action would be condemnable irrespective of motive. In most inquiries into abuse of power, that line of reasoning would never find abuse of power. See Andrew C. McCarthy, "The IG's Report May Be Half-Baked" (*National Review*, Jun. 14, 2018).

4.   Isikoff and Corn, *Russian Roulette, supra*.

5.   Lee Smith, "Unpacking the Other Clinton-Linked Russia Dossier" (RealClearInvestigations, Apr. 26, 2018).

6.   James Comey, *A Higher Loyalty: Truth, Lies, and Leadership* (Flatiron Books, 2018); Matthew Yglesias, "James Comey admits that his read of the polls may have influenced his handling of the Clinton email probe" (Vox, Apr. 13, 2018); cf. Justice Dept. Inspector General Report, *supra*, p. x ("Much like with his July 5 announcement, we found that in making this decision, Comey engaged in ad hoc decisionmaking based on his personal views even if it meant rejecting longstanding Department policy or practice. We found unpersuasive Comey's explanation as to why transparency was more important than Department policy and practice with regard to the reactivated Midyear investigation while, by contrast, Department policy and practice were more important to follow with regard to the Clinton Foundation and Russia investigations.").

7.   Del Quentin Wilber, "In FBI Agent's Account, 'Insurance Policy' Text Referred to Russia Probe" (*The Wall Street Journal*, Dec. 18, 2017). The same cannot be said, alas, for any irresponsible person. Katie Leach, "Fox News guest suggests FBI employees plotted Trump's assassination" (*Washington Examiner*, Dec. 19, 2017).

8.   Ashley Parker and David E. Sanger, "Donald Trump Calls on Russia to Find Hillary Clinton's Missing Emails" (*The New York Times*, Jul. 27, 2016).

9.   Always long on innuendo and short on incriminating proof, Special Counsel

Mueller's prosecutors dutifully alleged that, hours after Trump's sophomoric statement, a Russian military intelligence unit unsuccessfully targeted candidate Clinton's personal office with malware, attempting to compromise email accounts. There is, naturally, no evidence offered of a causative link between Trump's statement and Russia's malevolence. Not do prosecutors offer an evidence-based reason to believe that anyone (Trump, Russia, *anyone*) believed the private-server emails—to which Mueller acknowledges Trump was referring—were stored in office accounts. Indeed, Mueller concluded that there was Trump–Russia conspiracy, so he implicitly found that the misconduct he insinuates did not happen—though that doesn't stop him from making the insinuation, resuscitating the Democrats' political collusion narrative. Mueller Report, Vol. I, p. 49.

10.   Later, at their Helsinki summit, Trump appeared to side with Putin against the conclusion of American intelligence agencies that Russia is responsible for hacking Democratic emails; moreover, he seemed to take seriously Putin's laughable offer to have Russia's investigators work with Special Counsel Mueller on the hacking case. And at a cabinet meeting at the start of 2019, the president made the astonishingly ignorant claim that the reason the Soviet Union had invaded Afghanistan in 1979 "was because terrorists were going into Russia.... They were right to be there." Andrew C. McCarthy, "Trump Bites on Putin's 'Incredible Offer'" (*National Review*, Jul. 21, 2018).

11.   Donald J. Trump (@realDonaldTrump) May 25, 2019, Tweet.

12.   Phillip Rucker and Josh Dawsey, "'We fell in love': Trump and Kim shower praise, stroke egos on path to nuclear negotiations" (*The Washington Post*, Feb. 25, 2019).

13.   "'Journalism for rent': Inside the secretive firm behind the Trump dossier" (*The Washington Post*, Dec. 11, 2017).

14.   Simpson further told congressional investigators that his postelection contact with Ohr was either at Ohr's request or orchestrated by Steele. In fact, it was set in motion by Simpson, who asked to meet Ohr on December 10, gave Ohr a memory stick that Ohr believed contained Steele's dossier, and pressed Ohr to have the Justice Department investigate the Alfa Bank server connection that purportedly served as a Trump–Russia back channel. Bruce Ohr House Testimony, pp. 13, 40-42, 73-74, 175-89; Simpson House Testimony, pp. 77-80; Byron York, "Ohr, Simpson—with Russian oligarch in the background" (*Washington Examiner*, Aug. 8, 2018).

15.   York, "Ohr, Simpson—with Russian oligarch in the background," *supra*; "Judicial Watch Uncovers DOJ Records Showing Numerous Bruce Ohr Communications with Fusion GPS and Christopher Steele" (Judicial Watch, Mar. 7, 2019).

16.   *Gubarev et al. v. Orbis and Steele*, Defendants' Response to Claimants'

Request for Further Information, *supra*, p. 8; Chuck Ross, "Here's How the Steele Dossier Spread through the Media and Government" (The Daily Caller, Mar. 18, 2019).

17. Michael Isikoff, "U.S. intel officials probe ties between Trump adviser and Kremlin" (Yahoo News, Sept. 23, 2016).

18. Micah Morrison, "Hillary Clinton's rogue agenda: Why Sidney Blumenthal matters" (*New York Post*, Oct. 31, 2015); John Cook, "Hacked Emails Show Hillary Clinton Was Receiving Advice at a Private Email Account From Banned, Obama-Hating Former Staffer" (Gawker, Oct. 1, 2015); David Goldstein, "2 Clinton supporters in '08 reportedly shared Obama 'birther' story" (McClatchy, Sept. 16, 2016).

19. Shearer's brother-in-law is Strobe Talbot, President Clinton's close friend from Oxford who was a deputy secretary in Clinton's State Department, and his brother was a Clinton State Department ambassador. Shearer and his sister are alleged to have worked with Clinton enforcer Terry Lenzner to intimidate women positioned to accuse President Clinton of sexual improprieties. Shearer was also enmeshed in a bizarre controversy during the Bosnia war, in which he persuaded Serbian elements to pay him $25,000 to orchestrate negotiations with the Clinton administration that would prevent President Radovan Kardzic—the war criminal who directed the Srebrenica genocide—from being captured by military forces. Shearer worked closely with Blumenthal over the years, and was involved in composing the confidential intelligence memos about Libya that Blumenthal emailed to Clinton. Brendan Bordelon, "Meet Cody Shearer, the Strangest Character in Hillary's Vast Left-Wing Conspiracy" (*National Review*, Jun. 1, 2015); Rowan Scarborough, "Clinton's 'Mr. Fixer,' ally Sidney Blumenthal emerge on list of Russia collusion figures" (*The Washington Times*, Jan. 31, 2018).

20. Lee Smith, "Unpacking the Other Clinton-Linked Russia Dossier" (RealClearInvestigations, Apr. 26, 2018).

21. Jonathan M. Winer, "Devin Nunes is investigating me. Here's the truth." (*The Washington Post*, Feb. 8, 2018).

22. Jack Crowe, "Gowdy Claims FBI Relied on Clinton Ally Blumenthal to Corroborate Steele Dossier" (*National Review*, May 15, 2019).

23. Susan B. Glasser, "Victoria Nuland: The Full Transcript" (*Politico Magazine*, Feb. 25, 2018).

24. Eric Felten, "Victoria Nuland Can't Keep Her Steele Story Straight" (*The Weekly Standard*, Jun. 21, 2018).

25. Tom Hamburger and Rosalind S. Helderman, "Hero or hired gun? How a British former spy became a flash point in the Russia investigation." (*The Washington Post*, Feb. 6, 2018); Glenn Simpson Senate Testimony, *supra*, pp. 174-75.

26. Hamburger and Helderman, "Hero or hired gun," *supra*; Isikoff and Corn, *Russian Roulette, supra*, pp. 232-33; Jane Mayer, "Christopher Steele, the Man Behind the Trump Dossier" (*The New Yorker*, Mar. 5, 2018).

27. Byron York, "Years later, Trump dossier still frustrates verification efforts" (*Washington Examiner*, Mar. 21, 2019).

CHAPTER 15

1. Andrew C. McCarthy, "The Wall Truth" (*National Review*, Apr. 19, 2004).

2. See U.S. Const., Amendment VI ("In all criminal prosecutions, the accused shall enjoy the right to a speedy and public trial, by an impartial jury of the State and district wherein the crime shall have been committed...").

3. The firm later dubiously claimed that Sussmann was not involved in the firm's representation of the DNC and the Clinton campaign at the time of the meeting with Baker. As we have already detailed, Sussmann was the Perkins Coie lawyer who retained CrowdStrike on behalf of the DNC when its computers had been hacked. Baker testified that he had read in the press that Perkins Coie was representing the Clinton campaign and the DNC, but he did not recall whether Sussmann told him that at the time of their meeting. Baker House Testimony, *supra*, pp. 52-53.

4. James Baker Testimony before the House Judiciary and Oversight Committees (Oct. 3, 2018), pp. 43-51.

5. Baker House Testimony, *supra*, pp. 43-51, 113-17. The House Intelligence Committee later noted in its report on Russia's interference in the election that Baker had taken anti-Trump information from a person—now known to be Sussmann—who was concurrently supplying that information to the press. House Intelligence Committee Report on Russian Active Measures, *supra*, p. 57 & n.43; Kimberley A. Strassel, "Who Is Michael Sussmann? FBI's general counsel met with a Clinton lawyer in September 2016" (*The Wall Street Journal*, Oct. 11, 2018).

6. At the time of his testimony, Baker was under investigation for media leaks. He admitted sharing information related to the Russia investigation with Corn, but declined to say what the information was. Baker House Testimony, *supra*, pp. 35-51. See also Jeff Carlson, "Baker Testimony Reveals Perkins Coie Lawyer Provided FBI With Information on Alfa Bank Allegations" (*The Epoch Times*, Jan. 21, 2019).

7. David Corn, "A Veteran Spy Has Given the FBI Information Alleging a Russian Operation to Cultivate Donald Trump—Has the bureau investigated this material?" (*Mother Jones*, Oct. 31, 2016); FBI Director James Comey Letter to Various Senate and House Committee Chairmen (Oct. 28, 2016).

8. House Report on Russian Active Measures, *supra*, p. 143 (Nunes Memo, *supra*, at p. 2).

9. Glen Caplin, "Hillary for America Statement on Bombshell Report About Trump Aide's Chilling Ties to Kremlin" (*Milwaukee Courier*, Sept. 24, 2016).

10. Carter Page Letter to FBI Director James Comey (Sept. 25, 2016).

11. Carter Page Letter to Frank Walter-Steinmeier, Chairman-in-Office, Organization for Security and Co-operation in Europe, and Dame Audrey Glover, Head of OSCE/ODIHR Election Observation Mission, United States (Oct. 28, 2016).

12. Page-Strzok Texts, *supra*; Andrew McCabe-Lisa Page Texts, Oct. 12-15, 2016; Sharyl Attkisson, "Senate probes FBI's heavy-handed use of redactions to obstruct congressional investigations" (*The Hill*, Jun. 14, 2018); Gregg Re, "FBI clashed with DOJ over potential 'bias' of source for surveillance warrant: McCabe-Page texts" (Fox News, Mar. 22, 2019); John Solomon, "Steele's stunning pre-FISA confession: Informant needed to air Trump dirt before election" (*The Hill*, May 7, 2019).

13. Matthew Rosenberg and Matt Apuzzo, "Court Approved Wiretap on Trump Campaign Aide Over Russia Ties" (*The New York Times*, Apr. 17, 2017) (FISC issued the warrant, an unidentified government official said, "after investigators determined that Mr. Page was no longer part of the Trump campaign, which began distancing itself from him in early August"; "The Justice Department considered direct surveillance of anyone tied to a political campaign as a line it did not want to cross, the official added"; "The official was not aware of any instances in which an active member of Mr. Trump's campaign was directly surveilled by American law-enforcement or spy agencies, though some Trump associates were swept up in surveillance of foreign officials.").

14. See Page Letter to Walter-Steinmeier et al. (Oct. 28, 2016), *supra* ("I am not currently affiliated with any political campaign"); David Cohen, "Conway denies Trump campaign ties to Russia figure" (*Politico*, Sept. 25, 2016); Margot Cleveland, "Carter Page: Obama's FBI, DOJ May Have Spied on Trump Admin, Not Just Campaign" (*The Federalist*, May 21, 2019) (Page continued to stay in touch with Trump officials, including during transition and into new administration).

15. See, e.g., Gina Stevens and Charles Doyle, "Privacy: An Overview of Federal Statutes Governing Wiretapping and Electronic Eavesdropping" (Congressional Research Service, Oct. 9, 2012) (see especially Chapter 121, "Stored Communications Act," explaining that standards for government access to stored wire and electronic communications are less demanding than showing required for real-time eavesdropping warrants); Stored Communications Act, Title 18 U.S. Code, Sec. 2701 et seq.; compare Edward C. Liu, "Surveillance of Foreigners Outside the United States Under Section 702 of the Foreign Intelligence Surveillance Act (FISA)" (Congressional Research

Service, Apr. 13, 2016) p. 2 (noting that focus on "electronic communications" includes "electronically stored information").

16. Nicholas Fandos and Adam Goldman, "Barr Asserts Intelligence Agencies Spied on the Trump Campaign" (*The New York Times*, Apr. 19, 2019).

17. In re Carter W. Page, a U.S. Person, U.S. Foreign Intelligence Surveillance Court, four warrant packages.

18. See, e.g., House Intelligence Committee Report, *supra*, p. 142; Gregg Re and Catherine Herridge, "FBI clashed with DOJ over potential 'bias' of source for surveillance warrant: McCabe-Page texts" (Fox News, Mar. 22, 2019).

19. House Intelligence Committee Chairman Devin Nunes Letter to Attorney General Jeff Sessions (Mar. 1, 2018); Nick Short, "FISA Court, Woods Procedures and Carter Page" (PoliticallyShort.com, Apr. 20, 2019); Sharyl Attkisson, "Nunes memo raises question: Did FBI violate Woods Procedures?" (*The Hill*, Feb. 4, 2018).

20. On May 23, 2019, President Trump issued an order conferring on Attorney General William P. Barr the authority to declassify documents. The exercise of that authority is taking place in consultation with relevant intelligence agencies to ensure the safeguarding of intelligence that should remain classified, particularly intelligence methods and sources. The fact that information may be declassified, moreover, does not mean that it will perforce become public. It may be a long time before we have a full picture—or as full as we will be permitted to have. The White House, "Presidential Memorandum on Agency Cooperation with Attorney General's Review of Intelligence Activities Relating to the 2016 Presidential Campaigns" (May 23, 2019); Andrew C. McCarthy, "Bill Barr's Declassification Kerfuffle" (*National Review*, May 28, 2019).

21. See, e.g., Grassley-Graham memo, *supra*; House Intelligence Committee Report, *supra*, p. 51.

22. Ellen Nakashima, Devlin Barrett, and Adam Entous, "FBI obtained FISA warrant to monitor former Trump advisor Carter Page" (*The Washington Post*, Apr. 11, 2017).

23. Compare the testimony of Director Comey's then-general counsel, James Baker, who explained that he reviewed only the probable-cause section of the application, not the accompanying sections mandated by statute. Baker House Testimony, *supra*, pp. 94-95.

24. Title 50, U.S. Code, Section 1804.

25. The other eight sections do not bear on probable cause. They direct the government to supply: the identity of the applying officer and the target, a statement of the "minimization procedures" the FBI will use to avoid unauthorized monitoring, a description of the nature of the information sought (i.e., foreign intelligence), certifications by high-ranking national-security officials

that the government is seeking foreign intelligence, an explanation of how the eavesdropping will be carried out, a recitation of any prior applications related to the target, and a statement of the proposed duration of the surveillance.

26. The FBI's then-General Counsel, James Baker, explained that when he reviewed the FISA warrant application, he confined himself to the section addressing probable cause because most of the rest of the application deals with legal requirements that are standard in all FISA applications. Baker House Testimony, *supra*, pp. 93-95.

27. Oct. 21, 2016, FISA Warrant Application, pp. 15-17 n.8.

28. Schiff Memo, *supra*.

29. Smith, "Unpacking the other Clinton-Linked Russia Dossier," *supra*.

30. Schiff Memo, *supra*.

31. October 21, 2016 FISA Warrant Application, pp. 23 n.18.

32. January 2017 FISA Warrant Renewal Application, p. 17 n.8.

33. FISC Rules, *supra*, Rule 13 (p. 5).

34. Margot Cleveland, "Has the DOJ Closed Its Inquiry Into Dossier Fabulist Christopher Steele" (*The Federalist*, Apr. 19, 2019); Elena Schor, "Grassley, Graham release copy of request for criminal probe of dossier author" (*Politico*, Feb. 5, 2018).

35. Inspector General's Report, *supra*, pp. xii, 395-424 (describing "cultural" problem: "although FBI policy strictly limits the employees who are authorized to speak to the media, we found that this policy appeared to be widely ignored during the period we reviewed"). Note that Deputy Director McCabe was fired after the inspector general found that he "lacked candor" in answering investigator's questions during a leak investigation. See U.S. Dept. of Justice, Office of Inspector General, "A Report of Investigation of Certain Allegations Relating to Former FBI Deputy Director Andrew McCabe" (Feb. 2018); Andrew C. McCarthy, "McCabe: Leaking and Lying Obscure the Real Collusion" (*National Review*, Apr. 21, 2018). Moreover, as this book goes to press, the inspector general has released a curt investigative summary indicating that a thus-far unidentified Bureau official who matches the description of Strzok (a former FBI deputy assistant director) committed misconduct by leaking sensitive information to the media, though the Justice Department declined to prosecute. U.S. Dept. of Justice, Office of Inspector General, "Findings of Misconduct by an FBI Deputy Assistant Director for Unauthorized Contacts with the Media, Disclosing Law Enforcement and Other Sensitive Information to the Media, an Accepting a Gift from the Media" (Investigative Summary, May 29, 2019). As already noted, the FBI's former General Counsel James Baker refused to answer some questions by House investigators, explaining that he was under criminal investigation in connection with media leaks.

36. U.S. Dept. of Justice, Practice Manual, "Electronic Surveillance—Title III Affidavits"; see also Title 50, U.S. Code, Section 1804(a)(6)(C) (FISA); Title 18, U.S. Code, Section 2518(1)(E) (Title III criminal wiretaps).

37. As we saw in Chapter 13, the Russians had far better ways to approach Trump, such as the Kremlin-connected oligarch Aras Agalarov, who had a personal relationship with the now-president and orchestrated the infamous June 2016 Trump Tower meeting.

CHAPTER 16

1. Letter of Senators Charles E. Grassley and Lindsey O. Graham to The Honorable Susan Rice (and counsel) (U.S. Senate Judiciary Committee, Feb. 8, 2018), excerpting Rice email-to-self (Jan. 20, 2017, 12:15 p.m.).

2. Jeff Jacoby, "Obama repeats the myth that his administration was free of scandal" (*Boston Globe*, Mar. 6, 2018).

3. Andrew C. McCarthy, "Completely Missing the Point on Lisa Page's Obama Text" (*National Review*, Feb. 18, 2018).

4. Andrew C. McCarthy, "The Strzok-Page Texts and the Origins of the Trump–Russia Investigation" (*National Review*, May 14, 2018).

5. Jack Holmes, "Here Are Some of the Propaganda Facebook Ads Russia Ran During the 2016 Election—Some are funny, but they're all sad" (Esquire. com, Nov. 1, 2017).

6. House Permanent Select Committee on Intelligence (HPSCI), "Report on Russian Active Measures" (Mar. 22, 2018), pp. 44-45; Greg Miller, Ellen Nakashima, and Adam Entous, "Obama's secret struggle to punish Russia for Putin's election assault" (*The Washington Post*, Jun. 23, 2017).

7. Isikoff and Corn, *Russian Roulette*, *supra*; Christian Datoc, "Obama's cybersecurity coordinator confirms Susan Rice ordered him to 'stand down' on Russian meddling" (*Washington Examiner*, Jun. 20, 2018).

8. "Transcript: Obama's end-of-year news conference on Syria, Russian hacking and more" (*The Washington Post*, Dec. 16, 2016).

9. See, e.g., Andrew C. McCarthy, "The Transies and the Treaty" (*National Review*, Dec. 16, 2010); John Bolton, "New Start is Unilateral Disarmament" (*The Wall Street Journal*, Sept. 8, 2010); James Jay Carafano, "Why New START Is a Non-Starter" (The Daily Signal, Nov. 23, 2010).

10. Redacted Caption (U.S. Foreign Intelligence Surveillance Court, Apr. 26, 2017), Memorandum and Order, pp. 19-20.

11. HPSCI Report on Russian Active Measures, pp. 54-55.

12. Jessie Hellmann, "Trump: 'I don't want to hurt the Clintons' over private email server" (*The Hill*, Nov. 22, 2016).

13. See Andrew C. McCarthy, *Faithless Execution: Building the Political Case for Obama's Impeachment* (Encounter Books, 2014).

14. House Intelligence Committee Report, *supra*, p. 38.

15. President Barack Obama, Executive Order 13757 of Dec. 28, 2016, Federal Register, Vol. 82, No. 1 (Jan. 3, 2017).

16. *Ibid.*, Sec. 1(a)(2)(E); see also, e.g., Missy Ryan, Ellen Nakashima, Karen DeYoung, "Obama administration announces measures to punish Russia for 2016 election interference" (*The Washington Post*, Dec. 29, 2016).

17. DAG Yates was already effectively running the Justice Department, though she would not formally become acting attorney general until Loretta Lynch left office upon President Trump's January 20 inauguration.

18. Office of the Director of National Intelligence, "Background to 'Assessing Russian Activities and Intentions in Recent US Elections': The Analytic Process and Cyber Incident Attribution" (Jan. 6, 2017).

19. It has now been widely reported that Brennan wanted Steele's farfetched allegations incorporated but was shot down because they could not be corroborated. By 2019, especially after the Mueller report found no Trump–Russia conspiracy, the dossier stood in such disrepute that Brennan was posing as a longtime skeptic and claiming that it had been Comey, not he, who tried to force official ICA reliance on Steele. Andrew C. McCarthy, "Was Brennan's 'Intelligence Bombshell" the Steele Dossier?" (*National Review*, May 29, 2019).

20. Isikoff and Corn, *Russian Roulette*, *supra*; Michael Isikoff, "Top FBI officials were 'quite worried' Comey would appear to be blackmailing Trump" (Yahoo News, May 15, 2019); Byron York, "New Revelations shed light on Comey, Trump, and that 'loyalty' demand" (*Washington Examiner*, Apr. 20, 2018).

21. James Comey, Senate Select Committee on Intelligence, Statement for the Record (Jun. 8, 2017); Comey Memo to File, "My notes from private session with [President-elect] on 1/6/17."

22. Mollie Hemingway, "Comey's Memos Indicate Dossier Briefing of Trump Was a Setup" (*The Federalist*, Apr. 20, 2018).

23. Asked, "Did you confirm or corroborate the contents of the dossier with CNN journalist Jake Tapper," Clapper responded: "Well, by the time of that, they already knew about it. By the time it was—it was after—I don't know exactly the sequence there, but it was pretty close to when we briefed it and when it was out all over the place." The reference to "when we briefed it" clearly refers to the briefings of Obama and Trump. Clapper later told *The Washington Post* that the first time he "had any interaction with Jake Tapper

was on May 14 [of 2017]." Notwithstanding the *Post*'s game effort, that does not square with his House testimony. (House Intelligence Committee Report, *supra*, p. 107: "Clapper subsequently acknowledged discussing the 'dossier with CNN journalist Jake Tapper,' and admitted that he might have spoken with other journalists abut the same topic. Clapper's discussion with Tapper took place in early January 2017, around the time [intelligence officials] briefed President Obama and President-elect Trump, on 'the Christopher Steele information,' a two-page summary of which was 'enclosed in' the highly classified version of the ICA.") Conveniently, Clapper does not mention the leak to Tapper or CNN's January 10 report that the intelligence chiefs had briefed Trump on the dossier in his memoir, instead claiming he first heard the dossier was leaked when he learned that BuzzFeed had published it—which, of course, happened after the CNN report. Clapper, *Facts and Fears, supra*, p. 379; Glenn Kessler, "The Unsupported claim that James Clapper tipped Jake Tapper about the dossier" (*The Washington Post*, May 3, 2018); Madeline Osburn, "4 Different Lies James Clapper Told About Lying to Congress" (*The Federalist*, Mar. 6, 2019).

24. Senator Ron Johnson (R., Wisc.) Letter to FBI Director Christopher Wray (May 21, 2018) (including snippets from McCabe's emails). Besides DAG Yates, McCabe's email to the Justice Department was also directed to then–Principal Deputy General Matthew Axelrod.

25. Evan Perez, Jim Sciutto, Jake Tapper, and Carl Bernstein, "Intel chiefs presented Trump with Claims of Russian efforts to compromise him" (CNN, Jan. 10, 2017, updated Jan. 12, 2018); Ken Bensinger, Miriam Elder, and Mark Schoofs, "These Reports Allege Trump Has Deep Ties to Russia" (BuzzFeed, Jan. 10, 2017); Chuck Ross, "Emails: Jake Tapper Tore Into 'Irresponsible' BuzzFeed Editor for Publishing the Steele Dossier" (The Daily Caller, Feb. 8, 2019).

26. Peter Schweizer and Seamus Bruner, "Ex-officials actually use security clearances to get rich" (*New York Post*, Aug. 22, 2018).

27. This description is taken from Kramer's deposition testimony in a libel suit arising out of BuzzFeed's publication of the dossier. *Gubarev v. BuzzFeed*, No. 17 Civ. 60426 (S.D.N.Y. 2017), Deposition of David Kramer (Dec. 13, 2017). U.S. First Amendment jurisprudence makes libel a very difficult claim to prove against journalists, and the suit, as expected, was tossed out by a federal judge in December 2018. See Josh Gerstein, "Libel suit against BuzzFeed thrown out" (*Politico*, Dec. 19, 2018). For more on Kramer and his interactions with Steele, through Sir Andrew Wood, see Tom Hamburger and Rosalind S. Helderman, "Hero or hired gun? How a British former spy became a flash point in the Russia investigation" (*The Washington Post*, Feb. 6, 2018); see also Victor Morton, "John McCain reportedly defends giving Trump dossier to James Comey in new Book" (*The Washington Times*, May 9, 2018); Jerry Dunleavy and Daniel

Chaitin, "John McCain associate behind dossier leak urged BuzzFeed to retract its story: 'You are gonna get people killed!'" (*Washington Examiner*, Mar. 14, 2019). For more on the McCain Foundation, see, e.g., Bill Allison, "McCain-Linked Nonprofit Received $1 Million from Saudi Arabia" (Bloomberg, Mar. 31, 2016); Michelle Ye Hee Lee, "John McCain's claim he has 'nothing to do with' the McCain Institute" (*The Washington Post*, Apr. 8, 2016) (rating the claim "Two Pinocchios" because the senator was better understood as having misspoken then misled).

28.   Kramer did not reveal the names when he was deposed.

29.   Ayesha Rascoe, "Trump accuses U.S. spy agencies of Nazi practices over 'phony' Russia dossier" (Reuters, Jan. 11, 2017).

CHAPTER 17

1.   Compare Notes of Comey Communications with Trump, e.g. Feb. 8, 2017, Comey conversation with then–chief of staff Reince Priebus ("I repeated what I had told the President about not wanting to create a narrative that we were investigating him.").

2.   P.L. 94-503, § 203; 90 Stat. 2407, 2427 (1976).

3.   See, e.g., Vivian S. Chu and Henry B. Hogue, "FBI Director: Appointment and Tenure" (Congressional Research Service, Feb. 19, 2014); Andrew C. McCarthy, "On the Limits of Loyalty" (*National Review*, May 13, 2017).

4.   Comey Senate Intelligence Committee Testimony (Jun. 8, 2017), *supra* (questioning by Senator Angus King (Ind., Maine)).

5.   Flynn supported Agent Robyn Gritz, a supervisor in the counterintelligence agent who implicated McCabe in the retaliation aspect of the case. Flynn wrote a letter commending Gritz on Defense Department stationary and offered to testify on her behalf. Daniel John Sobieski, "Could Flynn's Unmasking be McCabe's Revenge?" (*American Thinker*, Jun. 30, 2017) (unidentified FBI witnesses are said to have heard McCabe disparage Flynn before and during the time he emerged as a figure in the Trump–Russia probe) (excerpting Circa report, no longer available, by Sara A. Carter and John Solomon); Paul Mirengoff, "Report: Top FBI Official Had It In For Flynn" (Power Line, Jun. 27, 2017).

6.   Kristen Welker, Dafna Linzer, and Ken Dilanian, "Obama Warned Trump Against Hiring Mike Flynn, Say Officials" (NBC News, May 8, 2017).

7.   *United States v. Michael Flynn*, No. 17 Cr. 232 (RC) (District of Columbia, 2017), Statement of the Offense, pp. 4-5 (Dec. 1, 2017); Andrew C. McCarthy, "Outrageous Redactions to the Russia Report" (*National Review*, May 7, 2018).

8.   Flynn Statement of the Offense, *supra*, pp. 2-3.

9. As noted, *infra*, Flynn was also the subject of a counterintelligence investigation in 2016, but there is no public indication that he was under targeted FISA surveillance, something that, one assumes, would have been disclosed in his false-statements prosecution if it had happened.

10. Peter Baker, Glenn Thrush, Maggie Haberman, Adam Goldman, and Julie Hirschfield Davis, "Flynn's Downfall Sprang From 'Eroding Level of Trust'" (*The New York Times*, Feb. 14, 2017).

11. Not even Christopher Steele has accused Flynn of involvement in Russia's hacking of Democratic email accounts, although there have been efforts to tie him to an effort by a now-deceased Republican activist to locate tens of thousands of emails from Hillary Clinton's private server—suspected of being hacked but never proved to be. Director Comey was prepared to close the counterintelligence investigation of Flynn in late 2016, so it is unlikely to have been part of the Trump–Russia investigation, which continued well into 2017. In 2015, Flynn, who had started his own security company, took a trip to Moscow, where he was paid $45,000 to speak at a gala for RT, a regime-controlled news outlet—not exactly chump change, though not nearly as much the $500,000 Bill Clinton got for his speech to a regime-connected financial institution. At the gala's head table, Flynn sat next to Vladimir Putin (also seated at the same table were Jill Stein, then the U.S. Green Party presidential candidate, and other dignitaries). Flynn disclosed his 2015 trip to the Defense Department; he and his son, who worked at his company, met with Kislyak before he flew to Moscow. Flynn made other unsavory professional choices after leaving military service, including work for the repressive Islamist regime of Recep Tayyip Erdogan in Turkey. In fact, some of Flynn's business associates have been charged with illegally lobbying on Turkey's behalf (an investigation in which Flynn has cooperated with prosecutors). On the other side of the coin, Flynn also cowrote with historian (and close friend of mine) Michael Ledeen a bestselling book, *The Field of Fight: How We Can Win the Global War against Radical Islam and Its Allies* (St. Martin's Press, 2016), which argues that Putin's regime is at the core of a global, anti-American alliance with Iran, and that it would bolster U.S. interests to attempt to pry Russia out of that relationship. See House Intelligence Committee Report, *supra*, pp. 52-54; Robert Windrem, "Senate Russia investigators are still interested in Jill Stein" (NBC News, Dec. 19, 2017) (report with accompanying photograph of those seated at head table); Rebecca Kheel, "Turkey and Michael Flynn: Five things to know" (*The Hill*, Dec. 17, 2018); McCarthy, "Outrageous Redactions to the Russia Report," *supra*; McCarthy, "Intramural GOP Strife Over Russia? Not So Fast…" (*National Review*, Jan. 3, 2017); McCarthy, "Collusion as Farce: The Hunt for Hillary's Hackers" (American Greatness, Jul. 6, 2017).

12. David Ignatius, "Why did Obama dawdle on Russia's hacking?" (*The Washington Post*, Jan. 12, 2017).

13. The Logan Act is codified at Title 18, U.S. Code, Section 953.

14. Dan McLaughlin, "Repeal the Logan Act" (*National Review*, May 5, 2018); compare Director Comey's rationalization for recommending against the indictment of Hillary Clinton: even though her actions fell within the ambit of the applicable statute, he was unable to find a case the Justice Department had prosecuted on similar facts.

15. Sally Yates and James Clapper, Senate Judiciary Committee Testimony (May 8, 2017) (questioning by Sen. Lindsey Graham (R., N.C.)).

16. Andrew C. McCarthy, "Of Course There Is Such a Thing as a 'Perjury Trap'" (*National Review*, Aug. 11, 2018); McCarthy, "Flynn: Fact, and Narrative" (*National Review*, Dec. 19, 2018).

17. Jonathan Turley, "No glory in James Comey getting away with his abuse of FBI power" (*The Hill*, Dec. 15, 2018).

18. Evan Perez, "Flynn changed story to FBI, no charges expected" (CNN, Feb. 17, 2017).

19. House Intelligence Committee Report, *supra*, p. 54, n.97 (citing Comey testimony on Mar. 2, 2017); Byron York, "Comey told lawmakers FBI agents saw 'no physical indications of deception' in Michael Flynn" (*Washington Examiner*, May 4, 2018).

CHAPTER 18

1. Comey House testimony (Mar. 20, 2017), *supra*.

2. Michael S. Schmidt, Mark Mazzetti, and Matt Apuzzo, "Trump Campaign Aides Had Repeated Contact With Russian Intelligence" (*The New York Times*, Feb. 14, 2017).

3. John Solomon, "Intelligence chairman accuses Obama aides of hundreds of unmasking requests" (*The Hill*, Jul. 27, 2017).

4. Andrew C. McCarthy, "On Susan Rice, the Issue Is Abuse of Power, Not Criminality" (*National Review*, Apr. 5, 2017).

5. Manu Raju, "Exclusive: Rice told House investigators why she unmasked senior Trump officials" (CNN, updated Sept. 18, 2017); David French, "Did Susan Rice Lie, Again?" (*National Review*, Sept. 14, 2017); Andrew C. McCarthy, "Did the DOJ Misuse the Steele Dossier—to Spy on the Trump Campaign?" (*National Review*, Dec. 9, 2017); Claudia Rosett and George Russell, "Obama ambassador's testimony on intelligence unmasking raises new questions" (Fox News, Oct. 20, 2017).

6. Evelyn Farkas Interview (*Morning Joe*, Mar. 2 2017); Alex Diaz, "Who is Obama administration official who spilled beans?" (Fox News, Mar. 29, 2017).

7. Sessions recused himself from the Russia *counterintelligence* investigation based on a regulation that applies to *criminal* investigations. He should have acknowledged the potential for conflicts related to the Trump campaign (of which he was a top surrogate) and announced that he would recuse himself if individual criminal investigations arose out of the campaign. He could then have recused himself from, for example, the Flynn false-statements investigation, and even the Manafort/Gates investigation (Trump-campaign officials whose crimes were unrelated to the campaign), without recusing himself from the overarching Russia intelligence probe. By doing the latter, and doing it in such sweeping language, he set himself up for such claims as that he should not weigh in on the removal of the FBI director and the appointment of the director's replacement—even though an attorney general who cannot supervise the FBI cannot truly function as attorney general. In fact, Sessions's conflict was not as serious as that of Rod Rosenstein, the deputy attorney general who never recused himself (and who never faced media–Democrat pressure to do so because he appointed Special Counsel Mueller against Trump's wishes and was seen as supportive of the Trump–Russia investigation). See Andrew C. McCarthy, "Attorney General Sessions's Recusal Was Unnecessary—The regulation he cited applies to a different type of investigation" (*National Review*, Jun. 13, 2017); McCarthy, "Rod Rosenstein's Subpoena Threat: He's Conflicted and He's Acting Like It" (*National Review*, Jun. 13, 2018).

8. Comey Senate Testimony (Jun. 8, 2017), *supra* (questioning by Senator Tom Cotton (R., Ark.)); Becket Adams, "'Not True': James Comey denounces NYT report on Trump campaign collusion with Russia during testimony" (*Washington Examiner*, Jun. 8, 2017); Scott Johnson, "Almost Entirely Wrong" (Power Line, Jun. 8, 2017).

9. Dan McLaughlin, "Comey Wasn't Investigating Trump—But Look Who Said He Was" (*National Review*, Jun. 8, 2017) (Collecting headlines and public statements by members of Congress, e.g.: "It's Official: The FBI Is Investigating Trump's Links to Russia" (*The Atlantic*); "The President Is Under FBI Investigation. Is This Normal?" (*Slate*); "Donald Trump is under investigation for ties to Russia. What happens now?" (*The Guardian*); "Schumer: Delay Gorsuch while Trump Is Under FBI Investigation" (*Huffington Post*)).

10. Comey Senate Testimony (Jun. 8, 2017), *supra*.

11. Chris Kahn, "Despite report findings, almost half of Americans think Trump colluded with Russia: Reuters/Ipsos poll" (Reuters, Mar. 26, 2019).

12. Mueller Report, Vol. II, pp. 62-77 (citing Comey Senate Judiciary Committee Testimony, May 3, 2017).

13. *Ibid.*

14. Rod J. Rosenstein, Memorandum for the Attorney General, "Restoring Public Confidence in the FBI" (May 9, 2019).

15. President Donald J. Trump letter to FBI Director James Comey (May 9, 2017).

16. Andrew C. McCarthy, "Trump's Berating of Comey for the Consumption of Our Enemies" (*National Review*, May 20, 2017).

17. Matthew Nussbaum, Josh Dawsey, and Tara Palmieri, "In interview, Trump contradicts Pence on Comey" (*Politico*, May 11, 2017).

18. Donald J. Trump (@realDonaldTrump) May 12, 2017, Tweet.

19. Donald J. Trump (@realDonaldTrump) Jun. 22, 2017, Tweet. ("With all of the recently reported electronic surveillance, intercepts, unmasking and illegal leaking of information, I have no idea...whether there are 'tapes' or recordings of my conversations with James Comey, but I did not make, and do not have, any such recordings."); Stephen Collinson, "Trump ends his self-made crisis where it started: Twitter" (CNN, Jun. 23, 2017).

20. Andrew C. McCarthy, "The Special Counsel: The Swamp's Watchdog for Trump" (American Greatness, Jun. 14, 2017).

21. Comey Senate Testimony (Jun. 8, 2017), *supra*.

22. See, e.g., Executive Order 13256, "Classified National Security Information" (Dec. 29, 2009); Andrew C. McCarthy, "Comey Confirms: In Clinton Emails Caper, the Fix Was In" (*National Review*, Apr. 28, 2018); McCarthy, "Report: Comey Memos Are Government Documents...and Some Are Classified" (*National Review*, Jul. 10, 2017).

23. FBI Director James Comey's Testimony before the Senate Judiciary Committee (May 3, 2019) (questioning by Senator Patrick Leahy (D., Ver.)).

24. *Ibid.* (questioning by Senator Mazie Hirono (D., Haw.)).

25. Adam Goldman and Michael S. Schmidt, "Rod Rosenstein Suggested Secretly Recording Trump and Discussed 25th Amendment" (*The New York Times*, Sept. 21, 2019).

26. Kelly Cohen and Diana Stancy Correll, "Rosenstein rejects report saying he talked about getting rid of Trump with 25th Amendment" (*Washington Examiner*, Sept. 21, 2018).

27. The president has claimed that one of these candidates was Robert Mueller, who is said to have interviewed for the job a day or so before Rosenstein named him special counsel. In the obstruction volume of his final report, Mueller appears to refute this claim. According to then-presidential adviser Steve Bannon, Mueller was invited to the White House to give the president advice about the FBI as an institution. By law, Mueller is not eligible to serve as FBI director, and Bannon said he did not come looking for the job. Mueller Report, Vol. II, pp. 80-84; Sonam Sheth, "One paragraph in the Mueller report refutes Trump's claim that Mueller asked him to be FBI director" (*Business Insider*, May 30, 2019).

28. McCabe recorded Rosenstein's suggestions in memoranda on which the *Times* reported. McCabe repeated the allegations in a later *60 Minutes* interview. The FBI's then–general counsel James Baker was consulted at the time and confirmed the incidents in congressional testimony. "Andrew McCabe: The Full 60 Minutes Interview" (CBS News, Feb. 17, 2018); Nicholas Fandos and Adam Goldman, "Former Top F.B.I. Lawyer Says Rosenstein Was Serious About Taping Trump" (*The New York Times*, Oct. 10, 2018).

29. Michael S. Schmidt, "Comey Memo Says Trump Asked Him to End Flynn Investigation" (*New York Times*, May 16, 2017).

30. The Mueller investigation alleged 11 potential episodes of obstruction, though it did not determine if any of them was worthy of prosecution. I do not believe they are, but addressing them is beyond the scope of this discussion—a question for another day. For now, we are considering the 2 episodes that were under consideration at the time Rosenstein appointed Mueller: the firing of Comey, and weighing in on the investigation of Flynn. See, e.g., Bill Barr, Memorandum to Deputy Attorney General Rod Rosenstein and Assistant Attorney General Steve Engel, "Mueller's 'Obstruction' Theory" (Jun. 8, 2018); Andrew C. McCarthy, "It Would Still Be Foolish for Trump to Talk to Mueller" (*National Review*, Apr. 7, 2018); David B. Rivkin and Lee A. Casey, "Can a President Obstruct Justice? Yes but not by doing any of the things we know Trump to have done." (*The Wall Street Journal*, Dec. 10, 2017); Anna Giaritelli, "Alan Dershowitz: You cannot charge a president with obstruction of justice for exercising his constitutional power" (*Washington Examiner*, Dec. 4, 2017).

31. Though adamantly opposed to the appointment of a special counsel, I too attested to Mueller's credentials. Andrew C. McCarthy, "Robert Mueller: A Solid Choice for Trump–Russia Investigation 'Special Counsel'" (*National Review*, May 18, 2017).

32. Mueller Report, Vol. II, pp. 78-80.

33. Byron York, "From former Trump lawyer, candid talk about Mueller, Manafort, Sessions, Rosenstein, collusion, tweets, privilege, and the press" (*Washington Examiner*, Apr. 3, 2019) (linking to Byron York podcast interview with the president's former personal lawyer, John Dowd). In September 2018, Jody Hunt became the Assistant Attorney General in charge of the Justice Department's Civil Division.

34. Sari Horwitz, Ashley Parker, and Ed O'Keefe, "Trump angrily calls Russia investigation a 'witch hunt,' and denies collusion charges" (*The Washington Post*, May 18, 2017).

Index